W9-AQW-086

Understanding
Interpersonal Communication

SECOND EDITION

Understanding Interpersonal Communication

SECOND EDITION

Richard L. Weaver, II
Bowling Green State University

Scott, Foresman and Company   Glenview, Illinois
Dallas, Tex.   Oakland, N.J.   Palo Alto, Cal.   Tucker, Ga.   London

To Robert G. Gunderson and Edgar E. Willis—

teachers who have contributed to my growth and development

An Instructor's Manual is available. It may be obtained through a local Scott, Foresman representative or by writing the English Editor, College Division, Scott, Foresman and Company, 1900 East Lake Avenue, Glenview, Illinois 60025.

Library of Congress Cataloging in Publication Data

Weaver, Richard L   1941-
    Understanding interpersonal communication.
    Includes bibliographies and index.
    1. Interpersonal communication.   I. Title.
BF637.C45W35   1981   158 .2   80-27088
ISBN 0-673-15436-X

iv

ACKNOWLEDGEMENTS

Prologue   Olson—From *The Art of Hanging Loose in an Uptight World* by Ken Olson. Published by O'Sullivan Woodside & Co., 1974. Prather—From *Notes to Myself: My Struggle to Become a Person* by Hugh Prather. Published by Real People Press, 1970.

Chapter 1   Alinsky—From *Rules for Radicals* by Saul D. Alinsky. Published by Vintage Books, 1971. Beier—From *People-Reading: How We Control Others, How They Control Us* by Ernst G. Beier and Evans G. Valens. Published by Stein and Day Publishers, Inc., 1975. Classified ads—Reprinted with permission from *The New York Review of Books*. Copyright © 1977 Nyrev, Inc. Fast—From *Talking Between the Lines: How We Mean More than We Say* by Julius and Barbara Fast. Published by The Viking Press, 1979. Time—From "The Bodacious New World of C.B." Reprinted by permission from *Time*, The Weekly Newsmagazine; Copyright Time Inc. 1976.

Chapter 2   Christophers—From *Christopher News Notes*, November 1976. Reprinted by permission of The Christophers. Goodman—"People Are What They Seem to Be" by Ellen Goodman from *The Blade*, July 3, 1979. Copyright © 1979, The Boston Globe Newspaper Company / Washington Post Writers Group. Reprinted with permission. Huseman—From *Interpersonal Communication in Organization, A Perceptual Approach* by Richard C. Huseman, James Lahiff and John D. Hatfield. Copyright © 1976 by Allyn and Bacon, Inc. Reprinted by permission. Olson—From *Can You Wait Till Friday?* by Ken Olson. Published by O'Sullivan Woodside & Company, 1975. Reprinted by permission. Reed—"Naming of Parts" from *A Map of Verona* by Henry Reed. Reprinted by permission of Jonathan Cape Ltd. Woods—"Gorilla 'Talks' to The Humans" by Michael Woods from *The Blade*, July 3, 1979. Reprinted by permission of *The Blade*.

Chapter 3   Cicero—From "Alone For The Holidays: Finding Contentment From Within Is Key" by Linda Cicero, *The Blade*, December 9, 1979. Reprinted by permission of KNT News Wire. Coudert—From *Advice From a Failure* by Jo Coudert. Published by Stein and Day, 1965. Hamacheck—From *Encounters with the Self* by Don E. Hamacheck. Copyright © 1971 by Holt, Rinehart and Winston, Inc. Reprinted by permission of Holt, Rinehart and Winston. McGrath—"As a Navaho" by James A. McGrath, *Arizona Highways*, August 1976. Reprinted by permission of the author. Weinberg—From *Self Creation* by George Weinberg. New York: St. Martin's Press, 1978. Reprinted by permission of St. Martin's Press, Inc. Young—From *Your Personality and How to Live with It* by Gregory G. Young. New York: Atheneum Publishers, Inc., 1978, pp. 2–3 and 32–33. Reprinted by permission. Zimbardo—Reprinted from *Shyness, What It Is, What to Do About It* by Philip G. Zimbardo, copyright © 1977, by permission of Addison-Wesley Publishing Co., Reading, Mass.

Chapter 4   Associated Press—From " 'Listen Here!' Possible Motto For Man Who Is All Ears," *The Blade*, August 16, 1975. Reprinted by permission of The Associated Press. Egan—From *The Skilled Helper*, by G. Egan. Copyright © 1975 by Wadsworth, Inc. Reprinted by permission of the publisher, Brooks/Cole Publishing Company, Monterey, California. Harris—From *Strictly Personal* by Sydney J. Harris. Copyright © 1975 Field Enterprises, Inc. Courtesy of Field Newspaper Syndicate. Ignatow—"Two Friends" by David Ignatow. Copyright © 1963 by David Ignatow. Reprinted from *Figures of the Human* by permission of Wesleyan University Press. Landers—From *Ann Landers* column, *The Blade*, Toledo, Ohio. Copyright © 1979 Field Newspaper Syndicate. Reprinted by permission. Olds—From "Why Compliments May Make You Uneasy" by Sally W. Olds from *Today's Health*, February 1975. Reprinted by permission of the author.

Chapter 5   Communication Research Association—From Communication Research Association: *Communicate! A Workbook for Interpersonal Communication*, Second Edition. Copyright © 1978 by Long Beach City College Department of Theater Arts and Speech. Kendall/Hunt Publishing Company, Dubuque, Iowa. Reprinted by permission. Cooke—"Words Can Hurt You" by Janet Cooke from *The Blade*, June 11, 1978. Reprinted by permission of *The Blade*. Harris—From *The Best of Sydney J. Harris*, published by Houghton Mifflin Company. Copyright © 1975 by Sydney J. Harris. Reprinted by permission of Houghton Mifflin Company. Landers—From *Ann Landers* column, *The Blade*, Toledo, Ohio. Copyright 1980 Field Newspaper Syndicate. Reprinted by permission. Newman—From *Strictly Speaking* by Edwin Newman. Published by Bobbs-Merrill Company, Inc., 1974. Peter—"Educational Jargon Phrase Indicator" (p. 129) *The Peter Prescription* by Dr. Laurence J. Peter. Copyright © 1972 by Laurence J. Peter. By permission of William Morrow & Co.

Photography Credits

Preface

Like the first edition, this second edition of *Understanding Interpersonal Communication* is designed not only to help students understand interpersonal communication in general, but also to help them improve their own skills in this area. Interpersonal communication is sometimes described as if it is an activity the reader observes or studies from the outside but does not actually practice. An important part of the course in interpersonal communication, and of this book, is teaching a body of information—concepts, principles, theory. This can be interesting in itself. But understanding the concepts, principles, and theory without putting them into practice has little value in the beginning course, in my view, and so I have emphasized throughout the book the practical skills needed to improve our communication with others.

This dual emphasis on concepts and skills underlies both the overall approach of the book and the organization within its chapters. Each chapter begins with a discussion of concepts and concludes with a discussion of skills. The final chapters on communicating with family, friends, and co-workers (an extension of this concern with both concepts and skills) ask students to apply what they've learned in earlier chapters to the situations in which they most often find themselves.

For most instructors, the beginning chapters on perception and on the self will provide a base on which to build their course. Although Chapters 4 through 11 develop in a logical way out of each other, they are written so that they can easily be used in a different order to suit different course needs. Chapter 11, "Entering the World of Work: Communication and Your Job," is a new chapter in this edition. Because of increased interest in how communication affects familial, social, and work relationships, I split the former Chapter 10, expanding the coverage of family and friends and of the job into two chapters. Students will find both chapters relevant and specific.

I have tried to write a *teachable* book that will permit flexibility but cover essential content, and a *readable* book that will have an impact on the student. To these ends I have presented information in terms students will understand and have suggested skills that are practical. The "Consider This" readings scattered throughout the book sometimes agree with and support the text and sometimes disagree, but in all cases should stimulate thought and discussion. The special "Try This" materials suggest exercises and projects that reinforce the concepts in the text. The additional readings section at the end of each chapter lists, for the most part, popular books of high interest to students, usually available in paperback. The photos, the design, the informal writing style—all these are intended to engage the reader in the fascinating subject of interpersonal communication.

An Instructor's Manual, available from the publisher, provides suggestions on how to use the "Try This" exercises and "Consider This" material to enhance students' understanding of the text. It includes test and discussion questions, lists of important concepts and terms, numerous exercises for the class to try as a group, and a list of references of special interest to the instructor. The 8½-by-11-inch format allows the teacher to duplicate relevant materials directly for distribution to students.

Even though one author's name may appear on a book, seldom is a book the work of just one person. In the preparation and development of this one, I have had the pleasure of working with some fine individuals. My editors, JoAnn Johnson, Isobel Hoffman, and Kathy Kleinheksel, have helped me every step of the way. The suggestions of manuscript readers have also been important. For reading the first edition, I thank James J. Bradac of the University of Maine at Orono, Jo-Ann Graham, Bronx Community College of the City University of New York, and Theodore Hopf, Washington State University. Their concerns are still reflected in this revision. For the ideas they suggested for this second edition, I thank Mary E. Lunz of Illinois Benedictine College, Lisle, and Paul M. Seland, Niagra City Community College, Sandborn, New York. And to all those who responded to the Scott, Foresman survey that offered me many valuable comments, thank you.

I also wish to acknowledge Mary Ann Bowman at Western Michigan University for asking her students to read and critique the first edition. Her ideas and those of her students have helped to strengthen this new volume.

For a considerable amount of the supplementary material that appears in the sections labeled "Consider This," I thank Charles A. Wilkinson, Communication Counselor.

Special thanks are extended to *The Key*, the yearbook of Bowling Green State University, for permission to use photographs from their files.

Others who have contributed to the development of the manuscript are Gloria Gregor and Mary Lou Millmarth, Jim and Judy Harris, and Florence Miskovic. I express my appreciation to the assistant directors and teaching assistants connected with the basic communication course at Bowling Green State University, and to Allen S. White, Director of the School of Speech Communication at Bowling Green.

I also thank my friends and the friends of my family. Although the names have been changed, many of the illustrations in the book have come out of my experience with them.

Finally, and most importantly, I thank the members of my family. They are the greatest. Writing necessarily becomes a family project, and I thank Scott, Jacquelynn, Anthony, and Joanna for being who they are. Their contributions, although unfootnoted, are evident at many points. I also express my deepest appreciation and love to my wife Andrea, not only for her continuing support and love, but also for her reading and typing of the first edition manuscript and for thoughtful, critical comments throughout. Without the support and love of my family this book would never have been completed. And the second edition is no exception.

Dick Weaver

Contents

Understanding Interpersonal Communication

SECOND EDITION

Prologue

Finding Your Way: Values and Goals

You are beginning to read a book about interpersonal communication. This book and the course you are taking work toward two things: (1) increasing your knowledge about interpersonal communication and (2) improving your skills in interpersonal communication. You may say "I get along all right now" or "What difference does it make?" or "How can it possibly help me?" I can't answer for you. But I can speak for my self.

I am writing this book out of the belief that clear and open communication between people is generally a good thing. That's one of my values: clear and open communication. If you asked me why, I'd say because with clear and open communication I have a chance to build closer relationships with people. And close relationships—where we both give something of our selves—are something else I value. I could go on and say that in relationships with other people I learn about my self and growth may take place. Self-knowledge, growth, and change are other values that are important to me. You know now some of the values that I bring to the writing of this book.

I cannot prove these values. You probably could not prove the truth of your values to me. Still, these ideas and beliefs shape how I live and determine how I communicate with others. Our lives and therefore our communication are guided by our value systems, and it's safe to say that no two people in the world have identical value systems. We learn and share our value systems through experience. Since no two people have identical experiences, no two of us have precisely the same set of values.

If you haven't already, I hope this book and this course will start you thinking about

— how you express your values when you communicate with others
— how your values control and shape the way you communicate
— how your values may change as a result of communicating with others
— how you can come to have confidence in the values you hold

You, too, have certain values that you consider important, even if you don't think or talk about them very much. What are some of these? Do you value cooperation? Love? Knowledge? Comfort? Play? Religion? Workmanship? Ambition?

Just for a moment, let's consider that last value—ambition. How might being ambitious affect a person's communication? Ambitious people tend to seek out other ambitious people in business and social relationships. They are goal oriented. They know what they want and have some idea of what direction they have to take in order to get there. We'll probably find this same orientation in their communications: they may be bored very quickly by information that doesn't pertain to their goal; they may put a high premium on efficient transmission of messages; they may be anxious to keep communications brief and to the point; they may show lots of energy and enthusiasm for anyone or anything that could help them reach their goals faster. The high value they place on ambition affects whom they talk to, how they talk, and what they say.

This works both ways. Even as our values affect our interpersonal communications, our communication skills affect how close we come

Consider This _____

As I look back on my life, one of the most constant and powerful things I have experienced within myself is the desire to be more than I am at the moment—an unwillingness to let myself remain where I am—a desire to increase the boundaries of myself—a desire to do more, learn more, express more—a desire to grow, improve, accomplish, expand. I used to interpret this inner push as meaning that there was some one thing out there I wanted to do or be or have. And I have spent too much of my life trying to find it. But now I know that this energy within me is seeking more than the mate or the profession or the religion, more even than pleasure or power or meaning. It is seeking out more of me; or better, it is, thank God, flushing out more of me.

—Hugh Prather, *Notes to Myself*

_____ **Consider This**

to satisfying our values. If we are ambitious, weak communication skills can stand in the way of our ambition. We'll have a hard time moving toward any positive goals if we have trouble communicating with other people.

Although values and goals are not identical, they are related. The goals we set are often determined by our values. Satisfying a particular value can become a goal. We may value cooperation and want, as a goal, to become more cooperative. We may value knowledge for its own sake and yet want, as a personal goal, to become more knowledgeable. The goal is the ideal end. It is the reality of what we value—it is where we would like to be as a result of valuing certain things above others.

Only you know what your own goals are. The goal of this book is to help you understand interpersonal communication, in general, and to help you improve your own skills, in particular. I hope that your goals and this book's will coincide, at least temporarily! Each chapter in this book includes concepts and skills that should help you achieve the goal of effective interpersonal communication.

In the course of the book I'll be making some assumptions about your desire to grow—growth is important to me and I'm hoping it's important to you. Growth hardly ever takes place in total isolation. It takes communicating with people—understanding them and being understood by them. People who want to grow often have certain other motivations, things they hope to accomplish along the way. James L. Jarrett has identified these motivations and I think they describe the intermediate goals of any serious student of interpersonal communication.[1] As you read them, think about how well or how poorly they describe your own goals:

To Learn

The desire to learn cannot be instilled in us from the outside. It must come from within. As children we had a natural desire to explore, to find out about things. To the very young child, learning and playing are the same thing—any new discovery is exciting. As growing adults, we need to recapture that excitement of discovery.

To Broaden Range of Experience

Our routine—how we think and behave—becomes a kind of security blanket. Few people are eager to leave their security blankets behind for something they do not completely understand. But it is only by breaking out that we will meet new people, confront new ideas, and

discover new frontiers. The more experience we have, the more options we have open to us and the more flexible we become.

To Repeat Pleasant Experiences

We all know what it is to do something for no other reason than that it was enjoyable the last time. We'll talk to Pam because last time we talked to her she was friendly. We'll talk about our trip to Montana because last time we brought up the subject we got a good reaction. The better we understand interpersonal communication, the better we'll be able to control the variables in a communication situation and recreate pleasant experiences.

To Internalize Insights

It is one thing to be able to comprehend an idea; it is quite another to be able to internalize it, to know what it means to us. We need to make insights personal if we're going to grow through them. These insights determine how we look at things, feel about them, and respond to them. Learning empathic interpersonal skills will help us with the internalizing.

To Savor Feeling

When we have a good feeling, we want to hold on to it. To know what our reactions are made of and what stimulates them in us will help us to savor such feelings. It can help us to make the most of an otherwise unmemorable experience. Do you know what you like? Knowing what we like is the first step toward recognizing pleasure when we see it. Though of course we never seek them out, even painful feelings can be savored, in a way. That is, we can explore the pain and try to understand what brought it on and at least appreciate the fact that we are not numb to sensation. That's what savoring means—experiencing a feeling to the utmost.

To Intensify Sensation

Whenever we can, we're likely to try to control communication situations so as to intensify whatever sensation that situation produces in us. It's like the kind of ride in an amusement park that lets us control the speed or spin of our own car. We can go faster when *we* want to, slower when *we* want to. Having communication skills is like having our own controls; we can get the most of what *we* want out of interpersonal communication situations.

To Become Discriminating

It is rare to find a person who is totally undiscriminating. We learn in early childhood how to sort color, shape, and meaning—how to be discriminating. This does not mean assigning value, saying one thing is better or worse than another. Discriminating simply means recognizing samenesses and differences. A good communicator will be discriminating in this way—not judging "up" as better than "down," but at least always being able to tell them apart.

To Recognize Relevance

In order to deal with the millions of stimuli we encounter every day, we must be selective. We usually base our selection on relevance, not "What difference does it make?" but "What difference does it make *to me?*" This is how we begin to make sense out of our environment and our communications. An effective communicator learns to choose and cope with only the most relevant of the many available stimuli.

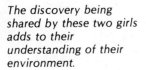

The discovery being shared by these two girls adds to their understanding of their environment.

It is not easy to learn patience; to be still and look within yourself; to risk taking off all the masks that you hide behind; to end the destructive games with people. But I believe that if an individual can do such a pilgrimage into self, what he will find will not be that he is so bad, but that he is so rich in unused potential; that he has a great capacity to love and become alive.
—Ken Olson, *The Art of Hanging Loose in an Uptight World*

To Increase Human Potential

It is not uncommon to hear someone describing his or her philosophy of life as "to be everything I *can* be" or "to do everything I am capable of." There is a strong motivation on the part of many of us to live life to the fullest. The effective communicator wants to explore all known possibilities and, when they are exhausted, to discover even more. This is really what growth is all about: reaching out, discovering how far we can go in any given direction.

To Create

There is a real excitement about the creative impulse, the irresistible desire to invent and to put things together in a new way. We don't have to be artists in the traditional sense of musicians and sculptors to want to and to be able to create. We have more opportunities to exercise our creativity in communication than in any other area simply because we communicate more than we do just about anything else. As we engage in interpersonal communication we need to find our own personally effective ways of getting along. And this takes real, creative imagination. As you begin to read about interpersonal communication, think about which of these goals and motivations are important in your life. You undoubtedly have others not listed here and you might want to argue about some of the ones I listed. That's fine. The idea is for you to think about the interpersonal communication process in general and to see how it applies to you as a communicator. We can read and read and not really understand if something is important to us until we try it out. The skills section of each chapter should help you to reach your goals by suggesting how to put concepts into practice.

Now that you have some idea about where I am coming from—a values-growth approach to clear and open communication—we need to find out more about the communication process itself. Chapter 1 provides a perspective on interpersonal communication. It should give you an overview so that as we discuss specific concepts within the communication process you'll have a better idea of how the parts relate to each other and to the whole.

OTHER READING

Leo F. Buscaglia, *Love* (Thorofare, N.J.: Charles B. Slack, Inc., 1972). Love is discussed as it relates to people's daily lives. Buscaglia believes that love is the creative force for change. He supports the need to speak honest convictions and feelings. This book is full of warmth and sincerity.

Wayne W. Dyer, *Pulling Your Own Strings* (New York: Avon Books, 1978). This is a book about freedom: finding it, securing it, and maintaining it. It is about the joy and fulfillment that come from controlling our own lives. Dyer includes specific strategies and techniques that can help keep us from being victims of others' behavior. His suggestions can become routes to constructive, self-fulfilling behavior.

Albert Ellis and Robert A. Harper, *A Guide to Rational Living* (North Hollywood, Calif.: Wilshire Book Company, 1975). Self-analysis can be useful. Here is a practical, straightforward, well-explained approach to help people become creatively and actively involved in the world around them. The thesis of this book is that the best way to achieve a highly satisfying emotional existence is through reasoning powers.

Reuel L. Howe, *The Miracle of Dialogue* (New York: The Seabury Press, 1963). A sensitive examination of communication. Howe presents practical guidelines for those who want to become dialogical—in communication with the environment and open to the communication that environment offers.

Ken Olson, *The Art of Hanging Loose in an Uptight World* (Greenwich, Conn.: Fawcett Publications, Inc., 1974). Olson's purpose is to provide ways for people to deal with change, crisis, chaos, and stress. The book treats negative thoughts and negative emotions and explains how to break or control emotional reactions. It is a practical, sensible approach toward living more comfortably with yourself.

Robert M. Pirsig, *Zen and the Art of Motorcycle Maintenance* (New York: Bantam Books, 1974). The story of a man in search of himself. Pirsig challenges readers to work well and to care and to be aware. It will make you question what you are, your values, and the quality of your life. This is a book about feeling.

Philip G. Zimbardo, *Shyness* (New York: Jove Publications, Inc., 1977). A
thorough examination of shyness—what it is and what to do about it.
Full of examples and specific information, the book provides useful
techniques for people who want to understand themselves, build their
self-esteem, and develop social skills.

NOTE

[1]From *The Humanities and Humanistic Education* by James L. Jarrett,
p. 147. Copyright © 1973 by Addison-Wesley Publishing Company, Inc.
Reprinted by permission.

1

Speaking Interpersonally:
A Perspective

We are all interpersonal communicators—that is, we all communicate with other people. We have been communicating since we were born. And most of us are fairly good at it. At least we are usually able to share ideas when we need to and get information that is important to us. Then why read a textbook or take a class in interpersonal communication? The answer is: Just because we communicate a lot does not necessarily mean that we do it as well as we can. We can all improve.

We engage in interpersonal communication innumerable times every day. Whether it is conversing with our family, talking with team-mates, discussing a problem with a teacher, talking with friends over a cup of coffee, or planning a party, we are sending and receiving messages and those messages are having some effect. Even when we wave at someone we know or tap a person on the shoulder in passing, an interpersonal transaction occurs. All the transactions we engage in have certain elements in common. The better we understand these elements, the more likely we are to improve our own communication and to change our behavior for the better.

In this chapter I will present an overview of the whole process. I'll discuss what interpersonal communication is and what it isn't. I'll look at nine communication principles that affect every interpersonal situation we are involved in. And I'll examine the human and environmental contexts in which communication occurs. Finally, I'll offer some general suggestions on how we can all improve our interpersonal communication skills.

ELEMENTS OF AN INTERPERSONAL COMMUNICATION SITUATION

Figure 1 shows the skeleton of the communication process. It describes in the most basic terms the three elements necessarily involved in any communication situation: people, messages, and effects.

People

At any point in an interpersonal communication situation we may be a sender of a message, a receiver of a message, or a sender and a receiver simultaneously. Although Figure 1 suggests that messages begin with one person and are received by another, the process can be reversed at any time. We send and receive messages simultaneously when the person we're talking to says or does something as we talk that influences what we say next. Even as we speak, we receive the verbal and nonverbal messages our listener sends us.

Messages

Messages may be verbal and/or nonverbal. Both kinds of messages are equally valid communications. A lot of the feedback we get—cues that tell us how our message is being received—is mostly nonverbal. We get it in the form of head nodding, eye squinting, large and small gestures, shifts in posture, and in many other ways.

When we think of messages, however, the first thing we usually think of is words, or verbal communication. An important thing to remember is that words mean different things to different people.

Figure 1.
The skeleton of the communication process.

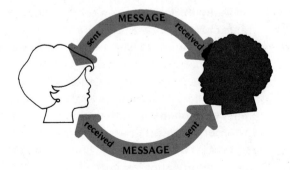

Consider This _____

One can lack any of the qualities of an organizer—with one exception—and still be effective and successful. That exception is the art of communication. It does not matter what you know about anything if you cannot communicate to your people. In that event you are not even a failure. You're just not there.

Communication with others takes place when they understand what you're trying to get across to them. If they don't understand, then you are not communicating regardless of words, pictures, or anything else. People only understand things in terms of their experience, which means that you must get within their experience. Further, communication is a two-way process. If you try to get your ideas across to others without paying attention to what they have to say to you, you can forget about the whole thing.

—Saul D. Alinsky, *Rules for Radicals*

Words are personal. Words depend for their meaning on the experiences, reactions, feelings, contexts, and ideas of the people using them. All words have these kinds of associations. It is vital to be aware always of the reactions other people have to the words we use.

Effects

Notice that in Figure 1 the "message" arrow penetrates the heads: this is to show that the message is having an effect. An effect may be a mental, physical, or emotional response to a message. We may say something that causes another person to reconsider his or her position on a subject: mental effects. We may say something that causes someone to break out in a sweat, run away, or fight: physical effects. Closely tied to these effects are emotional ones. Our message may cause the other person to feel angry, affectionate, or joyous: emotional effects.

A message that has no effect serves no useful purpose in interpersonal communication. However, we must remember that all effects may not be readily observable. A person might respond to a message with silence. Silence is an effect. It could be based on a mental, physical, or emotional response and it could mean any one of a number of things. The point is, just because another person responds to a message with silence does not mean no effect has occurred. The silence itself is the effect. Another response that may appear to show no effect is that of boredom or apathy. But just because people do not care about what we are saying does not mean there is no effect. They have chosen not to care. We have produced an effect. Sometimes, too, an effect occurs only after some time has elapsed—a delayed effect. Some effects that take a long time to appear are more significant because they have been thought out better. The point is, for communication to take place every message must produce some effect, even if that effect is not immediately apparent.

CHARACTERISTICS OF INTERPERSONAL COMMUNICATION

Having briefly examined the basic elements of interpersonal communication, let us look at some of the unique features of the interpersonal process that define it and distinguish it from other forms of communication. Interpersonal communication:

1. Involves two or three people,
2. Involves feedback,
3. Need not be face-to-face,
4. Need not be intentional,
5. Produces some effect,
6. Need not involve words,
7. Is affected by context, and
8. Is affected by noise.

Interpersonal Communication Involves Two or Three People

The fact that interpersonal communication involves people may seem too obvious to mention, but by saying it involves people we rule out the communication we have with our pets, with our car (especially when it's running poorly), with our plants, or with other objects of affection. Such communication may be important and healthy, but it is not "interpersonal" as the term will be used in this book.

To say that interpersonal communication involves at least two people rules out the kind of communication we have within our selves. *Intrapersonal communication* is the name usually given to these kinds of internal messages. In Chapter 3 we'll look more carefully at intrapersonal communication—communication within the self—as the self is the starting point for all messages we exchange with others. But for the most part, the primary focus of this book will be on communication situations involving two people.

For our purposes, we will think of interpersonal communication as involving no more than three people. Three is an arbitrary number

Try This

Pretend that someone made each of the following comments to you. This person is someone you know but do not consider a close friend. Categorize the comments according to the effect they might have on you. Is the effect mental, physical, or emotional?

1. "Have you ever considered changing your major?"

2. "Why don't you grow up?"

3. "You know, you really have a lot of friends."

4. "You're always complaining."

5. "What do you like best about this class?"

6. "For somebody taking interpersonal communication you sure don't know much about it."

here—it was selected because it is a likely and useful cut-off point between interpersonal and group communication. As soon as there is a larger group of people interacting, we move into an area called small-group communication and many new factors enter in. The problem in defining interpersonal communication in terms of the number of people involved is that (1) small-group communication is really an extended form of interpersonal communication, and (2) interpersonal communication may actually occur between two people who are part of a larger group.

Sometimes within a group of people, splinter groups of two or three participants occur. As groups increase in size, this becomes more likely. When two people in a larger group argue over a point, they are definitely engaged in interpersonal communication. We've all been in discussion groups where two members dominated the conversation until the discussion became simply an exchange of ideas between those two people. This kind of interpersonal communication often occurs in a group setting.

7. "Are you really cut out for college?"

8. "You can give advice, but you can't take it."

9. "I really hate the way you are acting toward me."

Effects differ. Just because these comments have certain effects on you does not mean they would have the same effect on others. A lot depends on who makes the comments and in what context. Can you think of other factors that might determine how you would react to them?

CHARMING, SOPHISTICATED LONELY WOMAN, 40, (comfortable in Pucci gown, tennis dress, sneakers and patched jeans, on the ski slopes, at symphony, or curled by fireplace, wine, good book, someone special to share mood with). Seeks full relationship with gentleman of similar interests. Recently migrated to Ohio (prefer 50 mile radius of Akron, unless you have your own Jet). Hobbies, many and diversified. Gestaltist: basic needs; awareness, sensitivity, giving, sharing, receiving, spontaneous, and total enthusiasm to enjoy life. Please, only honest, mature, intelligent and emotionally together reply.

FARMER WITH BUSINESS INTERESTS, articulate, non-drinker, non-smoker, ambitions in left wing politics. Seeks liaison with compatible woman. No triflers or swingers.

WEST OF MILWAUKEE, single male, 50, tops mentally, physically, into Jung, Yoga. Want independent, confident, intelligent, educated woman in good physical condition for equal-sided relationship. Good manners fine, but turn-ons (unconscious) count. Seek replies from nearby, California and Southwest for trip in March.

FEMALE GOLF ENTHUSIAST, 42, wishes meet male counterpart. Am also tall, blonde, attractive, very feminine, gentle natured.

—*New York Review of Books*, March 3, 1977

Interpersonal Communication Involves Feedback

When we use the term "interpersonal" we do not include TV news-casters or radio disc jockeys, whose messages go from source to audience but do not return. (See Figure 2.) We do not include public-speaking situations either, where the message goes from a speaker to a large audience with only a limited amount of return. (See Figure 3.)

Feedback is the message sent by the receiver back to the speaker. Interpersonal communication involves direct feedback. It is often immediate, obvious, and continuous. (See Figure 4.) It is important to note that the process includes not only an arrow from the source to the receiver but also an equal arrow from the receiver to the source. This direct relationship between the source and the receiver is a feature unique to interpersonal communication.

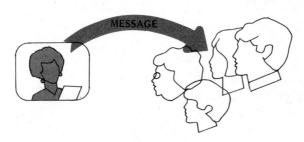

Figure 2.
A no-feedback situation.

Interpersonal Communication Need Not Be Face-to-Face

Sitting on a bus, we may be affected by a noisy conversation between two people sitting in front of us (even though it does not involve us) and choose to move to another seat as a result. We may speak to a person on the telephone; we may pass nonverbal messages to a friend across the room by using facial expressions or gestures; we could even be in another room altogether and pass messages to another person by tapping on the wall. We need not be in a face-to-face situation to experience interpersonal communication.

It is true, though, that in a face-to-face situation we receive more information because we can see more of the other person. Communication is less likely to break down during a face-to-face encounter because we're more apt to catch each other's subtleties, special inflections, and emphases. We can perceive moods more accurately when we are face-to-face, and consequently we have a better chance of getting the whole message.

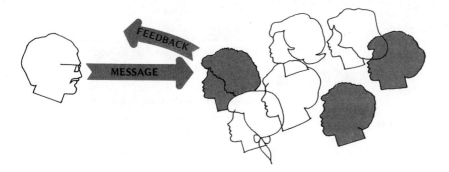

Figure 3.
A limited-feedback
situation.

Interpersonal Communication Need Not Be Intentional

Interpersonal communication does not have to be intentional. We might find out, for example, that someone has lied to us through a slip of the tongue. We could discover that a person is very nervous around us by the constant shifting of weight from one foot to another, continual fumbling over words, or by other nervous reactions. We might decide that we do not want to be around a person at all because of a certain abrasiveness or disagreeable manner. The person probably didn't intentionally communicate these things, but they are messages because they are signals that affect us.

Interpersonal Communication Produces Some Effect

To be truly considered interpersonal communication, a message must produce some effect. As we saw earlier, this effect need not be im-

Figure 4.
A direct-feedback situation.

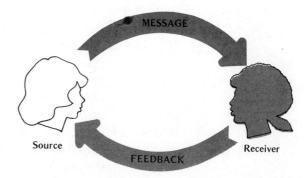

Next time you have a long, chatty telephone conversation with someone, see how it affects the communication when you do the following things:

1. Let the other person talk for a while with absolutely no response from you.

2. See what kind of feedback works best to encourage the other person to talk:
A. No feedback
B. "Ummm," "Uh-huh," "Oh," "Ah"
C. Questions
D. Comments
E. Paraphrasing (restating the other person's words in your own words)

3. Instead of silence, engage in parallel talking: you talk on a subject parallel to your telephone partner's but with no response to his or her communication.

4. Try to provide vocal responses only with no words. How many meanings can you provide without using words?

5. Try to affect the context of the message by your responses to your telephone partner's. Can you change business to pleasure? Can you change a serious message to a humorous one? Can you take the initiative in directing the conversation if your partner originally assumed it?

mediately apparent, but it must occur. If we walk along the sidewalk toward a person we don't know, wearing our broadest, warmest, I-want-to-get-to-know-you-better smile, and the other person doesn't see us and walks on by, no interpersonal communication has taken place. A similar situation occurs if we are talking to someone while that person is listening to music on stereo headphones or using a hair dryer and doesn't hear us. These are not interpersonal communications if the messages are not received and have caused no effect.

Interpersonal Communication Need Not Involve Words

Though I've already mentioned some of the ways we can communicate without words, this characteristic needs a specific statement because nonverbal communication is so important. Picture two people secretly in love with each other who are standing on opposite sides of the room at a party. A quick glance between them can reaffirm their whole relationship and love for each other. Often a look or a touch can convey much more than words. Nonverbal messages are a powerful and significant form of interpersonal communication.

Interpersonal Communication Is Affected by the Context

When we speak of the context of an interpersonal communication we mean all the human and environmental factors which preceded, will follow, and are at work during the actual exchange of messages. Communication does not occur in a vacuum. There are countless stimuli that affect what is meant, what is said, and what is understood in a message exchange. Obviously, the people involved in interpersonal communication must be in a position to receive cues from each other; however, they could be two inches apart, two feet, or two miles. The kind of communication that takes place depends heavily on just such factors of circumstance.

Context often determines content. We usually talk about different kinds of things depending on whether we are alone with a friend or surrounded by people who can listen in on our conversation; on whether we're speaking over the phone at long distance or talking face-to-face; on whether we're both happy or depressed. These factors all make up the communication context and have great effect on the quality of the communication that takes place.

Interpersonal Communication Is Affected by Noise

In every communication situation noise is a factor. It can take two forms and in most cases, both forms are present. *Physical noise* is the kind we are most familiar with. We are talking to someone and a door slams, people walk by, a child yells, a car horn blows, and a stereo blares in the background. Our environment is filled with physical noise. There is another kind of noise, however, that often we do not think much about. Because it is hard to detect, because it is difficult to compensate for, and because we may not have thought much about it before, we tend to overlook it. It is *psychological noise* and it exists in the minds of both the sender and receiver.

Try This

Which of these common forms of psychological noise distract you when you are talking to other people?

1. Thinking about what you are going to say next?

2. Worrying about what the other person thinks of you?

3. Thinking about where you should be right now, or where you are going?

4. Wondering when the other person is going to finish talking?

5. Worrying about how you look? How you sound? How you are acting?

The kind of psychological noise that distracts you is likely to vary with the people you talk to, what you talk about (the message), and the context or circumstances in which you find yourself.

Becoming more aware of psychological noise is part of the process of becoming more aware of all behavior that affects your communication. Such awareness precedes control. What we want to do is control our behavior and reactions.

We have all caught our selves thinking while another person was talking to us, "I wonder when this story is going to end?" or "I probably should get to class" or "Why is she telling me all this?" or any of a large number of other things. We are not listening to what is being said as well as we could because we are distracted by psychological noise. It could be a letter from home, how we did on an exam we just took, or how we are feeling that distracts us. It could also be a comment that the other person makes that triggers a specific response in us. The possibilities are endless.

As a speaker in an interpersonal situation we may have thought, "I wonder how he is going to take this?" or "Maybe she doesn't understand what I mean" or "Why did I say that?" We are communicating with our selves about a message we are sending and we are, in a sense, momentarily distracted from sending that message. Both physical and psychological noise interfere with the message. Both must be overcome, at least in part, if we are to communicate effectively.

SOME PRINCIPLES OF COMMUNICATION

There is more to understanding interpersonal communication than knowing its irreducible elements of people, messages, and effects. When we study this form of communication closely, we notice that there are nine principles operating that affect every interpersonal communication situation. They are inescapable. To understand these nine principles will help us to analyze, evaluate, and improve our own communication habits. They provide an important foundation. In the discussion of many of the concepts developed in later chapters, it will be assumed that these principles are affecting what takes place in any interpersonal communication situation. These nine principles are, then, the fundamentals on which other concepts depend:[1]

We Cannot Not Communicate

Think of a time when you sat in the classroom waiting for class to begin, in a rotten mood, not wanting to talk to anybody, staring blankly ahead of you and not making a movement or a sound. Anyone coming into the room could see that you didn't want to talk. You may not have wanted to speak but you were communicating. Just as *you* were communicating, so were those people who decided not to speak to you. Communication is more than the exchange of words.

All observable behavior is communication and can be considered a message. No word, gesture, or mannerism is neutral. Even people who dress and speak inconspicuously do so for a reason. The fact that they choose anonymity communicates something about them. Knowing that we cannot *not* communicate should make us more aware of our behavior at all times. In the presence of others, we probably reveal far more about our selves than we realize.

Communication Can Be Verbal or Nonverbal

When we communicate with others we use either nonverbal messages, verbal messages, or a combination of the two. Words are either sent or not sent just as a light switch is either on or off. They have an all-or-nothing feature built in. Nonverbal cues are not as clear-cut.

Nonverbal communication includes such things as facial expressions, posture, gestures, voice inflection, and the sequence and rhythm of the words themselves. Just as a dimmer switch on a light can be used to adjust intensity, nonverbal cues often reveal shades or degrees of meaning. We may say, for example, "I am very upset," but *how* upset we are will be conveyed more by tears and frantic gestures than by the actual words.

What messages are being sent by this couple's body positions? their facial expressions? their clothing?

"I didn't know you felt so deeply about that sales territory."

Surprised, Martin said, "What do you mean, deeply? I'd like to see it split up, and I'm glad we decided to, but it's no big deal."

Puzzled, his friend protested, "But you spoke so vehemently about it. You were so angry."

"Me angry?" Martin shook his head. "You must be kidding. I wasn't angry at all. I was just presenting my ideas."

Frowning, his friend dropped the subject, but from that point on he no longer trusted Martin. "The thing is," he confided to another member of the board, "I think he's two-faced."

—Julius and Barbara Fast, *Talking Between the Lines: How We Mean More Than We Say*

Every Communication Contains Information and Defines Relationships

Imagine initiating a conversation with a woman by asking, "How about joining me for a cup of coffee?" The informational part of this message refers to what we expect of her—namely, that we want her to join us for coffee. The relationship aspect of the message is the meaning behind the words that says something about our relationship to her.

The relationship aspect tells her how to deal with the message. She recognizes, for example, that this is not a command, but a friendly invitation that implies no status difference between the two of us. What if this same suggestion were made to us by her and she happened to be one of our teachers? The relationship aspect of the message would be quite different. What if she commanded, "Come, have a cup of coffee with me!" The relationship implied here is one of unequal status—known as a complementary relationship. When the status is equal the relationship can be labeled symmetrical. Often, relationships between people change from complementary to symmetrical and back again depending on the content of the message or the situation.

The messages, "Please, won't you come and have coffee with me?" and "You are going to have coffee with me!" contain the same information but imply a different relationship. The message, "Could I please see your notes from yesterday's lecture?" has essentially the same relationship level as "Please, won't you come and have coffee with me?" but the content is very different. For people with whom we have an ongoing relationship, we tend to operate on the same relationship level for all our communication, no matter what information we're exchanging. This relationship level changes only when one of us perceives a change in status in relation to the other.

When we speak to another person we reveal something about how *we* see the relationship between our selves and that person, not necessarily how that relationship *should* be. In our simple opening comment, "How about joining me for a cup of coffee?" we have offered the woman a definition of our selves that implies we are her equal—that we have a symmetrical relationship. She can make any of three general responses:

1. She may *confirm* our definition of self. She might say, "I'd love to," and verify our equality.
2. She may *reject* our view of self by saying, "I'm really not interested." This response implies that her view of the relationship is not the same as ours.
3. She may *disconfirm* by ignoring us—denying our right to definition of self. By ignoring our question, she could be saying she thinks we have no claim to a relationship at all.

True, these responses are extreme. There are many intermediate kinds of responses the woman could make. She could say no without rejecting our view of self by adding, "Could I take a rain check on it?" But clearly, the kind of response she makes has significant implications for the definition of our selves and the relationship that we have offered.

Problems in communication most often occur in the relationship dimension rather than in the content dimension. Consider a situation where you have to do a major project and need to use your roommate's desk to spread out your materials. You do this without asking your roommate's permission first. He returns to find your things spread out all over the room and flies into a rage, saying, "What the hell do you think you're doing?" There is really no question about the content of that question or how you would answer it on that level: you are doing your project and you are using his desk. But that isn't really what he is asking. On the relationship level, he's saying, "You are taking advantage of me. You are acting as if I didn't matter. You think you are superior to me." To put that response into a communication framework, your roommate could be saying, "I thought we had a symmetrical relationship, but now you have proven that all *you* want is a complementary one."

To cope with the situation you need to address the fact that your roommate feels you have threatened the relationship of equality that existed before. To have asked his permission earlier would have acknowledged his equality with you—it would have said, "You are a person capable of helping me solve my problem."

The trouble is not that the communication occurs on the relationship level—all messages imply something about a relationship. But

Try This

"I would really like to get to know you better."

Briefly describe what changes you would make in saying the above phrase if you were speaking to each of the following people:

—a member of the opposite sex whom you just met for the first time

—the parents of your best friend

—one of your teachers

—one of the cafeteria (or lunchroom) personnel

—a student (same sex) in one of your classes

Would you make different kinds of changes if the statement were the following, instead of the one above? What kinds?

"You know, you are wrong; I was there and I saw exactly what happened."

problems occur when there is a discrepancy between the content and the relationship conveyed. In the above example, your roommate does not describe his feelings accurately. He asks an aggressive question (the literal answer to which he already knows) when what he really wants to do is reestablish the equal relationship that seems to have been threatened. There is a discrepancy between the content and relationship aspects of his message. The healthier a relationship is, the less discrepancy there is, because we are more likely to say exactly how we feel. And we will be more secure in our status regarding the other person, less likely to feel the balance is being threatened by the smallest word or action. Weak relationships are often characterized by constant struggles over the nature of the relationship.

This is not to say that arguments cannot occur over the information dimension of a message. But this kind of conflict tends to be more manageable because the content level of a message generally refers to something external to both parties. The content level refers to something that exists in the real world and can often be verified. An example of an argument on the content level is: "Did the newspaper come this morning?" "No, it didn't." "I thought I heard it hit the door." "Well, I didn't see it when I looked." "But I *heard* it." The content question raised in this argument can be resolved by both people looking to see if the paper is actually there. Either it is or it isn't. Relationship questions are not as easily resolved. Often the people arguing think they are arguing about content when actually it is the nature of their relationship that they are questioning.

We may find that questions of content can be raised and resolved using a minimum of nonverbal communication. Words and sentences are an effective medium for dealing with informational aspects of messages, both simple and complex. When questions of relationship arise, and particularly when these questions are buried in matter that is supposedly concerned with content, the intricacies of such questions are often better expressed nonverbally. That is, if all we care about is knowing where someone is going, we can simply ask, "Where are you going?" If we want to show what we see as our superiority over that person, we might say very loudly, "Where are *you* going?" with our hands on our hips and exasperation in our voice. We express the relationship aspect of our message nonverbally.

It's good to remember that every communication is a combination of content and relationship factors and is expressed with verbal and nonverbal elements together. If we're unsure about the information someone is trying to pass on to us, we should try not to be distracted by nonverbal messages. If we're trying to understand what that person is saying about the nature of our relationship, nonverbal cues might be more helpful to us.

Try This

Plot several conversations you have had with other people recently. Put down the other person's name and a representative comment he or she made to you. Consider both the content and relationship aspects of the message. For example, let me transcribe part of a recent conversation:

Name
Wife

Comment
"Remember to write."

Content
Wants me to spend morning writing.

Relationship
Controlling (in this instance), as if she directs my life.

Consider This _____

A very "nice" friend of ours was upset because a man she liked responded to her with total indifference one evening. However, she was perfectly cool about it. At their next—and last—meeting, the man apologized for his previous indifference; the woman merely shrugged and said, "Oh, that was nothing." She felt she had handled the situation thoughtfully and smoothly, and she later wondered why he did not call again. We said, without thinking, "Because you <u>lied</u>." The woman turned with a look of sharp surprise at our relabeling effort. Then she said quietly, "Yes," and cried for some time.

—Ernst G. Beier and Evans G. Valens, *People-Reading: How We Control Others, How They Control Us*

Communication Relationships Can Be Equal or Unequal

The communication relationships we have with people are all based on whether we see our status as basically equal or basically unequal. This status depends on many factors—circumstance, personality, age, wealth, job position, and so on. We may, at different points in life, feel unequal with our parents, teachers, siblings, or authority figures. This can change at any time. We may find we feel equal or superior to people we once felt inferior to.

When we not only feel, but are, on an equal level with another person, the two of us tend to mirror each other's behavior—sometimes intentionally, sometimes not. We may discover we are depressed at the same time, cheerful at the same time. In relationships based on equality, both people usually try to minimize the differences and emphasize the similarities between them, whether or not they do this on purpose. These are the relationships labeled symmetrical in the previous section.

People involved in an unequal relationship do just the opposite. These relationships are often defined by social or cultural context. There are generally unequal relationships between doctor and patient, employer and employee, parent and child. These relationships are labeled complementary.

Complementary relationships also exist in more informal relationships. Two friends may slip into a pattern of one being the decision maker, the other less decisive; one levelheaded, the other scatterbrained; one the agitator, the other the soother. Sometimes there are very subtle arrangements where one person is the decision maker on matters of where to eat, but the other is the decision maker on matters of finance. One may be superior in matters of entertaining but the other is superior in matters of car purchase and maintenance. People some-

Try This

In the situations described here, do you see your self assuming an equal or an unequal relationship with the people indicated?

1. With your best friend: making plans for the weekend.

2. With your parents: deciding what you will do after you graduate.

3. With your roommate: determining when the record player or television will be on or off.

4. On a date: choosing where the two of you will go.

5. In working with another student on a project: deciding who does what part of the work.

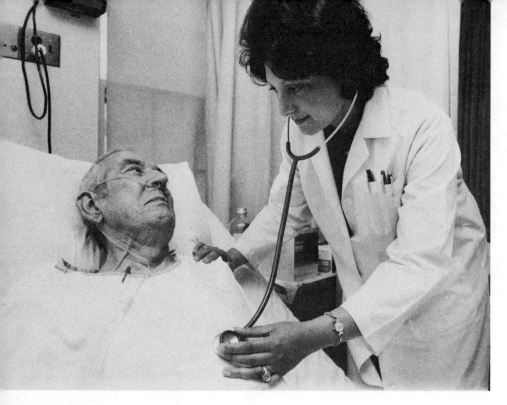

When we are young we generally feel inferior to people older than ourselves, but this can change. Here an older man finds himself in an inferior position to a physician much younger than he is.

times work out an equilibrium or balance of complementary relationships. In each case it is important to note the interlocking nature of the roles; the superior behavior of one person often evokes and reinforces complementary behavior from the other person.

There can be problems in both symmetrical and complementary relationships, and one form is not being suggested as better than the other. Some people respond best in symmetrical relationships, others in complementary relationships. Problems can arise in a symmetrical relationship where partners mirror each other's negative behaviors, creating a vicious cycle. Trouble may surface in a complementary relationship when one person's inferior behavior reinforces superiority in the other person to such an extent that the superior person becomes unreasonably rigid or powerful. The nature of our communication relationship depends upon who the other person is, what position he or she holds, what message is being conveyed, and when and where the interaction is occurring.

We see these first four principles operating in every communication situation: We cannot *not* communicate, even when we choose not to speak. We use both verbal and nonverbal channels when we talk. Our communications with others relate information and define a relationship between us at the same time, and that relationship can be symmetrical, complementary, or both at different times. Knowing this may raise certain questions for us about our own interpersonal communication, such as:

1. Why am I having trouble communicating?
2. How much more am I saying than I mean to? How much more could I say that I am not?
3. How can I be certain my nonverbal communication agrees with and reinforces my verbal communication?
4. What kinds of relationships is my communication defining for me? Can or should this be changed?
5. Are the symmetrical and complementary relationships that I have with others satisfactory, or should they be changed? How can I control the nature of the relationships I have with others?

If we are going to begin to question our own communication behavior, we do not need to stop with these first four principles. Dean Barnlund mentions five other characteristics that will help us gain a broader perspective of the interpersonal situation.[2] He says that our need to communicate "arises out of the need to reduce uncertainty, to act effectively, [and] to defend or strengthen the ego." To understand this, Barnlund suggests, we must view communication as a process that is circular, complex, irreversible, unrepeatable, and involving of the total personality.

Communication Is a Process

When we look at communication as a process, we mean that each communication situation is part of an ongoing series of actions. To fully understand any single communication, we really need to know all that has come before. Each communication experience is accumulative—a result of what has preceded. And each experience affects all the ones still to come. For example, as we talk with another person, we may discover an attitude or prejudice that we hadn't known about. That new information will change how we communicate with that person in the future. The present conversation is a point of development for all future conversations with that person. It is a point in a process.

Think about the kind of conversation you would have if you, at your present age, could talk to the person you were at sixteen, at thirteen, at eight. Each of the "you's" would be a completely developed person *for that age*, yet each would be merely a developmental point for the "you's" to follow. Communication builds on itself. The process goes on as long as we are alive.

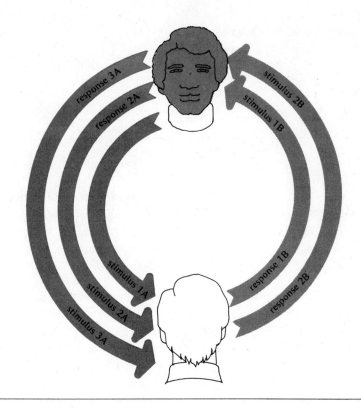

Figure 5.
Communication is circular.

Communication Is Circular

To view each of our interpersonal communication situations as circular means that we are concerned not only with the effect of our initial message on someone else, but also with the effect of his or her response on us. We then respond based on this new message. This act of going around, back and forth in this way, is important to grasp. (See Figure 5.) Though it may sound as if we're going in circles, we are not. We are both constantly changing and making corrections in our thinking as we interact.

Although a minimum number of stimuli and responses are depicted in Figure 5, this figure reveals the cyclical nature of communication triggered by the first stimulus. For example, if your initial stimulus is, "How was the party last night?" I might reply, "Dull!" You might inquire, "Oh, how come?" and I would answer, "Nothing happened." You might follow with, "What do you mean?" and so on. The conversation builds on itself. Each remark makes sense only in terms of what preceded it. Remember that in real conversations, many stimuli can occur and be considered at once. Either person may, at any time, provide a new stimulus which can start off its own chain reaction.

Communication Is Complex

In every interpersonal communication we share with another person, there are at least six "people" involved:

1. The person we think we are,
2. The person our partner thinks we are,
3. The person we believe our partner thinks we are,
4. The person our partner thinks he or she is,
5. The person we think our partner is, and
6. The person our partner believes we think he or she is.

Even the most apparently simple interpersonal encounter is actually quite complicated.

Notice how many variables are operating in the relationship shown in Figure 6 when the six "persons" are described. With only four constants, mathematicians can come up with close to fifty possible relationships; thus, even in a simple communication situation the number of variables involved is large. When we talk with others, what we say depends on how we perceive each of the variables, just as what others say to us depends on the variables they perceive. The more honestly we talk, the more we can be sure that the variables we perceive are accurate. If the people in Figure 6 take the time to get to know each other, he may discover she's not as self-confident as she first appeared to be and she may find that his "enthusiasm" is nothing more than undirected nervous energy. She may start to appreciate his sincerity or ambitiousness instead, if those traits seem to apply to him. If our perceptions

Figure 6.
There are at least six "people"
involved in every interpersonal
communication.

aren't accurate, we correct them. Thus, as open communication proceeds, it becomes better and better because:

1. It becomes grounded on perceptions that are more accurate — perceptions that are tested through actual interaction.
2. It becomes better adapted to the person we're talking to because we have a better idea of where he or she is coming from.
3. It becomes less open to chance. We need to do less guessing about the other person and less guessing about the nature of the message.
4. There is less chance for breakdowns to occur. Breakdowns often involve simple misperceptions and misinterpretations. These can never be avoided completely. But big breakdowns based on gross error become less likely. We know better who and what we are dealing with.

Communication is complex. There is no way to control all the variables involved, but the more accurate our perceptions are, the better chance we will have of minimizing the complexity of the communication.

Communication Is Irreversible and Unrepeatable

Each interpersonal experience is totally unique. It can never occur again in just the same way under any circumstances. Sometimes we wish we *could* take back things we've said. Have you ever said, in the heat of an argument, "You're hopeless! You'll never amount to anything!" or something equally cruel? You can't ever take the sting out of a remark like that, no matter what you say or how you apologize later. The remark cannot be taken back.

It is impossible to recreate a communication situation because the knowledge, feelings, and impressions a person brings to an experience change with time, even within a matter of seconds. Saying "I love you" because we want to in a particular situation is quite different from repeating it because we are asked to, even if the words are the same both times. The communication can never be precisely repeated, no matter how many times we say the very same words, because both people are different as a result of the words' having been said in the first place.

Despite thorough organization and planning, most of what occurs interpersonally is spontaneous — open to chance. Every moment is, indeed, a once-in-a-lifetime moment, made unique by the once-in-a-lifetime set of circumstances that came together at that point in time.

Have you ever tried to repeat a funny story or describe a hilarious incident only to have your listeners say, "What's so funny about that?" You end up saying, "I guess you had to be there." It is impossible to reconstruct past communication experiences. Even when we come close, new and different factors over which we have no control arise to change the situation and the communication.

Communication Involves the Total Personality

Our whole organism is involved in communication, not just our body or mind, reason or emotion. We find meaning in communication by involving our entire personality. Just as every message we send reveals, in a way, where we are, how we have developed, right up to that point, so we should look at the messages we receive from others as revealing the same things about them. From the various cues that others reveal to us, we construct a total picture of them. Whether the image is accurate or not does not matter as much as the fact that it is *our* configuration and we use it when we respond to them.

Consider This

SON: Well, when we didn't go fishing it seemed to throw my whole day off. I didn't have any schedule anymore. I started doing other things and the next thing I knew the day was gone.

FATHER: Bill, I'm awfully sorry about the fishing, but your mother and I were out late Friday night and I was very tired. If you didn't study because of the fishing, it sounds like you're blaming me.

SON: Not exactly, but this is the third time in a row you haven't done what you said you would.

FATHER: It is? Let's see. I guess you're right. Looks like I haven't been handling my responsibilities well either. I guess you were pretty annoyed about the whole thing and it got in the way of your concentrating on your studies.

SON: Well, I was pretty upset. Somehow I didn't feel like doing any homework.

FATHER: I can understand that, Bill. Look, let's go fishing next Saturday, real early. I'll make it a point to get to bed early Friday night.

SON: Great!

FATHER: And, Bill, what about your studying? I know you were angry about the fishing but you're only hurting yourself when you get low grades. Even if I do the wrong thing in slipping up on my promises, is there any point in your doing the wrong thing by not studying?

SON: No, I guess not. I just wasn't thinking. I'm going to set aside a study period every day and stick to it.

As we receive additional cues about people's whole personalities, we change our image of them. Communication provides information for this change. The fact that we depend on communication for the data we use to keep up with other people's development, and they with ours, is due to what is called the transactional nature of communication, or *communication as transaction*.[3] Communication is the tool used to gain the information. As the overlapping and interlocking circles in Figure 7 indicate, the personalities of the people become intertwined as they communicate.

Most of the communication we engage in is intended, consciously or unconsciously, to change the other person. The change need not be big. We might only want Sue to stop reading and listen to us. We might want Bob to consider our opinion on the upcoming election. Simply asking someone to focus his or her attention on us for a minute is asking that person to change, in a way.

Think of the last interpersonal communication you had where you may have unintentionally tried to get the other person to accept your ideas or simply to understand where you were coming from.[4] Can you see how your interpersonal behavior was purposeful, even if you can't verbalize the purpose?

When we *consciously* set out to persuade or change another person, we will not only bring our total personality to bear in order to effect the desired change, but we will summon even greater

Figure 7.
The transactional nature of communication.

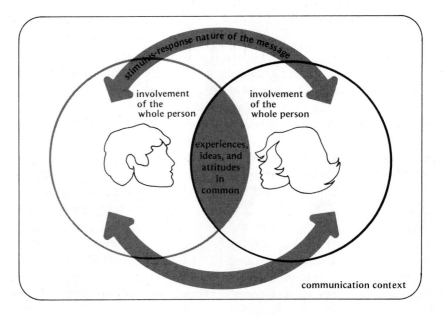

stimulus-response nature of the message

involvement of the whole person

involvement of the whole person

experiences, ideas, and attitudes in common

communication context

resources—more effective language, stronger evidence, and more powerful delivery—to create the change. In analyzing any interaction, we must consider the purposes of those involved—that is, the reason they are bringing their total personalities into the relationship.

CONTEXTS

Human communication does not occur in a vacuum. It *always* takes place in a complicated context and the context *always* influences the kind of communication that occurs. Interpersonal events cannot be understood by looking just at each individual in isolation, or by looking at the people but ignoring the environment. Who, what, when, where, and how are all important variables and the way these variables interact with each other is also important.[5] Unfortunately, it is impossible to be aware of *all* possible contextual elements, much less the way they affect each other. Some elements, like very personal and private feelings, are never revealed overtly. And always it seems there are so many elements at play at one time that we could never sort them out. Here, we will examine the human context and the context of environment.

The Human Context

Picture this: You are talking to a teacher in his office about the grade you think you ought to get for a course. Your communication is affected, simultaneously, by what your friend Karen told you about this teacher, your own past experience with him, your feelings about teachers in general, your feelings about education in general and your own in particular, the teacher's actual expectations of you, what you perceive as the teacher's expectations of you, etc., etc. The point is, we cannot separate the communication that is occurring from the people who are communicating. We must look at their wants, needs, desires, and goals if we are to understand the whole interpersonal communication situation.

In talking with this teacher, your communication will be affected by how well you know him. Just as his appearance, clothing, language, posture, and mannerisms will affect you, yours will also affect him.

It is people who give life to communication, and how well they know each other helps define the context. If you feel comfortable with teachers, you may not be affected by the role teachers play. If you've never known a teacher as a friend (or a friend as a teacher, for that matter) you might find the situation awkward and artificial. There are hundreds of other human context factors that will contribute to the

This communication context is a complicated one because it includes so many varied elements.

ultimate success or failure of this interpersonal encounter. Communication contexts are complicated because they consist of so many varied elements.

The Context of Environment

Consider the following interpersonal communication encounter, as described on the left, and the specific environmental variables that bear on the situation, on the right:

Encounter	Variables
You are studying in the library late one evening and are ready to call it a night when in walks a friend who has just finished studying and is headed back to the dormitory. Your friend asks, "Care to go for a walk?" You decide to walk across campus together.	Location: Library (sterile and cold) Time: 11 p.m. Light: Bright fluorescent lights Persons: Two friends Furniture Arrangement: Uncomfortable and awkward (large table, straight chairs) Temperature: Cold and damp Physical Space: Comfortable but distant

How would this encounter be different if it took place at noon on a crowded public beach on a hot summer day? Would you say different things? Talk louder? Laugh more? Walk slower?

All human communication is affected by the physical circumstances under which it takes place, whether it be a job interview, a pizza party, a formal cocktail hour, a classroom speech, a public lecture, or whatever. People's words and behavior change according to the context. Having a phone conversation with someone is not the same as talking to that person face-to-face. Each situation has its own set of variables and cues that may determine whether an exchange is friendly and comfortable or cold, hostile, and tense.

IMPROVING SKILLS IN INTERPERSONAL COMMUNICATION

The overall goal of this book is to help you to understand interpersonal communication and to become a more effective sender and receiver of interpersonal messages. Each chapter includes a list of specific skills that are tied to the concept developed in that chapter. There are some general skills, too, that relate to interpersonal communication as a whole. Developing these skills will make it easier to master those listed at the end of each chapter. They are practical. They can be started at once:

Broaden your experience.   We should actively search out new relationships and not shy away from potential encounters just because they appear to be unlike what we've dealt with before. Interpersonal communication must occur between people—between us and someone else—and often this means reaching out for new relationships.

Consider This _____

The macho world of CB is part soap and part horse opera. Says Amitai
Etzioni, the eminent Columbia University sociologist: "A CB allows you to
present a false self: to be beautiful, masculine, tall, rich, without being any of
those things. Like the traveling salesman who drops into a singles bar and says
he's the president of his company, a person can project on the air waves
anything he wants to be." The person who installs a CB set and adopts a
"handle" (nickname) and starts "modulating" on the air, is creating a
character and reaching out to others while still maintaining anonymity. Adds
Etzioni: "People in our kind of society, torn from our roots, want to relate
without fully investing ourselves in a relationship, as we would if we joined a
church group or worked on a campaign. With a CB, you can have personal
contact with the turn of a dial. It is very controllable and protects you from
getting too involved."
—*Time*, May 10, 1976

We can take steps toward forming new associations rather than
waiting to let them simply happen to us. Growth will not necessarily be
immediate, but there is no doubt that we will open up to many new
kinds of experiences. Willingness to reach out requires risk, but exciting
relationships are often built on just that kind of risk.

- Plan to attend more activities (parties, athletic events, lectures, so-
  cials, movies, etc.)
- Plan to meet more people. Break out of your small group of friends
  and acquaintances. Make contact with at least one new person a day.
- Eat breakfast, lunch, or dinner with new people. Sit somewhere different. Join a new group.
- Join a new club, organization, or program. Look for new ways to use
  your talents and abilities.

Realize that growth takes time.   Wonderful, satisfying relationships
don't develop overnight. Like getting to know one's self, really getting
to know another person takes time. Give it time. It's a good idea, if we
have known someone in one way only—in the college context, for example—and would like to know more about that person, to try interacting in different social settings, talking about different things, and sharing reactions to the new things we have experienced together.

People are often quite different in the context of their own families
than they are in the context of college. We may discover a new side of a
person by observing him or her in a setting other than the one we're accustomed to. Traveling, shopping, eating, or simply spending hours at a
time with a person can be very revealing if the two of us usually don't
do these things together. Only through time can we become familiar

enough with the feelings and motivations of another to really understand the person. The key to relationship building at this stage is simply patience.

- Ask new acquaintances to do things with you.
- Don't push yourself on other people.
- Allow relationships to develop—slowly.
- Begin to spend time with other people.
- Practice being a social animal—feeling the energy that other people transmit and all their unique qualities.
- Decide what you need from other people and what you can give them.
- Let them know you are ready and open to sharing.

Use existing relationships in new ways.   We might try using existing relationships as a testing ground for the information we'll be picking up about interpersonal communication. Try things out with a friend. Practice new patterns of sending and receiving messages. Create hypothetical situations similar to some of the ones described in this chapter and develop other ways of coping with these situations. Allow "communication" to be the subject for conversations and discussions. (Don't give up if this feels strange at first!) Talk about communication with reference to the principles discussed in this chapter. Be specific about how to improve skills.

- Begin to talk about your behavior. Share your impressions and be responsive to those of your friends and acquaintances. (Remember that as you encourage feedback, you are likely to get as much negative as positive.)
- Do not be defensive and refute comments or defend your behavior. It is important to get honest reactions; defensiveness may encourage dishonesty.
- Experiment with things that you are learning about communication. Do some of the "Try This" activities suggested in this book with your friends. It is better to experiment in a warm, trusting environment first, before taking new behaviors beyond the confines of such security and protectiveness.
- Engage in *metacommunication*: talking about the communication you engage in. Is it effective? . . . offensive? Can it be strengthened or improved? What can I do better?

Develop openness.   Skill development in any area begins with an awareness that something can and should be done. We need to be open to change. We can start by simply trying to become more aware of the kinds of things we do, the feelings we have toward our selves and

Try This

Think about the last communication you shared with the person you consider your closest friend. What contextual variables affected your communication? How many can you remember? Try to be specific. Here are several variables that may have affected it:

— time of day

— noise or distractions

— how you met (at this time)

— furniture

— weather

— smells

— what you talked about

— what you wore

— touch

— location

— other people present

Explain the significance of each variable and how it affected your communication.

others, the way we view life and what we want our place in it to be. We should learn to monitor our own behavior and feelings as objectively as possible, becoming more open and responsive to our internal experiences.

Openness also means being receptive to all that goes on around us. As we open up to our environment, we will begin to be more sensitive to the small details of things that we may once have overlooked. This sensitivity will increase our ability to recreate situations in our mind to better analyze and dissect their parts. Our new behavior may be more carefully considered than before in light of our past successes and failures. This is growth, change, development—maturity. A lot of people would discover a great deal more if only they would pause and look and feel and care just a bit more than they do.[6]

- Be prepared to find things about yourself that need changing.
- Realize that you are not perfect: there *is* room for improvement.
- Be ready to take action wherever necessary. As you open yourself to discovery, be conscious of those things about which something can be done. Commit yourself to those areas.
- Keep your sights on progress—moving forward in a positive direction. Do not worry about past failures and do not try to anticipate the future; deal with what can be done *now*—in the present.

Improve the exactness of your communication.   We could all stand to improve the exactness of our communication. It's a great help to be able to convey to others just what we mean to convey and to receive from them just what they mean to send to us. This has been labeled *fidelity*. Improving the exactness of our communication is a skill. If we're aware of the need for fidelity, we will become more sensitive to those situations where some of the fidelity is lost. We will be better able to detect when meaning is becoming distorted. And, it is hoped, we'll be able to take steps to correct the situation.

- Think about what you intend to say before opening your mouth. Plan it out rather completely.
- Think about ways you can elaborate on or enumerate the things you have to say. Practice the art of skillful repetition—how many different ways can you say the same things?
- Be responsive to the feedback you get and use it to alter your message as necessary. Plan to make changes in your message to assure that the other person will hear what you intend him or her to hear.

Make a contract with yourself.[7]   Vague, general plans for improvement or change generally do not work. What is needed is an explicit contract which lays out the objectives and enumerates specific measures you can use to achieve them. In this way progress can be charted.

- What changes do you want to make? Be realistic about this. You may want to divide your goal into smaller, more manageable parts. For example, if one of your goals was to make more friends, your first step might be to say hello to one new person each day, or four new people each week.
- How will you monitor your progress? Charts and journals may help you keep track. You might also ask your friends to monitor your behavior.
- What rewards will you get for fulfilling each part of your contract? For every new person you say hello to, you might reward yourself with a long walk, a movie, or a meal out. How about a day off? Reinforcement is essential for making the contract work. It helps you meet your own desired standards of performance. Don't be stingy here. Generosity and verbal approval will help you continue with the contract. There is no harm in patting yourself on the back or whispering words of praise in your own ear. Why be unduly modest if no one else hears you exulting: "That was a good thing I did," or "I'm pleased with the way that turned out," or "That is one quality I really like about myself."
- How will you know when you have completed the contract? At the end of two weeks you will have said hello to eight new people and you will be ready to move on to the next step in making friends. Set daily or weekly goals.
- What will you do if you fail to meet the contract? Appropriate punishments can be just as effective as appropriate rewards, provided they are realistic and established in advance of the contract period. But plan to make them stick. Some possibilities are: cleaning your closet (or room); washing your car; raking leaves (or cleaning up litter); straightening out drawers (or a collection).

It is a good idea to write out the contract. This makes it more official and increases the chances you will honor it. With concentration and practice, many of the skills you set for yourself will soon become second nature to you. You can form a contract around many or all of the skills and activities in this book.

In this chapter we have examined the three basic elements of interpersonal communication: people, messages, and effects. I have tried to show how interpersonal communication is unique by describing some of its characteristics. We looked at nine principles — things that occur in every communication situation. We mentioned two important contexts that must be considered whenever we communicate: the human context and the context of environment. Finally, I talked about goals and skills. In the next chapter we will examine methods we have for acquiring information—information that is essential for effective interpersonal communication.

OTHER READING

Barbara Fast, *Getting Close: Daring to Be Really Intimate with Friends and Lovers* (New York: Berkley Publishing Company, 1978). A description of intimacy that helps us learn how to risk and how to communicate with others on a deep, richly rewarding, emotional level. The author also writes about being intimate with ourselves, guiding readers to discover a new source of strength, comfort, and creativity. Full of examples, this is a warm, enjoyable book.

Frederic F. Flach, *Choices: Coping Creatively with Personal Change* (New York: Bantam Books, Inc., 1979). How can creativity help solve our problems? How can we open our minds and increase the flow of new ideas? How can we abandon self-defeating attitudes and values and gain more realistic and rewarding ones? Flach's suggestions will help us gain a sense of personal importance and direction.

Erving Goffman, *The Presentation of Self in Everyday Life* (Garden City, N.Y.: Doubleday Anchor Books, 1959). A description of how people present themselves as characters who wear masks which others acknowledge, like performers before an audience. The author illustrates how people often form teams to help define and support their roles, how inconsistent roles are enacted, and how people manage impressions.

Thomas A. Harris, *I'm OK—You're OK: A Practical Guide to Transactional Analysis* (New York: Harper & Row, Publishers, 1969). Provides practical methods for understanding and analyzing the complicated and destructive games people play. Helps those who are bound by the past to become free to respond to the needs and aspirations of others in the present and, thus, to become responsible people.

Muriel James and Dorothy Jongeward, *Born to Win: Transactional Analysis with Gestalt Experiments* (Reading, Mass.: Addison-Wesley Publishing Company, 1971). Straightforward methods concerned with discovering and fostering awareness, self-responsibility, and genuineness. A useful study guide for people who want to increase their awareness, direct their own lives, make decisions, and enhance the lives of others. Encourages people to see their uniquenesses.

Jess Lair, *I Ain't Well—But I Sure Am Better: Mutual Need Therapy* (Garden City, N.Y.: Doubleday & Company, 1975). The thesis of this book is that people will come to a greater appreciation of life once they see their mutual need for each other. Lair challenges readers to establish relationships with a few intimate friends they can trust—people they care about and who care about them.

Alan Lakein, *How to Get Control of Your Time and Your Life* (New York: New American Library, 1973). Practical, sensible suggestions on how to get more accomplished each day by setting goals and establishing priorities and getting organized. Tips include how to achieve better self-understanding, how to build willpower, and how to keep oneself on target.

John Powell, S.J., *Why Am I Afraid to Tell You Who I Am?* (Niles, Ill.: Argus Communications Co., 1969). An interesting, enjoyable, and basic approach that offers insights on self-awareness, personal growth, and interpersonal communication. Chapters on how to deal with emotions and the games and roles people play are realistic and down-to-earth.

David Viscott, *Risking* (New York: Pocket Books, 1977). A common-sense approach to seizing opportunities and taking risks without fear. Viscott offers a guide that will help you understand what happens when you take risks. He challenges you to examine your life—to find objectives worth taking risks to achieve. When you identify these, your actions become purposeful and your life begins to make sense.

Leonard Zunin and Natalie Zunin, *Contact: The First Four Minutes* (New York: Ballantine Books, 1972). The authors examine the way people meet and relate during the initial phase of interaction. They offer suggestions for developing more control over the first four minutes which will make relationships warmer, closer, and more significant.

NOTES

[1] Paul Watzlawick, Janet Helmick Beavin, and Don D. Jackson, *Pragmatics of Human Communication: A Study of Interactional Patterns, Pathologies, and Paradoxes* (New York: W. W. Norton & Company, Inc., 1967). See Chapter 2, "Some Tentative Axioms of Communication," pp. 48–71.

[2] From "Toward a Meaning-Centered Philosophy of Communication" by Dean C. Barnlund, *Journal of Communication*, Vol. 12:4 (1962), pp. 202–203. Reprinted by permission.

[3] John Stewart, "An Interpersonal Approach to the Basic Course," *The Speech Teacher* 21 (1972): 10.

[4] Dean C. Barnlund, "Communication: The Context of Change," in *Perspectives on Communication*, Carl E. Larson and Frank E. X. Dance, eds. (Milwaukee: University of Wisconsin Communication Research Center, 1968), p. 27

[5] See Harold D. Lasswell, "The Structure and Function of Communication in Society," in *The Communication of Ideas*, L. Bryson, ed. (New York: Harper & Row, 1948), p. 37.

[6] Arthur Gordon, *A Touch of Wonder* (Old Tappan, New Jersey: Spire Books, 1976), p. 11.

[7] Philip G. Zimbardo, *Shyness* (New York: Jove Publications, Inc., 1977), pp. 229–30.

2

Creating Meaning:
Perception

Have you ever thought about how people form impressions of other people? We do it all the time. If our perceptions of each other are correct, effective interaction can occur. But *how* do we form the impressions? Say a woman is at a party and she notices a man to whom she is at least superficially attracted. She is aware of his movements, his voice, his clothes. From her observations she draws conclusions about how this man thinks and feels. She may make inferences about his needs, goals, and attitudes. She will guide her action toward him and her prediction of future interactions by her perceptions. As she made judgments about him, he may also have been making judgments about her. If the observations and predictions being made are incorrect, communication between the two may get off to a bad start or may never start.

This chapter is about perception—how we create meaning. I'll talk about how we select, organize, and interpret information. I'll discuss some factors that affect what we perceive, such as our tendency to label things, physical and psychological distance, and the restrictive roles we sometimes play. Finally, I'll discuss how we can improve our skills in perception so that genuine, effective interaction is more likely to occur.

As you read this chapter, bear in mind that we develop, create, and maintain our self-concept, in large part, by the information we process. At the same time, our self-concept helps to determine *what* we process. How we see our selves influences the kind of information to which we are likely to be receptive. The self-concept and the perceptive process are closely related. The self-concept will be discussed in the next chapter.

WHAT YOU PERCEIVE IS WHAT YOU GET

You have just come out of a movie with a friend feeling that it was one of the best you have ever seen. You turn to share your exhilaration and quickly realize that your friend's reaction was completely different. You saw the same movie but your friend says that he was restless and bored, that the movie was too long and did not include enough action.

You have just completed your third week of the term and are walking away from class with a classmate who says, "Finally, I understand what is going on in there!" You look at her, surprised, and reply, "Not me. I have no idea what's happening. I'm more confused now than on the first day of class!"

These are normal, everyday occurrences, and they show that perceptions vary between people. What one person thinks is not necessarily the same as what another person thinks. Clearly, what each person perceives is a function of something unique and personal.

Perception is the process of gathering information and giving it meaning. We see a movie and we give meaning to it: "It's one of the best I've seen." We come away from class after the third week and we give meaning to it: "It finally makes sense." We gather information from what our senses see, hear, touch, taste, and smell, and we give meaning to that information. Although the information may come to us in a variety of forms, it is all processed, or *perceived*, in the mind.

———————————————————————— **Try This**

For just a moment now, exercise your imagination. Listen to the messages being sent from the following environments. What are your perceptions in each case?

1. You see a slum with trash spilling out on the sidewalk. A child is looking down at the concrete from steps going into an apartment. What do you hear?

2. You are in a gray, bleak, and barren back ward in a state mental hospital with people sitting on benches. Their drab appearance is heightened by baggy clothes, and there's a smell that is only too common in such a ward. How would you feel in that environment?

3. There is a beautiful, royal blue ocean with whitecaps breaking against a sparkling, sandy beach. The beach is outlined by palm trees and a few fluffy, white clouds. How do you feel about that message?

4. A warm fire is crackling in the fireplace. The lights are dimly lit and outside the picture window snow is falling quietly. Soft music is playing in the background, and you are there with the person with whom you want to share that environment. What are your feelings now?

—paraphrased from Ken Olson, *Can You Wait Till Friday?*

 Try This ——————————————————————————

Communication and perception are so closely related that we can't really talk about one without the other. To understand interpersonal communication we need some understanding of perception, for it is through perception that we give meaning to our world, become aware of our surroundings, and come to know our selves and others. Most of the time we engage in the process without paying attention to what we are doing. We rarely think of *how* it is occurring or how we could improve it. Perception is a complex activity, but by understanding the process we can improve our chances for more effective interpersonal communication. We will expand the perimeters of our own personal world.

THE PERCEPTION SIEVE:
HOW YOU CREATE MEANING

One way to view the general process of perception is to visualize a large sieve with holes of different shapes and sizes. (See Figure 1.) Each hole represents a category we understand or with which we have some experience. The largest categories are those areas we're most familiar with or have given preference to—special needs and interests. The number of holes in the sieve changes constantly as we encounter new experiences, just as the size of the holes changes according to our changing values—what we consider to be most important.

Our perceptual categories develop as we grow. Our interests, experiences, and knowledge create them. Our culture, parents, religion, education, and peers are probably the strongest influences on how we perceive the world. As our interests change, we drop old categories and form new ones. As a child of six you may have wanted to be a firefighter; as an adolescent you may have wanted to be a veterinarian; as a student you may want to be a lawyer; as an adult you may choose to become an electronics technician. Think of how many of your other interests have changed over the years. Sometimes we may expand a perceptual category to include a related piece of information; sometimes, when we can't relate the new information to the old, we create a whole new category. ·

Notice in the figure that certain holes are black. There are some areas where we make a determined effort *not* to gain any more information. We may no longer want to hear any more rumors about our roommate. We may no longer want to read science fiction. We might no longer want to taste any drinks containing rum and coconut milk. These are experiences we choose to close our selves off from.

Notice, too, that the sieve holes are irregular in size and shape. If information comes to us that does not exactly fit one of our present

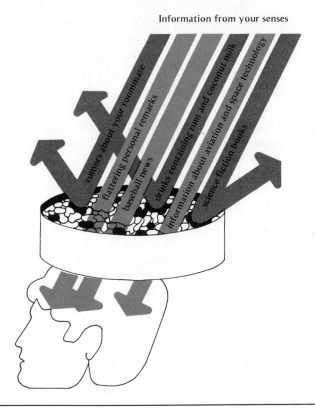

Information from your senses

rumors about your roommate
flattering personal remarks
baseball news
drinks containing rum and coconut milk
information about aviation and space technology
science fiction books

Figure 1. The perception
sieve.

categories, we might distort that information so that it does fit. One function of our perceptual filtering process is to protect us from information we dislike or disagree with. We do not let that information through, or we adjust it as necessary. For example, if we heard some unflattering remarks about our roommate but one good comment like, "You must admit she has a sense of humor," we might hear only about the sense of humor and filter out all the other comments. We tend to hear what we want to hear.

No Two Are Alike

Every person has a unique perceptual filtering system, although there is some cultural overlap. If we are white, middle-class, urban eighteen-year-olds, our perceptions are likely to resemble those of other white, middle-class, urban eighteen-year-olds more than those of any other group in society. But ours still won't be exactly like those of any other person. Each individual's system depends on numerous elements which either broaden or limit the size of the categories.

Our physiological make-up affects how much information we are able to gather. The number of visual stimuli we take in is limited by how well our eyes work, for example. And although the number of stimuli we ordinarily sense is impressive, it is still little compared with the maximum amount of which we are capable. Most of us are physiologically able to distinguish 7,500,000 different colors.[1] Our ears can pick up sounds ranging from 20 to 20,000 vibration cycles per second. We can distinguish among 5,000 different smells and 10,000 different tastes. Even our sense of touch is more sensitive than we might have thought. Our fingers can feel the separations between objects as little as 3 to 8 mm apart.[2] Our bodies are extremely sensitive instruments for taking in sensory information.

The kind of information we perceive is strongly affected by our expectations, attitudes, beliefs, interests, emotions, needs, language, experience, and knowledge. What is important to realize is (1) that what new information we pick up depends on the perceptual categories we have available, and (2) that each of our systems is unique. Although several of our categories may be similar to someone else's, we must never assume that all of ours are like all of his or hers or even that *any* are identical.

THE FAMILY CIRCUS®   **By Bil Keane**

1-27

Copyright 1979
The Register and Tribune
Syndicate, Inc.

"This is nothing. When I was your age we had snow that came all the way up to here on me."

Implications

What does this perception-sieve analogy imply? First, that perception is not a passive process. Our perceptions are our own and we have some control over them; we do not have total control because our culture, environment, and upbringing create categories we might not even be aware of. But because we have most of the control, we do not record everything our senses take in. Perception is selective. We block out some sights, sounds, and smells. For the most part, we actively apply our perceptual filter to incoming stimuli. Our perceptual system gives us a way of dealing with outside reality in terms of inside reality—our own thoughts, feelings, and attitudes.

Although our perceptions may be well established, they can and do change. The more open we are to new experiences, the more likely it is that our perceptions will change. If we aren't willing to try new things, we may not allow information through that does not correspond with established categories. We may adapt some of the categories to keep up with the times, but we are generally rather inflexible.

We can become less rigid if we realize we have a lot of room for new information and if we are willing to take in information unrelated to what we already know. We might develop conditional categories for information we consider risky, for information we're not sure what we're going to do with yet. We will have a hard time with information totally unrelated to our present knowledge and experience because we have no familiar way of processing it. But knowing that we do have room for new experiences, if we'll only let them in, is a good start toward flexibility. And sometimes just realizing how little we know is an education in itself.

Another implication of the perception-sieve analogy is that we do not accept stimuli just as they are presented. We hear a teacher talking; what is actually being said may *not* be what we hear. Just as we reject some information altogether, we also shape some to make it fit in with our existing perceptions. If we do not understand an assignment, we might make what the teacher says come as close as we can to an assignment we had in the past. We change what the teacher says to make it fit. We are actively involved in making things fit whenever we receive information from our senses. The more we adapt stimuli to fit in with what we already know, the less likely it is that our views will reflect what actually occurred.

Finally, whatever meaning we are left with is based on *how* we process the information rather than on what actually happened. When someone says she sat through a doubleheader on a 90° day, what that experience means to us is a result of all our attitudes and feelings about

Figure 2. Our perceptions are based on our own attitudes and experiences.

baseball and hot weather. The experience could mean something quite different to her. (See Figure 2.)

Our interpretation of something is just that—an interpretation. Objects, events, and words don't *mean* in themselves. Their meanings are in us, in the way we evaluate them. When we talk with someone else, we make up what that person says just as when we see an object, we make up what that object looks like. Our filtering system determines how we view the world. The world exists for us as we perceive it. We cannot "tell it like it is"; we can only "tell it like we perceive it." Understanding this is a big step toward more effective interpersonal communication: it will help us become more sensitive to reactions to experiences, both ours and others', as personal interpretations of events. It's useful to think in terms of how and why we respond to something rather than in terms of the "something" as an experience in itself. Experiences have meaning only as we respond to them.

THE PERCEIVER: DOING YOUR PART

To develop the concept of perception in greater detail, let's think in terms of *selecting, organizing,* and *interpreting* information. These steps occur simultaneously and often instantaneously. The perception process is complicated by the fact that each process depends upon and is affected by uncountable numbers of factors occurring within us and within our environment.

Selecting: Choosing the Pieces of the Puzzle

We perceive selectively. That is, we limit the quantity of stimuli to which we attach meaning. We are selective simply because we are exposed to too many stimuli each day to be able to deal with all of them. Notice, for example, how our selectivity works in reference to advertising messages:

> . . . the average American adult is assaulted by a minimum of 560 advertising messages each day. Of the 560 to which he is exposed, however, he only notices seventy-six. In effect, he blocks out 484 advertising messages a day to preserve his attention for other matters.[3]

We usually choose to focus on those messages we agree with or which are most meaningful to us. During an election campaign, we tend to recall acceptable comments made by the candidate we support and unacceptable comments made by the other person. And we tend to ascribe statements with which we agree to the person we support.[4]

We select what we will perceive on the basis of our experiences. The next time you go to a party, pay attention to what seems most important to the people there. One person may observe the "performance" of the host and hostess. Another person might be totally absorbed with what people wear. Only the handsome men might catch one person's eye, while somebody else is aware of all the vivacious women present. The pretzels and cheese dip might be the center of attention for a number of people.

Each person chooses what is most meaningful on the basis of his or her experiences. One person may have been brought up to believe that how a host behaves is an essential element at a party. Another person may have parents who attach great importance to clothes. We will usually select for perception stimuli related to matters we've already given some thought to or had memorable experiences with. The act of selecting stimuli is the first one in the perceptual process. Once we have it, what do we do with that information?

Organizing: Putting the Pieces Together

Because information comes to us in a random, unstructured manner, we must do something with it to make sense of it. We must determine relationships: how the new information relates to other information we are receiving and to information we already have. To get an idea of how we need to organize cues, stop reading and look at this page and the marks on it as if there were no structure to it. Look at the room you are sitting in right now as if it contained no structure, as if you didn't know that chairs were for sitting on, floors for walking on, lamps for providing light. How about the view from the nearest window? Can you look at nature as if there were no structure? Our world, for us to understand it, requires organization, and we organize it by perceiving relationships.

Understanding structure helps us to understand our world.

If we see a swallow flying by, we know from experience that it is not the only bird in the world. We know there are many swallows like it and many other birds unlike it. We know that birds eat insects or seeds for food, and that birds can be, in turn, eaten by larger forms of life. We know that birds are warm-blooded as we are, and feathered as we are not. They walk as we do and fly as we do not. We organize our information about birds by noting relationships between this particular bird and all other birds of our experience. We organize information more

Find a picture or two of several people interacting. It should involve some strong emotional reactions: hostility or violence, for example. The picture should be fairly large. Write a paragraph describing the picture.

Now, take this same picture and show it to a variety of your friends (or classmates). Have them describe the picture; they could even write down their own descriptions in a paragraph or two.

1. Compare the descriptions you obtained.

2. Were there differences among them?

3. How can you account for the differences?—differences in backgrounds—differences in experiences?

4. Did some people interpret what was happening?

5. Did others simply describe what they saw?

6. What difference does this make to their perceptions?

or less consciously, in more or less detail, with all incoming stimuli. We can think of the organizational process as involving three steps—enlarging, simplifying, and closing—which occur simultaneously and instantaneously.

Enlarging.   The information our senses receive is in small pieces. Think of words as tiny pieces of information. In any communication situation, we try to put the words we hear into a larger context so that we can understand them better. We call this enlarging, looking for a frame of reference for the message. We might start by observing the whole nonverbal picture—the facial expressions, gestures, and body movements of the person sending the message—placing the words into that picture.

Think of your self as you talk with George. You listen to his words for a moment, then shift to the sincerity in his face, then back to his words, then to the pleasantness of his voice, then back to his words, then, perhaps, to the hole in his sweater. As you focus on what seems to you the most important aspect of George's total communication, other aspects fade into the background. You enlarge on the one important aspect—which may be his sincerity—to try "to gain the big picture." You need all the pieces to the puzzle of George's message, of course, but it helps to have an idea what the completed puzzle is supposed to look like, so that you can better anticipate the meaning and significance of each piece. You want to understand the expressions and feelings George reveals in his nonverbal cues to better understand the words you hear.

Simplifying.   Just as we search for a relationship between pieces of information and a larger framework into which we can place those pieces, we also look for ways to simplify complex or confusing stimuli. Complex stimuli are anything that we have difficulty understanding. We simplify them by finding patterns, an order that will help us make sense of the message.

For example, if we drove into a gas station to get directions, we might hear the attendant say something like, "You go up here to your first stoplight and turn left on Broadview. At your next light turn right. Then just after you pass Wiley High School, turn right, and the street you are looking for will be your next left." As a simplifying response we might reply, "So it's a left, two rights, and a left." We find order in the stimuli that will help us remember the essential information.

We do the same thing when we hear a teacher explaining an assignment or when we are taking notes in a lecture. We do not need, and we don't have time to record, all the teacher says. We simplify the message so that we have the essentials when it comes time to complete the assignment or to study our notes for a test.

Closing.   Because we get information in scraps, we must also fill in gaps. We tend to think in unified wholes. That is, we tend to see things as complete rather than separate. For example, in Figure 3 we tend to see a triangle, a square, and a rectangle rather than a series of disjointed, unorganized lines.

We probably engage in closing (or closure) more often than we realize. For example, how often have you completed a sentence for the person you were talking to? The more we get to know people, the better we know how they think, and the more often we will find we think ahead and close their thoughts. Very close friends can say a great deal to each other with few words — without knowing it, they may depend on closure for their messages to get through. Another example of closing is when we overhear others talking but are able to pick up only fragments of their conversation. From the fragments we fill in the rest of the conversation. Have you ever sat in a bus station or airport and made up

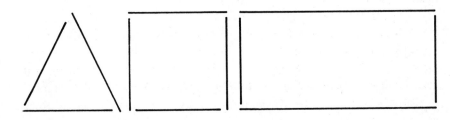

Figure 3. We tend to think in unified wholes.

_____

I know many other people who live with their ideas of each other. Not with a real person but with a "really." They doggedly refuse to let the evidence interfere with their opinions. They develop an idea about the other person and spend a lifetime trying to make him or her live up to that idea. A lifetime, too, of disappointments.

As James Taylor sings it:

> "First you make believe
> I believe the things
> that you make believe
> And I'm bound to let you down.
>
> Then it's I who have been deceiving
> Purposely misleading
> And all along you believed in me."

But when we describe what the other person is really like, I suppose we often picture what we want. We look through the prism of our need.

I know a man who believes that his love is really a very warm woman. The belief keeps him questing for that warmth. I know a woman who is sure that her mate has hidden strength, because she needs him to have it.

Against all evidence, one man believes that his woman is nurturing because he so wants her to be. After 20 years, another woman is still tapping hidden wells of sensuality in her mate which he has, she believes, repressed.

—Ellen Goodman, "People Are What They Seem to Be"

stories about the people you observed around you? From a minimum of cues we can put together a fairly complete story, making sense of the available information by closure.

Interpreting: Giving the Puzzle Meaning

Not only do we select and organize information, we also interpret it. That is, we assign some meaning to information, making evaluations and drawing conclusions about it to better predict future events and thereby minimize surprise.[5] Most of the interpreting we do takes either of two forms: *identification* or *evaluation*. Again, these processes occur rapidly and often simultaneously.

Stop reading for a minute and just listen. Can you label every sound you hear? Most of the sounds that go on around us are common ones and easily identifiable. Sometimes, however, there is a strange one—a scream, a bang, or an unrecognizable sound. After we identify the source of the noise, we evaluate it. Was it startling? Disruptive?

Harmful? In identifying, but more significantly, in evaluating information, we bring to bear all of our experiences and knowledge. The interpretation of information is a subjective judgment; it is a product of our own creation and it may or may not be valid.

We should realize that in interpreting what we sense, we seldom stop with apparent, observable cues. We almost always infer other characteristics. Such things as a person's attitudes, values, beliefs, motives, personality traits, interests, or background are not directly observable. Identification can be fairly reliable — interpretation is usually open to some question. We need to remember that if appearances are deceiving and untrustworthy, then our own inferences are even more tenuous. They may be little more than guesses based on uncertain facts.

THE PERCEIVED: OTHER INFLUENCES

Although the perceiver has been the main focus of this chapter so far, there are other factors that directly influence our perceptions. In a sense, these factors — stereotyping, proximity, and role[6] — are restricting forces. To understand them will help us to detect, analyze, and cope with them as we engage in interpersonal communication.

Stereotyping: Labels Are Restricting

We can usually tell fairly quickly just by looking at another person whether or not we would like to strike up a relationship. How? The appearance of a person often provides us with just enough cues to stereotype him or her. Stereotyping is the process of assigning fixed labels or categories to things and people we encounter, or, the reverse of this, placing things and people we encounter into fixed categories we have already established. When we stereotype a person, we assume things to be true about the individual because that person reminds us of someone else about whom those things may really have been true. We assume that the pattern that holds for one person holds for another, even though these people may actually have little in common. Stereotyping simplifies the task of making judgments about things and people. It is a commonly used device; all human beings employ it to deal with the tremendous flow of events around them.[7]

It does, however, tend to distort our perceptions. Instead of recognizing what is unique in each person, stereotyping places people into categories, much as mail is pigeonholed according to route. She is not wearing a bra, thus she is "liberated" (a category); he has a full beard and glasses, thus he is an "intellectual" (a category); he plays football, thus he is a "jock" (a category). We do this with individuals, events, ideas — anything. To each category we attach an extensive set of corresponding labels, or stereotypes.

Take the man who plays football, for example. If we assign him the label of "jock," we may jump to the conclusion that he is insensitive, not very bright, and a male chauvinist. The man may or may not be any of these things. The point is, we can't know anything about him for certain simply by knowing he plays football. Many of our stereotypes are so conditioned into us that it is hard to see that we have them, much less get rid of them.

Besides the fact that stereotyping doesn't take into account the unique qualities of individuals, it also implies that all the people, events, ideas, or things we pigeonhole are static, when in reality they are ever changing. Nobody is witty or bright all the time. Everyone has his or her moments. And yet we tend to attribute static qualities and respond to others as if those qualities were appropriate *all the time*. Think carefully about the last time you made comments like, "Sam is really the life of *any* party," or "Carolyn *always* looks so nice." We use statements like these because they are the best predictors we have about how a person "should" act, if everything we know is right.[8]

If you were a job interviewer and had to decide between two applicants who were equally qualified for a particular job, would you spend hours agonizing over the decision if you could make it quickly on the basis of a stereotype, whether appropriate or not? If one applicant had long, straight hair, for example, and the other had short, styled hair? Or if one spoke with an accent and the other spoke as you do? If one applicant were a man and the other a woman? One stereotype, perhaps, would be enough to tip the scales.

Everyone stereotypes, to a degree that varies with the individual and with the groups to which the individual belongs. Take college freshmen as an example of a group: A study was done in which college freshmen, male and female, looked at photographs of men with different amounts of facial hair. The students were to rate the men in the photos on masculinity. The results? The more hair a man had on his face, the more likely the students were to see him as "masculine, mature, good-looking, dominant, self-confident, courageous, liberal, nonconforming, industrious, and older."[9] The students didn't know anything about these men except what they looked like; they formed their judgments on the basis of a stereotype.

Physical attractiveness is another category by which we stereotype people and, unfortunately, we tend to give it disproportionate emphasis as we communicate with them. An attractive appearance creates a

Pretend you are the interviewer for a large business. You are looking for a person in public relations—one who will represent your company. All of the following individuals had essentially similar qualifications for the job. But each had one outstanding, conspicuous personal characteristic. What might be your impression of the following people, based on just the one quality noted?

1. He had a beard.

2. She wore too much makeup.

3. He did not comb his hair.

4. Her dress was very short.

5. He wore sandals.

6. She wore jeans.

7. He slouched in his chair.

8. She chewed gum.

9. He bit his fingernails.

10. Her fingernails were very long and pointed.

"halo effect": this appeal influences all other impressions a person makes on us. For example, research has shown that the defendant was given a harsher sentence in a criminal trial if either the victim was attractive or if the defendant was unattractive.[10] It has been shown, too, that an attractive female has a better chance of changing the attitudes of males than an unattractive one.[11] This is probably not news to anyone. And studies have proven that attractive people, regardless of their sex, will be perceived as having higher credibility.[12] How fair is this? Can you think of any situations where such stereotyping is justified?

Proximity: Distance Discovers / Distance Distorts

Proximity is simply nearness to something in place, time, or relationship. It can strongly affect the way we perceive. There are two types of proximity: physical and psychological.

An example of how physical proximity can influence perception is the experience of thinking one of our lecturers was quite young and not realizing the mistake until we went down to ask a question. Then the hair we thought was blond might turn out to be gray and the skin that looked unblemished might be crossed by age lines blurred by the distance at which we sat. Middle twenties might turn out to be late forties. Have you ever been in this situation, making judgments that later proved to be inaccurate because you were either too close to or too far from the object to perceive accurately?

Psychological proximity may have several effects on us. One is that the extent to which we are attitudinally similar to someone else may determine how well we understand him or her. You must know some people you feel you always have to be explaining your self to. You don't have psychological proximity with them—you don't understand each other. Then there are people with whom you just seem to get along; the two of you "click." With such people you rarely have to say, "I *meant* that! I was serious" or "I was only kidding." They know without your telling them. Don't you feel you *understand* this other person? With this person you have achieved psychological proximity.

The second effect is that when we are attitudinally similar to someone, we give this person a more positive evaluation than if we are not. You probably like teachers you perceive as having tastes similar to yours—teachers you see buying your favorite record or wearing a parka very like yours. Research has been done that showed when teachers are attitudinally similar to the students, they are rated higher by them. Attitudinally dissimilar teachers are rated lower. The instructors in this test were rated on open-mindedness, their ability to be stimulating and interesting, personal attractiveness, and desirability as instructors.[13]

A third effect of psychological proximity involves our readiness to respond in a specific way. For example, if we witness an automobile accident along with some other people, viewpoints may differ although physical proximity is the same for all of us. A police officer might look at the accident from the point of view of what driving violations were incurred. A doctor might be most concerned about the injuries sustained by the people involved. A highway worker might notice broken curbs or uprooted sewers. Each person would bring his or her own experiences or psychological set to the accident. Each would be psychologically near to a different aspect of the accident. Too, the testimony of each would be necessary to learn all the important details of the accident. What we bring to an event such as this often influences our perceptions of it more than the actual facts of the event.

Role: A Limiting Point of View

The roles we play affect our perceptions strongly. Our roles are simply positions we assume in relation to someone or something else. In relation to your parents, your role is that of son or daughter. In a classroom, your role is that of student. A role is the stance we take or are assigned in a particular situation; the role we play affects our expectations, needs, attitudes, and beliefs about that situation; it restricts how we

Consider This

Both Koko and Washoe were taught to converse in AMESLAN, the acronym for American sign language. Used by about 20,000 deaf Americans, AMESLAN consists of a series of gestures, each of which represents a word or an idea.

Miss Patterson began working with Koko 6 years ago, when the animal was about 13 months of age. She did so despite the advice of some prominent authorities on animal behavior and intelligence.

Some experts felt that the gorilla did not possess enough manual dexterity to form the sometimes-intricate signs used to communicate in AMESLAN. Others believed that the gorilla was mentally dull, incapable of the conceptualization and abstraction necessary for communication.

"Gorillas are tragically misunderstood animals," Miss Patterson stated. "In fact exceedingly shy, placid, and unaggressive, they are conceived to be ferocious, slavering, man-killers."

—Michael Woods, *The Blade: Toledo, Ohio,* September 29, 1978 perceive that situation. There are job roles, family roles, sex roles, friendship roles, and many others.

Your father, for example, may have experienced some parental-role restrictions. He may have thought that he maintained open and harmonious relations with his children, welcoming their ideas on any problem that occurred. For him, in the position of father, it may really have seemed like that. It is possible, however, that his children, because of their role or position, did not see it the same way. Our own perceptions may be limited by our roles.

Each of us plays roles defined by our culture, by our upbringing, and by how we personally see those roles. We are all familiar with the sex roles that have come to be traditional in our society. Think of how our perceptions are affected by the degree to which we accept these traditional roles. A strong-minded man may be perceived as assertive and a natural leader while an equally strong-minded woman is perceived as pushy and castrating. An unpleasant woman may be called a bitch; an unpleasant man is a son of a bitch (he can't help it?). How often do we see male children dressed in pink? Our acceptance of traditional sex roles has a direct effect on our perception of the color pink as appropriate or inappropriate in certain situations. A woman wearing an apron at the kitchen sink is a natural and acceptable sight; we have been conditioned to squirm or laugh at a man in that same apron at that same sink. Our perceptions are affected.

We have learned to expect to hear a woman's voice in certain situations, a man's in others. Think of telephone operators, airplane pilots, and doctors' receptionists. Listen hard to television commercials. In how many of them is the "voice-over" provided by a man, even in advertising of products intended for use by women? Advertisers are banking on the fact that potential consumers will listen to a persuasive man's voice more closely than to a woman's. They know society has trained us to perceive men's voices as being more reliable and authoritative. How many other instances can you think of where acceptance of traditional sex roles affects perception in a directly observable way?

Certain roles carry higher prestige or credibility than others. What we see as another person's role will affect our perceptions of that person in certain situations. The role of professor, for example, might carry higher credibility and prestige in a faculty meeting on curriculum than the role of student. On the other hand, any student would probably be better able to discuss the availability of drugs on campus than a professor. In this case, the role of student is perceived as the more reliable source of information. If we see a person in a certain position fulfilling the duties and responsibilities of that job and serving our own best interests, then we are likely to overlook what we see as that person's

Try This

What is the first image that comes into your mind when you think of the following people?

A. A gas-station mechanic.

B. Someone who walks with a cane and lives in a rest home.

C. A rock-musician.

D. A hairdresser.

E. Someone who sells vacuum cleaners door-to-door.

F. Someone who has five children and is on welfare.

G. A rapist.

H. A business executive for a large corporation.

I. A nurse.

J. Someone who is in the army.

What sex did you think of for each of these people? What age? What political persuasion? What ethnic background? What stereotypes are you aware of holding? What do your stereotypes simplify for you? What do they complicate?

shortcomings. Our perceptions are affected by the fact that the responsibilities of the position are being satisfied. Anything else matters less to us.

IMPROVING SKILLS IN PERCEPTION

Because of the broad range of factors affecting our perception and because of the number of ways these factors interact, there are no universal rules that will guarantee improved, accurate perception. But there are several courses of action that might help. Some seem obvious and easy to put into practice; others may require more time to develop and use. All will contribute to the improvement of our perceptual skills. Since our perception influences and directs our reactions to others, improvement becomes crucial to improving our interpersonal communication.

Don't jump to conclusions.   One error we may tend to make that affects the accuracy of our perceptions is generalizing or drawing conclusions based on weak evidence. Just because we see something happen once, we may automatically assume it happens that way regularly.

We may see a bus stopping at a new location and assume a new route was established to include that location. We may see a person go into a bar and assume the person drinks heavily. Our perception will improve if we temper our thoughts and comments with conditional clauses like, "*I wonder if* the bus route has been changed to include . . ." or "*Maybe* he drinks heavily, because I saw him. . . ." Even better, stick strictly to the simplest facts: "I saw the bus stop at a new location today" or "I saw Ralph going into a bar downtown." If we are not reporting firsthand information, we should identify our source to indicate the potential believability of the observation. That is, if we have heard information from someone else or read it someplace, we should label what we report: "*Bill says* he saw Jane and Dave together downtown" or "*I read in the paper* that. . . ." This allows those who hear our information to gauge its believability without having our judgment interfere with it.

But often the problem is not in the labeling. Sometimes we believe our own judgments despite weak evidence. We convince our selves by phrasing the idea in a certain way, stating it to someone else, or repeating it. If we can learn to restrain our selves—suspend judgment—until we receive more evidence, we will improve the accuracy of our perceptions.

Maintaining a balance between openness and skepticism is difficult in our society. Forced to produce, make decisions, act, and respond quickly, it is hard to stand back and judge the worth of the information we hear daily. The point is not to doubt the validity of everything we hear; the point is to place new evidence into the context of other evidence we already have before drawing conclusions. If no other evidence exists, it is wiser to continue to have doubt than to make inferences. If a conclusion is necessary, the cautious skeptic will label the conclusion as a conditional one. We can never anticipate the decisions other people may make based on what we have told them—all we can do is be responsible in reporting what we actually do know.

- Broaden your personal experience. The more experience you have, the better the frame of reference into which new information can be placed.
- Try to find out what other yardsticks can be used to measure the phenomena. Do not depend on your own yardsticks alone.

  —Are you depending on what others have told you?
  —Are you focusing primarily on the situation?
  —Are you looking simply at role relationships?

The older child, with more experience, perceives the enormous bear as harmless and can (cautiously) accept it—but his younger brother is overwhelmed.

- Encourage communication. The more people who talk the more likely that new evidence and impressions will emerge.
- Encourage others to define the language they use. Even when two people hear the same cluster of cues and receive similar impressions, the language they use to express those impressions may be so different that one might suspect different perceptions.
- Be on guard for selective perception. Try to deal with contradictory information rather than overlook or deny it.
- Try to assume the role of detached observer—like a third person who can be objective about what is being observed.

Give it time. Physical togetherness helps to increase the accuracy of our perceptions. We have all had the experience of being impressed by a person from a distance only to change our impression radically upon closer contact. The same phenomenon occurs after knowing people better or working with them.[14] Accurate perceptions of another person do not occur instantaneously like the picture on a solid-state television set. They require both time and spatial closeness. Give your self time to be with someone. Even so, long-term, face-to-face, physical togetherness provides only the opportunity to understand how another person interprets the world; it does not guarantee that we will understand it.

- Try to reserve judgment. "I need time to think this over," is an easy way to admit this need and make it known to others.
- Be patient. Slow down a little. Let time and experience have an effect. It is amazing how much information can be acquired simply by waiting. Your mind has an opportunity to sift through the relevant material.
- Study the situation. Learn all you can about it. Find out what you need to know to make a decision or identify an impression.
- Use your intelligence to help articulate the impression or perception you wish to convey. Try to reconstruct the cue as accurately as possible and rephrase, in your mind, the response to it until you feel it is accurate.
- Do not use time as an excuse for not responding or for doing nothing.

Make your self available. It's important to be available to other people, both physically and psychologically.[15] This means trying to get on another's "wave length" or "into another person's head." An old Sioux prayer stated it this way: "O Great Spirit! Let me not judge another man without first walking a mile in his moccasins." So often in this hurry-up, get-things-done society, we do not spend much time really making our selves available to others. Physical togetherness does not necessarily mean psychological availability.

Psychological availability requires an active commitment to openness on our part. We have to make time for other people—time not only to share but also to be aware. To improve the accuracy of our perceptions, we must be willing to go beyond cliché-level exchanges that require little time and demand no commitment from us.

- Much of psychological availability will become clearer in the discussion of self-disclosure and how to improve it presented in the next chapter.
- Strive for "peak communication" based on absolute openness and honesty.[16]
- Whenever possible, move toward complete emotional and personal communion with others. This communion may not be a permanent experience, but a time when you feel almost perfect and mutual empathy.
- Be willing to share your reactions with others. Enjoy sharing in their reactions as well—whether the occasion is one of happiness or grief.

Make a commitment. Any self-improvement requires active commitment, but it is especially important if we are truly seeking to increase our perceptivity. If we want our perceptions to be accurate, we must make a conscious effort to search out as much information as possible on any given topic or question before we make a judgment or form an opinion. The more information we have, the greater the likelihood of accurate perceptions.[17] We should make a real effort to search out possibilities, asking "What if . . . ?" and "What about . . . ?" and "What else . . . ?" at every turn. We cannot hope to have reliable perceptions if we are indifferent and passive about acquiring information.

- Nothing happens unless you want it to. Change your attitude. Decide that change is good.
- Begin now to want to seek new information, knowledge, and experience. Decide that change is beneficial. There are personal benefits to be gained. The more information you have, the more accurate your perceptions are likely to be.
- Life can go by and you may take little part in what happens. On the other hand, you can be a responding, actively immersed participant.
- Remember that the "commitment" is a frame of mind—an attitude—and it can be changed. Notice the people who are having fun, who are getting so much out of life. What do they have? Check it out. Think about it. You only go around once.

Establish the proper climate. Our perceptivity will improve if we establish a climate conducive to communication. This means maintaining an atmosphere in which self-disclosure is likely to occur. Where open communication can be sustained, the likelihood of accurate perception will increase simply because people will trust each other enough to exchange honest messages. The more we know about the needs and feelings of other people, the more likely our actions toward them and our prediction of future interactions will be accurate. We must establish an environment in which truth is free to surface, so that our perceptions may be based on that truth. Face-to-face encounters where both visual and vocal ingredients are part of the interaction help us gain the information we need.

Part of creating a proper climate also means recognizing that each of us is unique; that is, recognizing that our view of the world is entirely our own. The world does not revolve around us, and if we see that everyone does not share our perceptions of the world, we will have at least acknowledged the need for a proper climate.

- Stop manipulating, dominating, and running other people's lives.
- Be authentic. Be yourself, honestly, in your relationship with others.
- Drop pretense, defenses, and duplicity.
- Stop "playing it cool."
- Don't use your behavior as a gambit to disarm others — to get them to reveal themselves before you reveal yourself to them.[18]

Be willing to adjust.   Perception involves a perceiver, something perceived, and a context within which the process occurs. These components are so interwoven that they cannot be analyzed apart from each other. Changes in any one affect all others. The most we can do is to recognize that as these components vary, so must our perceptions. The flawless friend of two weeks ago may now be the most disliked and despised creature on earth. The arrogant and unfair teacher of yesterday may be the humble and helpful teacher of today. To be unwilling to change our perceptions, and righteous in our inflexibility, can only cause us perceptual problems. What we need is perceptual sensitivity: full recognition that our perceptions will change as our interests and experiences change. We cannot expect today's perceptions to be accurate if we are basing them on yesterday's attitudes.

- Take a hard look at your spontaneity. Can you open up to something new? Do you rigidly adhere to your perceptions of what is expected of you?
- Take a hard look at your prejudices. Can you change your impressions of people, ideas, or activities?
- Take a hard look at your life. Are you living according to a rigid, well-defined plan that allows no deviation? There is certainty and security in such a life — but little excitement and growth. Change brings both.[19]

Consider This _____

To-day we have naming of parts. Yesterday,
We had daily cleaning. And to-morrow morning,
We shall have what to do after firing. But to-day,
To-day we have naming of parts. Japonica
Glistens like coral in all of the neighboring gardens,
    And to-day we have naming of parts.

This is the lower sling swivel. And this
Is the upper sling swivel, whose use you will see,
When you are given your slings. And this is the piling swivel,
Which in your case you have not got. The branches
Hold in the gardens their silent, eloquent gestures,
    Which in our case we have not got.

This is the safety-catch, which is always released
With an easy flick of the thumb. And please do not let me
See anyone using his finger. You can do it quite easy
If you have any strength in your thumb. The blossoms
Are fragile and motionless, never letting anyone see
    Any of them using their finger.

And this you can see is the bolt. The purpose of this
Is to open the breech, as you see. We can slide it
Rapidly backwards and forwards: we call this
Easing the spring. And rapidly backwards and forwards
The early bees are assaulting and fumbling the flowers:
    They call it easing the Spring.

They call it easing the Spring: it is perfectly easy
If you have any strength in your thumb: like the bolt,
And the breech, and the cocking-piece, and the point of balance,
Which in our case we have not got; and the almond-blossom
Silent in all of the gardens and the bees going backwards and forwards,
    For to-day we have naming of parts.

—Henry Reed, "Naming of Parts"

Our own interpersonal communications will be a great deal more effective when we realize the role that perception plays. Each of us, in our own unique way, is responsible for our method of arriving at the meaning of things through selecting, organizing, and interpreting the information we receive. No one gives us meaning, and no one can control the meanings we determine for our selves. It is we who create meaning out of our own experiences.

The more accurate our perceptions, the more likely we are to communicate effectively with others. By acquiring more information, we increase the number of ways we can respond to other people and we strengthen our ability to grow in a positive direction. And since our first step in communicating with others involves forming some impression of them, how well we form those impressions becomes crucial to interpersonal success. Other people are also the mirrors through which we learn about our selves. The self and self-disclosure are essential parts of the perception process. They will be discussed in the next chapter.

OTHER READING

Ernst G. Beier and Evans G. Valens, *People-Reading: How We Control Others, How They Control Us* (New York: Warner Books, Inc., 1975). The focus is on how to read the signals we receive from others. A book that starts us thinking about our lives and relationships, it is both theoretical and practical.

Kenneth E. Boulding, *The Image: Knowledge in Life and Society* (Ann Arbor, Mich.: The University of Michigan Press, 1956). People's behavior depends on the image—the sum of what they think and what they know. The way that image grows tends to limit the direction of future growth. Boulding emphasizes communication and feedback as sources for orderly and organized growth.

Arthur Gordon, *A Touch of Wonder* (Old Tappan, N.J.: Pillar Books, 1974). The author challenges readers to look at things more closely—even the simple things. There is more to commonplace happenings than what normally meets the casual eye.

Edward T. Hall, *Beyond Culture* (Garden City, N.Y.: Anchor Books, 1977). Part of perception concerns increasing knowledge. This book may open up new dimensions of understanding and provide new capacities for perception. Hall challenges readers to rethink their values.

R. D. Laing, H. Phillipson, and A. R. Lee, *Interpersonal Perception: A Theory and a Method of Research* (New York: Harper & Row, Publishers, 1966). What kind of perceptions occur when two people meet? The authors present concepts which indicate both the interaction and interexperience of two people. They describe each person's own experiences and behavior within the context of the two-party relationship.

Ken Olson, *Can You Wait Till Friday? The Psychology of Hope* (Greenwich, Conn.: Fawcett Publications, Inc., 1975). This book is on patience. Everyone wants everything immediately. People do not know how to deal with frustration. It is a warm book full of laughter, love, human insight—and, especially, hope.

John Powell, S. J., *Fully Human, Fully Alive: A New Life Through a New Vision* (Niles, Ill.: Argus Communications, 1976). Powell argues that change in the quality of people's lives must result from a change in their vision of reality. Emotions, according to Powell, grow out of how people see themselves and out of their perceptions. He challenges readers to examine their perceptions. The book is written in a warm, personal style.

NOTES

[1]Frank A. Geldard, *The Human Senses* (New York: John Wiley & Sons, Inc., 1953), p. 53.

[2]Donald R. Gordon, *The New Literacy* (Toronto: University of Toronto Press, 1971), pp. 25–47.

[3]From *Future Shock* by Alvin Toffler. (New York: Random House, Inc., 1970).

[4]Hans Sebald, "Limitations of Communication: Mechanisms of Image Maintenance in Form of Selective Perception, Selective Memory and Selective Distortion," *Journal of Communication* 12 (1962), 142–49.

[5]J. S. Bruner, "Social Psychology and Perception," in *Readings in Social Psychology*, E. Maccoby, T. M. Newcomb, and E. L. Hartley, eds., (New York: Holt, Rinehart and Winston, 1958), pp. 85–94.

[6]Richard C. Huseman, James M. Lahiff, and John D. Hatfield, *Interpersonal Communication in Organizations: A Perceptual Approach* (Boston: Holbrook Press, Inc., 1976), pp. 28–32.

[7]George J. McCall and J. L. Simmons, "Identities and Interaction: An Examination of Human Association in Everyday Life," in *Speech Communication: A Reader*, Richard L. Weaver, II, ed. (San Diego, Calif.: Collegiate Publishing, Inc., 1979), p. 64–66.

[8]Ibid., p. 65.

[9]Robert J. Pellegrini, "Impressions of the Male Personality as a Function of Beardedness," *Psychology* 10 (February 1973), 29–33.

[10]D. Lancy and E. Aronson, "The Influence of the Character of the Criminal and His Victim on the Decisions of Simulated Jurors," *Journal of Experimental Social Psychology* 5 (1969), 141–52.

[11]J. Mills and E. Aronson, "Opinion Change as a Function of the Communicator's Attractiveness and Desire to Influence," *Journal of Personality and Social Psychology* 1 (1965), 73–77.

[12]R. N. Widgery and B. Webster, "The Effects of Physical Attractiveness upon Perceived Initial Credibility," *Michigan Speech Journal* 4 (1969), 9–15.

[13]Katherine C. Good and Lawrence R. Good, "Attitude Similarity and Attraction to an Instructor," *Psychological Reports* 33 (August 1973), 335–37.

[14]J. W. Shepherd discusses how people's conceptions of each other change as a result of working together. See J. W. Shepherd, "The Effects of Valuations in Evaluations of Traits on the Relation Between Stimulus Affect and Cognitive Complexity," *Journal of Social Psychology* 88 (December 1972), 233–39.

[15]For more on psychological availability, see John Stewart and Gary D'Angelo, *Together: Communicating Interpersonally* 2nd ed. (Reading, Mass.: Addison-Wesley Publishing Company, 1980), pp. 110–112.

[16]John Powell, *Why Am I Afraid to Tell You Who I Am?* (Niles, Ill.: Argus Communications, 1969), pp. 61–62.

[17]See Frederick W. Obitz and L. Jerome Oziel, "Varied Information Levels and Accuracy of Person Perception," *Psychological Reports* 31 (October 1972), 571–76.

[18]Sidney M. Jourard, *The Transparent Self* (New York: D. Van Nostrand Company, 1971), p. 133.

[19]Wayne W. Dyer, *Your Erroneous Zones* (New York: Avon Books, 1976), pp. 126–31.

3   Getting in Touch:
The Self and Self-Disclosure

I am going to begin the discussion of how we can improve our skills in communicating with others by discussing how we communicate with our selves. This may sound contradictory, but before we can really be in touch with someone else, we must be in touch with our selves. This process of communicating with our selves is called *intrapersonal* communication. The interesting thing is that the way we learn most about our selves is through communicating with others. Let's look at an example of how this works.

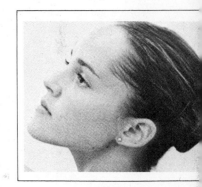

If you grew up with strong-minded parents or siblings who made all the decisions, and if the only interpersonal contacts you ever had were with your own family, you could end up thinking of your self as an indecisive person. But among your friends you may be very opinionated and action oriented. Your friends may look to you for leadership and decisions. Conceivably, other communication contexts could bring out even more strongly the bully or the shrinking violet in you. You may be more or less decisive depending on if you're talking to a small child or to a salesclerk or to a police officer. The point is, you would have no way of evaluating your own decision-making ability if it weren't for the communication contacts you had with other people.

YOUR SELF-CONCEPT

The starting point for all our interpersonal communication is our concept of self. After discussing the development of self-concept and the importance of disclosing that self to others, I will outline the skills necessary for improving our ability to self-disclose. This ability is the key to discovering the self and continuing to grow.

Look at yourself in the mirror. Spend about ten minutes doing this. Look at each part of your body carefully. Study it. What do you see?

— What is your best feature? How would you describe yourself to a stranger who is going to meet you at an airport or train depot?
— Imagine meeting yourself for the first time.
— What would be your first impression?
— How could you make a more positive impression?
— What is your worst physical attribute?
— Imagine that it is as bad, as ugly as it could possibly be.
— Now laugh at that image as you do when seeing your body deformed in a curved mirror at a carnival.
— What features of your body would you like to trade in? For what in return?

— Reprinted from *Shyness, What It Is, What to Do About It* by Philip G. Zimbardo, copyright © 1977, by permission of Addison-Wesley Publishing Co., Reading, Mass.

Who Are You?

If you had to use *one* word to characterize your self, what would that one word be? Shy? Enthusiastic? Loving? Confident? Your characterization of your self will probably involve more than one word. You may think of your self as interesting and friendly once people get to know you; you may think you are intelligent, attractive, and generally concerned about other people and what happens in the world. Whatever words you select, this idea of your self — your self-concept — is directly related to how you behave. It works both ways. If you've always had the knack for making new friends, you've probably come to think of your self as friendly and outgoing. And if you think of your self as basically outgoing, it can actually make meeting other people and making new friends easier. Your behavior reflects the opinion you have of your self.

Your success in college and in life may depend more on *how* you feel about your self and your abilities than on your actual talents. And your self-concept will affect your skill in dealing with other people. You can see how your communications with people could go haywire if all the time you are thinking of your self as a friendly, warm person, people around you see you as a loud, offensive boor. What you consider a concerned inquiry into a friend's health could be perceived by that person as nosy, prying into something that is none of your business. Interpersonal communication, to be effective, depends upon a realistic perception of self.[1]

How Did You Get to Be This Way?

Think back to the word or words you used to describe your self just now. Chances are you arrived at that self-concept ("I'm popular") by the reactions other people have to you ("Glad to see you!"). But then you had to think about those reactions and decide what they meant to you ("They like to have me around. They appreciate my sense of humor."). In other words our self-concept is created through both interpersonal and intrapersonal communication. Much of this goes on without our being really conscious of it. There are four processes we all more or less unconsciously engage in as we build our self-concepts. By becoming more aware of the processes and working at them, we will gradually be more in touch with our true selves. Those processes are: (1) *self-awareness*, (2) *self-acceptance*, (3) *self-actualization*, and (4) *self-disclosure*.

SELF-AWARENESS

You have some understanding of your self—how attractive, intelligent, influential, and successful you are. You derive these perceptions from experiences and interactions with others. (See Figure 1.) Not all your

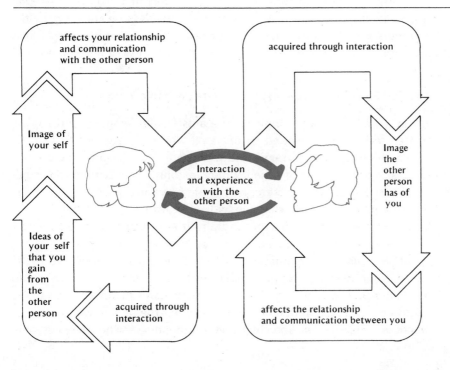

Figure 1. We derive information about our selves from our interactions with others.

Try This

Lie down comfortably and close your eyes. Pretend that you are going to watch an hour-long movie of your life. Okay, begin the film:

1. Where does the movie take place?

2. What's the plot outline?

3. Who are the major characters?

4. Who are the minor characters?

5. Who is directing the movie?

6. What is the audience doing as it watches the movie?

7. What are the various turning points of the story?

8. How does it end?

9. Are there any morals to be derived?

10. What does the audience do when the movie is over?

beliefs about your self are realistic—some are beliefs about what you would *like* to be rather than what you are.

For example, if you would like to be chosen as the leader of a certain organization, you may behave the way you feel will get you the leadership role. What you would *like* to be—a leader—makes you more careful about your clothes, your speech, your associates. Both what you are and what you would like to be are important factors in making up your identity. Self-awareness involves comprehending the sum total of beliefs you have about your self.

As another example, a woman who thinks of her self as fragile, elegant, and sophisticated may avoid anything that does not match her self-concept. She may avoid things that require physical effort, like a touch-football game or backpacking, activities that could force a compromise in her ideal self. Toward these activities she builds defenses. Getting dirty or injured wouldn't fit her image of her self. Activities more satisfactory to her might be going to the theater, belonging to social organizations, or playing bridge.

Different experiences have different impacts on her self-image. She can accept more easily experiences consistent with her values; she will probably reject those that don't seem to fit. We all do this. Some experiences may be rationalized to fit our needs if they are inconsistent with our perceptions of our selves. For example, if at a club meeting the woman is asked to do something she considers inappropriate, like sitting on the floor, she may do it because she needs to be accepted by the members of this club. She may rationalize the activity as one that is novel or amusing—even though it is inconsistent with her values.

The Self-Fulfilling Prophecy: Like a Dream Come True

If the woman in the example above acts fragile, elegant, and sophisticated, others will respond to her as if she is. This is not to say the woman is not *genuinely* fragile and sophisticated—she may well be. The feedback or responses of others will help confirm her perception of her self. And she will feel more comfortable behaving in accordance with her self-image. This is what we call a self-fulfilling prophecy: your behavior reflects feelings you hold about your self, others respond to your behavior, and the original feelings are confirmed.

Now, think what might happen to this same woman if everyone she met thought of her as tough, vulgar, and simple. Her self-image would be compromised or threatened. She might react in several ways: she might change her self-image; she might reject the people who provided negative feedback; or she might seek out people who give her only positive reinforcement. Faced with a similar situation, most of us would be unlikely to change our self-image. More probably, we would seek confirmation by associating with people who reinforce our own feelings about our selves and by avoiding people who give us negative messages.

Your self-concept develops over a long period of time. Periodic and regular reinforcement from others is necessary to help confirm your feelings about your self. You can see the obvious problems if you have negative feelings about your self. The self-fulfilling prophecy can work to strengthen both negative and positive self-concepts. If you want to change some quality in your self, the best way to begin is by believing in the characteristic you want to possess. For example, if you want to be considered dependable, begin by thinking that you *are* dependable.

This sounds easy but it isn't. You might have to get rid of some self-defeating ideas about your self you didn't even know you had. This kind of change requires hard work.

Negative Self-Concepts: The Power of Negative Thinking

What happens when your feelings about your self are weak or negative? Since you tend to act consistently with the feelings you have about your self, this can be a damaging or destructive situation. For example, what if you perceive your self as a failure in school? This attitude may be a

Consider This _____

I celebrate myself, and sing myself,
And what I assume you shall assume,
For every atom belonging to me as good belongs to you.
I loafe and invite my soul,
I lean and loafe at my ease observing a spear of summer grass.
My tongue, every atom of my blood, form'd from this soil, this air,
Born here of parents born here from parents the same, and
their parents the same,
I, now thirty-seven years old in perfect health begin,
Hoping to cease not till death.
Creeds and schools in abeyance,
Retiring back a while sufficed at what they are, but never forgotten,
I harbor for good or bad, I permit to speak at every hazard,
Nature without check with original energy.

—Walt Whitman, "Song of Myself"

result of something as insignificant as misunderstanding directions for an assignment, or it may have developed over a long period of time: having to compete with a very successful brother or sister, having a string of unsympathetic teachers, or not gaining enough positive reinforcement at home for schoolwork. Whatever the cause, it is likely that once you start seeing your self as a failure, you will begin to act the part. Poor study habits, inadequate reading, lack of participation in class, and, in the end, a poor grade may result, reinforcing your feeling. You can see how such negative feelings feed upon themselves and become a vicious, growing cycle, a cycle which will begin to encompass all of your thoughts, actions, and relationships. (See Figure 2.)

Figure 2. A negative cycle.

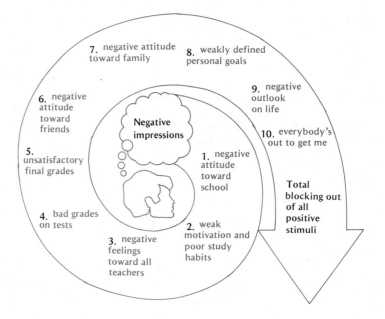

You may know people whose negative cycle is already well developed. It may be the person, for example, who can't accept criticism or who is over-responsive to praise. It may be someone who complains constantly, or someone who withdraws into self-imposed isolation. We all know people who couldn't think of a self-promoting thing to say if their lives depended on it. Why a person behaves this way, or how the feeling came about is too complex a topic to go into here. We are concerned with changing negative self-concepts to positive ones because of the effect such a change can have on interpersonal communication.[2]

Positive Self-Concepts: You Can Do It

We all know people who are confident about their ability to deal with problems. Given a difficult situation, they seek answers or ways of approaching it. They feel equal to other people and have self-respect. These people accept praise simply and graciously. They can admit to a wide range of feelings, behaviors, and desires, some of which are socially approved and others of which are not. They are realistic in their assessment of self.

People with a positive self-concept can accept as normal, negative feelings, behaviors, and desires if they are balanced and kept in perspective. They recognize that nobody is all good. Finally, these people are also capable of self-improvement. When they see they have an unlikable aspect or a negative quality, they find ways to change it.[3] And they are *likely* to discover personal faults because they are open and responsive to the way they behave and do not expect perfection. A positive self-concept creates a framework that is stable and well-balanced so that mistakes and failures can be successfully integrated into the behavior pattern without a shattering effect.

Few of us have entirely negative or entirely positive self-concepts. Either would be unrealistic and difficult to maintain. You probably fall into some middle-ground position. It would be healthy for all of us if we could be aware of our negative self-concepts and move away from them as well as we are able. Our self-concept affects how we view life, how we want to be viewed, how we view others, and how we interpret messages. Our self-concept holds a controlling influence on our life.

How you view life.   Do you see the world as generally threatening and unfriendly? Or does it seem basically a friendly place where you feel at home? Your images of your self, whether positive or negative, form the framework for your intrapersonal and interpersonal communications. If you have a positive self-concept and rewarding and enjoyable relationships with others, you probably will hold a generally positive overall view of life. You'll be able to sort out what is important and what is irrelevant to you. A warm, open, and significant relationship with even one other close person often makes you look on *all* others with a more positive outlook.[4]

How you want to be viewed.   If you think of your self as a "super salesman" or as a "terrific storyteller," then you want that view confirmed by others. You're going to try to live up to the label, whether you chose it yourself or someone else chose it for you. Labels can be limiting if you don't think beyond them. It's not a good idea to let them

Draw a model or diagram of your "ideal" self—the self you would like to be. As you draw the model or diagram

1. Include all the significant aspects of your ideal life:

   a. its past,

   b. its future,

   c. the present environment,

   d. thinking and feeling activities.

2. Try to show the relationships of the various parts.

What insights does your model or diagram reveal? Does it raise any important questions? In what ways does this "ideal" self that you have diagramed differ from your "real" self model? Can you discern ways that you could move from the real to the ideal?

come to *define* who you are and what you want to be. But on the other hand labels can be useful for providing direction, for helping you make choices.[5] If you decide to aim for the label of "popular," you will behave in such a way that certain people will admire you. If the people whose esteem you're after—referred to as significant others—insist on a neat and fashionable appearance, non-stop smiles, and sociability, then you will choose to comb your hair carefully, wear stylish clothes, smile a great deal, and seek the company of others. Your self-concept determines how you wish to be responded to and will encourage you to seek that response.[6]

How you view others.   Your view of other people also will be affected by how you label your self. If you chose the label "popular," you might suddenly become very aware of the relative popularity of other people. You'll be more anxious to keep as friends those people who are generally considered popular. You'll be more likely to avoid people who seem to be unpopular. Because the label is important to you, you'll see other people in terms of it. If you view your self as reliable, you are likely to judge others according to how reliable or unreliable they are. If you're very conscious of how well dressed you are, you'll become extra aware of how other people dress. How you view others often results from how you view and label your self.[7]

How you interpret messages.   Your self-concept also affects the kinds of messages you accept and the way you interpret them. If you see your self as "popular," you are likely to see people around you in terms of

How aware are you of your self? Write ten statements that begin with the words "I am." We'll get back to your statements later in this chapter.

how they respond to your label. You'll probably keep as friends those people who accept you on your own terms. If it's popularity you're after, then your friends will be not only friends but also admirers. You're likely to see people you don't get along with as nonadmirers—they do not help you cultivate your "popular" self-image. You accept messages that confirm your popularity. You might distort, misinterpret, or ignore messages that don't confirm your popularity in order to protect your self-image.

I've been taking a long look at self-awareness here because if we want to be more effective in our communications, this is where it all must start. It starts specifically with coming to grips with a realistic view of our selves. We've seen the control our self-image has in our intrapersonal and interpersonal communications—this image had better be realistic. We've seen how the self-fulfilling prophecy works, and we'd all like it to work for us rather than against us. It makes sense to be careful about the labels we assign our selves because we're probably going to live up to them sooner or later. This might sound like a warning to you, but think of it as encouragement. We all face similar problems in this respect. Realistic self-awareness is difficult to come by, but it is crucial if we want our communications to matter.

SELF-ACCEPTANCE

You begin by being aware of your self, but you must also be satisfied with your self. You must accept your self. By this I do not mean you are smug or uncritical of negative qualities, but rather that you see your shortcomings for what they are, making neither too much nor too little of them. Accepting your self means seeing how your positive and negative qualities are equally valid, equally *you*, equally normal to have. It means building on those qualities you're satisfied with and working to change the ones you're not happy with.

Like self-awareness, self-acceptance doesn't come easily. It isn't easy to accept your self when you are constantly being measured by other people's standards. There are the standards of your parents ("Your friend Jimmy Bentley has been accepted by both Harvard *and* Yale. Have you heard from any schools yet?"), your teachers ("If you don't love *Moby Dick* you might just as well give up on American literature because you'll never understand it"), and even of advertisers ("Use *Whammo* lemon-herbal-avocado shampoo and get out there and have fun like you're supposed to"). If you are unsure of your self and doubtful about how acceptable you are to others, if you cannot accept your self much of the time, your communication will suffer. Accepting your

This girl appears to feel good about herself. Her self-acceptance will provide a basis for a satisfying life.

feelings, beliefs, goals, and relationships with others provides the base for a healthy, integrated self. What are some of the things that stand in the way of your accepting your self?

Living Up to an Image

If you are always trying to live up to the image of a perfect or all-A student that your parents expect, you may have difficulty with your self-concept. Whenever someone else tries to impose an image on you, it may be an unrealistic one or one that demands things that simply are not important to you. Setting your own goals too high, in much the same way, may cause you to have a negative self-concept if you can't achieve fulfillment or satisfaction.

Teachers sometimes have a habit of setting students' goals for them. Have you ever been told, "You know, you're not working up to your potential"? With little or no positive reward, or with little or no definition about specific expectations, students often feel frustrated, confused, or depressed, which may result in low self-esteem. Parents, teachers, employers, and friends all seem to have goals for you—standards they want you to or think you should meet. Trying to live up to someone else's goals or image of you will make it more difficult to accept your self.

Living Without Answers

Add to these pressures the ones imposed upon you because of your age, your family situation, the decade, the place you live. There are pressures on you to make personal decisions, many of which seem to conflict with each other. These conflicts can make it difficult to accept your self.

At probably no other time in life will you be faced with so many momentous decisions about who you are, what to do with your life, what to believe, what principles to value highly, what standards to follow. Increasingly, most of us have to face and answer these questions without the answers family, school, and church once provided. Such a barrage of questions can make decisions, interaction, and life itself difficult.

Living with Constant Change

In addition to having to cope with the high expectations of others and the struggle to find answers to important personal questions, you also live in a society where a great deal of rapid technological and social change is occurring. This makes self-acceptance difficult. How do you relate your self to things that are always changing? How can you accept your self when your own standards—and society's—change constantly?

Consider This _____

There is an assumption here that perhaps should be argued out rather than taken for granted. This is that the self is worth being. There is a philosophical dialogue that turns on the question of whether people are born good and become corrupted or are born evil and become civilized. My own opinion is that each is equally true. Thus, I cannot claim that if you strip yourself of the encrustation of attitudes and defenses, you are going to expose an angelic, euphoric, and expansive person. But, certainly, neither are you going to find the cretinous and willful monster that most of us fear is lurking underneath. There will be a human being, with the assets and limitations inherent in the definition of human being but, for the first time and most importantly, with the choice not to be ugly and cruel and stunted. If I look back at my own life, the hurtful things I have done have been out of defensiveness or an effort at adaptation or toward the end of becoming more comfortable with myself. Never once was the hurt of someone else gratuitous and unmotivated. Deliberate, yes, and wrongly motivated, but never gratuitous. Very, very few people are vicious without cause; and the cause, when the usual person is vicious, is archaic fear and defensiveness. It is the things that are not self, the pulp of notions around the self, that are the source of what we deplore and fear and long to change in ourselves. The dropping away of that pulp will not expose an ungovernable, reprehensible being but a self that can expand and afford to act with decency and generosity and courage. To give the self permission to be the self, a leap must be taken across the chasm of dread that the self is little and mean and nasty to a certain faith that it is a good thing to be and that spontaneous behavior can be trusted.

—Jo Coudert, *Advice from a Failure*

Try This

Work toward independence in your life. That is, make a habit of setting and working toward your own standards. Some things you can do to establish adaptability—and independence at the same time—would be:

1. Be more independent. Listen when others tell you, "You can do it. You know what to do."

2. Act rather than react. When you make a decision, carry it out. Do not make excuses or rationalize about why you could not do it.

3. Rather than say, "I have to . . . ," say "I've decided to . . . ." Take responsibility for your life.

4. Set your own standards. Stop looking over your shoulder for other significant standard setters.

5. Listen to praise and compliments. People are telling you that you are capable.

6. Learn to say "no" and really mean it.

7. Take chances. Test what happens when you let your desires be known.

8. Explore freedom—freedom to be yourself, to love and to be loved on your own merits.

—Gregory G. Young, *Your Personality and How to Live With It*

Try This

Alvin Toffler labels as "future shock" our reaction to this "stream of change so accelerated that it influences our sense of time, revolutionizes the tempo of daily life, and affects the very way we 'feel' the world around us."[8] This pace, he says, creates in all of us a sense of impermanence which affects how we relate to other people, things, ideas, and values. And, assuredly, such rapid change affects the level of self-acceptance we are able to achieve. Change in our environment affects our work. Are you preparing for an occupation that will be obsolete ten years from now? Change will affect your acquaintances. What kind of a permanent relationship can you establish with someone you may never see again after two or three years? It will affect your family. Will the ties in the family you form be the same as those in the family in which you were raised? What are the forces that cause a splintering of the family? Change will affect your religion. Do you want rigid dogma or a philosophy that is adaptable to you and to a changing world? It affects your sexual relationships. How much stability do you want or need in your intimate associations? With all these changes, it's easy to become disoriented. How can you accept or measure the person you are when the measuring stick is different from one day to the next?

If these pressures and influences worry or upset you or make you uncertain, then you are normal. The adjustments you need to make to cope with the pressures of life end up changing your life and your concept of who you are. Self-acceptance will always be a problem when we are not certain of who we are. But actively working to accept our selves is an important step toward healthy interpersonal communication.

Putting It All Together

If we get our self-concept mainly from our interaction with the people and world around us, and if those people and that world are constantly changing, then you can see how difficult it is to get in touch with your self and feel confident in accepting it. It is very important to recognize the significance of change and its effect on your self-concept and on knowing your self.

The more realistic your self-concept is, the more value it will have for you. To make it realistic means to consider the expectations that others have of you, to answer or at least confront the most important personal questions you face, and to fit your self-concept with your current environment, not the high-school or grade-school world. These expectations others have of you, the questions you must answer, and your environment all are continually shifting, and if your responses do not change accordingly, you may develop an unrealistic picture of the world and of your relationship to it.

The part of your self-concept that evaluates your self is called *self-esteem*. The less distance between your ideal self and your real self, the higher your level of self-esteem. Your real self is the self you reveal as you function in daily life; your ideal self is the self you want to be. The greater the distance between ideal and real, the lower the self-esteem. This is nothing new—we all know we're much prouder of our selves when we act according to our best impulses than when our hopes lie in one direction and our behavior in another. (See Figure 3.)

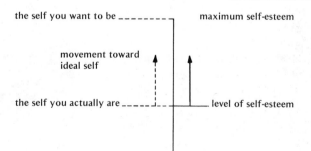

Figure 3. The less distance between the ideal self and the real self, the higher the level of self-esteem.

As a Navaho
I entered the Southwest
  on my striped blanket of rainbow
  in the 11th or 12th Century:
      may be earlier,
      may be later.

As a Navaho
Our rainbow stretched
  from the icy Northwest
  beyond the tallest trees
  to the desert Southwest
  among the tallest pinnacles
  of Monument Valley.
Our lands continually reach
  toward the sun —
      even when we sleep.

We Navahos
  are of all land and no land
  finding the canyons of our
  earth equalling the canyons
  of our travels.
  The canyon depths are as if
  carved by our moccasin
  feet walking and walking
  back and forth —

  always forward —
  across the earth
  again and again,
  sometimes herding
  sometimes schooling
  sometimes going to a Squaw Dance
  sometimes crossing the mountain over there. . . .

We Navahos
  carried with us our Yei
  who teach us from one end
  of the rainbow . . .
  who teach us all things.
  Who take us through
  all life in streams of beauty —
  flowing deeply in our rains
  flowing shallowly in our dry times.

The Yei gives eyes and fingers
and hearts to learn from Spide
Woman,
or learn from our grandfathers
or learn from the many yous
of the world.

We Navahos
  are always learning,
  it is our way,
  it is our eternal Transformation
  like a seed . . .
  we are seeds,
  and we plant ourselves.

—James A. McGrath, "As a Navaho"

How close do you come to measuring up to the standards you've set for your self as ideal? The closer you come, the more likely you are to respect your self.[9] Self-confidence, self-respect, self-esteem—these are words we hear all the time and they all mean pretty much the same thing. If your self-esteem is high, your behavior will reflect that.

Whether or not you can accept your self and feel that you are worthwhile may depend on your beliefs about who you are. Go back and briefly review your responses to the "I am" phrases you listed earlier. Having completed those statements, put each into one of the following categories: (1) Your *physical attributes*—such bodily characteristics as age, height, and weight; (2) Your *emotional attributes*—the feelings you possess: shy, happy, cynical, cheerful, frustrated, etc.; (3) Your *mental attributes*—your intellectual characteristics: smart, average, or dumb; (4) Your *roles*—functions you fulfill in relation to others: your class-level in school, whether you are single or married, your major, your profession, etc.; (5) Your *relationships with others*—the characteristic stance you take toward others such as whether you are accessible and open, closed and withdrawn, or neutral and moderate.[10]

You may find you tend to describe your self more in one way than in another. One person may be very role conscious ("I am a son." "I am an account executive." "I am a sophomore.") while another is more aware of emotional traits ("I am often depressed." "I am sensitive to criticism." "I am generally optimistic."). While you should not take a listing of only ten such statements too seriously, what you've said about your self can give you a rough idea of what's important to you. You're likely to have listed personal attributes that you've given some thought to, possibly had doubts about, or tried to improve. If you were honest, your responses can give you an approximate profile of what we've been calling your real self.

The next step is to evaluate your responses either positively or negatively. Chances are, you listed some characteristics you feel good about having and some you feel bad about having. Put a plus (+) or a minus (−) next to each statement. The statements you've marked with a minus are probably areas where you feel you don't come up to your own standards, where you are less than your ideal self. If you've marked mostly minuses, it could be a sign of low self-esteem, at least in those areas. Bear in mind that this exercise is only a very crude measuring tool, and that the person who can label every response with a plus is rare indeed.

Check your statements once again for accuracy. Were you being unduly modest? Selling your self short is just as dishonest and useless as being pompous. Your statements should tell it like it is, not as you'd like

Try This

Write down three negative characteristics of your real self—your true, authentic self. You might say, for example, "I lack self-confidence" or "I am too domineering." Now write down one ideal correlate for each negative characteristic. This positive correlate should correspond exactly to the characteristic above. The ideal gives you direction, a model for growth. For example, you might say, "I want to have pride in my abilities and accomplishments" or "I want to give others a chance to control their own lives" as a response to the above examples. How far from your ideal self (in these respects) are you? Do you think this is a good way to measure self-esteem?

it to be. The more accurate your observations are here, the more likely it is that you have a realistic self-concept. And only if you have a realistic self-concept can you fairly measure where you are in relation to your ideal self, and, consequently, your level of self-esteem. It could also reveal the distance between your ideal and real self, and could, thus, be reflective of the level of your self-esteem.[11]

Self-acceptance is always a difficult process, but it need not be painful. It's valuable for all of us to become conscious of and sensitive to the pressures that stand in the way of self-acceptance—the pressures of living up to an image, coping with environmental factors, and living with constant change. Acquiring such sensitivity is an important first step, but it is not enough. Learning to accept your self is an ongoing, lifelong process. It involves continuous awareness and evaluation of your self. Your standards and values are probably quite different from what they were five years ago. Five years from now they'll be even more different still. As you continue to re-evaluate your own standards honestly, you'll probably find some things you want to change.

This brings us to what I'm going to talk about next—self-actualization. What I've been talking about so far—self-awareness and self-acceptance—are pretty much internal changes. They do not involve taking positive action in your life. Self-actualization is a term for the change that comes when you really work at getting in touch with your self. This kind of change requires real commitment.

SELF-ACTUALIZATION

Self-awareness on some level and then self-acceptance are necessary prerequisites for self-actualization. Self-actualization is an important term to know because it is an important idea in interpersonal communication. To actualize means simply to make something (in this case, your self) *actual*, to make it happen. Self-actualization involves growth that is motivated from within. It means willingness to pursue your ideal self on your own—to grow and change because *you* think it is important. If you see a need to change in your interpersonal relationships or communication with others, the motivation to do this, if you want positive results, must come from within you.

The self-actualized person is one who has taken steps to make things happen. Such people know their potential and actively strive to realize it. The question is, of course, how do you know what your potential is? The preceding discussions on self-awareness and self-acceptance should give you some clues. What it amounts to, again, is being com-

Develop a skill or become an authority on something that you would be able to share with others in a social setting. Develop some attribute that others will enjoy, profit from, be entertained by, or be wiser for.

Some of the following suggestions might be helpful to you in your quest:

A. Learn to play an instrument (guitar, harmonica, or piano).

B. Learn to tell jokes well.

C. Learn to do magic tricks.

D. Learn how to dance well.

E. Be up-to-date on current events.

F. Specialize in some particular world issue of importance (overpopulation, hunger, ecology, the decline of heroes in our culture, etc.).

G. Read and be able to discuss some good books (from both the fiction and the general best-seller lists).*

The purpose of this exercise is to become a more social being. To succeed in social situations is positive reinforcement for further development of one's self—further self-actualization.

*Reprinted from *Shyness, What It Is, What to Do About It* by Philip G. Zimbardo, copyright © 1977, by permission of Addison-Wesley Publishing Co., Reading, Mass.

pletely honest about your real self, your real abilities. The real self is not some fantasized version—positive *or* negative—of your self, but a real picture of the you other people see, the you that functions in the real world, the you that has been proven by experience to be your true self.

People who have a good idea of their potential are likely to do things they know are right for them, to set and maintain personal standards, to become open to new experiences, and to trust themselves. That is, they have fairly assessed their own personal characteristics and have come to accept and believe in the self they discover. And, most important, they are able to act on that belief. They tend to realize the importance of change in their lives, and are willing to be forever in the process of "becoming."[12]

How might the behavior of a self-actualized student be different from one who is not self-actualized? Such a student is aware and accepting of his or her self. If this person consistently gets A's and B's it is likely to be more out of a belief in the value of learning than out of a desire to play the role of perfect student for parents, peers, or professors. Such a student will work chemistry problems and write English papers by acting on his or her own best judgment, without constant reinforcement or prodding or praise from other people. This student does

Have you ever simply recorded some of your personal goals so that you have a specific set of guide-lines, a direction in which you want to move? Write down five of your most important personal goals— things <u>you</u> want to achieve and things <u>you</u> want to accomplish. Be as idealistic as you like. How do you want to accomplish these goals? For each of them, write three things you can do that will help you reach them. Be as concrete and practical as you can. Setting goals is one thing; working toward them is another. Are your methods realistic?

not panic when a course in economics turns out to be tougher than expected, or a grade lower than hoped for. The self-actualized student interacts on an equal basis with the people he or she lives with and socializes with. This person might really enjoy belonging to a choir, working on the yearbook, and leading a Scout troop all at the same time, getting satisfaction from each activity. Such a student enjoys searching, seeking, and pursuing. This person might decide that after graduation he or she will live in California and work for a film-production company, taking college courses accordingly, at the same time remaining open to the possibility of living somewhere else and doing some other kind of work.[13]

You probably already know some people who seem to have it all together, who know who they are and act on that knowledge. You may even know some for whom the whole process is pretty much unconscious, people who may have never even heard or considered the words "self-actualization." What would you add to our description of a self-actualizing person? It might be helpful for you to study such a person carefully and to try to pinpoint the kinds of things he or she does differently from you. Of course this person cannot and should not be a model for your own behavior; your goal, after all, is to be true to *your* self.

The self-actualized person is motivated from within.

There are certain characteristics essential to the self-actualized person. If you are self-actualized, you:

1. Are willing to stand on your own two feet. This simply means appreciating and capitalizing on your own strengths and abilities.
2. Trust your self. You believe that you can make decisions for your self, and you trust that those decisions will serve your own (and others') best interests.
3. Are flexible. Flexibility is the willingness to broaden your own interests by experiencing as much as possible. It is also the willingness to change when you see that certain decisions or alternatives are wrong.

Making What You Have Count

You may wonder why all this is so important. Why emphasize this phase of personal development we call "self-actualization"? The reason is that the self-actualized person is usually more capable of using interpersonal communication skills in an effective, healthy way. As I have said, the self is at the heart of intrapersonal communication, and it is also at the heart of interpersonal communication. How well you'll be able to apply the concepts treated in the following chapters of this book depends on how well defined your self-concept is. It will be to your benefit if you know your self well and are able to act on what you know.

Most of us are painfully aware of our shortcomings and failures. We can learn to be as *realistically* aware of our strengths. To do this, first find qualities you already possess that you can emphasize. These can be very simple qualities. You might begin with: I am good at tennis. I can make people laugh. I like animals. Make what you already have a starting place upon which you can build.

Then think about how often you act on your own likes and strengths. Do you play tennis often? Do you always wait for someone else to ask you to play? Try initiating getting together with someone the next time *you* feel like playing. Do all your friends think you have a good sense of humor or is it something you reserve for a few select people? Maybe you're holding back without knowing it. Do you own a pet? If you do, find out as much as you can about how to take care of it. If you don't or can't have a pet, join an animal welfare society. Make a small donation to a zoo. This is what your parents and teachers may have always encouraged you to do: Pursue your own interests! It makes sense. It can lead you to new, deeper interests and relationships. And it's the beginning of self-actualization.

_____

I cannot emphasize too strongly the need for and the potential value of your recognizing and responding to your personality strivings. This might be a basic definition of health. When you are able to look at the positive, constructive aspects of your personality style, you have certain options and alternatives open to you, as well as a frame of reference to explain your meaning, value, and humanity. You can be more aware of feelings of tension, helplessness, and meaninglessness. And you will be able to deal with them more appropriately. In short, by knowing yourself better, you can better deal with both your strengths and your weaknesses.

—Gregory G. Young, *Your Personality and How to Live With It*

SELF-DISCLOSURE

Think of the last interpersonal communication you had with someone where you exchanged ideas and information freely and came away feeling the relationship had been strengthened, or at least better defined. What are the ingredients that cause one encounter to be memorable and another to be meaningless and forgotten? Perhaps one ingredient was the amount of self-disclosing that occurred. "Self-disclosure" simply means disclosing or revealing your self, showing what you know about your self. Isn't it true that when somebody reveals private, personal information you could acquire from no other source except him or her, that the quality of communication increases?

What probably made your latest encounter significant was that both of you shared information. It did not come from just one of you. The information, too, probably had to do with your feelings about each other, the social situation, or about other people in your social situation. For example, you might say, "I feel great just knowing you" or "I'm glad I could do this with you" or "Can you imagine what Mike would say if he could see us now?" You would be revealing personal feelings that result from your interaction with the other person. These are potentially high-disclosure messages; that is, they say something particular about the circumstances of your relationship. Such messages need not be intimate exchanges, but they can be. They can also be quite simple. But they do depend for their complete meaning on your having shared certain experiences with the other person.

Potentially low-disclosure messages might relate to situations that the two of you do not share. For example, to reveal the name of a book you just read, or the fact that you did not like the eggs you had for breakfast, or that your roommate has a cold, is to share low-disclosure

Write down some of your positive traits, characteristics, abilities, and accomplishments. What is there about your self that you would like to emphasize? For example, are you in good health? Are you comfortable meeting new people? Are you good at math problems and puzzles? Do you have a good memory? List as many things as you can think of—they don't have messages. They may, however, pave the way for high-disclosure messages. Self-disclosing is important because you need to know your self in order to do it, and because by disclosing your self you come to define your feelings toward your self more clearly.[14]

It's likely the last significant interaction you thought of involved a friend. It is in such close relationships that most self-disclosure occurs because revealing your self involves risk, and we are not as likely to take a risk with a new acquaintance. We do not want to share feelings with a person we don't trust. The interesting thing is that we cannot create trust in a relationship, and thus diminish the amount of risk in that relationship, without self-disclosure. And the more we trust another person, the more likely it is that we will self-disclose. Self-disclosure creates trust, and trust encourages self-disclosure. As in so much of what we talk about in interpersonal communication, a positive interacting circle creates growth.

What Happens in Self-Disclosure?

Before any further explanation of self-disclosure, we might consider some of the benefits to be gained. What happens when you self-disclose? One of the first things you might notice happening is *increasing accuracy in communication*. Because self-disclosure involves the expression of personal feelings, you not only pass along information ("Your philodendron died while you were gone") but you can also say how you feel about delivering that message ("I'm sorry to have to tell you your philodendron died while you were gone. I know how much it meant to you"). Otherwise, the other person would have to guess how you feel from your behavior. Feelings are often interpreted from

to be earth-shaking skills or accomplishments. Then, for each skill, write down the last time you can think of that you acted on that preference or ability. If it's been so long that you can't remember, list concrete steps you can take to revive that particular skill. This can be as simple as talking to someone, writing away for information, looking something up in the library, joining a club or musical group. As you discover new preferences and skills, add to your list.

Self-disclosure creates trust which encourages further self-disclosure. This positive circle creates growth, which can continue throughout life.

Remember the last time you self-disclosed something to someone else? Try to recall exactly what it was. Who were you with? Where were you? Now, with this example of self-disclosure in mind, answer the following questions:

1. What did this self-disclosing reveal about your

   — values?   — attitudes?

   — beliefs?   — needs?

2. What happened after you self-disclosed?

   — Was there silence?

   — Did you continue to talk?

   — Did the other person say something?

   — Did he or she also self-disclose? (about as much as you did? — more?)

3. Was this a positive experience? Why or why not?

   — Would you do it again?

   — Would you do it differently if you had to do it again?

   — If you could, how would you change the experience?

   — Has the groundwork been laid for still more self-disclosure?

behavior, and we hope that others interpret our feelings correctly. But we know from experience that other people do not always guess correctly how we feel unless we tell them. The first benefit of self-disclosure, then, is that it ensures a certain level of accuracy in communication.

Another thing that happens has to do with *getting to know others better*. Interpersonal relationships are built upon self-disclosure. If you want to deepen your friendships, discover more about how others think and feel, and increase the intensity of your associations, self-disclosure provides one means. Think of the person you consider your closest friend. Chances are more mutual self-disclosure has taken place with this person than with anyone else you know. As you find out more about both your self and others, you will realize how little you know about both, and how much room there is for growth.

Self-disclosure also is a way of *increasing your number of contacts and enlarging your group of friends*. Getting to know a larger number of people can add knowledge, interest, and a degree of excitement to your present life. It might provide opportunities for you to experiment—to try out new attitudes, to experience new behaviors, and to encounter new relationships. It is not necessarily dishonest in your interpersonal encounters to be one thing to one person, something a little different to another. You have many sides. You are not composed of a single set of attitudes, behaviors, or relationships, but many times routine, habits, or laziness can prevent you from sharing certain aspects of your self. The self you reveal in every situation should be an honest one, but that does not mean it must be the same one exposed to everyone, or that it cannot change.

Perhaps the most important personal benefit to result from self-disclosure is simply the possibility of *gaining increased insight into the "real" you*. Self-disclosure is the window you use to see your self. The more self-disclosure you engage in, the more likely it is you will discover attributes, uniquenesses, and peculiarities you may not have been aware of, thus opening a window into your self.

The Johari Window: Here's Looking at You

Joseph Luft and Harrington Ingham created a diagram that looks at the self-disclosure process as a means of expanding what you know of your self. They called it the Johari Window (Joseph + Harrington).[15] (See Figure 4.)

The Johari Window identifies four kinds of information about your self that affect your communication. Think of the whole diagram as representing your total self as you relate to other human beings. Remember that for every person you relate with, a new window can be

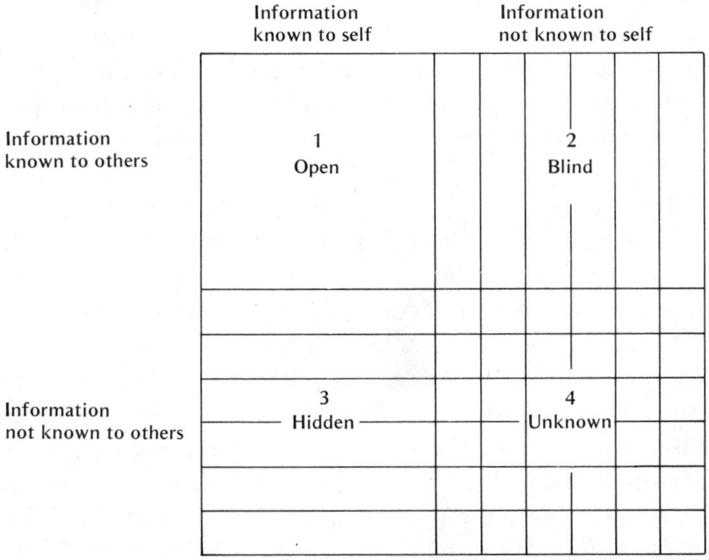

Figure 4. The Johari Window identifies different kinds of information about our selves.

drawn. The panes of the window change in size according to your awareness, and the awareness of others, of your behavior, feelings, and motivations. While the size of the panes can change according to different levels of awareness, the size will also be different for different people because your behavior, feelings, and motivations are actually different with them. Every relationship you have can be described by a Johari Window, and no two would be alike.

The open pane.   The size of the *open* pane reveals the amount of risk you take in relationships. As relationships become deeper, the open pane gets bigger, reflecting your willingness to be known. This pane comprises all aspects of your self known to you *and* others. It includes such things as the color of your eyes, your sex, and whether you are standing up or sitting down at the moment. It may also include things you know and don't mind admitting about your self, such as the fact that you are married or a teacher or happy or depressed. Information included in this pane provides the substance for the biggest part of your communications with others. This is where everybody's cards are on the table.

The blind pane.   The *blind* pane consists of all the things about your self that other people perceive but that are not known to you. Others, for example, may consider you abrasive and unpleasant while you may see your self as optimistic and pleasant. You may think of your self as genuinely humorous; others may find your humor forced and vulgar. Or you may think of your self as confident and self-assured, but because of your nervous mannerisms, others may see your insecurities. The more you learn about the qualities in your blind pane, the more you will be able to control the impressions you make on others, understand their reactions to you, and learn to grow beyond them. Growth requires such discovery of things unknown to you, though known to others.

The hidden pane.   In the *hidden* pane, you are the one who exercises control. This pane is made up of all those behaviors, feelings, and motivations that you prefer not to disclose to someone else. These things could be events that occurred during your childhood that you do not want known. They could include the fact that you failed biology in high school, that you like soap operas, that you eat peanut butter with every meal. They could concern other people besides you, and need not be things you are ashamed of or think are wrong. Everyone is entitled to some secrets. There are certain things that can remain private and personal and need never be disclosed. These things remain in the hidden pane: things unknown to others but known to you.

Plot a Johari Window for the following encounters in your life —
as specifically as you can:

A. your roommate (if you have one)

B. your best friend

C. someone you recently met for the first time

D. the teacher of this course

E. one of your parents

F. someone you know but who does not know you (and has not spoken to you)

Note that a Johari Window represents a relationship between you and this
other person. The relative size of the various panes of the window depends on
the amount of self-disclosure that has occurred between you.

The unknown pane.   The *unknown* pane is made up of everything
unknown to you and to others. No matter how much you grow and
discover and learn about your self, shrinking the size of this pane, it can
never completely disappear. You can never know all there is to know
about your self. This pane represents everything about your self that
you and other people have never explored. This pane includes all your
untapped resources, all your potentials, everything that currently lies
dormant. It is through interpersonal communication that you can
reduce the size of this pane; without communicating with others, much
of your potential will remain unrealized.

The interdependence of the panes.   The four panes of the Johari Window are interdependent: that is, a change in the size of one pane will affect the others. For example, if through talking with a friend you
discovered something you never knew before (something that existed in
the blind pane), this would enlarge the open pane and reduce the size of
the blind one. Your discovery could be of something rather insignificant, like the fact that your socks don't match, or it could be something
crucial to your relationship, like the fact that Sam really doesn't care
about you as much as you thought he did.

It can be rewarding and satisfying to add to your open pane,
whether by revealing or by discovering things about your self. It can
also be painful; enlarging the open pane involves some risk. You need
to use discretion here, as inappropriate disclosure can be damaging
whether you are giving it or receiving it. Be sure you are ready to cope
with the consequences before you try to empty your hidden and blind
panes into your open pane.

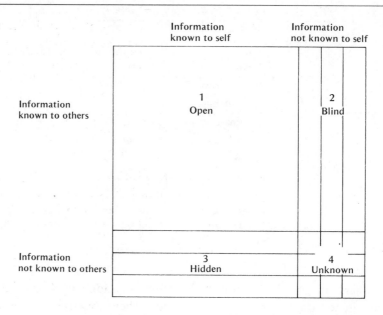

Figure 5. This window describes a relationship with a great deal of free and honest exchange.

Generally, though, the more you reveal your self to others so that they can know you better, the more you will learn about your self. And the more truth about your self you are willing to accept from others, the more accurate your self-concept will be. This increased knowledge of your self can result in greater self-acceptance. After all, if your friend is not shocked by your C average, perhaps you can accept it too. A Johari Window representing a close relationship between two people in which there is a great deal of free and honest exchange has a very large open pane. (See Figure 5.)

Sidney Jourard, a researcher, has concluded that humans spend an incredible amount of energy trying to avoid becoming known by other human beings. The acts of avoidance keep us from healthy human relationships. According to Jourard, allowing your self to be known to at least one other person who is important to you and whose opinions and judgment you value and respect highly is one characteristic of a healthy personality.[16]

What Are You Afraid Of?

Why are we afraid to reveal our selves to others? Why is it easier to hold back than to express our real being? In *Why Am I Afraid to Tell You Who I Am?* John Powell suggests that one reason is that each of us thinks, "If I tell you who I am, you may not like who I am, and it is all that I have."[17] We fear rejection. We fear discovering that we might be not totally acceptable to others or that we are unworthy. Another reason is that we feel we may not get reinforcement. What if I open my self to you and you offer no support or positive feedback? Even the possibility of some slight negative reaction scares us. Or we might be afraid of hurting another person or making him or her angry. You may have wanted for a long time to tell someone that if she continues to treat her boyfriend callously she will lose him. Your fear of angering her may have kept you from telling her.

Research on self-disclosure has indicated that the primary reason why people avoid it is because they feel that if they disclose themselves they might project an image they do not want to project. Research showed, further, that beyond protecting their image, males and females avoid self-disclosure for different reasons. Males, for example, do not want to give information that might make them appear inconsistent. They also do not want to lose control over other people, nor do they want to threaten relationships they have with others. For males, the predominant concern is to maintain control.[18]

For females, beyond protecting their image, research showed that they did not want to give other people information that might be used against them. Also, females felt that self-disclosure is a sign of emotional disturbance. Further, they did not want to hurt a relationship. Their object, according to the research, was to avoid personal hurt and problems with a relationship that might result from self-disclosure.[19]

We may not self-disclose if we believe that no one else is interested in our thoughts, feelings, or view of the world.[20] Or we simply may not know how to self-disclose constructively. Since this disclosure is the primary channel for gaining information about our selves, some of the basic skills for successful, constructive self-disclosure will be outlined next.

Consider This _____

Risk rejection by reaching out to communicate with someone else, even if it is only a casual conversation in a grocery store. "You can become a prune, shriveled up in a world of misery, or you can say to yourself: 'I may have been hurt, but I am going to survive.' Sure, it feels lousy to lose someone, to be alone. And if your belief is strong enough that you can't live without them, you'll die. But within each of us is the ability to make change, to grow," [says Pat Berman, a Miami nurse and mental-health therapist].
—Linda Cicero, *The Blade: Toledo, Ohio,* December 9, 1979

IMPROVING SKILLS IN SELF-DISCLOSURE

How can we disclose our selves more successfully than we do now? Perhaps it would be more accurate in this chapter on the self to talk about improving attitudes rather than skills. Without the proper attitude, it is unlikely that our skills in self-disclosure will improve.

Commit your self to grow.[21]   If we have no desire to grow or change, no commitment to improve our relationship with another person, we are not likely to self-disclose. We have to care about another person before taking the risk necessary to build a trusting relationship. The fact that we acknowledge the value of a relationship shows the other person our level of commitment and makes the self-disclosure even more useful.

It takes courage to let another person know he or she means something special to us. To say, "It has been fun talking to you," sounds superficial, but it may be enough to trigger further interaction. So, feeling a commitment to a relationship is part of it, but we also need to disclose that commitment to the other person. How often do we tell other people that we need them or appreciate them?

- Cultivate the ability to see—and enjoy—people as individuals. Look for the qualities in others that make them unique.
- Learn to enjoy life more. Take time to savor the things you do. Get involved in the world around you. Look for good experiences, expect them to happen, celebrate them when they do.
- Avoid cynicism. Cynics feel that everyone is out for his or her own personal gain. No one is genuine or generous; everyone wants to get something from others—this is the cynic's view. Allow yourself to act as if you expect the best from others.
- Try to be more positive in the things you do. Do not blame others for your troubles or trace your choices to their advice or example. Take responsibility for your behavior, ideas, and decisions.

Share your feelings.   Beyond sharing with another person what we consider the value of the relationship, it helps if we both agree to share feelings and awarenesses. This sharing often occurs naturally when the relationship is already comfortable and mutually supportive. Other times it might help if we simply make a comment like "I hope we can be honest with each other. I know I'm going to try." Self-disclosure operates best in a situation where both people know the value of sharing. Each should be willing to share feelings about the other person's actions, being careful not to confuse honest communication with thoughtless or cruel remarks.

We all need some reinforcement in our communications. Have you ever come out of a movie really excited and talking about it, wanting to share your enthusiasm, only to have your companions say nothing at all? You don't know if they agree with you or don't agree with you or are simply thinking about something else! Sharing is a two-way process and without give *and* take, one person might stop giving anything at all. To be ready and willing to share means each partner views the relationship from nearly the same viewpoint, lessening the feeling of risk.

• Cultivate the ability to empathize—the ability to feel and to care about other people's experiences. This not only makes your own life richer, it connects your life to that of others and makes you more likable as well. To develop empathy:

  —study your own experiences,
  —remember the way you felt—or imagine the way you might feel—in similar situations,
  —relate your feelings—or probable feelings—to the other person.

• Encourage other people to talk about their feelings and their lives. Try to remember what they say and to get a sense of what their experiences feel like.
• Be ready to confront people when you disagree with them about a matter that is important to you. This helps give yourself purpose and identity. It also lets others know you are capable of strong beliefs and feelings.
• Root for your friends. Can you rejoice at other people's successes? Not being able to—because of envy or fear—makes you less a friend and less confident and secure in your own life.

Try This

Engage in some self-analysis by answering the following questions:

1. What are your chief goals?
2. What do you love?
3. In what situations are you most likely to show courage?
4. How do you work at getting what you want?
5. What four potentially true sentences would you most like written on your tombstone?
6. What four sentences would you least like written there?
7. If you were on a life raft in a raging ocean and could save six people among everyone you know, who would they be and why?

—George Weinberg, *Self Creation*

Take a chance.   We must be willing to take chances in self-disclosure. There is no guarantee that we will not get hurt or that we will not be rejected. If a relationship is important, it is worth risking being honest so that both people can learn and grow. One of us may become angry or defensive at something the other says, but if we aren't willing to express our real feelings, the result is superficiality and facade building.

If it bothers you that a friend always dominates conversations by griping about her parents, you might say, "Let's make any discussion of parents off-limits for tonight." This takes some courage, but it allows your real feelings to show. And your friend may not even have been aware that she *was* dominating the conversation. It's worth taking the chance of telling her how you feel as long as you have her best interests at heart and care about preserving an honest relationship with her. The habit of honesty in all matters, no matter how small, makes it easier to be honest in more difficult, personal areas. For example, to tell a friend that he seems to be feeling sorry for himself takes a lot of courage. But taking such a chance often pays off and the other person values us even more because of our honesty.

- Don't suppress strong emotions—especially anger. If you spend many long hours working on a project or paper, and receive a low grade, tell the teacher that you are annoyed. Don't just let it go by saying, "It's no big thing." It *is* a big thing. Resigning yourself to mistreatment makes you believe that you *deserve* mistreatment and that you'll always get it.
- Meet all the challenges you possibly can. Decide for yourself—honestly—what you can and cannot do with respect to each one. Even if you know others will excuse you, do not excuse yourself from challenges you *can* meet with an effort.
- Act ethically toward others. How you treat others *does* matter—even in small things. Remember to thank people for small favors as well as great ones.
- Force yourself to do things you've never done before—talk to people you've never spoken to; engage in activities you haven't tried. Taking chances in some areas of your life makes it more likely that you will take chances in other areas.
- Snatch at all fleeting moments of intense feeling. Avoid the repetitive and automatic. Look for opportunities to inject freshness and emotionality.

Don't manipulate.   The best self-disclosure occurs when neither person tries to change or manipulate the other person. Despite the intense emotions that may surface, conversation should never turn to who is at fault but, rather, focus on making the relationship more satisfying and productive for both parties. For example, if your friend seems to be indulging in self-pity, it would be more helpful to point out to him that this seems (to you) to be so than to tell him to stop it. Stopping or not stopping is his choice to make. Any change that occurs in a relationship should result from one of us acting freely in response to information provided or acquired. This nonmanipulative atmosphere is created when we truly care for and accept the other person.

- Do not tell other people how they feel. "I'm sure you don't like this." "I know how Sue makes you uncomfortable, so I won't invite her." People's feelings change, as yours do. You can ask others how they feel, but don't tell them.
- Do not tell other people what they should do. "You should never be angry," or "You should control your temper." Let the other person decide what is or is not appropriate behavior.
- Do not always try to be the powerful one in your relationships. You may be forceful, but not dominating. Listen, and be aware of your own weaknesses.
- Don't be passive and let others control your life. Do not feign helplessness and stupidity. Learn to be willing to express your own convictions strongly.

Watch your timing.   It's a good idea to express our feelings and reactions as closely as possible to the time we actually feel them. Both parties must realize what behavior caused the reaction. Parents usually find a reprimand means more to a small child if they say "No!" just as the child is about to do something wrong than if the incident goes undiscovered for an hour and the "No!" comes too late. This is true for adult interactions, too. Even disturbing reactions should be discussed at once. Sometimes feelings are saved up and then dropped on the other person; this does not aid healthy self-disclosure. Of course there are times when immediate expression of our reaction may be inappropriate. For example, we would not want to share highly personal reactions with a friend in a crowded elevator. It's almost always better to wait until no one else is around.

- When someone asks you how you feel about something, answer as quickly as possible. Don't censor your response. You have the right to any reaction you feel. A quick answer is often more authentic and accurate than a slow one.
- Make your comments to the people you think are affecting you and to no one else.
- Do not object to another person's behavior in front of others. Objections often come across as personal attacks. Unless waiting would be costly, waiting until you are alone reveals your concern for fairness to the other person and your consideration for his or her feelings.

- Avoid comparisons. Nobody likes being described as inferior to anyone else. Comparisons may predispose others not to listen to what you have to say.
- Make your comments as soon as you can. Speaking up becomes more difficult the longer you postpone it. Also, if the comments are tied to a strong emotional reaction—like anger—waiting allows the reaction to build with the possibility that irrelevant comments will be added. If you comment on things that happened a long time ago, too, you will look as if you have been holding a grudge.
- Try to make only one comment at a time. Too many comments—especially criticisms—might demoralize the other person and may obscure and detract from the major point.

Clarify, clarify.   If we're not sure we understand what another person means, we should try stating his or her comments in other words. If we offer this paraphrase of the other person's remarks before supplying our own response, there's less chance of our misunderstanding each other. (Ralph: "I'm sick of taking this bus with you every day." Mike: "I hear you saying you're sick of riding to work with me. Is that right?" Ralph: "No, I just meant I'm sick of this bus. I wish we had a car.") Check, also, to make sure the other person understands your comments in the way you mean them.

As we respond to another person, we can try to eliminate any kind of personal judgments ("Don't you *ever* listen?"), name-calling ("You really are a hypocrite"), accusations ("You love walking all over people, don't you?"), commands or orders ("Stop running his life"), or sarcasm ("You really want to get to the top," when another person just flunked an exam). Instead, talk about things the other person did—actual, accurate descriptions of the action that took place. We can try to describe our own feelings, letting the other person see them as temporary rather than absolute. Instead of saying "I hate sitting next to you in class," we might try "I can't stand it when you crack your knuckles." We should make certain, too, that our assumptions about the other person are correct in the first place.

According to research, the clearest self-disclosure messages are those that are:

- mutually relevant. That is, they are based on the immediate situation—the here and now—not something which is past or unrelated to the present situation.
- personally owned. To say "I feel" is much more exact than the more general "People feel."
- source specific. Saying "I feel x toward you, Allen" rather than "I feel x around people."

- based on a clear causal connection with your feeling or perception. Try to use the word "because" rather than omitting a reason or alluding to the cause indirectly by saying something like "there may be a reason."
- behavior specific. Rather than saying that someone is irresponsible or can't be counted on, it is better to say, "You were late for our appointment."[22]

Your success in college and, indeed, in life, will depend on *how* you feel about your self and your abilities. Your self-concept is a product of intrapersonal and interpersonal communication. What you think about your self affects your behavior toward others. And it is what other people say about you and to you that is the information you use in thinking about your self. Thus, intrapersonal communication and interpersonal communication are intricately entwined. We see this especially in the process of self-disclosure. Disclosing your self is the key to discovering your self, but productive, worthwhile self-disclosure requires interaction with other people. Self-disclosure is an important method of acquiring information. Other practical methods by which we acquire new information and broaden our perceptions are listening and feedback. These subjects are treated in the next chapter.

OTHER READING

Raymond Gale, *Who Are You? The Psychology of Being Yourself* (Englewood Cliffs, N.J.: Prentice-Hall, Inc., 1974). A challenging book for those concerned with expanding their awareness of who they really are. Comprehensive, well-documented, easy-to-read humanistic approach to becoming an authentic person. A book for those who want a thorough, well-organized presentation.

Sidney M. Jourard, *The Transparent Self* (New York: Van Nostrand Reinhold Company, 1971). Jourard describes how people can gain health and full personal development once they have the courage to be themselves. One of the best books written on the self and self-disclosure. It is lively, straightforward, interesting, and relevant.

Sam Keen and Anne Valley Fox, *Telling Your Story: A Guide to Who You Are and Who You Can Be* (New York: New American Library, 1973). Includes many simple and useful exercises to foster self-discovery and discover personal potential. Basic but enjoyable material. A good place to start.

Eugene Kennedy, *If You Really Knew Me, Would You Still Like Me?* (Niles, Ill.: Argus Communications, 1975). Kennedy develops a procedure through which people get to know themselves, identify strengths and weaknesses, and build self-esteem by building on their strengths. A simplified approach to achieving self-confidence.

Jess Lair, *I Ain't Much Baby—But I'm All I've Got* (New York: Doubleday & Company, Inc., 1972). Building on his own experience, Lair develops a philosophy of living based on getting in touch with the self. He discusses acceptance, trust, search, and change among other topics. This is an engaging, personal book that successfully holds the reader's attention.

Maxwell Maltz, *Psycho-Cybernetics* (New York: Pocket Books, 1960). The thesis of this book is that the self-image is the key to human personality and human behavior: to change personality and behavior, one must change the self-image. Maltz encourages the reader to experience.

Maxwell Maltz, *The Search for Self-Respect* (New York: Bantam Books, 1973). This is an expansion of *Psycho-Cybernetics*. In this book, Maltz tells the reader how to set and achieve goals, how to reinforce positive qualities and overcome negative ones, and how to gain freedom.

Mildred Newman and Bernard Berkowitz, *How to Be Your Own Best Friend* (New York: Ballantine Books, Ltd., 1971). Light, easy, popular approach that suggests people will find themselves richer than they ever imagined if they can learn to love and nurture themselves. Readers are encouraged to make their own possibilities available to themselves.

Everett L. Shostrom, *Freedom to Be: Experiencing and Expressing Your Total Being* (New York: Bantam Books, Inc., 1972). Shostrom writes about us, in the here-and-now, daring to be ourselves, fully and freely. Do you know your self? —your strength? —your weakness? —your anger? —your love? Shostrom urges the reader to move in this direction on an inner journey toward interdependence.

Everett L. Shostrom, *Man, The Manipulator: The Inner Journey from Manipulation to Actualization* (New York: Bantam Books, Inc., 1968). This practical book will help the reader recognize manipulative behavior. Further, it clearly describes actualizing behavior and indicates the kinds of changes we must make to achieve it.

George Weinberg, *Self Creation* (New York: Avon Books, 1978). "You are what you create." Weinberg provides specific guidelines for controlling the forces behind your life, for the striving to do this makes life meaningful and fulfilling. Since you are responsible for your life, Weinberg makes specific suggestions that will help you in taking charge.

Gregory G. Young, *Your Personality and How to Live With It* (New York: The New American Library, Inc. [A Signet Book], 1978). Young offers an examination of 12 basic personality types. If readers can find themselves among these, they can use his suggestions for becoming themselves more effectively. There is a great deal of information here—perhaps more than most readers will want.

John O. Stevens, *Awareness: Exploring, Experimenting, Experiencing* (New York: Bantam Books, 1971). Awareness experiments designed to help readers adjust to themselves and to discover their own reality, their own existence, and their own humanness. Enlightening and stimulating ideas.

NOTES

[1]Donald Washburn, "Intrapersonal Communication in a Jungian Perspective," *Journal of Communication* 14 (September 1964): 131–35.

[2]Paul Watzlawick, Janet Helmick Beavin, and Don D. Jackson, *Pragmatics of Human Communication: A Study of Interactional Patterns, Pathologies, and Paradoxes* (New York: W. W. Norton and Company, Inc., 1967), pp. 98–99.

[3]D. E. Hamachek, *Encounters with the Self* (New York: Holt, Rinehart and Winston, 1971).

[4]Charles T. Brown and Paul W. Keller, *Monologue to Dialogue: An Exploration of Interpersonal Communication* 2nd ed. (Englewood Cliffs: Prentice-Hall, 1979), pp. 82–105.

[5]John C. Condon, Jr., *Semantics and Communication* (New York: Macmillan Co., 1966), p. 60.

[6]The following writers maintain that the self-concept is a direct result of the reactions of "significant others": Henry Stack Sullivan, *The Interpersonal Theory of Psychiatry* (New York: W. W. Norton and Company, Inc., 1953); John J. Sherwood, "Self Identity and Referent Others," *Sociometry* 28 (1965): 66–81; and Carl Backman, Paul Secord, and Jerry Pierce, "Resistance to Change in the Self-Concept as a Function of Consensus Among Significant Others," in *Problems in Social Psychology*, Carl Backman and Paul Secord, eds. (New York: McGraw-Hill Book Company, 1969), pp. 462–67.

[7]Experiments by Robert Rosenthal have confirmed that labels become self-fulfilling prophecies. See Robert Rosenthal, "Self-Fulfilling Prophecy," in *Readings in Psychology Today* (Del Mar, Calif.: CRM Books, 1967), pp. 466–71.

[8]Alvin Toffler, *Future Shock* (New York: Bantam Books, 1970), p. 17.

[9]Nathaniel Branden, *The Psychology of Self-Esteem* (Los Angeles: Nash, 1969), p. 103.

[10]From *Personal and Interpersonal Communication: Dialogue with the Self and with Others* by John J. Makay and Beverly A. Gaw, p. 28. Copyright © 1975 by Bell & Howell. Reprinted by permission of Charles E. Merrill Publishing Co.

[11]Ibid.

[12]Earl C. Kelly, *Perceiving, Behaving, Becoming: A New Focus on Education*, 1962 Yearbook (Washington, D.C.: Association for Supervision and Curriculum Development, 1962), pp. 9–20.

[13]From *Encounters with the Self* by Don. E. Hamachek. Copyright © 1971 by Holt, Rinehart and Winston. Adapted by permission of Holt, Rinehart and Winston.

[14]Sidney M. Jourard, *The Transparent Self* (New York: Van Nostrand Reinhold Company, 1971), p. 6.

[15]From *Group Processes: An Introduction to Group Dynamics* by Joseph Luft, by permission of Mayfield Publishing Company. Copyright © 1963, 1970 by Joseph Luft. See also *Of Human Interaction*.

[16]Jourard, *The Transparent Self*, pp. 32–33.

[17]John Powell, *Why Am I Afraid to Tell You Who I Am?* (Chicago: Argus Communications, 1969), p. 27.

[18]Lawrence B. Rosenfeld, "Self-Disclosure Avoidance: Why I Am Afraid to Tell You Who I Am," *Communication Monographs*, 46 (March 1979), 72–73.

[19]Rosenfeld, 73.

[20]Jourard, *The Transparent Self*, p. 193.

[21]David W. Johnson, *Reaching Out: Interpersonal Effectiveness and Self-Actualization*. © 1972, pp. 37–38. Reprinted by permission of Prentice-Hall, Englewood Cliffs, New Jersey.

[22]J. W. MacDaniels et al., "Openness: Personalized Expression in Interpersonal Communication" (Paper presented at the annual conference of the International Communication Association, Phoenix, April 1971), as cited in Mark L. Knapp, *Social Intercourse: From Greeting to Goodbye* (Boston: Allyn and Bacon, Inc., 1978), p. 150.

4

Responding to Others:
Listening and Feedback

You have just spent five minutes explaining to a friend the time and place of a birthday party and as you turn to go he asks you, "Oh, yes, where are we meeting and what time did you say?" You know he hasn't listened. And you know how it feels when someone hasn't listened to you.

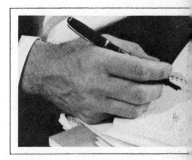

Do I listen well? Chances are this is a question we never ask our selves. After all, listening is something we have done all our lives with no special training. We take it for granted. Everything I've said in this book about successful interpersonal communication describes it as a circular give-and-take in which we really tune in to the other person. An essential part of that give-and-take is listening. This does not mean simply putting on a "listening" expression and nodding and grunting agreement now and then while mentally planning our evening; it means listening with our full and active attention—listening empathically, as though we are in the other person's place. We can never take this kind of listening for granted. It takes skill and constant practice, but the reward is greatly improved communication.

This chapter is about the importance of listening empathically and giving appropriate feedback. I'll talk about some of the bad listening habits we all have and ways we can improve our listening and feedback skills.

THE IMPORTANCE OF LISTENING

When we think of our selves in communication situations, we usually think more about getting our ideas to someone else than about receiving ideas from them. This is normal. We've come to think the word "communication" means a process that flows out from us rather than one in which we are the receiver. But communicating orally involves far more than just talking to a person. It involves sharing ideas, trying to exchange meaning with each other as perfectly as possible. In most interpersonal situations, we spend just as much time listening and responding to the other person as we do talking. Considering all the communication activities of a normal day—talking, listening, reading, writing—we probably spend more time in listening, on the average, than in any of the others.[1]

As I said, most of us do not think much about listening. We take it for granted until someone does not listen to us. We *do* get a great deal of experience in it. Think of all the things and people we listen to in an ordinary day: a clock radio to wake up by, roommates or friends at meals, teachers and other students in classes, piped-in music in stores, radios and tape players in cars, television and stereo at home.

Because we spend so much of every day in listening we may think it takes no great effort. Not true. Listening is not the same as hearing. Hearing is done with the ears and, unless our hearing is impaired, goes on virtually all the time. We have no mechanism in our bodies that lets us shut our ears as we shut our eyes. Listening is done with the mind as well as the ears. If we want to improve our listening we need to monitor our own listening habits and then actively work to improve. The kind of practice we get is important if we really want to get rid of bad habits.

The kind of listening we're concentrating on here is the most significant kind in interpersonal communication. We cannot and need not listen empathically to every gas station attendant or bank teller we exchange a few words with during the course of a day. Listening empathically—indeed, the kind of interpersonal communication skills this book is about—is appropriate in certain situations. There is also a place

HÄGAR the Horrible　　　　By Dik Browne

Consider This

I have something to tell you.	I will and you too.
I'm listening.	And let me know what's new.
I'm dying.	Certainly, though it can't be much.
I'm sorry to hear.	And stay well.
I'm growing old.	And you too.
It's terrible.	And go slow.
It is, I thought you should know.	And you too.
Of course and I'm sorry. Keep in touch.	—David Ignatow, "Two Friends"

for the simple exchange of information and for small talk. But empathic listening is quite different.

Empathic listening involves integrating physical, emotional, and intellectual inputs in a search for meaning and understanding. It is an active, not a passive process. We cannot just make sure that our ears are alert or open and let the rest come naturally. Because empathic listening involves both emotional and intellectual inputs, it does not just happen. We have to make it happen and it's not easy. It takes energy and commitment. We have a lot going against us—there are many influences that practically conspire to make us poor listeners. Some of them we can control, some we cannot.

Empathic listening also means listening to the whole person—to the gestalt. We listen to what is being said by the other person's facial expressions, gestures, posture, as well as body motion. (I'll examine nonverbal communication more fully in Chapter 6.) But it is the integration of these functional units—their combination—that tells us what we want to know. Thus, we must not limit our concentration and focus to words alone for that is restrictive and inhibitive. That is why empathic listening—the most effective kind of listening—means responding to the gestalt: the totality that is the other person.

WHAT INFLUENCES YOUR LISTENING?

Being aware of the factors that affect listening will help us improve our own listening skills but will also help us become more considerate of people who listen to us. Knowing what factors operate increases our understanding of the whole communication process and can help explain why breakdowns and confusion sometimes result. Here are some of the things that influence how well we listen:

As you listen to someone, notice the kinds of messages you receive from cues other than spoken words. Be aware of how many cues you are responding to and the nature of the specific message you are receiving from each.

Realize that this process is almost automatic. It is also a part of the whole perceptual process and, as such, takes less than a tenth of a second in most cases.

But to be conscious of the numerous cues to which you normally respond in a listening situation has two important advantages:

1. It increases your sensitivity to communication beyond words alone.

2. It increases your ability to control, or at least monitor, the numerous cues you yourself emit beyond words alone.

Things that influence how we listen.

Physiological Differences Affect What You Hear

Listening is part of the perceiving process. As a means of perception its effectiveness is limited by the mechanics of the physical process of hearing—to be able to select from aural stimuli we must first be able to hear them. If we are hard of hearing our listening will be affected simply because we won't have as many stimuli to choose from, organize, and interpret as someone who hears well.

You Process Words Faster Than They Can Be Spoken

The average person speaks at a rate of 100 to 200 words per minute. But as listeners, we can easily process 400 words per minute.[2] Though our minds can absorb words very rapidly, in our ordinary listening we are rarely challenged to process them as efficiently as we can. Even the most skilled speaker pauses and stumbles occasionally; even the most polished speech contains words that are not essential to the message. These hesitations and extraneous elements add up to many precious seconds of wasted time *within* a message. What do we, as listeners, do with this time? Let our minds wander, mostly. Unless we purposefully make use of that time to concentrate on the speaker's message, we can find it very easy to be distracted.

Effective Listening Requires Active Commitment

If we believe that listening is a passive process in which we simply monitor what we hear, we may misinterpret information or overlook important cues. We'll hear only what we want to hear or what grabs our attention. Productive listening involves real work. It takes emotional and

intellectual commitment. It's possible that our TV-watching habits contribute to our tendency to listen passively. Television, after all,
demands nothing from the viewer or listener. We don't have to respond
to TV, we just let it happen. But in interpersonal communication, if we
listen half-heartedly and passively we get only part of the message.

Those Hidden Messages . . .

Effective listening means listening with a third ear. By this I mean trying
to listen for the meanings behind the words and not just to the words
alone. The way words are spoken—loud, soft, fast, slow, strong, hesitating—is very important. There are messages buried in all the cues that
surround words.[3] If a mother says, "Come *in* now" in a soft, gentle
voice, it may mean the kids have a few more minutes. If she says,
"Come in NOW" there is no question about the meaning of the command. To listen effectively we have to pay attention to facial expressions and eye contact, gestures and body movement, posture and dress,
as well as the quality of the other person's voice, vocabulary, rhythm,
rate, tone, and volume. These nonverbal cues are a vital part of any
message. Listening with our third ear helps us understand the whole
message.

   The ability to expand on the obvious—to listen beyond words—allows us to really "see into" another person. People who seek help and
sympathy bear two messages—the one they speak and the one beneath
the surface. To help them we need to "see through" what they say. You

This girl seems to have found a friend who hears the hidden messages—who listens with the third ear.

may know a person to whom everyone goes with problems, a person other people seek out for counsel or just to share ideas. This person is probably an effective listener, someone who listens with the third ear.

Effective Listening Requires Empathy[4]

Another variable that works against effective listening is our tendency to evaluate what others say. We often want to judge, approve, or disapprove the statements we hear.[5] Then we act more on our evaluation than on what is actually said. There is a time for this kind of evaluative listening. The label "deliberative" has been given to the listening we do when we want "to hear information, to analyze it, to recall it at a later time, and to draw conclusions from it."[6] This is the kind of listening we do in a psychology lecture class or when we listen to a government official explaining a proposal to curb inflation. We judge the information we hear in these situations. We try to remember it and evaluate its significance—whether we think it is relevant or irrelevant to us, right or wrong.

Both empathic listening and deliberative listening are done in order to achieve accurate understanding. With deliberative listening we want to understand the message accurately because we want to make specific use of the information it contains; it's our evaluation of the information that matters most. But when we listen empathically, our first goal is to understand the other person, to see and feel what that person sees and feels. In deliberative listening, understanding the other person is a secondary goal.[7]

The overall reason interpersonal communication improves when we listen empathically is that our own responses to the other person are based, ideally, on maximum understanding of what that person says. Specifically, this happens because:

1. There are more message channels available; we have a better chance of getting cues that will clarify communication;
2. Our responses are more appropriate because we give ourselves time to consider them carefully, and we are more likely to deal with the other person as he or she actually is instead of on the basis of a stereotype; and
3. We have a better picture of the other person's point of view, as a frame of reference for his or her remarks.

To understand where the other person is coming from requires a broader base than what we are probably accustomed to using. Empathic listening is one means to obtain that more comprehensive framework: the total image that is the other person.

Consider This

I happened to overhear some conversations of strangers on a plane not long ago, and it struck me that each of them was using the other as a sounding board and little else. One would speak about himself, the other would dutifully listen: then the second would take his turn, and the first would listen.

But the "listening" was a matter of surface courtesy and nothing more. Each was going through a set of verbal gymnastics, a kind of exercise in self-disclosure, but no contact was really made. They were like golfers taking turns addressing different balls; they walked the same course, but no genuine transaction ever took place.

Mostly, they were seeking to reassure themselves that all was well; they were looking for identity and stability and acceptance, by means of constructing an image in the other person's mind. This is a futile and unsatisfactory way to do it—for in personal relations, the only structures that can stand are bridges, not skyscrapers. Unless we reach across, we are reaching out in vain.

—Sydney Harris, "Strictly Personal"

WHY DON'T YOU LISTEN EMPATHICALLY?

If it is so important, and if there are so many advantages, you might wonder why more people are not empathic listeners. Actually, there are three reasons—all of them directly tied to each other. First, listening empathically is not easy. It is far more difficult than simply taking note of actual words spoken and responding to them literally. Second, empathic listening requires that we get outside of our selves by trying to share in the meaning, spirit, and feelings of another person. We're not always willing to do this. Our egos get tied up in our communication; we get involved in our own thoughts and problems. The next time you are involved in an interpersonal encounter, notice how hard it is to concentrate on what the other person is saying if you are preoccupied with your own next remark. Do you begin to plan what you are going to say before the other person even has a chance to stop talking? Instead of listening, you may find you are figuring out how to impress him or her with your next comment.[8]

The third reason we may not listen empathically is because of lifelong poor listening habits. We may listen too literally or too judgmentally by habit. We may habitually think of communication as a talking medium rather than as a listening medium. Here are some other habits we may have that get in the way of effective listening:

Tuning out.   Habit may cause us to tune out much of the talk we hear. Our society is a talk-oriented one. We tune out to avoid listening, to protect our selves from the communication babble that sometimes seems to surround us. It is necessary to tune out some things. We must be selective or we would be inundated. But we cannot listen empathically if habit has caused us to avoid the very basics of the process—tuning *in*!

This does not mean we need to tune in to everything we hear. But good listeners do tend to discover interesting elements in almost all communications. They are able to cope with the bombardment of stimuli. Whereas poor listeners tend to find all topics uniformly dry and boring, effective listeners concentrate their attention well and learn efficiently through listening.

We can't expect to be fascinated by every subject. But if we too often find our selves bored by the communication in a certain situation—eating lunch with the same people every day, for example—we might ask our selves, "What were my reasons for going to lunch with these people in the first place? Do those reasons still hold?" Perhaps we started eating with these people because they are politically active and we wanted to discuss politics with them. If we still feel the same way, remembering the original motive can help us focus our listening in this group's communications. We may be able to pick out useful bits of information from conversations that would otherwise seem pointless.

Wanting to be entertained.   Another habit that can affect our listening might be labeled the "Sesame Street Syndrome." We want to be entertained. We may mentally challenge a speaker: "Excite me or I won't listen." If we think ahead of time that the message we're going to hear will be dull, we're not likely to listen well. And if we expect to be bored, there's a good chance we will be. We generally prefer a lively, entertaining presentation to a straight, unembellished delivery. Think of the way local television news programs present the news. You may notice a real difference from one station to another in how many program elements are included mainly for their entertainment value.

Avoiding the difficult.   Another version of the "Sesame Street Syndrome" is that we tend to stay away from difficult listening. That is, given a choice, we are likely to avoid listening that requires mental exertion. Any kind of communication that deals with unfamiliar subjects can seem tough to follow, especially if the speaker moves quickly from one point to the next. If we're not used to a speaker's reasoning, we may give up on the message rather than try to follow his or her thought processes. Editorial comments on TV, panel discussions, and some lectures can be hard to follow if we're not used to really concentrating.

Criticizing the superficial.   Think about a recent interpersonal encounter you had with people you do not know well. Can you remember what they looked like? What they were wearing? What they said? We often let externals distract us from what the other person is saying.

Especially if we don't know someone well, we're likely to be diverted by that person's lisp or hairstyle or purple sweater. We may find our selves criticizing some unimportant characteristic of the person instead of listening to what he or she is saying. Think of how you and people you know size up a political candidate. Do you notice the candidate's hairstyle? Smile? Clothing? These nonverbal cues are important, but they shouldn't distract us from really listening to what the person is saying.

Letting your emotions take over.   Finally, we may habitually either (1) block things out; (2) distort things; or (3) agree too readily to everything. Often, when we hear things that don't fit in with our own beliefs, we put up a mental block so we don't get frightened or angry. Sometimes we hear just what we want to hear. We may have a conviction so strong that we twist whatever we hear to conform. Some words ("mother" "I love you") may appeal to our emotions to such an extent that we agree to anything that follows. If we loved every minute we spent at Barnwood High School, meeting someone else from old Barnwood automatically produces a favorable emotional climate for our conversation.

Our emotions may be triggered by a single word or phrase that seems to leap out. Suppose we meet a woman at a party who says, "I just got back from Colorado." Some emotional reactions we may have are "I never get to go anywhere" or "Colorado is overrun by crazy outdoor types. I wouldn't go there if you paid me" or "*Colorado!* I love Colorado! Mountains! Fresh air! Good times!" Any of these thoughts will color how we hear the rest of what the woman says to us. Once we hear that trigger-word ("Colorado"), we listen to nothing else. Instead we plan a defense, rebuttal, supportive example, argument, or other way to involve our ego. Effective listening means controlling emotional responses—trying to break old habits.

Try This

Next time you catch your self being distracted by another person's clothes, mannerisms, or looks, <u>stop</u> and try to:

1. <u>Refocus</u> your attention on the message.

2. <u>Paraphrase</u> what is being said.

3. <u>Review</u> the important elements of what has been communicated.

The idea is to redirect your attention to the message and away from distracting elements.

HI AND LOIS

RESULTS OF EFFECTIVE LISTENING

Animated, cooperative, and responsive listeners help the person they are talking to because their reactions produce an immediate effect. They can influence what the other person will say next. And the listener will benefit from the improved communication that results. (See Figure 1.)

Specifically, what are the rewards of effective listening? The first is that we will get a more stimulating and meaningful message—the other person may subconsciously adapt the message specifically to our knowledge and background. The more closely we listen to a person and indicate what we do and don't understand, the more likely we are to end up with a message that makes sense. And we're more likely to remember it. By improving our listening habits we should be able to recall more than fifty percent of the information we hear, rather than forget it.[9]

For example, if we respond to a friend's description of a recent trip with partial or complete silence, our friend will probably cut the description short. But if we ask such questions as, "Where did you go?" or "What did you do?" or "Was it fun?" or "Who did you see?" he or she will be more interested in providing the details. Our understanding of our friend's experience will be far more complete. Of course, we can

Figure 1.
The cycle of improved communication through effective listening.

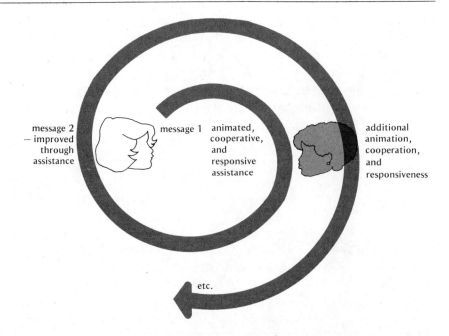

message 2 — improved through assistance

message 1 animated, cooperative, and responsive assistance

additional animation, cooperation, and responsiveness

etc.

Kirk Martin listens, in person and by appointment only.

"I will talk, if a customer asks me to, or if he looks like he wants me to," Mr. Martin explained. "I can talk eyeball-to-eyeball to anyone who comes through my front door."

Mr. Martin, 48, a professional truck and taxi-cab driver who sells one-family homes and farms on the side, began his listening enterprise with a newspaper ad.

"Did you know men are allotted 27,000 words per day, and women 31,000? I will listen to you talk for 30 minutes, without comment, for $5," the ad said.

"I get about 10 to 20 calls a day now, but only a few of those make appointments," Mr. Martin reports.

He says his clients are from all walks of life, many of them troubled people who need some-one to hear them out, just once.

"Just the other day a man from the upper-income group came because he felt stilted in his exclusive neighborhood," Mr. Martin said. "He couldn't grow a garden in his yard or hang his laundry out to dry if he wanted for fear of what the neighbors would think."

Mr. Martin says he's not sure why he began listening professionally.

"I guess because I feel the Lord gave me a capacity to work with people," he said. "I almost went into psychiatry. And this is an inexpensive alternative to a psychiatrist."

Mr. Martin said he has a bachelor's degree in business administration, and studied sociology, math, law, and psychiatry at the University of Missouri.

He says that the key to good listening is to avoid interference—"You can't communicate if there's a lot of static and noise."

—(AP) *The Blade: Toledo, Ohio,* August 16, 1975

purposely cut short a conversation by showing no interest or involvement. But we might miss out on a stimulating and meaningful message.

The second reward of effective listening is improvement in our own communication techniques. By paying closer attention to the communication of others and by observing their methods, we will be able to analyze our own efforts more completely.

For example, we may notice that a friend ends every other sentence with the words "you know." If this interferes with our listening, we'll be more alert to certain phrases or words that *we* overuse ourselves. Once we see how distracting such things are, we'll be more inclined to ask a friend to point out mannerisms *we* have that we are not aware of.

We may find that another reward of effective listening is an enlarged circle of friends. Good listeners are in great demand. People have an emotional need to be heard; the person who is willing to take the time to listen is often sought out.

Finally, in becoming effective listeners we are likely to become more open and involved human beings. The ultimate reward is more meaningful interpersonal relationships. Effective listening habits will increase our capacity to meet the demands of modern life. It is one of the most important communication skills needed for human interaction.

Next time you are in a conversation with someone, listen with the goal of finding out as much as you possibly can. Plan to ask the other person a series of probing questions to gain the necessary information. Some sample questions might be:

1. How did you discover that?
2. What else happened?
3. Why do you suppose that is so?
4. What was the outcome?
5. Would you do the same again?
6. Do you think it could happen again?
7. What do you think you gained from this experience?

Do not interrupt the other person with your probes. Listen closely so that your questions will be relevant to what is being said. Maintain a positive, supportive spirit of inquiry.

Wouldn't it be fascinating if we had more time to do this on a regular basis? We would become not only better listeners, but more retentive learners as well.

THE IMPORTANCE OF FEEDBACK

These benefits of good listening occur only when the cues we give back to a speaker allow that person to know how we received the message, permitting the speaker to adjust the message as needed.[10] This important process is known as *feedback*. Feedback consists of responses made *as* communication occurs. Feedback provides reinforcement for the speaker. It shows if he or she is being clear, accepted, or understood.

The heart of this feedback process is the adjustment or corrective function. Feedback can be words ("Yes, I get it") or physical messages (a smile) or responses that show the other person that we are, indeed, sharing in the spirit of what he or she is saying. It can also show if we do *not* understand or agree. Just as we know, by the response we get, whether or not we are being listened to, the other person is in the same situation. We recognize that mutual understanding has or hasn't occurred through feedback. An atmosphere which promotes honest feedback is a necessary condition for understanding and for being understood.

In any communication setting, each of us is both a source of messages and a receiver of messages simultaneously. This means that we are at all times responding and being responded to. Feedback exists

Consider This _____

DEAR ANN LANDERS: Mary Lou was depressed because she said, "I talk too much." She then asked, point-blank, "How can I learn to shut up?" Because Mary Lou has rescued me from boredom and discomfort many times, I would like to respond. She may not be Oscar Wilde, but she is darned good company.

   DEAR MARY LOU: Why are you so sure your listeners are bored to death? Do their eyes dart around the room while you are talking? Do they try to avoid you? While this happens occasionally to us all, next time you are suffering from post-party depression, ask yourself if that person asked you any questions. If so, it means he (or she) was interested.

   The genuine bore tries to engage the entire room with his strident bragging. But you say you behave "normally" until you are with someone who is not much of a talker. You have the right to feel used by your listeners, because actually, you are not monopolizing them, they are monopolizing you.

   A lively talker takes the pressure off and helps people relax. If everyone at the party said to his or herself, "This time, dummy, listen," so many of us would be ill at ease, searching desperately for something to say.

   People like me who are not scintillating are glad to see you come in the door. Please don't shut up. You are performing a useful service.—**READER IN VICTORIA, B.C.**

—syndicated in *The Blade: Toledo, Ohio*, December 19, 1979

_____ **Consider This**

when each person affects the other—each is a cause and an effect.[11] Just as we cannot *not* communicate, we cannot *not* send some kind of feedback. We send messages even when we do not speak.

Receiving Feedback

Imagine your self, for a moment, as only a source of messages; you gain no feedback to any message you send out. You say hello and nobody answers. You ask, "How are you doing?" and nobody answers. You say, "It sure is a beautiful day" and nobody reinforces or acknowledges what you've said. You have no way of knowing if you were heard or understood. You have no way to gauge your effectiveness. It's understandable how someone in this hypothetically one-way-communication situation could become frustrated, feeling unacceptable and unloved.[12] What's the use in talking if there is no one to respond? Receiving feedback is one of the best ways we have of modifying our behavior. Monitoring feedback is our way of assuring that the message we intend is as closely related as possible to the message received.

   Think of some people with whom you enjoy communicating. Do these people provide you with honest feedback as you speak? Their feedback affects not only *how* you communicate with them, but *why*

How do you think the speaker who gets this response feels?

you express your self as you do and *why* you treat them as you do. The cues we receive may cause us to keep talking, restate our ideas, become silent, begin to stumble or stammer, or stop short. Whatever the case, we need feedback for insight into our own communication and to aid us in understanding the communication behavior of others.

Giving Feedback

Just as we need to receive feedback, we also need to give it. Listening attentively and giving appropriate feedback let us know that we are coping successfully with our environment; we are active participants, not passive observers of life. We can act in direct response to a specific stimulus.[13] The feedback we give people can make them feel unique and worthwhile and heighten their sense of well-being—it's personally rewarding to know that our reactions matter.

Communication does not exist for long when the direction of flow is one-way. A person who receives no feedback, whose feelings are not encouraged and reinforced, will look somewhere else for support. Effective communication assumes a two-way flow of information.

The Effects of Feedback

If you ever think that your feedback is insignificant and makes no difference, remember that in a two-person interpersonal situation, you are

In your next conversations with people, notice the feedback you receive as you talk:

1. How extensive is it?

2. What are the primary cues that provide the feedback? (eyes, face, gestures, posture, body movement?)

3. Do different people use different kinds of feedback? — Do they depend on different cues?

4. Does the amount of feedback differ between friends and strangers? — Does it depend on the nature of the message or situation?

5. How much do you depend on the feedback you get from others?

6. Do you find yourself adjusting your message when you receive feedback? In what ways?

If nothing else, this exercise should encourage you to become more conscious of feedback in any communication situation. As you grow more sensitive to it, your messages can become more exact and specific.

the *only* source of reactions for the other person. Without you, there is no one else. If you do not provide feedback, the other person can't know how well he or she is getting through. It's up to you to help the other person make the message as accurate as possible: your influence is felt strongly. How much feedback you give is also important.

In a landmark study, researchers investigated how differing amounts of feedback affected how the message was conveyed.[14] In all cases, students were to draw geometric patterns according to directions given to them by the instructors. In one situation the researchers allowed no feedback between the instructor and the students. In a second situation, the students and teacher could see each other, but ask no questions. In a third environment, students could answer yes or no to the instructor's questions. In a fourth circumstance, students could ask any questions and get information—a free-feedback situation. The researchers discovered that as the amount of allowed feedback increased, it took students longer to complete their tasks but they also drew their geometric figures more accurately. And they felt far more confident about their success in drawing the figures in this condition of free feedback. We can conclude from this that feedback in an interpersonal communication encounter takes extra time but results in more accurate message transmission and more confidence in the message-transmission process.

CATHY   **by Cathy Guisewite**

Styles of Positive Feedback

Feedback begins within us. Internal feedback takes place all the time as we communicate with others.[15] As we speak, we anticipate certain responses from the other person; our process of getting set depends on internal feedback. As we receive feedback from another person, we adapt and correct our own message; the process of adapting and correcting depends on internal feedback.

As we look forward to an interpersonal encounter, we may even quiz our selves on how we should behave in this situation. This process is internalized feedback.[16] You have probably caught your self going over the message you want to give another person or rehashing his or her ideas long after you have received them. For example, what kinds of feelings might you have if you were planning to meet a close friend for coffee after class? A professor in her office to discuss your final grade? A friend for a drink in the evening? An interviewer for a job interview? In each case your expectations would be different. But you could predict what behavior would be appropriate on the basis of similar experiences you've already had. You would use internal feedback.

Giving positive feedback to another person begins with our own internal feedback. If we want to give someone positive reinforcement as he or she speaks, we must first be very attentive to that person's communications. We can't give helpful feedback if we aren't listening effectively to start with. To be ready to respond appropriately we must be alert to the other person's overall message—we should try hard to see where he or she is coming from so that our feedback is not insensitive or confusing.

Positive feedback is supportive. Giving it may be as simple as nodding "yes" or smiling or saying, "Mm-hmm. Go on." It can be just enough to let the other person know we're there and tuned in. It should mean the message is being received and understood—it's pointless and not helpful to nod and smile and say yes if we don't mean it. Feedback that expresses agreement is not the only kind of positive feedback; in most open, honest exchanges there will be times when we disagree with the speaker. But we can still give positive feedback; that is, we can still show that we are there and receptive.

In a conversation where both parties give positive feedback, certain kinds of distractions are less likely to cause problems. Each person's meaning is likely to get through to the other in spite of jet planes passing overhead or small children interrupting to ask questions. Exchanging positive feedback is a way of saying, "I want to hear what you want to tell me." If both people have this attitude, meaning is likely to survive problems in message transmission.

David W. Johnson suggests three kinds of response styles for giving positive feedback to others.[17] The three styles are called *supportive*, *probing*, and *understanding*.

Consider This _____

Why am I so discomfited by a compliment? According to a recent sociological study, I am, in fact, very typical. Praise seems to make most of us uneasy. . . .

Why do so many of us accept a gift-wrapped word as gingerly as we might a beribboned time bomb? Usually, say Professors Turner and Edgley, for one of six reasons: the felt obligation to return the compliment; the need to keep up a modest front and avoid seeming conceited by agreeing with the praise; suspicion of ulterior motives; fear that commendation is but a prelude to criticism; resentment at being evaluated at all by

someone else; or worry that we won't be able to keep up whatever we're being praised for at the moment. . . . Reciprocity is a fact of social life. Just as we feel obliged to "return" a dinner invitation or a Christmas card, the Turner-Edgley study shows that most people feel they must return a compliment. . . .

Many respondents felt extreme anxiety about returning kind words; some felt the very relationship depended on it. Most, however, didn't like the feeling that they were "beholden" to their complimenters and wanted to even out the relationship as soon as possible.

Sidney B. Simon, Ed.D., professor of education at the University of Massachusetts, calls this rush toward reciprocation the "compliment-flick" syndrome. "Many people get rid of a compliment as fast as they can by giving one back," he says. "They just can't stand hearing themselves praised. That's because so many of us have been trained from an early age to be humble and modest and not to toot our own horns. We can't even enjoy hearing anyone else toot them, either, because that might imply that we think something of ourselves."

—Sally Wendkos Olds, *Today's Health,* February 1975

Consider This

An engaging example of the impact of attending behavior is given by Ivey and Hinkle. At a prearranged signal, six students in a psychology seminar switched from the traditional student's slouched posture and passive listening and note-taking to attentive posture and active eye contact with the teacher. In the nonattending condition, the teacher had been lecturing from his notes in a monotone, using no gestures, and paying little or no attention to the students. However, once the students began to attend, the teacher began to gesture, his verbal rate increased, and a lively classroom session was born. At another prearranged signal later in the class, the students stopped attending and returned to typical passive student's posture and participation. The teacher, "after some painful seeking for continued reinforcement," returned to the unengaging teacher behavior with which he had begun the class. In the nonattending condition, the teacher paid no attention to the students and the students reciprocated in kind. Both students and teacher got what they deserved: reciprocated inattention. But simple attending changed the whole picture.

—Gerard Egan, *The Skilled Helper*

Supportive.   If a friend comes to us with an upsetting problem, we probably want to reassure him or her that all is not lost. Pointing out alternatives he or she may not have thought of would be supportive. Our support should be calming, to reduce the intensity of our friend's feeling. Initially, our support may be no more specific than a look or a touch that says, "I'm on your side." Once the friend knows that we are empathic, we can discuss actions to correct the problem.

In being supportive, we must be careful we aren't really trying to teach our friend a lesson. Saying what we think the problem means, or putting words in our friend's mouth, may have a negative effect.

No matter how much we have the other person's best interests at heart, it's a bad idea to start out with, "I *told* you that would happen . . ." or "Next time you'll know better . . ." or "You should be glad you found out when you did . . ." We don't want to suggest what he or she ought to think. Remember, what our friend does think is what we have to deal with. To provide support we should first reassure, pacify, and reduce the intensity of *that* feeling. A comment like, "That is a serious problem and I can see why you are upset . . ." is a good beginning point. Being supportive means acknowledging the seriousness of the other person's feelings. We don't want to argue or suggest that these emotions are inappropriate.

Probing.   A probing response may also be supportive because it can draw out the other person. The purpose of probing feedback is to get him or her to discuss the problem. A probing response is a good beginning point, too, because it gives us information about the nature of the problem. It provides a better base to act on and an emotional release for the other person at the same time. This response often takes the form of a question: "What makes this situation so upsetting to you?" or "What do you suppose caused this to happen?" An implied question might be phrased, ". . . and you expect the situation to get worse, not better. . . ."

In probing, we don't want to be threatening or accusatory. Phrasing our questions carelessly can cause more problems than we solve. For example, we would probably not ask, "How did you ever get into this mess?" because that puts a value judgment on the experience. Questions like, "Didn't you know that was wrong?" or "You really weren't thinking, were you?" create defensiveness in the other person. If we tell our friend that the action was good or bad, appropriate or inappropriate, right or wrong, we are making a judgment. Again we don't want to imply what that person should have done or ought to do.

Understanding.   Our first comment to our friend could be, "I can see you're very upset about this problem. It must mean a great deal to you." In paraphrasing the other person's remarks we show that we understand. When we show that we care about correctly understanding our friend's situation, we are making an *understanding* response. When we reinforce our remarks with nonverbal gestures—eye contact, facial expressions of sincerity, touching—this response is very supportive.

In all three positive response styles we avoid judging the other person and the situation. Our choice of words is not as crucial as is an honest effort to understand the other person's problem and feelings and to convey that understanding. The idea is to indicate acceptance and respect for the other person. As these feelings are reflected back to us, an atmosphere of mutual respect, support, and trust develops. And our interpersonal relationships are likely to become more satisfying.

IMPROVING SKILLS IN LISTENING

As I said earlier, improving listening skills requires time and energy. I hope I have convinced you of the need for effective listening and will now discuss some ways we can improve our listening skills. As you read the suggestions, you may realize that many seem to be based on common sense. Some may seem obvious. Even so, the most common-sensical ideas are often not put into practice. If you simply read these

Consider This _____

DEAR ANN LANDERS: I need help with my grandfather. He's a nonstop talker. I mean, you can ask him, "How are you?" and he goes on and on for as long as you stand there. It takes an hour for him to tell you anything because he must relate every detail. He goes back 40 years and never leaves anything out. He knows the exact hour, remembers precise dates, places, faces, towns, prices, colors—you name it.

You tell him you have to go and he acts like he never heard you. The worst of it is he tells the same stories over and over and you could just die of boredom.

Please don't say I should put up with it because he is old and lonely. Grandma says he has been like this ever since she has known him—which is 55 years. How do you tell such a person—in a polite manner—to shut up or shorten the story?—EARACHE IN TOLEDO

> **DEAR EARACHE: Nothing you say will make a particle of difference. The compulsive talker has a sick need to talk and he will continue to do it. He's helpless. Your best bet is to listen for what you consider a reasonable period of time—then point to your watch, take his arm, lead him to the door, and wave good-by.**
>
> —syndicated in *The Blade: Toledo, Ohio*, May 11, 1979

and do not incorporate them into your own listening behavior, they will serve little purpose. Perhaps these suggestions will also bring to mind other practical ideas you can put to use in listening settings.

Prepare to listen. In many cases we do not listen well because we are not physically or mentally prepared. Our attention span—how long we are able to attend to a single stimulus (like someone talking)—is directly related to our physical and mental condition. This is obvious if we recall that listening involves an integration of physical, emotional, and intellectual elements. Think how impatient or short-tempered we become when we are mentally run-down, or physically tired. We stayed up all night studying for an exam and now everyone around us pays for it! We do not want to listen to anyone!

Control or eliminate distractions. Anticipating situations where we might have to listen helps prepare us. There may be something we can do to improve the situation: turning off a television, closing a door, asking the other person to speak louder, or moving to a less distracting location. If we can't eliminate distractions, we'll have to concentrate with greater effort.

When we concentrate on the speaker the message becomes more memorable and meaningful.

Anticipate the subject. Whenever possible, think ahead about the topics or ideas that might be discussed. The more familiar we are with the subject matter, the more likely we will learn, and the more interested we will be. Also, thinking ahead may prompt questions to ask. Becoming actively involved in interpersonal situations makes them more memorable and meaningful.

Anticipate the speaker. Anticipating the speaker means adjusting in advance (or being prepared to adjust) to the other person. We cannot control how the speaker will look or talk, but we can make sure, in advance, that distracting appearance or faulty delivery does not dominate our attention. Our aim should be to try to find out what the other person is saying. We should try not to be bothered by peculiarities or eccentricities. If we are always ready to adjust, we will find it becomes a natural part of our behavior when we *must* adjust.

Create a need to listen. We do not enjoy listening to some people as well as to others. We do not listen as well to some topics as we do to others. We often know in advance that we may not listen as well as we might in a certain situation. To try to counteract this situation, become a "selfish listener."[18] What can the speaker do for *you?* The key to being interested in another person or in a topic is making it relevant or useful to our selves.

Try to discover if the message has any personal benefits for you. Can it provide personal satisfaction? Does it stimulate new interests or insights? Good listeners are interested in what they are listening to whereas poor listeners find all people and all topics dry and boring. True, some topics are dull but we often decide this in advance and don't give the speaker a chance.

If the speaker or the material does not satisfy a need, ask your self, "Why am I here?" Try to remember what caused you to be there and see if the motive is still active. You might also try to discover a reward—some immediate way to use the material that will make the experience personally profitable.

Monitor the way you listen. Even if we are prepared to listen and need to listen, our listening will not necessarily be effective. We need to check occasionally to make sure our thoughts are not wandering and that we are keeping an open mind to the other person's ideas. Because of the time difference between speaking and listening rates, we need to use the spare time that results wisely.

Concentrate on the message. To keep your mind on the message, try to review what the speaker has already said so that you can keep ideas

Try This

To practice your supportive, probing, and understanding responses, think of one response of each kind for each of the following situations:

1. Your best friend comes to you with the following information: "I just flunked my second exam in my psychology course. It's all over. I just don't care about anything anymore . . ."

2. Your roommate says: "Someone stole my books and notebooks. I left them on a table in the cafeteria and when I came back they were gone . . ."

3. A friend down the hall laments: "Oh, I can't stand it, I can't stand it anymore! My roommate leaves the room a mess, plays the stereo at full volume, and sleeps only during the day. It's driving me out of my mind . . ."

together and remember them. Listen for the main ideas. Try to go "between" the words. Listen with your third ear. Listen for words that may have more than one meaning and discover, if possible, how the other person is using the word. Try to anticipate what the speaker will say next and compare this with what he or she actually says. This keeps your mind focused on the message.[19] Concentrate on the message, not on the other person's blue eyes or Hawaiian shirt.

Suspend judgment. Some words, phrases, or ideas evoke an automatic reaction. We may overreact to bad grammar, ethnic slurs, or vulgarity. We must learn not to get too excited about certain words until we have the whole context. Suspend judgment until you thoroughly understand where the speaker is coming from.

Think about those words you react strongly to. Why do they affect you like that? Sharing our reactions with others will often help us see that our reactions are entirely personal. Finally, try to reduce the intensity of your reaction by convincing yourself that the reaction is extreme and unnecessary, that the word does not merit such a reaction.[20] Our listening will always be affected when certain words touch our deepest prejudices or most profound values. Knowing that such reactions can happen is the first step toward overcoming them.

Empathize. Try to see the other person's ideas from his or her perspective. If Sam is telling you how angry he is with his brother, try to discover why he says what he does. Listen for his reasons, his views, and his arguments. You needn't agree with him. Sam's brother may be a friend of yours. But just because Sam's feelings differ from yours does not mean they aren't valid. Since you differ from Sam as a result of different past experiences, search for the message he is *really* trying to communicate. Look for elements he may have left out. What is he basing his evidence on? How did he come by his opinion? Through personal experience? Other people's observations? Guesswork? Try to see the problem through Sam's eyes.

IMPROVING SKILLS IN FEEDBACK

Effective feedback is as important as good listening. As listeners, we have a duty to respond, to complete the communication cycle. Although we can't avoid giving some feedback even if we don't say a word, there are ways we can improve.

Be prepared to give feedback. Feedback can be verbal, nonverbal, or both. Nonverbal feedback usually can say more about our sincerity than words alone. Our verbal feedback is more likely to be believed if

Try This

As you are listening to someone or just after a conversation ask yourself the following questions:

1. What did the other person do—as far as effective communication goes—that was particularly strong? What aspects of the other person's presentation were especially powerful or convincing?

2. What did the person do that was especially weak? What would you change in his or her presentation?

The purpose here is growth and change. Try to learn something from each communication experience that will help you improve your own communication patterns and behaviors.

we support it with appropriate gestures, direct eye contact, and possibly touching. Be certain that you are close enough to the other person—face-to-face if possible—that your feedback will be perceived. We will discuss nonverbal communication in more detail in a later chapter.

Although we must be prepared to give feedback, we shouldn't enter a situation with our specific reactions already planned. Spontaneity is important. The best feedback arises naturally as a result of an immediate and specific stimulus. But being prepared to give feedback does not preclude being spontaneous; it simply means that we are alert and sensitive to the need for feedback and are ready to give it.

Make your feedback prompt. Your response to the other person should be clear and prompt. The more closely tied feedback is to the original message, the less ambiguous it will be. The longer the delay between message and feedback, the more likely we are to confuse the other person.

Make your feedback accurate. Accuracy means making feedback specific to a single message and not general to the whole conversation. You probably know people who continually nod and smile the entire time you're talking to them. In addition to being distracting, this also appears insincere. It makes you want to ask, "All right, what exactly do you agree with? How will I know when you disagree?" Try to provide only necessary feedback.

React to the message, not the speaker. Our accuracy in giving feedback will also improve if we remember to direct it to the message and not to the person communicating. In addition to being distracting, personal comments may create hostility or frustration and a breakdown in communication.

Oddly, both complimentary and critical feedback may be better received if we phrase our responses in a slightly impersonal way. If we wish to praise someone for playing a piano sonata well, saying "I've never heard that piece done so beautifully. I really heard it in a new way" may make the performer less uncomfortable than "Sarah, you really did that well. I didn't know you were that good." Too, personal comments can imply, however subtly, "That was good, for *you*" when what we mean is "That was good." Effective feedback is message-oriented.[21]

Monitor your own feedback. If our feedback is not interpreted by the other person as we mean it, it serves no purpose. Check the effect you're making. You might have to repeat or clarify a feedback response. If Louise says, "I can never think of what to say to Alvin," and our response is "I know," it can either mean, "I know. I've noticed you never have anything to say" or it can mean, "I know. Alvin is hard to talk to." We must monitor our feedback to make sure we're being understood. Like any message, feedback can be blocked or distorted.

Concentrate on exchanging meaning.   Finally, our feedback will be perceived more accurately and sent more accurately if both parties are committed to the honest exchange of meaning. Think about how to help the other person express ideas more effectively. We are more likely to provide constructive feedback if we are motivated by a sincere desire to enhance communication.

Effective communicators respond to others through listening and feedback. We should work to increase listening and feedback skills. Try to develop sensitivity to the feedback and listening of others. We will be using our listening and feedback skills to learn more about the process of communication; applying what we learn to our own behavior will help us grow. Just as listening and feedback are essential in human communication, so are the words that make up a good part of the message. The words—verbal communication—are the subject of the next chapter.

Try This

The next time you are communicating interpersonally, do not respond to what the other person says until you do three things:

1. Wait until the other person <u>finishes</u> what he or she has to say.

2. Fully <u>paraphrase</u> what he or she has said.

3. Receive an <u>affirmative response</u> to the question, "Is that what you mean?" directly following your paraphrase.

Following an affirmative response, you may make any appropriate comment you wish to keep the conversation going. If the other person says your paraphrase was inaccurate, keep trying until you get it right.

Although in many situations we don't need to wait until the other person finishes talking before we respond, forcing your self to wait will indicate how often you do <u>not</u> wait. Does this kind of communication seem awkward or labored to you? Do you think it is a good way to get at the other person's meaning?

OTHER READING

Edmond G. Addeo and Robert E. Burger, *EgoSpeak: Why No One Listens to You* (New York: Bantam Books, Inc., 1973). EgoSpeak is the art of boosting our own egos by speaking only about what *we* want to talk about. This is an entertaining and systematic catalog of the major types of this disease: JobSpeak, BusinessSpeak, NameSpeak, SpeakSpeak, and many more.

Larry L. Barker, *Listening Behavior* (Englewood Cliffs, N.J.: Prentice-Hall, Inc., 1971). A textbook, this is one of the most comprehensive and thorough investigations of listening and feedback currently on the market. It is short, well written, and carefully documented.

Ernst G. Beier and Evans G. Valens, *People-Reading: How We Control Others, How They Control Us* (New York: Warner Books, Inc., 1975). The focus here is on life and relationships and how to become more sensitive to the controls that operate. Ten percent of the book treats listening directly, including a section on how to listen to feelings.

Eric Berne, *Games People Play: The Psychology of Human Relationships* (New York: Grove Press, Inc., 1964). A classic book that calls attention to the little "games" we play with each other. A realistic analysis of listening and feedback must place them into the framework of everyday encounters. This book offers various frameworks.

Adelaide Bry, *Friendship: How to Have a Friend and Be a Friend* (New York: Grosset & Dunlap Publishers, 1979). This book is listed because of its emphasis on empathy. A warmhearted, sensitive study of both making friends and being one, it describes the joy and comfort that come from sharing moments of happiness and sorrow.

Jard DeVille, *Nice Guys Finish First: How to Get People to Do What You Want . . . and Thank You for It* (New York: William Morrow and Company, Inc., 1979). DeVille's primary focus is on cooperation. Acting on and understanding other people's personalities will attract their support and commitment. This involves both interpersonal awareness and effective listening.

Jess Lair, *I Ain't Well—But I Sure Am Better: Mutual Need Therapy* (Garden City, N.Y.: Doubleday & Company, Inc., 1975). Realizing that we have a stake in others means understanding their value in our growth and development. This book suggests that both parties in a relationship gain. Lair causes us to examine our relationships and shows us what it is like to communicate our whole hearts.

Gerard I. Nierenberg and Henry H. Calero, *Meta-Talk: Guide to Hidden Meanings in Conversations* (New York: Pocket Books, 1974). This is a popular, uncomplicated approach to listening and feedback. Many examples are included. The author cautions the reader that no meaning is absolute; meaning lies in the speaker or listener. The book is important for pointing out some of the meanings behind or beyond words.

Jesse S. Nirenberg, *Getting Through to People* (Englewood Cliffs, N.J.: Prentice-Hall, Inc., 1963). To read the contents of this book is to see its relevance to interpersonal communication: encouraging cooperativeness, drawing out people's thoughts, dealing with people's emotions, listening between the lines, and giving and getting feedback, to name but a few relevant chapters. Nirenberg is practical and specific. This is an interesting, useful source.

Carl H. Weaver, *Human Listening: Processes and Behavior* (Indianapolis, Ind.: The Bobbs-Merrill Company, Inc., 1972). This textbook proves that listening is a type of behavior difficult both to understand and to change. By doing the exercises provided, one can learn how to improve listening skills.

NOTES

[1] Larry L. Barker, *Listening Behavior* (Englewood Cliffs, N.J.: Prentice-Hall, Inc., 1971), pp. 3–5. The studies Barker summarizes suggest that close to 40% of all time spent in communication activities is spent in listening.

[2] Ernest G. Bormann, et al., *Interpersonal Communication in the Modern Organization* (Englewood Cliffs, N.J.: Prentice-Hall, 1969), p. 197.

[3] G. Egan, *Encounter: Group Processes for Interpersonal Growth* (Belmont, Calif.: Brooks/Cole, 1970), p. 248.

[4] Based on "Empathic Listening" by Charles M. Kelly, published in *Small Group Communication: A Reader*, 2nd Edition, Wm. C. Brown Company, 1974. Reprinted by permission of the author.

[5] Carl R. Rogers, *On Becoming a Person* (Boston: Houghton Mifflin, 1961), p. 330.

[6] Kelly, "Empathic Listening," p. 340.

[7] Ibid., p. 342.

[8] This phenomenon is called "EgoSpeak." Edmond G. Addeo and Robert E. Burger, *EgoSpeak* (New York: Bantam Books, Inc., 1973), p. xiii.

[9] The retention rate of orally communicated messages is approximately 50% immediately after the message is communicated and only 25% two months later. Ralph G. Nichols, "Do We Know How to Listen?" in *Communication: Concepts and Processes*, Joseph A. DeVito, ed. (Englewood Cliffs, N.J.: Prentice-Hall, Inc., 1971), pp. 207–8.

[10] Norbert Wiener, one of the first persons to be concerned with feedback, defined it as "the property of being able to adjust future conduct by past experience." Norbert Wiener, *Cybernetics* (New York: John Wiley & Sons, 1948), p. 33, and Norbert Wiener, *The Human Use of Human Beings: Cybernetics and Society* (Boston: Houghton Mifflin, 1950). Also see discussion of the monitoring function of feedback in David K. Berlo, *The Process of Communication* (New York: Holt, Rinehart and Winston, 1960), p. 111.

[11] Arnold Tustin, "Feedback," in *Communication and Culture*, Alfred G. Smith, ed. (New York: Holt, Rinehart and Winston, 1966), p. 325.

[12] Warren G. Bennis, et al., eds., *Interpersonal Dynamics: Essays and Readings on Human Interaction* (Homewood, Ill.: Dorsey Press, 1968), p. 214.

[13] William C. Schutz, *The Interpersonal Underworld* (Palo Alto, Calif.: Science and Behavior Books, 1966), p. 13.

[14] Harold J. Leavitt and Ronald A. H. Mueller, "Some Effects of Feedback on Communication," in *Interpersonal Communication: Survey and Studies*, Dean Barnlund, ed. (Boston: Houghton Mifflin, 1968), pp. 251–59.

[15]See Wendell Johnson, *Your Most Enchanted Listener* (New York: Harper & Row, Publishers, 1956), p. 174.

[16]See Richard L. Weaver, II, "'Internalized Feedback': The Process of Asking Questions," *The Report* III (June 1970), 24–35.

[17]David W. Johnson, *Reaching Out: Interpersonal Effectiveness and Self-Actualization.* © 1972, p. 125. Reprinted by permission of Prentice-Hall, Inc., Englewood Cliffs, New Jersey.

[18]Barker, *Listening Behavior*, p. 74.

[19]Ibid., pp. 75–76.

[20]Ibid., pp. 76–77.

[21]Ibid., p. 124.

5   Creating Messages:
Verbal Communication

Words, words, words! We live in a sea of words. If we are not talking, we are reading or writing or listening to others talk.[1] So many words—so much talk—it's no wonder we take most of it for granted. From birth we are confronted with people making noises at us trying to get us to do this, believe that, buy this, or think about that. Even so, sometimes we feel that not very much is being communicated. We rarely give the words themselves much thought.

Have you ever said something to someone and, in return, gotten an odd answer or none at all? You may have wondered, "What's wrong with me?" Words can be strange or, at least, can appear to be strange, but can you imagine a civilization without them? Their role and function in interpersonal communication is crucial. Understanding how language works will help us make sure we come across just the way we want to.

Think about the transactional nature of communication. In any communication transaction we are involved in constructing a mental image of the other person, just as he or she is constructing a mental image of us. We base all future communication with each other on these mental images. Our use of language, and especially the way we view each other's use of language, will affect how we construct those mental images. The closer we can make the other person's mental image of us conform to the one we have of our selves, the more effective our interpersonal communication will be. We use words to communicate ideas and describe feelings. We use them to reason and to transform experience into ideas and ideas into experience. Knowing how to use them well will increase our effectiveness in interpersonal communication.

In this chapter I will discuss language from the perspective of you, the language user. Since the problem of abstract language is major, I will spend some time talking about how we can modify our use of words for more precise meaning. I'll explore the way words shape our world by influencing our perceptions. Finally, I will suggest some specific things we can do to improve our language skills.

WHAT WORDS CAN AND CANNOT DO

If we see a series of stones lying across a stream, we know they will help us get across to the other side. But our experience with such stones tells us that some stones may be loose or covered with slime and could cause us to slip. Like these stones, words can help us to reach our goals or they can cause us to stumble and fall. Let's look at some characteristics of language that affect our interpersonal communication.[2]

What Did You Have in Mind?

When we talk to people we often assume too quickly that we are being understood. If we tell people we are going to put on some music, we probably don't think about whether they are expecting to hear the kind of music we intend to play—we just turn it on. But think about the word "music" and how many different interpretations there are of it. (See Figure 1.)

We depend on context and on nonverbal cues to give us the meaning of words. If we said we were going to put on some music, our friends might predict from knowing our taste and from nonverbal cues (our mood) what we might play. But they have a good chance of being wrong. In our daily conversation we use about 2,000 words. Of those 2,000, even the 500 we use most often have over 14,000 dictionary definitions.[3] Think of the possibilities for confusion! The problem of figuring out what a person means by a certain word is compounded by the fact that even dictionary meanings change and new words are constantly being added to the language.

Connotative meanings. Dictionary definitions would probably not help our friends predict the kind of music we would play or what we mean by "music." But their experience with us and with music will give them a clue as to what we mean. If "music" connotes the same thing to us and to our friends, there's less chance of misunderstanding.

When we hear a word, the thoughts and feelings we have about that word and about the person using it determine what that word ultimately means to us. This is the word's *connotative* meaning. Con-

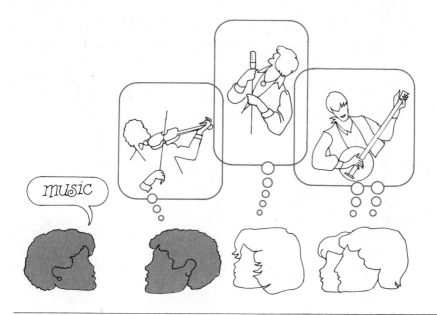

Figure 1.
One word may have many different interpretations.

notative meanings change with our experience. Just as we experience something different in every second of life that we live, so does everyone else. And no two of these experiences are identical! It's no wonder there are infinitely many connotations for every word we use.

If a word creates pretty much the same reaction in a majority of people, the word is said to have a general connotation. Actually, the more general the connotation of a word, the more likely that meaning will become the dictionary meaning, because most people will agree what that word represents. The more general the connotation of a word, the less likely people are to misunderstand it.

Denotative meanings.   The denotative meaning of a word is its dictionary definition. Some words have relatively stable meanings. If several people were to define a particular word special to their discipline, they would probably use about the same definition—an agreed-upon interpretation. In the legal profession, the word "estoppel" has one precise, *denotative* meaning. Doctors would probably agree upon the definition of a "myocardioinfarction." Many disciplines depend on certain words having precise, unchanging meanings in order to carry on their work. Denotative words give sharpness and accuracy to our ideas.

There is little likelihood of confusion with denotative meanings because there is a direct relationship between the word and what it describes. Although we must process every word if we're to understand it, connotative meanings depend a lot more than denotative meanings on our subjective thought processes.[4] (See Figure 2.)

Problems in interpersonal communication increase as we use words with many connotative meanings. Because these meanings are so tied to the particular feelings, thoughts, and ideas of other people, we have a bigger chance of being misunderstood when we use them. On the other hand, richly connotative words give our language power. Note, for example, the differences between the following lists of words:

freedom	book
justice	piano
love	tree
liberty	teacher
music	fire

The words on the left have many connotations; the words on the right are more strictly denotative. "The teacher put the book on the piano" is a sharp, unambiguous statement. The sentence, "The love of freedom burns like a white flame in all of us" can be interpreted numerous ways.

What does all this have to do with our use of words? First, we should recognize that words evoke sometimes unpredictable reactions in others. We should try to anticipate the reactions of others to our words as much as we can. For example, if we are talking to an art major we may cause confusion or even produce a hostile response if we use English-major jargon we have picked up. If we anticipate this negative reaction, we'll leave the jargon in the English classroom.

Second, most words have both connotative and denotative meanings and we should recognize that these meanings vary from person to person. People will react to words according to the meaning *they* give them. An effective communicator tries to recognize different reactions and to adapt to them. Remember as you communicate that meanings do *not* reside in the words themselves. Meanings are in the minds of the people who use and hear the words.

Coping with Levels of Abstraction

Words vary in their degree of abstraction.[5] (See Figure 3.) The word "cow" means different things to different people. Think of experiences you have had with cows. It is considered a low level of abstraction when we perceive not the word "cow," but the cow itself as an object of our experiences. If we think of "Bessie," a particular cow, the name of this cow stands for one cow and no other. Or we may think of cows in general, all the animals that have the characteristics common to cows. This is a higher level of abstraction. At a higher level yet, we might think

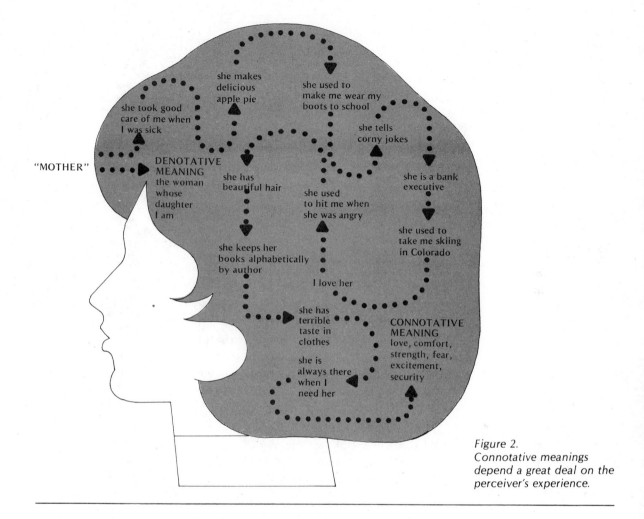

she took good
care of me when
I was sick

she makes
delicious
apple pie

she used to
make me wear my
boots to school

she tells
corny jokes

"MOTHER"   DENOTATIVE
MEANING
the woman
whose
daughter
I am

she has
beautiful hair

she used
to hit me when
she was angry

she is a bank
executive

she used to
take me skiing
in Colorado

she keeps her
books alphabetically
by author

I love her

she has
terrible
taste in
clothes

CONNOTATIVE
MEANING
love, comfort,
strength, fear,
excitement,
security

she is
always there
when I
need her

Figure 2.
Connotative meanings
depend a great deal on the
perceiver's experience.

of "cow" as part of the broader category of "livestock." Going higher
up the abstraction ladder, Bessie may be thought of as a "farm asset,"
an "asset," or as "wealth."

You can see how these references to the word "cow" have become
more and more abstract. At each higher level of abstraction, more items
could be included in the category. The more that can be included in a
category, the less possible it is for someone to know exactly what we
are talking about.

We may have been in conversations where different levels of
abstraction were at work without being aware of it. We can see from the
abstraction ladder how easy it would be, when dealing with something
specific, to jump to a higher level and avoid answering or responding to
the specific issue. If someone asked us, "What do you think of Dr. Smith

Figure 3.

ABSTRACTION LADDER[6]

Start reading from the bottom *UP*

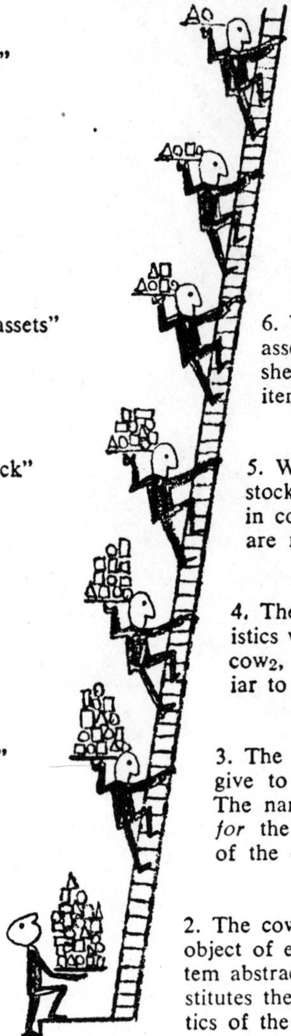

8. "wealth"

8. The word "wealth" is at an extremely high level of abstraction, omitting *almost* all reference to the characteristics of Bessie.

7. "asset"

7. When Bessie is referred to as an "asset," still more of her characteristics are left out.

6. "farm assets"

6. When Bessie is included among "farm assets," reference is made only to what she has in common with all other salable items on the farm.

5. "livestock"

5. When Bessie is referred to as "livestock," only those characteristics she has in common with pigs, chickens, goats, etc., are referred to.

4. "cow"

4. The word "cow" stands for the characteristics we have abstracted as common to cow_1, cow_2, cow_3 . . . cow_n. Characteristics peculiar to specific cows are left out.

3. "Bessie"

3. The word "Bessie" (cow_1) is the *name* we give to the object of perception of level 2. The name *is not* the object; it merely *stands for* the object and omits reference to many of the characteristics of the object.

2.

2. The cow we perceive is not the word, but the object of experience, that which our nervous system abstracts (selects) from the totality that constitutes the process-cow. Many of the characteristics of the process-cow are left out.

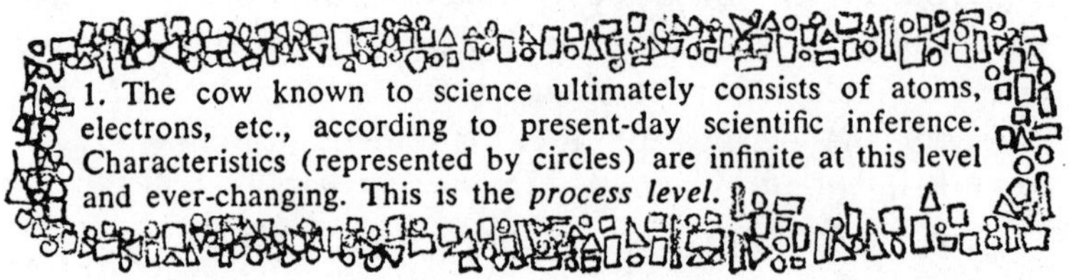

1. The cow known to science ultimately consists of atoms, electrons, etc., according to present-day scientific inference. Characteristics (represented by circles) are infinite at this level and ever-changing. This is the *process level.*

as a lecturer?'' we could say, ''I do not like Dr. Smith's lecturing,'' which would be answering at the same level of abstraction. But if we think such a commitment is risky, we might respond that ''lecturers just do not seem to care about the students in their audiences.'' By doing that, we move to a higher level of abstraction. If we respond that teachers at this institution just do not care anymore, we go to a higher level. Saying ''education has sure gone to pot'' is even more abstract. Teachers and politicians often try to avoid difficult questions by escaping to a higher level of abstraction when pressed on a specific issue.

As we escape to a higher level, we depend more on the connotative meanings of words than on the denotative meanings. Moving up the abstraction ladder causes the meanings of words to be less directly related to the thing they represent and more dependent on the perceiver of the word. If we actively work to keep our language at a low level of abstraction, there's much less chance for ambiguity and misunderstanding.

There are always some teachers who deal only in principles and theories and do not tie these abstractions to concrete reality. When we ask, ''What does that have to do with me?'' or ''How can I apply that in *my* life?'' we are asking to have the level of meaning brought down the abstraction ladder. We are asking for concrete particulars so that we can make sense out of the abstract principles.

Consider This

EDUCATIONAL JARGON PHRASE INDICATOR

1	2	3
perceptual	maturation	concept
professional	guidance	process
environmental	creative	articulation
instructional	relationship	philosophy
homogeneous	motoric	activity
developmental	culture	resource
sequential	orientation	curriculum
individualized	cognitive	approach
exceptional	accelerated	adjustment
socialized	motivation	interface

To use the Indicator I selected at random one word from the first list, one from the second, and one from the third. This produced as many phrases as I needed. By sprinkling a few common Anglo-Saxon words among these phrases I was able to quickly compose answers to questions, speeches, letters to government agencies, and so forth.

—Laurence J. Peter, *The Peter Prescription*

To get a feel for abstract words, the next time you are in class listening to a lecture, write down every word which you think could be (or is being) misinterpreted — every word for which you could have a definition different from that of your instructor.

1. How many words did you come up with?

2. How could you verify the definitions for these words? — dictionary? — other source?

3. In what ways might these differing definitions affect you? Is the fact that definitions might be different in this situation detrimental for you?

4. What suggestion could you make to the instructor that might improve the clarity of the words he or she uses?

The point of this exercise is to increase your sensitivity to the words others use. Practice tying words to specific definitions and interpretations. It will help clarify your communication with others, and it will help make certain that your interpretation of their communication is accurate.

Usually when we talk to people we go continually up and down the abstraction ladder. We adapt our words to each other's experiences. Knowing that certain words are more abstract than others will help us stay flexible. Words like "love" and "beauty" and "truth" are highly abstract and open to the possibility of confusion and error.

Limiting Your Horizons

In Chapter 2 we looked at how we select and organize incoming data and how we stereotype things. We process stimuli as they come to us, taking what we find meaningful and putting it into a form we can use. There are a number of bad language habits we get into that restrict the meaning exchanged in our communications:

"Have a nice day!" We simplify stimuli to make them understandable and we do this in our use of language as well. Since we depend on relatively few words to describe our many experiences, we may find it hard sometimes to describe fine differences between experiences — our language loses precision.

One reason, for example, that some teachers do not permit students to use the word "good" in speeches or papers is that the term is almost meaningless. What is good to one person can be so far from what is good to another that the term has no descriptive significance. When a word's meaning is restricted to the experience of the person who uses it, it will be difficult or impossible for listeners to understand that person. Codes are intentionally restrictive in that way, since only a few people know them. Our purposes are quite different; unlike the sender of a code, we *want* listeners to understand us.

"I know that."   Another restriction on meaning shows up in the language of children. Children often get into the habit of saying "I know it" to whatever they are told—they assume that their experience is already complete. We cannot tell them anything they do not already know! Some adults do the same thing. They respond to others with "I know" so as not to appear stupid or naive. When we do this we are not only lying to our selves and to others, we are closing our selves off to other people's insights, ideas, and feelings. The words "I know" can close the door to sharing. Often, too, they simply aren't true. We restrict our experience with the language we use in order to appear "in the know."

"Everybody knows that."   When we assume everybody shares our experiences and feelings, we overgeneralize, which is another way of restricting meaning. We overgeneralize when our words imply that *our* interpretation is the best, right, or only one. We may say, "How can

Consider This _____

There is no way to measure the destructive effect of sports broadcasting on ordinary American English, but it must be considerable. In the early days sports broadcasting was done, with occasional exceptions such as Clem McCarthy, by non-experts, announcers. Their knowledge of the sports they described varied, but their English was generally of a high order. If they could not tell you much about the inside of the game they were covering, at any rate what they did tell you you could understand.

Then came the experts, which is to say the former athletes. They could tell you a great deal about the inside, but—again with some exceptions—not in a comprehensible way. They knew the terms the athletes themselves used, and for a while that added color to the broadcasts. But the inside terms were few, and the nonathlete announcers allowed themselves to be hemmed in by them—"He got good wood on that one," "He got the big jump," "He really challenged him on that one," "They're high on him," "They came to play," "He's really got the good hands," and "That has to be," as in "That has to be the best game Oakland ever played."

The effect is deadening, on the enjoyment to be had from watching sports on television or reading about them, and, since sports make up so large a part of American life and do so much to set its tone, on the language we see and hear around us.

—Edwin Newman, *Strictly Speaking*

anyone think such a thing?" or "Who would ever want to see that movie?" We don't let other people possess their own meanings for their own experiences. Obviously, communication suffers when this happens.

"You've seen one, you've seen 'em all." Another way our language restricts the meaning exchanged in a communication is when we assume that everything stays the same. When we do this we don't allow for the possibility that things could ever be different. Time alone alters objects, things, people, and ideas—as well as the perceiver. To say, "Connie is like that" or "Bob always does that" or "That is just the way Sam is" allows for no flexibility or room for change in Connie, Bob, or Sam.

Try This

Begin monitoring your own communication behavior. How often are you guilty of restricting the meaning exchanged in your communications by the methods described here?

1. Do you oversimplify?

2. How often do you respond to another with "I know that"?

3. Do you assume others share your meanings?

4. How often do you assume that everything stays the same?

5. Do you presume that when things are clear to you, they are clear to everyone else as well?

6. What kind of language do you use to describe yourself? Can you see how this can affect your communication with others?

Whenever meanings are distorted, full fidelity does not occur. Since meanings are in people's heads and <u>not</u> in words, you must begin to understand what goes on in your head as you process words.

Try This

"What do you mean, what do I mean?" One of the most difficult barriers to successful human communication occurs when we assume that if something is clear to us, it is clear to everyone else. Even though few people are skilled in reading other people's minds, we still assume that because *we* said it, whoever is listening understood it! We sometimes assume this even when we have made no special effort to be clear: "You know *perfectly* well what I mean!" "What's wrong with you? *I* understand it!" We may even shout the same words again, assuming that repetition in itself is enlightening. It rarely is![7]

These problems are dangerous but we can't hope to avoid them completely since language itself is a body of generalizations. Perfect in-

Consider This

When I plead, as I often do, for greater precision in our use of words, perhaps it is because I am so prone to confusion. I remember as a little boy reading the signs on some highways and bridges: HEAVY TRAFFIC NOT PERMITTED.

It puzzled me for a long time how the individual motorist was going to decide whether the traffic was too heavy for him to continue on the road or over the bridge. It was a year or more before I realized that the sign meant: HEAVY VEHICLES NOT PERMITTED.

And I may have been more stupid than most, but when I heard in fourth grade that a special class was being formed for "backward readers," I silently wondered how many of my classmates possessed that marvelous gift of being able to read backward.

A friend recently told me of an incident in a veterans' hospital. The physician in charge of the mental ward had a sign on his door: DOCTOR'S OFFICE. PLEASE KNOCK. He was driven to distraction by an obedient patient who carefully knocked every time he passed the door.

Youngsters, and people out of their right minds, are likely to take words more literally than they are meant. Unless we say exactly what we mean, youngsters will read another meaning into it.

I am not suggesting that everything should be spelled out in a-b-c fashion, thus reducing us all to the condition of children or savages. But words should be accurate and explicit; except for poetry, they should say no more and no less than they actually mean.

As Mark Twain remarked, "The difference between the right word and the almost right word is the difference between lightning and the lightning bug."

A lovely example I ran across in California last summer was a sign in a public park: PEOPLE WITHOUT DOGS ON A LEASH NOT PERMITTED. I wonder if the good aldermen realized that this banned everyone not owning a dog from entering the park? As you see, I haven't changed much since the fourth grade.

—Sydney J. Harris, *The Best of Sydney J. Harris*

terpersonal communication is virtually impossible. But to recognize that we are likely to be misunderstood because of the restrictive nature of language will help make us better communicators because it will make us more cautious about the words we select.

The restrictiveness of our language affects how we view the world as well as our ability to accept change. Our category system is fragile and sensitive and requires constant attention—once a category becomes rigid, it is difficult to relax it again. We must recognize that we'll always need to alter our views to keep pace with changing conditions. Failure to update our views will cause us to become "stalled on the periphery of effectiveness as a communicator."[8]

Facts, Inferences, and Judgments

Yet another way to restrict meaning in communication is to confuse facts, inferences, and judgments. A fact is a verifiable statement. It can be, or has been, observed directly: seen, heard, felt, tasted, or smelled. If one were to draw a conclusion about what has been observed, this conclusion could be labeled an inference. Further, if one attaches to that inference a qualitative component that places a value on it, this would be called a judgment. Judgments indicate that someone feels that something is good or bad, beneficial or detrimental, justified or unjustified.

An example of each of these will help clarify the differences. What if your friend Linda said that she saw a man get out of a car, go into a store with an empty shopping bag, come running out of the store with the bag full, jump into the car, and speed away? These are facts that Linda verified through direct observation. To add an inference, what if Linda said, "You know, I have never witnessed a robbery before"? This is an inference because Linda does not actually know that this was a robbery—unless she heard the owner say, "I've been robbed," or paused long enough for the police to show up and begin their investigation. Indeed, the man may simply have been picking up some last-minute groceries—using his own shopping bag for ease, to save the store money, or to eliminate needless waste.

A judgment would be added to the process if Linda continued by saying, "I can't believe he would pull a dirty trick like that in broad daylight." The "dirty-trick" comment is the judgmental part of her statement.

Knowledge of these differences can help clarify conversation. Facts are often the substance of discussion. From facts we *must* draw inferences; this is how we make sense of our world. How important or unimportant these inferences are to us will determine whether and how we act. But it should be clear in our conversations:

1. What are facts and what are inferences.
2. That inferences may or may not be true.
3. Who drew the inferences or judgments.
4. On what (or whose) facts the inferences and judgments depend.
5. That the inferences and judgments are open to interpretation.

In another example, John has just told you that Bob must have received a promotion. Fact? Or was he just seen driving a new car? "Well, Sam told me he saw Bob in the boss's office." So, John drew the conclusion (inference) from these two facts. "After all," adds Mary, "his father is mayor of the city and probably pulled strings." Now the inference has been mixed with a rather dubious judgment from Mary. But it is easy to see from this example how meaning can be distorted if facts, inferences, and judgments are intermixed and unlabeled.

Labeling helps because it is less likely to cause misinterpretation. It may keep people from making erroneous statements or judgments or from taking needless or senseless action. It may also prevent people

Assume the following facts:

Joe and Tina walked from class together. They had lunch at the Union.

Now, label the following statements as F = Fact, I = Inference, or J = Judgment:

_____ 1. Looks like Joe and Tina have started dating.

_____ 2. "Joe and Tina left class at the same time, Bill."

_____ 3. "Joe and Tina even had lunch together at the Union."

_____ 4. "I don't think Joe and Tina are cut out for each other."

_____ 5. Joe and Tina have been studying together lately.

_____ 6. It certainly is ridiculous for Tina to be dating both Joe and Bill.

_____ 7. Joe and Tina saw each other after class.

Answers: 1. I; 2. I; 3. I (doesn't say they ate together); 4. J; 5. I; 6. J; 7. F.

from forming false impressions based on lack of sound evidence and spurious judgments. Accuracy in interpersonal communication often depends upon your ability to know the difference between facts, inferences, and judgments.

Speaking for Your Self . . .

Words are an indispensable mechanism of our lives. As our experiences accumulate, our vocabulary increases in size and in richness in order to describe those experiences. Although we probably spend little time thinking about language, unless to briefly consider a grammatical point, it reflects the basic features of our personality. Just as we adjust to changes in the physical climate, we also adjust our selves to changes in the verbal climate. We go from one type of discourse to another, from one set of terms to another, from listening habits for one kind of occasion to another kind, all without conscious effort. But we hardly ever acknowledge the relationship the words have to our personality or, for that matter, to our mental health or well-being.[9]

One thing we may not have thought about is that we describe our selves in some kind of language—words, mental pictures, idealizations. These descriptions are fairly clear: "I am an extrovert," "I am efficient," "I am self-motivated," and so on. These statements are more or less accurate descriptions of what we think of our selves. This self-concept determines how we dress, how we behave, what tasks we undertake, and even whose society we seek.

The language we use to describe our selves may have a direct effect on our self-concept. What kinds of self-concepts might develop in children who grow up thinking of themselves, variously, as "colored," "nigger," "Negro," or "black"? These are just words but they have come to connote a great deal about personal identity. Richly connotative words often acquire power beyond themselves. Such words can both draw meaning from, and lend meaning to, a person's sense of self.

What we think of our selves is also affected by the society we live in, the groups we belong to, the people we associate with, the family we were raised in, even the religious experiences we have had. There is no way we can escape from the values our environment imparts. Even if we reject them, they have influenced us—we have taken some action because of them. Language is designed and modified to meet the changing requirements of different cultures. That's why language differs from culture to culture. What we are, or even can become, is reflected in the language of our culture.

Language also differs among subcultures. Think about some of the subcultures that exist in our society. There are religious subcultures, ethnic subcultures, geographic subcultures, each with its own special

Try This _____

Place a check beside those adjectives you use to describe yourself, or that you find popping up in your conversations when you refer to yourself:

_____ proud	_____ cheerful	_____ stubborn	_____ trusting
_____ complex	_____ sarcastic	_____ selfish	_____ liberal
_____ realistic	_____ warm	_____ sexy	_____ happy
_____ aggressive	_____ outgoing	_____ trustworthy	_____ sincere
_____ prejudiced	_____ rude	_____ conservative	_____ fearful
_____ unfriendly	_____ negative	_____ uptight	_____ naive
_____ materialistic	_____ blunt	_____ vain	_____ wise
_____ open-minded	_____ boastful	_____ quiet	_____ free
_____ manipulative	_____ religious	_____ idealistic	_____ energetic
_____ studious	_____ confident	_____ mature	_____ cool*
_____ shy	_____ sensitive		

To what extent do these feelings (or labels) have a bearing upon your communication with others? Do they shape your reactions? Your attitudes?

*Communication Research Associates, *A Workbook for Interpersonal Communication*, 2nd ed. (Dubuque, Iowa: Kendall/Hunt Publishing Company, 1978), p. 75.

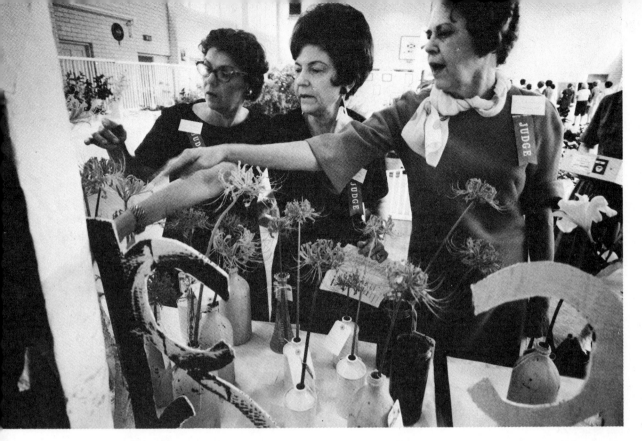

Judges at this flower show use a sublanguage to describe more accurately the features they are looking for.

vocabulary. Subcultures may form on the basis of disciplines of study, interests, and needs as well. A dormitory may have a code of its own that identifies other residents of the same dorm. One teacher who lectured to massive groups of students would give each term's group of students a way to identify each other or him if they met on campus. Sometimes they would use a code phrase like "spring-one" for the spring term of 1981. In each case, the lecturer formed a subculture and gave it a unique way to let everyone else in the subculture know he or she belonged to it. Language can be used, as in this instance, to define who is in the in-group and who is not.

It is because of the common interests, needs, and conditions of individuals in subcultures that sublanguages come into being. These sublanguages help members communicate with each other. The statement, "A Quartimax rotated factor matrix will have very high and very low loadings in each row,"[10] may sound like a foreign language, but to the subculture known as "behaviorists," it is not unusual at all. Besides letting members communicate with one another, sublanguages provide a sense of common identity, a means of identification, and a special-

We don't always realize
the influence that a per-
son's name, alone, may
have on other people's
reactions. What is your
first reaction to the
following names?

1. Jonathan
2. Bernard
3. James
4. Curtis
5. John
6. Darrell
7. Patrick
8. Donald
9. Craig
10. Gerald
11. Thomas
12. Horace
13. Gregory
14. Maurice

The names next to odd
numbers were considered
desirable and the names
next to the even numbers
were considered unde-
sirable in a study done at
Tulane University.* If it is
true that some names are
more desirable than
others, think about the effect that a name may
have on a person's self-
concept. Think about the
psychological effect on a
person who has the same
name as a famous person
or that of a television
character.

*In a study by S. Gray
Garwood, reported in "The
Importance of Not Being
Ernestine or Egbert or Elmo
or Beulah, or Percival . . . ,"
Detroit Free Press, December
5, 1976, pp. 13–14 of the
"Detroit" section.

ized vocabulary for members to describe more accurately those things that concern them. A member of the prison subculture might not call a prison guard a prison guard but, rather, a *screw, roach, hack, slave driver, shield,* or *holligan*.[11] And there could be nuances of meaning to these words not apparent to the outsider.

As the words of a sublanguage come into general use outside the subculture, they no longer serve the purposes they were designed for and are dropped. New words take their place. This is one way that new words enter our language. It is also one reason why we must be flexible, adaptable, and open.

As words of sublanguages come into general use, they can cause problems if everyone doesn't understand precisely what the words mean. The meanings of words used by subcultures may include nuances not readily understood by the outsider. If we recognize the diverse ways in which people of different subcultures communicate, and then think about the people of different *world* cultures, we begin to understand the possibilities for misunderstanding and conflict. Despite the tremendous potential for breakdowns in communication, some consensus and predictability *are* possible if we are alert and sensitive.

Language Affects Your Perceptions

If we label something "attractive" or "pleasant," we are already predisposed to perceive it in a certain way, probably with interest and enjoyment. If we think of people in terms of how much we like them rather than how little we hate them, we will probably respond more favorably to those individuals. Language shapes our ideas—the labels we attach to things are likely to affect the attitudes we hold. Doesn't a weather forecast of "partly sunny" make you feel better than "partly cloudy"?

To show how labels affect our responses, think of the possible confusion that might result if the person we label "professor" was also the person we label "best friend." If we are not accustomed to responding to "professors" in the same way as "best friends," conflicts occur and perceptual adjustments must be made.

Think about a person who seems to have a negative attitude toward life. Can you recall any conversations you've had with this person? What kinds of words did he or she use? Bob, a person with a pessimistic attitude if ever there was one, tends to label things as being different degrees of "awful." His perceptions cannot help but be reinforced by this labeling. Bob cannot approach a person he has labeled

Try This

Next time you watch television, pay special attention to the advertisements. Notice, especially, the "weasel" words—words that allow the advertiser to evade or retreat from any direct or forthright statement or position. Weasel words are not only a retreat or an evasion, they make you hear things that are not being said, accept as truths things that have only been implied, or believe things that have only been suggested. How many of the following weasel words can you find in advertisements?

1. <u>Help</u>—as in aid or assist. Examples: "Brand X <u>helps</u> keep you young." "Brand A <u>helps</u> prevent cavities."

2. <u>Like</u>—as used in comparison. Examples: "It's <u>like</u> getting one bar free." "Cleans <u>like</u> a white tornado."

3. <u>Virtual</u> or <u>virtually</u>—meaning essentially, but not in fact. Examples: "<u>Virtually</u> trouble-free." "<u>Virtually</u> foolproof."

4. <u>Acts</u> or <u>works</u>—as used to bring action to a product. Example: "<u>Works</u> like new."

5. <u>Can be</u>—as used to indicate an ideal situation. Example: "Brand Y <u>can be</u> of significant value when used in . . ."

6. <u>Feel</u> or <u>the feel of</u>—as used to imply that it is a matter of opinion. Example: "So-and-so has <u>the feel of</u> real leather."*

Can you find other weasel words not mentioned above?

*For more examples and further explanation, see Carl P. Wrighter, *I Can Sell You Anything* (New York: Ballantine Books, 1972), pp. 23–25.

"abusive" without fearing emotional or physical injury. Think how often we describe things as "not bad" when what we really mean is "great." Changing the labels we use to describe things is sometimes the first step toward changing our attitudes.

Examples abound of how language shapes the way we perceive things. In a grocery store, labeling techniques can trick us into thinking an item is "first" or "A-number-one" when it is really a third- or fourth-quality item. How, for example, is a shopper supposed to identify different grades of beef? Jennifer Cross, in *The Supermarket Trap*, explains the dilemma:

> The fact is that "Blogg's Blue Ribbon-Gold Ribbon-Gourmet-Good-Better-Best" has no objective meaning at all. It bears no relation to any U.S. Department of Agriculture meat grade, though in high quality stores "Blogg's Finest" is mostly choice, and occasionally prime. Elsewhere it could be choice, or even a lower grade like good or standard.[12]

The problem is in identifying different levels of quality without making one level appear to be inferior.[13] When we buy "U.S. No. 1" fresh fruits and vegetables or "U.S. Grade A" butter, we are getting second grade, because "U.S. Fancy" is first grade for most fruits and vegetables and "U.S. Grade AA" is first for butter. When we buy "U.S. Extra" nonfat dry milk we get first grade but "U.S. Extra" dry whole milk is second grade, and "U.S. Extra No. 1" in cucumbers or peaches is also second grade.[14]

When we purchase clothes, we want labels that make us feel comfortable or good about our selves. We want a "Fine Linen Handkerchief," not a "Nose Rag." Schools that came under fire when they offered courses in "Sex Education" received fewer protests when the same material was taught as "Social Hygiene" or "Family Health." At work, most people will try much harder and be much happier if they have a title. Think how much more motivated you would be if you were called an "assistant manager" as opposed to a "sales clerk," or in a theater, a "ticket-taker."[15] Ever wonder why large corporations have so many vice presidents? The difference between "Vice President in Charge of Widgets" and "Widget Director" may sound slight to an outsider, but it can make a great difference to those involved. The way things are labeled leads us to respond to them in a certain way.

IMPROVING SKILLS IN LANGUAGE

A word is simply a vehicle we use to produce a certain response in another person. If our words do not accomplish their mission, we say there is a breakdown in communication. There is no guarantee that our language will produce the responses we want even if we apply all the suggestions mentioned here. Interpersonal communication can never be perfect. But learning language skills can help us move closer to the goal of effective, efficient communication. It will increase the chances for our success.

Make the message complete.   Because there are so many ways for words to be misinterpreted, we must try to give listeners as much information as possible about our ideas, experiences, feelings, and perceptions so that they will know where *we* are coming from. There should be enough information so the other person can understand our frame of reference. But don't go too far! Too much information can create a negative effect. We would very likely bore or overwhelm our listener with more details than are necessary or manageable.

Our message will be more complete if we repeat the message with

Consider This

What you say may be hurting you.

An error of grammar could cost you a job. Your friends may enjoy private but delirious laughter each time you use a favorite word incorrectly. And the trite phrase which you utter with regularity may one day transform your loving spouse into a raving and violent stranger.

A social philosopher of the radical '60s said that close attention to the spoken and written word represented "the last vestige of a caste society." As the mood of the country relaxed during the '60s and early '70s, the standard rules of speech gave way to less rigid forms of self-expression. "Relating" became the name of the game.

Today, however, employers, educators, and the general public are clamoring for a time out in the game—and there are some who have called for an end to the auditory assault.

—Janet Cooke, *The Blade: Toledo, Ohio,* June 11, 1978

some variation; that is, if we add details to the original message that make it more accurate. If the listener does not "get it" one way, he or she will have another chance the second time with the added information. To simply restate a misunderstood word or phrase in precisely the same way does not serve the listener's purposes and perpetuates confusion. What we want to make sure of is that our message is as complete and "on the mark" as possible.

Remember that meanings are in people. If we're going to use abstract language, it's extra important to monitor the reception of our messages to see that they are getting through. It often helps to move to a lower level of abstraction. Remember that as we talk we tend to project meanings into words just as much as our listener does. These projections are the result of our own experiences. The higher the level of abstraction, the more we must deal with our own and our listeners' connotations for words. If we remember that meanings are in people, not in words, we'll have a better chance of avoiding error and confusion. What another person brings to a word is usually more important than the word itself.

Stereotyping can also create breakdowns. Developing a sensitivity to labeling will help us avoid some of it. More importantly, it will help us to be conscious of labels used by others. We can't control what other people think when they either use stereotypes themselves or hear ours. But rather than take a chance that we hold the same stereotypes, we should try to avoid generalizations. Be specific and concrete instead.

It is impossible to know everything about anything. The mental picture we get of this world is incomplete; no matter how we describe the

The workman and the supervisor have different occupational responsibilities but they need to talk the same language to get the job done right.

world, there will be distortion. To say that we "know all that" or that we "understand completely" is not recognizing that our picture of reality is partial. Too often we operate as if we know all the facts, and what's more, as if others see the facts as we do.

Talk the same language. If we can comfortably and naturally use words, including slang and jargon, that our listener understands, so much the better. If we adapt our language to the listener, very specifically, we show concern for him or her—an attempt at genuine communication to reach honest understanding. But to litter our speech with fancy words, "cute" phrases, or inappropriate slang will do little to help create understanding (and can make us look ridiculous and phony).

There is nothing "wrong" with any word that we have in our vocabulary or that occurs in any dictionary. Words are only "wrong" if they are used inappropriately. We might not talk to our roommate as we do to our parents; the language we use with our roommate may be inappropriate for our parents. We may have all kinds of names and profanities we use for a teacher who seems to be doing us in, but we reserve them for our friends or for our selves, not the teacher. There are ways other than name-calling to express our dislike to the teacher. It would serve a negative purpose to use abusive language with the teacher; it would be "wrong" in that context.

To use different language in different contexts and with different people is not necessarily deceptive or hypocritical. Some language may be more appropriate for a casual party with a group of friends, some language is better suited for dinner with our future mother-in-law. Hypocrisy and deceit do result from using language that is not our own, language that reflects a character or beliefs and principles that we do not really possess. We are being hypocritical when we try to appear as we are not or try to present a facade, when we are no longer adapting

Consider This

In the beginning, we are told, was the Word; but it is no more. The word is no longer honored, respected, or believed; not even the Logos of God, which has too often been perverted by men for selfish ends.

One of the most salient characteristics of young people today, not only in the United States but all over the world, is the rejection of the word. The young person will not communicate because he distrusts words; he prefers listening to music to reading books because music is incapable of lying.

We have devalued the currency of communication. The monetary inflation we so worry about is as nothing compared with the verbal inflation we have inflicted on the world. We have taken the most singular gift of man—expression—and forced it to serve our own proud, profit-seeking, or petty purposes.

This is what young people resent most of all. Like all innocent youth, they began by trusting the word, by taking it at face value. Slowly and painfully, they learned that society does not say what it means, or mean what it says. Idealism quickly corrodes into cynicism, and the sullen silence of the young in the presence of their elders is a deep repudiation of the whole medium of verbal expression.

The task before us—if any real reconciliation is at all possible—is far more than a political or social or economic one. It is a task that goes to the very roots of human existence: that of restoring the word to its pristine purity and its human authenticity.

Communication—and therefore communion—can survive only when there is a genuine "meeting" between persons, when truth encounters truth, clasps it, and returns it. But no genuine meeting is possible when we use words as bludgeons, as blackmail, as screens to hide our bad faith, or as brilliant lures to hook the fish we are preying upon.

Even without bad faith—even when our intentions, so far as we know them, are the best—we still manipulate the word to defend our weaknesses, conceal our vulnerability, justify our self-centeredness, and erect a "philosophy of lift" out of fear, prejudice, and ignorance.

We are told that "the letter killeth, but the spirit giveth life," and the letter has all but killed the spirit. Man's most precious gift has been perverted from the beginning, but only in this age of "mass communication" has the letter been able to extend its hegemony over the total range of men's relationships. If there is one resolution worth making, it is the resolve to treat the word as a holy thing, not a dark device for attacking, defending, or disguising.

—Sydney Harris, *The Best of Sydney Harris*

"I must say since we learned to talk, how well you express yourself in a crystalline and often aphoristic manner."

our language to the context in an honest manner. It is deceptive to manipulate others by using language that misrepresents who we really are.

Be flexible. Stereotyping paints an unrealistically black-or-white world because things either fit our categories or they do not. If we say, "Teachers are too tough," meaning *all* teachers are too tough, we haven't allowed for variations among teachers. Statements like "Blondes have more fun" or "Professors are absent-minded" apply evaluations indiscriminately. If we think in terms of what is unique to a person or a situation, our language will become more accurate and flexible.

We increase our flexibility if we avoid extreme language. If we say, "I am totally happy," we allow no room for increased happiness. Happiness is seldom total, just as success and failure most often occur in degrees. Saying "I am a complete failure" is a rigid, inflexible response.

True, there are some things that *do* appear to be either-or, such as whether a woman is pregnant or not, whether we are here or somewhere else, or whether or not there is another person in the room with us right now. We can describe these things in black-or-white terms. But generally we tend to be too rigid rather than too flexible in our use of language.

It's a good idea to think in terms of "sometimes," "possibly," "normally," and "now and then." Such words as "always," "never," "all," and "none" can cause problems. "Allness" language makes us tend to think in set, rigid patterns. And in doing so, not only do we fail to distinguish what is unique in each case, but we do not allow for change.

Get others involved. If we assume that our communication has a good chance of being *un*successful and if we accept the fact that misunderstanding is *likely* to occur, we will be more cautious in our use of words. It will help if we can get others to share in our frame of reference. Ask your listeners what they think about what you have said. It is very easy to overwhelm another person with a verbal barrage and not realize we have caused that person to withdraw or become defensive. Saying "Do you understand?" or "You *do* see what I mean?" can seem accusatory or severe. But asking "Am I making sense?" or, simply, "What do you think?" involves the listener and can help us find out whether we really have been understood.

Using words well is not as simple as it might first appear. Trying to put our finger on the problems of using words is hard because so much depends on the users of the words and the contexts in which they are used. And we have to use words even to describe the problems of using words! There's no way around it. Even if we understood all about users and contexts, we wouldn't have all the answers because things would change. Words, we have seen, are flexible in meaning. Our effectiveness

---

Consider This

DEAR ANN LANDERS: I was, ah—er—wondering if you, ah—receive other letters, ah—you know, well, er—ah—complaining about a person, ah—er—who says about 60 words—ah—you know, and never finishes a sentence, ah—you know—ah—er—just keeps stringing together words separated with ah, er, and you know.

Other members of the family interrupt her because it drives them crazy, too. But the ah, you know, er, continues as if she had no idea she is doing it.

What can be done to cure her? We are—BORDERLINE BANANAS (PS, I'm an English professor with a master's degree. My wife is the problem.)

DEAR BORDER: If you honestly believe "Ah, er, uh, you know" is unaware that her speech patterns are driving the family batty, I have a suggestion that might help.

Get a tape recorder and take down about 20 minutes of ah-er-you know. Play it back to her—privately, of course. Most people have no idea what they sound like and are shocked when they hear a recording of their own voice. Suggest a speech therapist. Your wife can overcome this habit if she will work at it.

—syndicated in *The Blade: Toledo, Ohio,* February 4, 1980

in using them depends upon our understanding how they can vary depending on different communication contexts.

Verbal communication has a tremendous impact on interpersonal relationships. Verbalizing our feelings can help us feel better about our selves and can strengthen our interpersonal interactions. Although verbal communication is important, it makes up only a fraction of our total communication with others. We communicate at least as much through nonverbal means as through verbal means, as we will see in the next chapter.

OTHER READING

Robert L. Benjamin, *Semantics and Language Analysis* (Indianapolis, Ind.: The Bobbs-Merrill Company, Inc., 1970). In this introductory textbook on language, the author examines *how* language, sentences, and words mean. He looks at the language of value, and, finally, offers the reader suggestions for clarifying language. This is a brief, readable approach.

Stuart Chase, *The Power of Words* (New York: Harcourt Brace Jovanovich, Inc., 1953). Enjoyable reading. A useful introduction to general semantics for

[11]See Joseph A. DeVito, *The Interpersonal Communication Book*, 2nd ed. (New York: Harper & Row, Publishers, 1980), p. 193.

Peter Farb, *Word Play: What Happens When People Talk* (New York: Bantam Books, 1973). Farb confronts the basic question first by laying out the ground rules for the interactions that take place between a person and his or her total environment. Then he develops the strategies available. He talks about the fairness of the language game and ends by discussing how the game has changed through time. A thorough, well-researched book.

Rudolf Flesch, *The Art of Plain Talk* (New York: Collier Books, 1951). Although over 25 years old, the need for this book is as great today as ever. Plain talk is colorful, precise, and easy to understand. This is a handbook that will help readers get across what they want to say.

S. I. Hayakawa, *Language in Thought and Action*, 3rd ed. (New York: Harcourt Brace Jovanovich, Inc., 1972). Semantics is the study of human interaction through communication. This is a study of semantics based on the assumption that cooperation is preferable to conflict. The principles explained here relate to thinking, speaking, writing, and behavior. Challenges are provided for undertaking actual semantic investigations and exercises.

Philip Lesly, *How We Discommunicate* (New York: AMACOM [A division of American Management Associations], 1979). Although his focus is broader than language alone, Lesly discusses the snobbery of jargon and the sloppy use of language as major parts of this examination of our failure to communicate. An interesting, down-to-earth book full of examples which also includes a program for improvement.

Edwin Newman, *On Language* (New York: Warner Books, Inc., 1980. This is a combination of his two books, *Strictly Speaking: Will America Be the Death of English?* and *A Civil Tongue.* In the first book, his underlying argument is that if words are devalued, so are ideas and so are human beings. This is an entertaining examination of the state of the English language. In the second book, Newman supplies examples that prove we receive a smog of jargon from the press, television, schools, business, politics, advertising, public relations, military, and bureaucracy. He makes a plea to us all not to accept nonsense and to speak plainly.

Neil Postman, *Crazy Talk, Stupid Talk: How We Defeat Ourselves by the Way We Talk—and What to Do About It* (New York: Delacorte Press, 1976). An examination of talk that does not work (stupid talk) and talk that promotes purposes that are unreasonable, trivial, or evil (crazy talk). Written in down-to-earth, straightforward language.

NOTES

[1]S. Chase, *Power of Words* (New York: Harcourt Brace Jovanovich, 1954), p. 3.

[2]For their ideas on characteristics of language, see Kim Giffen and Bobby R. Patton, *Fundamentals of Interpersonal Communication*, 2nd ed. (New York: Harper & Row, Publishers, 1976), pp. 161–72.

[3]Ibid., p. 161.

[4]C. K. Ogden and I. A. Richards, *The Meaning of Meaning* (New York: Harcourt, Brace and Co., Inc., 1953).

[5]For the discussion on levels of abstraction I am indebted to S. I. Hayakawa, *Language in Thought and Action*, 3rd ed. (New York: Harcourt Brace Jovanovich, Inc., 1972), pp. 150–54.

[6]From *Language in Thought and Action,* Fourth Edition, by S. I. Hayakawa, copyright © 1978 by Harcourt Brace Jovanovich, Inc. Reproduced by permission of Harcourt Brace Jovanovich, Inc. and George Allen & Unwin Ltd. "The Abstraction Ladder" is based on a diagram originated by Alfred Korzybski to explain the process of abstracting. See Alfred Korzybski, *Science and Sanity: An Introduction to Non-Aristotelian Systems and General Semantics* (Lancaster, Pa.: Science Press Printing Company, 1933), especially chapter 25.

[7]Virginia Satir, *Conjoint Family Therapy* (Palo Alto, Calif.: Science and Behavior, 1968), pp. 65–70.

[8]Richard C. Huseman, James M. Lahiff, and John D. Hatfield, *Interpersonal Communication in Organizations: A Perceptual Approach* (Boston: Holbrook Press, Inc., 1976), p. 61.

[9]Hayakawa, *Language in Thought and Action*, pp. 8–17.

[10]Gary Cronkhite and Jo Liska, "A Critique of Factor Analytic Approaches to the Study of Credibility," *Communication Monographs* 43 (June 1976), 101.

[11]See Joseph A. DeVito, *The Interpersonal Communication Book,* 2nd ed. (New York: Harper & Row, Publishers, 1980), p. 193.

[12]From *The Supermarket Trap* by Jennifer Cross (Bloomington: Indiana University Press, 1970), p. 75.

[13]Raymond Loewy Associates, *Super Market of the Sixties* (Chicago: Super Market Institute, 1960), p. 29.

[14]Cross, *The Supermarket Trap*, pp. 210–11.

[15]Ron Adler and Neil Towne, *Looking Out/Looking In: Interpersonal Communication,* 2nd ed. (San Francisco: Rinehart Press, 1978), p. 319.

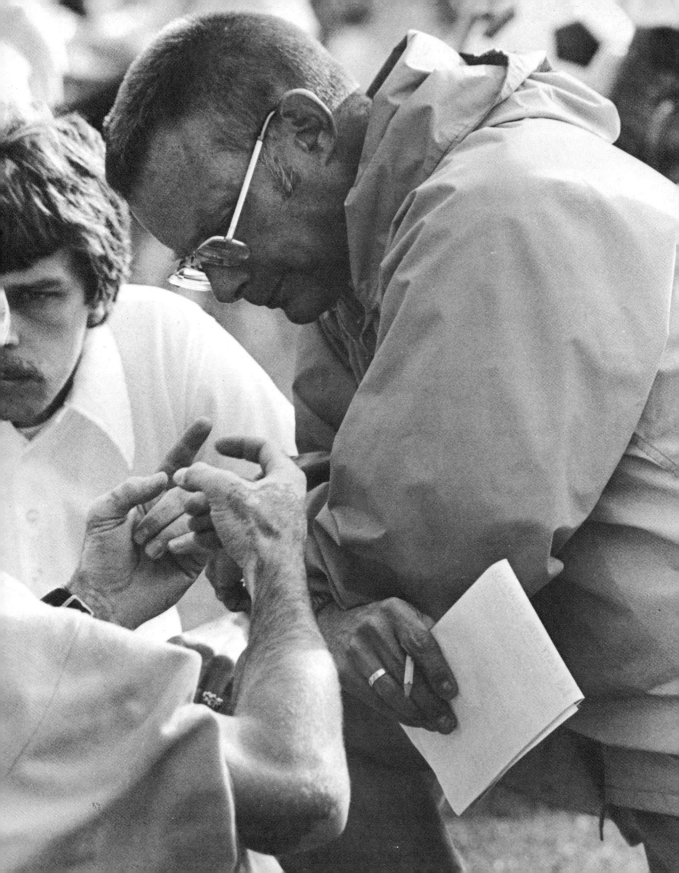

6   Communicating Without Words: Nonverbal Communication

Have you ever been in a public place and discovered someone was staring at you? You look away, but just to test your perceptions you look back at the person. "I wonder why he's staring at me," you think. You look away again, hoping his gaze will shift. This time when you look back at him, you do it quickly. If he continues to stare, you might become uncomfortable, angry, or even alarmed.

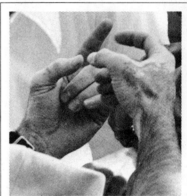

The direct, unwavering stare is a form of threat; it is an example of nonverbal communication.[1] Its meaning is clear and no words are necessary to drive the effect home. Too much eye contact, as with the unwavering stare, can serve to heighten intimacy, to express and intensify emotions, and in some cases to indicate possible sexual interest. What does it mean to "give someone the eye"? Americans often interpret prolonged eye contact as an indication of sexual attraction. You may have noticed a man give a woman a steady, challenging stare, with that stare followed by the woman lowering her eyes.[2] A great deal has been communicated without a word being spoken. Communicating without words is the subject of this chapter.

In this chapter I'm going to look at the many different ways we say things without using words. I'll discuss how our nonverbal communication conveys certain things better than verbal communication can—sometimes we reveal more about our selves than we may even want to! "Body language" is part of it. Vocal cues and spatial cues are just as important. Nonverbal language is not a precise language; we have to be careful we don't misinterpret nonverbal signals in our eagerness to understand what a person means by wearing those shoes or nodding that way or standing so close to us. But while we're not dealing with an exact science here, we can learn to send and interpret nonverbal messages in a way that enhances the total meaning exchanged in any communication.

THE RULES OF THE GAME

The stare is quite unusual in our society because of the connotations attached to it and because it is really opposite to the kind of behavior we have been programmed to accept. In the example just mentioned, the accepted rules require the woman to look away or lower her eyes. If she aggressively stares back or smiles or winks, the man might be pleased or frightened, but he would definitely know the usual rules were not in effect.

To be stared at is an invasion of privacy and can make us very uncomfortable. To be caught staring is an embarrassment. We've probably all at some time quickly looked away from someone we were staring at and pretended to be studying the clock or the wall just above the person's head. Erving Goffman, a sociologist who has investigated the behavior of human beings in public places, states that Americans meet one another with "civil inattention." Goffman means that we take enough visual notice of others to let them know that we know that they are there, but not enough notice to seem curious or to intrude.[3] You may take offense at the phrase "behavior we have been programmed to accept" in the first sentence of this section, because we don't like to think we are predictable. But our culture programs us from childhood, teaching us what to do with our eyes and what to expect of other people. Think of what happens when we shift our eyes to look away from another person's gaze. We produce a response that is out of all proportion to the small muscular effort we made.[4] The response is somewhat predictable since we both know what we mean by the eye contact—the response may be one of anger or hurt if it is a friend we have chosen to look away from. It is amazing that such a small movement can arouse strong feelings!

CATHY   **by Cathy Guisewite**

I HAVE CONVERSATIONS IN MY HEAD WITH IRVING ALL DAY LONG.

I DISAGREE. I PHILOSO-PHIZE. I MAKE JOKES. I FLIRT. I COMMENT ON WORLD EVENTS.

AND THEN WHEN I FINALLY SEE IRVING, I CAN'T THINK OF ONE THING TO SAY.

HOW CAN I BE SO FASCINATING IN PRIVATE AND SO BORING IN PERSON?

Do you recall one of your parents or teachers admonishing you to "take that look off your face"? The slightest suggestion of a smile at an inappropriate time can draw a lot of attention! It's the same with eye movements and physical touching and other forms of nonverbal communication. We all know what it is to share an inside joke with a friend and to express our understanding of the joke with a timely nudge when other kinds of communication would be out of place. That nudge can say a great deal, considering how little effort we put into it. Nonverbal messages are like that; they can pack a lot of meaning into otherwise small looks and gestures.

All nonverbal communication is influenced by a variety of factors—our personality, the situations we are in, the attitudes we hold toward people, the pecking order we maintain with others, our cultural upbringing. Nonverbal components almost always operate in conjunction with each other. At the same time we are establishing eye contact, for example, we are also dealing with the nonverbal variables of facial expressions, gestures, and larger movements. We draw conclusions from numerous nonverbal signals simultaneously and we do it very quickly. Whether accurate or inaccurate, we seldom have time to check. We respond, hoping that we have perceived accurately and hoping, too, that we'll get further cues.

THE IMPORTANCE OF NONVERBAL COMMUNICATION

Communication researchers have shown that the words themselves carry only a small part of the information exchanged between people when they talk. Ray Birdwhistell, a noted authority on nonverbal communication, estimates that, on the average, people speak words for only 10 to 11 minutes daily. The standard spoken sentence takes 2.5 seconds. Also, Birdwhistell notes, in normal two-person conversations, verbal components carry less than 35 percent of the social meaning while nonverbal components carry more than 65 percent of the social meaning.[5] It is easy to slip into the error of thinking that *all* communication must be verbal. But even when we think we are not consciously sending or receiving nonverbal messages, their influence is present and it is significant.

It Is Continuous

The more we think about nonverbal communication, the more we see how true it is that we cannot *not* communicate. Words come one at a

Try This _____

Recall the last conversation you had with someone. How many nonverbal cues did you use (or consciously control) to convey your message? Check each of them that you can remember:

_____	eye contact	_____	dress
_____	facial expression	_____	environment
_____	gestures	_____	space (closeness to other person)
_____	body motion	_____	attitude

It is likely that all cues came into play. But here, just check those that you made conscious use of in your last conversation. At different times do you depend on different cues? Do you use nonverbal cues better than verbal ones? Which do you think best conveys your message?

time, but nonverbal cues come continuously. Several, even many, may exist and are perceived at the same time. All these nonverbal signals are used as a foundation for understanding the words. Nonverbal cues can be sent slowly or quickly, while words become distorted if spoken too slowly or too rapidly. We send *and* receive nonverbal messages in an uninterrupted, persistent flow. All the time we are observing someone else's gestures and mannerisms, that person may also be observing ours.

It Conveys Emotions

When you think of it, objects and actions can generate more emotions than words because objects and actions are less abstract than words. To hear that someone cried or was injured is not nearly as powerful as seeing that person cry or get hurt. Words usually exert more of an intellectual appeal. If we want to convey sincerity, our facial and bodily gestures can probably do it better than our words, although words *reinforced* by nonverbal cues will convey the most unmistakable message.

Since nonverbal cues are so closely tied to the emotions, how well we understand nonverbal messages depends on how empathic we are. Everything I said earlier about empathic listening applies here as well. The empathic, alert perceiver will very likely understand (or at least be aware of) nonverbal cues. To understand verbal expression requires more skill. Nonverbal expression, learned much earlier and often closely tied to universal human emotions, is sometimes easier to attach meaning to, even though that meaning may be less than perfectly accurate.

It Is Rich in Meaning

Think of the last time you went to the doctor when you had certain symptoms but did not know what your illness was. You probably watched the doctor's face very carefully to see if you could detect how sick you really were. Ambiguous looks or "hmm-m-m" noises from the doctor could really make you uneasy. "My goodness, I'm dying!" you might think. In such situations, we look for even the most minute nonverbal signs to interpret.

Consider how the slightest sound or the most delicate movement can be fraught with meaning. Put these sounds and movements together into the larger context in which they occur and you realize how rich nonverbal communication can be. A raised eyebrow, a sly smile, a touch of the hand, can all say a lot in the right circumstances. Such nonverbal cues are especially useful when for some reason oral or written communication is inappropriate—during a concert or a lecture, perhaps, or even a movie. Nonverbal communication can be rich with meaning.

It Can Be Confusing

Although nonverbal communication may be rich with meaning, it can also be confusing. Certain cues may mean something entirely different than what we imagine. A man may be sitting on a sofa next to a woman with his legs crossed away from the woman. "Ahh-ha, obviously he has no interest in her, since his legs are crossed away from her," the enthusiastic reader of body language might think. "He is excluding her." Not necessarily. Some people *always* cross their legs right over left, no matter what. It's their habit, it's comfortable, and it doesn't mean a thing as far as nonverbal communication goes (except perhaps that they feel comfortable).

We can't assume that a woman with her arms folded in front of her is closed-minded and rigid—she may simply feel cold! We must be careful in interpreting nonverbal cues because they can be confusing. We do not always have enough information to make a judgment, and our guesses may be far from accurate.

DO YOUR ACTIONS MATCH YOUR WORDS?

FELLOW I KNOW says he went AWOL from the U.S. Navy in Japan shortly after World War II. He didn't speak a word of Japanese. He met no one who spoke English during his two-weeks' absence. Yet with facial expressions, hand waving, body language he was able to get food, drink, places to sleep, everything he wanted. His point: You can conduct countless transactions without saying anything. Quite on. Scientists have listed 700,000 different combinations of face and body movements that people use to convey meaning.

—L. M. Boyd, "Checking Up"

One of the best and most logical ways to check our interpretation of somebody's nonverbal message is through that person's words. He or she might say, "I like you" or "You are a wonderful person to be with," confirming eye contact that seemed affectionate. But it's rare that people come right out and express their feelings so directly. Usually we have to pay attention to more subtle verbal cues. What we should watch for is whether there is congruency between act and word. Do this person's words match whatever he or she is doing? Congruency makes it easy for us because we can be surer of our interpretations. When there is incongruency, we either try to get more information, we suspend judgment, or we tend to believe either what we hear *or* what we see.

Nonverbal and verbal communication usually work together, even if not congruently.[6]

A nonverbal message may *repeat* what we say, reinforcing it. For example, our message is reinforced when we wave and say "good-by" at the same time. Nonverbal *replaces* verbal when we wave without saying "good-by" or when we nod in agreement to indicate "yes." Nonverbal communication may *underscore* the verbal portion of a message much the way italics strengthen the written word; leaning toward another person with concern reinforces "Tell me about it."

Nonverbal behavior may *regulate* behavior, too. We can often tell

Consider This _____

We asked several people to act out six different moods on videotape. The moods were anger, fear, seductivity, indifference, happiness and sadness. Then we let our subjects review their protrayals and eliminate any that they felt were unrepresentative. The chosen portrayals, in other words, were emotionally authentic in the eyes of their creators.

When we played these videotapes to large audiences to discover if they could decode the moods intended, we found that most senders were able to project accurately only <u>two</u> of the six moods. The particular moods, of course, varied from sender to sender, but in general we were surprised to learn that everyone appears to send out misinformation. Their portrayals often failed to represent their intentions. This finding lent strength to the hypothesis that the discordance between our emotional expressions and our intentions may represent conflicting impulses. It is possible, admittedly, that our audiences were unusually poor judges of nonverbal behavior; our senders, moreover, may have been better actors in less artificial settings. But at least we found evidence for the notion that there are many people whose emotional intentions and self-images are out of harmony with their actual behavior.

I shall never forget two examples of this discordance. One girl, who tried like everyone else to appear angry, fearful, seductive, indifferent, happy and sad—and who subsequently edited her own performances for authenticity—appeared to her judges as angry in every case. Imagine what a difficult world she must have lived in. No matter where she set the thermostat of her emotional climate, everyone else always felt it as sweltering hot. Another girl in our experiment demonstrated a similar one-dimensionality; only in her case, whatever else she thought she was doing, she invariably impressed her judges as seductive. Even when she wanted to be angry, men whistled at her.

—From "Nonverbal Communication: We Send Emotional Messages" by Ernest G. Beier. Reprinted from *Psychology Today Magazine*, October 1974. Copyright © 1974 Ziff-Davis Publishing Company. Reprinted by permission.

when it is our turn to speak in a conversation through a nonverbal cue: the other person nods his or her head, changes position, or establishes strong eye contact with us. Similarly, we may show we wish to speak in a discussion group by leaning forward or suddenly looking very attentive—in so doing, we regulate the behavior of other people in the group to some extent. Finally, a nonverbal message can *contradict* the verbal message. We rarely send this kind of contradictory communication on purpose. Perhaps the most common example is when we look "down in the dumps" and someone asks us what's wrong and we reply, "Nothing." Albert Mehrabian suggests that when a person's actions and words contradict each other, we rely more on his or her actions to reveal true feelings.[7]

FORMS OF NONVERBAL COMMUNICATION

Nonverbal elements sometimes work separately from verbal communication; that is, we may receive a nonverbal message without any words whatsoever. The nonverbal component, in this case, is the entire message. But usually the nonverbal domain provides a framework for the words we use. If we think of nonverbal communication as including all forms of message transmission *not* represented by word symbols, we can divide it into the broad categories of sign language, action language, and object language.[8] These categories were first developed by Jurgen Ruesch, an early researcher in nonverbal communication.[9]

Sign Language

When we nod to signify agreement, when we shake a finger at someone as a threat, or when we raise our thumb to try to hitchhike, we are using a gesture in place of a word. If someone asks, "How many cards do you have?" and we show five fingers, we are using a gesture to replace a number—sign language. A smile is a form of sign language. If we pound our fist on the table at the end of a sentence, we are using sign language to show exclamation; we are using a gesture as a punctuation mark. Gestures used as sign language are generally unambiguous and readily understood.

Although most of us use sign language occasionally as a substitute for spoken words, deaf and hearing-impaired students at Gallaudet College in Washington, D.C., use sign language daily to communicate with each other.

Action Language

Have you ever thought much about the way you walk? When we are in a hurry or have an important appointment, our posture, motion, and pace reveal our excitement. If our mood, on the other hand, is sullen and blue—if we're worried about an exam we're not prepared for or a meeting we've been dreading—our posture, motion, and pace will reveal our concern.

Notice how much you can tell about someone's mood from observing his or her body movements. Although actions like walking and drinking are primarily functional activities, they also provide a kind of statement to others. Ruesch included such statements, even when unintended, in his category of action language. Intentional statements are just as common and they, too, are action language. We may intentionally stand near to someone at a party to show loyalty and affection for that person. We are making a nonverbal statement with action language.

Object Language

Think about what you are wearing right now—your hairstyle, glasses, jewelry, or other items. What do these things reveal about you? Ruesch labels as object language the statements we make with the books we carry, the car we drive, the clothes we wear, the furniture we have in our room. Whether we mean them to or not, these items transmit cues to observers. Our clothes, for example, will always reveal something about us. Even what we may consider a perfectly neutral set of clothes—jeans and a sweater, perhaps—says something about us, if only that we do not want our clothes to attract attention. Such statements made with *things* are object language.

TYPES OF NONVERBAL CUES

Let's look more closely at these cues that tell others about us or that tell us about them. Our own self-awareness and empathic skills will increase as we become more sensitive to these different kinds of nonverbal cues. The broader our base for understanding, the more likely we are to have meaning for the cues we perceive. But we know that nonverbal communication can be ambiguous and we must be careful not to overgeneralize from the behavior we observe. We may feel hurt by the listless "hi" we receive from a good friend unless we remember that

Try This

Classify each of the following into sign, action, or object language:

1. You jump out of bed in the morning.

2. You put on your best sweater.

3. You shake your head because your roommate borrowed the shoes that you wanted to wear today.

4. You storm out of the room slamming the door furiously.

5. You see your roommate in the cafeteria and shake your fist in anger.

6. You grab your books, walk slowly out of the building drooping with frustration.

Based on your own experience, is any one of these types of nonverbal communication more effective than any other in expressing how you really feel?

Consider This _____

Ties are said to be symbolic of romance. According to the Neckwear Association of America, psychologists consider them to be sex-oriented. Ernest Dichter, noted motivational psychologist, considers the necktie the "most revealing part of a man's dress."

The association points out that a man's necktie can tell you what he's all about romantically. Want an insight into your man? Try this quiz. (The right answers are at the bottom).

1. If a man you have met for the first time is constantly adjusting his tie, does it mean he is (a) wearing too tight a shirt, (b) uncomfortable around women, (c) unconsciously expressing his attraction to you?

2. If you see another woman adjusting your boyfriend's or husband's tie, is she (a) looking for the ring around his collar, (b) making a play for him, (c) trying to make you jealous?

3. A man who prefers neckties that are predominantly red is (a) an extrovert, (b) a frustrated fireman, (c) a passionate lover.

4. When a woman gave a man a tie in romantic 17th-century France, it meant (a) even then French restaurants required them, (b) it would protect the wearer from physical harm, (c) not all department stores carried them.

5. A woman who loosens a man's tie is (a) trying to help him relax, (b) keeping her hands busy, (c) subconsciously seducing him.

6. When a woman gives a tie to a man as a gift, does it mean she's (a) influenced by soap operas, (b) a believer in the body-language theory, (c) carrying on the romantic King Arthur tradition of giving her "colors" to her knight.

7. He says he "loves your intellect," but if he's constantly loosening his tie, (a) his next question is, "Your place or mine?", (b) he's saying how masculine he is, (c) he's indicating how relaxing it is to be with you.

Answers:

The right answers to this quiz, according to the National Neckwear Association, are: 1-c; 2-b; 3-a (but watch out for c); 4-b; 5-c; 6-a; 7-a or c (it's up to you to decide).

—(KNS) *The Blade: Toledo, Ohio,* March 12, 1978

Consider This

that listlessness could have been brought on by a headache, lack of sleep, preoccupation, or some other factor we don't know about. We would be unwise to assume we are being personally rejected if this friend doesn't smile and stop to talk with us every single morning.

We should always be alert to *all* cues and try to get as much information as possible on which to base our conclusions. One way to organize our thinking about nonverbal communication is to think in terms of spatial cues, visual cues, and vocal cues. In considering each of these, we should not overlook the fact that any communication occurs in a specific environmental setting. This setting will influence much of the nonverbal interaction that takes place. The weather can affect how we behave just as much as our actual setting—cafeteria, classroom, car, park bench, or whatever.

Spatial Cues

Each of us carries with us something called "informal space." We might think of this as a bubble; we occupy the center of the bubble. This bubble expands or contracts depending on varying conditions and circumstances:

- the personalities of the people with whom we are speaking
- our relationship with (or to) the other person
- the type of encounter
- what is being shared or discussed (nature of the message)
- the environment or situation

In his book *The Silent Language*, Edward T. Hall, a cultural anthropologist, identified the distances that we assume when we talk with others. He calls these distances intimate, personal, social, and public.[10]

Intimate distance.　At an intimate distance (0 to 18 inches), we often use a soft or barely audible whisper to share intimate or confidential information. Physical contact becomes easy at this distance. This is the distance we use for physical comforting, lovemaking, and physical fighting, among other things. At this distance, all of our senses can be activated—sight, scent, touch, sound, and even taste. Interestingly, we are forced in some situations to be with strangers at this intimate distance, in crowded buses or elevators, for example. At this range, sounds are intensified and even vision may be slightly distorted. However, vocalizations are minimal since most conversation need not be loud to be heard at this distance. The whisper can bring the participants closer together, reinforcing the psychological need to use this intimate distance even more.

Personal distance.　Hall identified the range of 18 inches to 4 feet as "personal distance." When we disclose our selves to someone, we are likely to do it within this distance. The topics we discuss at this range may be more or less confidential, and usually are personal and mutually involving. At personal distance we are still able to touch each other if we want to. This is likely to be the distance between people conversing at a party, between classmates in a casual conversation, or within many work relationships. This distance assumes a well-established acquaintanceship. This is probably the most comfortable distance for free exchange of feedback.

Social distance.　When we are talking at a normal level with another person, sharing concerns that are not of a personal nature, we usually

Try This

Would you like to know the size of "bubble" that a friend of yours carries around as his or her "personal space"? The next time you are involved in a conversation with your friend, get into a position where you are directly facing each other and there is nothing behind him or her. Then, as you talk, slowly inch closer and closer. As you infringe on the "bubble," your friend may begin to move backward. As the movement just begins, notice the size of the "personal space" that your friend is protecting. To test your perception of the size of the "bubble," slowly move closer yet. What distance did you find most comfortable for a casual conversation?

Think of two people you have recently conversed with at each of the first three distances and two recent situations where you used the public distance.

1. Intimate (0–18 inches)

2. Personal (18 inches–4 feet)

3. Social (4 feet–12 feet)

4. Public (12 feet or more)

What kind of subject matter did you discuss at each of these distances? Was it different for each of the distances? How formal was each of the encounters? Next time you are talking with others, notice the distance you maintain with them, and think about the factors that led you to choose that distance.

use the social distance (4 to 12 feet). Many of our on-the-job conversations take place at this distance. Seating arrangements in living rooms may be based on "conversation groups" of chairs placed at a distance of 4 to 7 feet from each other. Hall calls 4 to 7 feet the close phase of social distance; from 7 to 12 feet, it is known as the far phase of social distance.

The greater the distance, the more formal the business or social discourse conducted is likely to be. Often, the desks of important people are broad enough to hold visitors at a distance of 7 to 12 feet. Eye contact at this distance becomes more important to the flow of communication; without visual contact one party will likely feel shut out and the conversation may come to a halt.

Public distance. Public distance (12 feet and farther) is well outside the range for close involvement with another person. It is impractical for interpersonal communication. Our senses are limited to seeing and hearing; topics for conversation are relatively impersonal and formal; and most of the communication that occurs is in the public-speaking style, with subjects planned in advance and limited feedback opportunities.

Hall points out that his distances are based on his own observations of middle-class people native to the northeastern United States and employed in business and professional occupations. We should be cautious as we extend his generalizations to other ethnic and racial groups.

The important point regarding intimate, personal, and public distance is that space communicates. Our sense of what distance is natural for us for a specific kind of interaction is deeply ingrained in us by our culture. We automatically make spatial adjustments and interpret spatial cues. Can you imagine, for example, talking to one of your professors at the intimate distance? What would your most intimate friend say if you maintained the social distance for an entire evening? Try talking to people you interact with daily at a public distance. To be aware of how we and other people use space will improve our communication.

How close you sit or stand to someone may depend on numerous factors. The distance is likely to be dependent both on social norms and the idiosyncratic (unique) patterns of those interacting.[11] You are likely to stand closer to a member of the opposite sex than to one of the same sex.[12] There may be distance shifts during an encounter, too, because of important segments that occur: topic changes or beginnings and endings.[13] How pleasant, neutral, or unpleasant the topic being discussed is to the participants may also affect distance.[14] When a topic is pleasant,

Do some self-analysis with respect to the distances you select when you speak to other people. In your next encounter, for example, check the factors that affect the distance you choose:

_____ age
_____ sex
_____ cultural background
_____ ethnic background
_____ topic (or subject matter)
_____ setting
_____ physical characteristics
_____ attitude
_____ emotional orientation
_____ interpersonal relationship (friend, acquaintance, or stranger)
_____ personality characteristics (yours, others')

people stand or sit closer together. Also, one research study indicates that close distances may decrease the amount of talking between the partners.[15] There is little doubt that social setting can make a great deal of difference in the spatial relationships too. Just available space alone may be a factor besides light, noise, and temperature. Physical characteristics of the interactants may cause changes in distance just as attitudinal and emotional orientations do. Wouldn't you choose to stand closer to someone you thought was friendly and farther from one you were told was unfriendly? We also perceive closer people as being warmer, more empathic, understanding, and liking one another more.[16] It follows, then, that we interact more closely with friends than with acquaintances, and more closely with acquaintances than with strangers.[17] Closer distances are perceived, too, when people have a high self-concept, high affiliative needs (needs to associate with others), are low on authoritarianism, and are self-directed.[18]

Visual Cues

Greater visibility increases our potential for communicating because the more we see and the more we can be seen, the more information we can send and receive. Mehrabian found that the more we direct our face toward the person we're talking to, the more we convey a positive feeling to this person.[19] Another researcher has confirmed something most of us discovered long ago, that looking directly at a person, smiling, and leaning toward him or her conveys a feeling of warmth.[20]

Consider This

1. The person with a smiling countenance is always happy.

2. Some people smile when raging mad.

3. You should be wary of the "oblong smile" because it's as phony as a $3 bill.

4. There is one type of facial expression, which psychologists include in the smile category, that is universally employed to express the opposite of warmth and cordiality.

5. When a woman smiles at someone, she'll probably get more response than a man.

6. Smiles come in all shapes and sizes, but none mean what they seem to mean unless the eyes cooperate.

1. <u>False</u>. Many people who smile a lot are tense, fearful and unhappy. As psychologists Paul Ekman and Wallace V. Friesen observe in their study, <u>Unmasking the Face</u>, "smiles, which are part of the happiness facial expression, often occur when a person is <u>not</u> happy. You smile to mask other emotions or to qualify them. And smiles may indicate submission to anything unpleasant—a submissive response to ward off or call a halt to another's attack, for instance. Smiles also may be used to make a tense situation more comfortable because it is hard to resist returning a smile."

2. <u>True</u>. As pointed out in the above study, angry as the person is, the smile "informs the other person that he—the angry person—is still in control. . . . He is facially saying that he won't go too far, that his attack will be limited or suppressed." It's noted, however, that if the smile is blended with anger, rather than qualifying it, the person is saying that he enjoys being angry.

3. <u>True</u>. Psychological studies at the University of London classify the "oblong smile" as one of our

When we look at someone, we get a total impression; we are reading numerous cues at the same time. Often the combination of cues provides the information, not a single cue by itself. As you think about the following types of visual cues, remember that although we may discuss them separately, we send and receive all kinds of cues at the same time.

Facial expression.   The face is probably the most expressive part of the human body. It can reveal complex and often confusing kinds of information. It commands attention because it is visible and omnipresent. It can move from signs of ecstasy to signs of despair within a matter of seconds. Research results suggest that there are ten basic classes of meaning that can be communicated facially: happiness, surprise, fear, anger, sadness, disgust, contempt, interest, bewilderment, and determination.[21] Research has also shown that the face may communicate information other than the emotional state of the person—it may reveal phoniest facial expressions. It is produced by parting the lips from both upper and lower teeth and stretching the smile across the face, without curving the lips upward at the corners. This is the kind of smile in which the person pretends to enjoy something he does not.

4. True. Cited in a University of London study is the sneer—errant stepchild of the smile—in which the "center of the upper lip is drawn up to expose the teeth. Quite often this action is one-sided, with only one-half of the lip being drawn up." The expression signifies both contempt and derision.

5. True. Studies at Purdue University indicate that women, at least, tend to be more responsive when a woman smiles at them than when a man does. Why does a female get more mileage out of a smile? For one thing, when she is the recipient of a man's smile, her reaction is often inhibited because of uncertainty about the meaning of his smile. And it goes without saying that when a woman smiles at a man, it's likely to evoke a more interested response than when another man smiles at him.

6. True. Studies of communication via facial expression at the University of Illinois have demonstrated that the most foolproof way to tell the difference between a sincere smile and a counterfeit one is to check the eyes. When a smile communicates genuine warmth, it is usually enhanced by slight changes around the outer corners of the eyes. It's also observed that "even the broad smile, perhaps the most engaging of all (the mouth is slightly open, lips curled back, with both upper and lower teeth visible), is not always a convincing expression of surprise or pleasure unless accompanied by an elevation of the eyebrows." Other emotional impressions conveyed by a smile are also dependent upon a delicate use of the eye area. In short, a spurious smile is easy to detect if you know what to look for.

—John E. Gibson, *Family Weekly*, September 25, 1977

the thought processes as well.[22] In addition, it has been shown that we are capable of facially conveying multiple emotions at the same time, not just a single emotional state.[23]

The face can communicate more emotional meanings more accurately than any other factor in our interpersonal communication. Dale G. Leathers has determined that the face:

1. Communicates *evaluative* judgments through pleasant and unpleasant expressions;
2. Reveals level of *interest* or lack of interest in others and in the environment;
3. Can exhibit level of *intensity* and thus show how involved we are in a situation;
4. Communicates the amount of *control* we have over our own expressions; and
5. Shows whether we *understand* something or not.[24]

The face is crucial in revealing emotion. This man's hearty smile clearly conveys his happiness.

Because faces are so visible and so sensitive, we pay more attention to people's faces than to any other nonverbal feature. The face is an efficient and high-speed means of conveying meaning. Gestures, posture, and larger bodily movements require some time to change in response to a changing stimulus, whereas facial expressions can change instantly, sometimes even at a rate imperceptible to the human eye. As an instantaneous response mechanism, it is *the* most effective way to provide feedback to an ongoing message. What better way do we have, for example, to stop a confusing, digressive, or irrelevant message than by a negative facial response? We can usually change what someone is about to say by squinting in a certain way or raising an eyebrow or tightening our lips noticeably. Such feedback is immediate and very influential.

People seem to judge facial expressions along these dimensions: pleasant/unpleasant, active/passive, and intense/controlled. It has also been shown that no single area of the face is best for revealing emotions. For any particular emotion, certain areas of the face, however, may carry important information. For example, the nose-cheek-mouth area is crucial for conveying disgust, the eyes and eyelids for fear, the brow-forehead and eyes-eyelids for sadness, and the cheeks-mouth and brows-forehead for happiness. Surprise, it has been shown, can be seen in any of these areas.[25] The research has also confirmed that judgments of emotion from facial behavior are accurate.[26]

But, often, more than just facial expressions must be seen or known to make judgments of emotions. Some of these factors include the prior expectations of the person doing the observing. We often see what we want to see. Also, our familiarity with a person and prior exposure to his or her face will make a difference in the accuracy of our judgment. When we have seen someone express other emotions, we will identify more precisely an emotion we have not seen before. Information about the context may also affect our judgments. How long we have to see the face and how clearly we can see it also may make a difference in our perceptions.[27]

Eye contact.   A great deal can be conveyed through the eyes. If we seek feedback from another person, we usually maintain strong eye contact. We can open and close communication channels with our eyes as well. Think of a conversation involving more than two people. When we are interested in a certain person's opinion, we will look him or her in the eye, opening the channel for communication. If we are having difficulty finding the right words to say, we may break eye-contact. We not only signal our degree of involvement or arousal through eye contact, but we use eye contact to check on how other people are responding. Have they completed a thought unit? Are they attentive? What are their reactions?

Eye contact may be hard to maintain if we are too close to someone. We can use our eyes to create anxiety in another person. Eye contact also can show whether we feel rewarded by what we see, whether we are in competition with another person, and whether we have something to hide. Our eye contact habits may differ depending on the sex and status of the person we're talking to. If we are extroverted, in addition, our eye behavior is likely to be different than if we are introverted.[28]

Of all facial cues, eye contact is perhaps the single most important one. The fact that our culture has imposed so many rules regarding its use shows its significance. Think about your own patterns of eye contact. What rules do you follow? Until a certain age, children are rarely uncomfortable staring or being stared at. How long can you maintain eye contact with someone before it starts to feel awkward to you? It has been observed that as two people who do not wish to speak to each

Try This _____

In your next conversations with others, keep track of your eye contact. Which of the following motives for eye contact are you most aware of using? Does it depend on the other person? Does it depend on what you are talking about? Does it depend on the context? What other factors about the communication situation affect the kind of eye contact you use?

— monitoring the feedback

— regulating the flow of the communication

— expressing your emotions

— communicating the nature of the interpersonal relationship

Do you usually combine these as you talk? Are they ever used independently of each other?

other approach, they will cast their eyes downward when they are about 8 feet apart, so they don't have to look at each other as they pass. Goffman calls this "dimming your lights."[29] Eye contact can have a major impact on both the quality and quantity of interpersonal communication.[30]

Eye contact often indicates the nature of a relationship between two people. One research study showed that eye contact is moderate when talking to a very high-status person, maximized with a moderately high-status person, and only minimal when talking with a low-status person.[31] There are also predictable differences in eye contact when one person likes another or when there may be rewards involved.

There is likely to be more eye contact when we look at things that are rewarding to us. For example, you are likely to look more at a person with whom you have had a friendly conversation than a person who has made unfavorable comments to you.[32] Also, when you make a comment to someone else, it will be received more favorably if accompanied by more eye contact.[33]

Increased eye contact is also associated with increased liking between the people communicating. In an interview, for example, you are likely to make judgments about the interviewer's friendliness according to the amount of eye contact shown. The less eye contact, the less friendliness.[34] In a courtship relationship, more eye contact can be observed among those seeking to develop a more-intimate relationship.[35] One research study suggests that intimacy is a function of amount of eye gazing, physical proximity, intimacy of topic, and amount of smiling.[36] This model best relates to established relationships. It could also include body orientation, forms of address, tone of voice, facial expression, or other factors.[37] All the factors interact; a change in one causes changes in the others. One writer on nonverbal communication has summarized the factors that affect the amount of eye contact as follows:

1. Distance between the communicators;
2. Physical characteristics of the communicators;
3. Personal and personality characteristics of the communicators;
4. Topics and tasks of the involved parties; and
5. The cultural background of the participants.[38]

The body.   The body reinforces facial communication. But gestures, postures, and other body movements can also communicate attitudes. They can reveal differences in status, and they can also indicate the presence of deception. With respect to attitudes, as noted previously, body movements also reveal feelings of liking between people.[39]

A person who wants to be perceived as warm, according to other investigators, should shift his or her posture toward the other person, smile, maintain direct eye contact, and keep the hands still. People who are cold tend to look around a room, slump, drum their fingers, and, generally, they do not smile.

When a male or female in our society engages in courtship, he or she reveals this attitude, according to one researcher, through a

---

Consider This

Propriety of movement and general demeanor in company.—To look steadily at any one, especially if you are a lady and are speaking to a gentleman; to turn the head frequently on one side and the other during conversation; to balance yourself upon your chair; to bend forward; to strike your hands upon your knees; to hold one of your knees between your hands locked together; to cross your legs; to extend your feet on the andirons; to admire yourself with complacency in a glass; to adjust, in an affected manner, your cravat, hair, dress, or handkerchief; to remain without gloves; to fold carefully your shawl, instead of throwing it with graceful negligence upon a table; to fret about a hat which you have just left off; to laugh immoderately; to place your hand upon the person with whom you are conversing; to take him by the buttons, the collar of his cloak, the cuffs, the waist, etc.; to seize any person by the waist or arm, or to touch their person; to roll the eyes or to raise them with affectation; to take snuff from the box of your neighbor, or to offer it to strangers, especially to ladies; to play continually with your chain or fan; to beat time with the feet and hands; to whirl round a chair with your hand; to shake with your feet the chair of your neighbor; to rub your face or your hands; wink your eyes; shrug up your shoulders; stamp with your feet, &c;—all these bad habits, of which we cannot speak to people, are in the highest degree displeasing.

—Emily Thornwell, *The Lady's Guide to Complete Etiquette* (1884)

category of behaviors. The first stage is *courtship readiness*. This stage is
characterized by high muscle tone, reduced eye bagginess and jowl sag,
lessening of slouch and shoulder hunching, and decreasing belly sag.
The second stage is *preening behavior*. At this stage males and females
will stroke their hair, rearrange makeup, glance in the mirror, rearrange
clothes, leave buttons open, adjust suit coats, tug at socks, and readjust
knots. The third stage involves *positional cues* such as sitting in such a
way that third parties cannot enter the conversation, or moving arms,
legs, or torsos to inhibit others from interfering. The final stage, labeled
actions of appeal, includes flirtatious glancing, gaze holding, rolling the
pelvis, crossing the legs to expose a thigh, exhibiting the wrist or palm,
protruding the breasts, and other such cues.[40]

Body movement differences can also reflect status differences between people. Mark Knapp, a researcher and writer on nonverbal communication, summarized Albert Mehrabian's findings on nonverbal
indicators of status and power as follows:

> *"... high-status persons are associated with less eye gaze,
> postural relaxation, greater voice loudness, more frequent use of
> arms-akimbo [hands on hips], dress ornamentation with power sym-
> bols, greater territorial access, more expansive movements and
> postures, and greater height; and more distance.*[41]

These characteristics are in contrast to the low-status person's behavior.
Lower-status people communicating with higher-status people tend to
be more formal, rigid, and less adaptable.[42]

Deception has been associated with a variety of nonverbal body
behaviors. Research on lying indicates that liars will have:

1. Higher voice pitch,
2. Less-enthusiastic gestures,
3. Slower speaking rate,
4. Less immediacy (closeness) to others in body position,
5. Less eye contact,
6. More uncertainty in gestures,
7. More speech errors, and
8. Less nodding.[43]

Those cues that cause another person to notice or to become aware of
deception are called leakage clues. Leakage clues might be smiles that
are drawn out too long or frowns that are too severe—when they are
associated with the face. But other such clues are numerous and include gestures as well as body movement:

1. Hands digging into cheek,
2. Tearing at fingernails,
3. Aggressive foot kicks,
4. Soothing leg squeezing,
5. Abortive, restless movements,
6. Tenseness in leg positions,
7. Flirtatious leg displays,
8. Frequent shift of leg positions, and
9. Restless or repetitive leg and foot acts.[44]

Body movement is the heart of human nonverbal communication. We use it as:

1. an emblem (possessing a specific verbal translation), to
   a. give directions and commands
   b. indicate our physical state.
   c. provide replies
   d. reveal our feelings

2. an illustrator (linked to spoken discourse), to
   a. reveal the quality of an ongoing relationship through
      1. listening behavior
      2. rapport
      3. the degree of intimate interpersonal knowledge
   b. reinforce ideas that are
      1. difficult to conceptualize
      2. particularly exciting
      3. very important
   c. indicate the end of rhythmical units or as junctures between ideas, sentences, or parts of sentences

3. a regulator (used to maintain and regulate speaking and listening), to
   a. signal the beginning of interaction
   b. reveal the nature of a relationship
   c. help structure dialogue
   d. signal turn-taking within a dialogue
      1. yielding a turn
      2. maintaining a turn
      3. requesting a turn
      4. denying a turn
   e. signal leave-taking[45]

Clothes provide us with information about people. Which of these men is the college student and which is the businessman is easily determined by their dress.

Personal appearance.   Even if we believe the cliché that beauty is only skin deep, we must recognize that not only does our personal appearance have a profound effect on our self-image, but it also affects our behavior and the behavior of people around us. Our physical appearance provides a basis for first and sometimes long-lasting impressions. It also affects whom we talk to, date, or marry, how socially and sexually successful we will be, and even our potential for vocational success. It is unfair, but true.

The billion-dollar cosmetics industry provides testimony to the fact that people care about physical appearance and firmly believe it makes a difference. We apply all kinds of creams, lotions, and colorings to our skin. We may adorn our bodies in various ways with glasses, tinted contact lenses, ribbons, beards, hair ornaments, jewelry, and clothes. Body adornments are a big part of what Ruesch called object language.

Clothing is another communication medium over which we exert special control. Researchers have determined that our clothes provide three different kinds of information about us:[46]

1. Clothes reveal something about the *emotions* we are experiencing. This works both ways: how we feel affects what we wear and what we wear affects how we feel. We'll put on our most comfortable clothes in the morning if comfort is going to be our most important consideration that day. If we're going to speak as a student representative at a meeting of the board of regents of our college, chances are we'll choose our clothes less for comfort and more for the feeling we hope to convey at the meeting—confidence or maturity or whatever. In these cases we are dressing both for how we feel and how we intend to feel later on. We've all had the experience of feeling inappropriately dressed, either too formally or too informally, on some occasions, and we know how our clothes affect how we feel about those occasions.

2. Our clothes may disclose something about our *behavior*. If you have ever worn a uniform of any kind, you know how clothes can transform you and make you act differently than if you were not wearing those particular clothes. If we get dressed up for a job interview, we feel important; in our own mind our actions also take on importance. Because it occurs in our mind, it will also very likely affect how we actually behave. We will be more calculated, purposeful, and dynamic. We may stand rigid rather than slouched. We may tend to lower our voice, slow our rate of speaking, and use fewer nonfluencies ("uh's" and "um's"). Just as dress affects us, we are also likely to judge other people's behavior by the way *they* dress. What expectations do you have for a person dressed as a police officer, judge, nurse, or priest?

3. Our clothes function to *differentiate* us from other people. Twenty-year-old college students wear different clothes than twenty-year-olds with jobs in the business world. Clothing also differs between age groups. A single man, for example, of 20–25 spends twice as much on clothes as a man of 45–50 and three times as much as a man of

Consider This

You've got to make posture and gesture work for you. The "thoughtful" attitude, for example, is going to take more than a thoughtful <u>face</u> to get anywhere. You can't have a thoughtful expression on your face, for example, and sit just any old way. Use the way you sit to help get your message across. Here are some specific suggestions:

1. The <u>thoughtful</u> pose: Legs crossed and tucked under desk or just to the side of desk. Chin resting on one hand. It's <u>this</u> that makes you look studious. And also props your face up. Gives your face a nice line. Don't put your head sideways and put your cheek on your hand, though. (You can vary these positions, but always ask yourself what the effect would be. Here, it would be poor. Cheek on hand would distort your profile and really hide your face.) Now, bend slightly forward over your desk . . . to show you're intent on what's going on.

2. The <u>casual</u> look: Legs crossed or toe of one foot behind heel of the other foot. One hand in lap. Torso bent slightly back, but not so your back has an unnatural arch. The idea of this posture is to look completely natural, completely relaxed. As relaxed as though you were on a beach. You're facing the front of the room, but this is the only clue that you're absorbed in the lecture. The rest of you gives the idea that you can turn in a split second if anything else is worth your attention.

3. <u>Sexy</u>: Sit almost sideways in your chair. Legs crossed. One elbow on back of your chair. See what this does to the line of your body? Interesting. Careful, though, or you'll be too obvious. Don't for example stick your feet <u>way</u> out in the aisle or thrust your chest out too far. Elbow on back of chair will usually give you just the right line. One more thing. You're sitting slantwise. So be sure your face is to the front of the room ninety-five percent of the time. If you're not careful about this, the teacher could get the idea you're not paying attention. And then you're on risky ground.

—Ellen Peck, *How to Get a Teen-Age Boy and What to Do with Him When You Get Him*

65–70.[47] Clothing may also be used by people to raise themselves from a subordinate position, to raise self-esteem and apparent status.[48] Clothes serve to differentiate, too, between people who wish to be perceived as fashionable and those who don't care about fashion, between the formal and the informal, and between people with different social roles.

Personal appearance also relates to our body type. That is, our particular body configuration (fat, thin, or athletic) affects the way we are perceived and responded to by others, and even what they expect of us. In research studies, body types have been labeled endomorph (fat), ectomorph (thin), and mesomorph (athletic). People shown silhouette drawings of such body types in males were asked to respond on a variety of scales. Knapp summarizes the findings of these tests:

> *Their results show that (1) the endomorph was rated as fatter, older, shorter (silhouettes were the same height), more old-fashioned, less strong physically, less good-looking, more talkative, more warm-hearted and sympathetic, more good-natured and agreeable, more dependent on others, and more trusting of others; (2) the meso-morph was rated as stronger, more masculine, better looking, more adventurous, younger, taller, more mature in behavior, and more self-reliant; (3) the ectomorph was rated thinner, younger, more am-bitious, taller, more suspicious of others, more tense and nervous, less masculine, more stubborn and inclined to be difficult, more pessimistic, and quieter.*[49]

Although space does not allow a complete presentation of research findings in all areas of personal appearance, it should be noted that some of the other cues that may affect interpersonal responses are

Consider This

The darker the suit, the more authority it transmits. A black suit is more authoritative than a dark blue, although it is much too powerful for most men and should be rarely worn anyway because of its funeral overtones. The most authoritative pattern is the pinstripe, followed in descending order by the solid, the chalk stripe and the plaid. If you need to be more authoritative, stick with dark pinstripes. But if you are a very large man or if you already have a great sense of presence or if you have a gruff or swarthy appearance, it is best to trim down your authority so that people will not be frightened by you. This can be accomplished by wearing lighter shades of blue and grey and beiges.

Suits that will give you the most credibility with people of the upper-middle class are dark blue and dark gray solids and pinstripes of both colors. But note: Only the dark blue solid will give you high credibility with the lower-middle class.

If you must be authoritative and credible with both the upper-middle class and the lower-middle class at the same time—say you are a banker or a lawyer and must deal daily with a wide variety of people—light blue and light gray solids accomplish this, although the light blue is generally not considered an acceptable suit for the truly conservative businessman.

The suits in which men are more likely to be liked are again light gray and light blue solids and medium-range business plaids. Bright plaids sometimes turn off the upper-middle class.

—John T. Molloy, *Dress for Success*

Consider This

TRUE OR FALSE?

1. Even when a person is unknown and unseen—except for a thumbnail size photograph—appearance makes all the difference in the world in how people react in terms of helpfulness and consideration.

2. Regardless of whether a girl is plain, moderately attractive or outstandingly good-looking, how she fares in life so far as treatment by others (particularly males) is concerned—is directly affected by how well-turned out she is in terms of grooming.

3. You can be good-looking without being attractive, and you can be attractive without being good-looking.

4. While there are obvious advantages accruing to the exceptionally handsome man or the beautiful woman, there are also very definite drawbacks and hazards which would make the person of plain or average looks hesitate a long time before trading his 'look' for theirs.

ANSWERS

1. <u>True</u>. An interesting study of the effects of physical attractiveness by a team of behavioral scientists from Penn State U., Eastern Michigan U. and Earlham College (Indiana) reported this experiment: it was arranged that 600 male and female adult callers in public phone booths found a completed graduate-school application form, a photograph of the applicant and an addressed, stamped envelope. Findings: the more attractive the person in the photo, the more likely it was to be sealed, dropped in a mailbox and sped on its way.

2. <u>True</u>. Studies at Texas A. & M. University showed the important role that looking one's best plays in determining the help, consideration and cooperation received from others. For example, in one experiment a girl, appearing first attractively groomed and then indifferently so, asked 40 passersby to mail a letter for her. Results: 95 percent of the subjects mailed the letter for the girl when she was attractively turned out, and only 45 percent obliged when she was <u>not</u> looking her attractive best.

3. <u>True</u>. Findings of studies at the University of Chicago on the dynamics of interpersonal attraction show that with the emotionally mature adult, "attractiveness becomes increasingly a dimension of the personality rather than the body" but is a projection of what we really are, the essence of our thoughts, feelings and emotions. On the other hand, it is pointed out that some people who are well endowed with beauty that is superficial often engage in behavior which makes them less attractive to others than people of just average looks.

4. <u>True</u>. It is concluded in a Virginia Polytechnic Institute and State University study on this subject that "the individual who feels that in order to belong he must be beautiful or physically excellent leads a hazardous existence. Such a person, even if well endowed, wishes that he were more so. Even while he is enjoying what he has, ever present are the anxiety and fear of knowing that as the days and years pass he will no longer be so attractive or physically well equipped." . . . [There] is a great deal of loneliness, depression and feelings of being unloved lying beneath the glamorous surface of these Beautiful People who are invariably envied and admired by so many.

—John E. Gibson, *Family Weekly*, December 3, 1978

height, body color, body smell, body hair, and other body-related cues (freckles, moles, acne, and beauty marks). Even our own perception of our personal appearance—our self-image—will affect our interpersonal communication. It is the basic kernel from which our communication behavior grows and flourishes.

Vocal Cues

Vocal cues are all those attributes of sound that can convey meaning. Sounds (not words) are considered nonverbal communication. This includes how loudly or quickly we speak, how much we hesitate, how many nonfluencies we use. These vocal cues can convey our emotional state.

As we well know, all we have to do to reveal anger is change the *ways* we talk: we might talk louder, faster, and more articulately than usual. We may use our silences more pointedly. We can say exactly the same thing in a fit of anger as in a state of delight and change our meaning by how we say it. We can say "I hate you" to sound angry, teasing, or cruel. Vocal cues are what is lost when our words are written down. The word often used to refer to this quality—what occurs beyond or in addition to the words we speak—is *paralanguage*.[50]

If you don't think paralanguage is very important, think of the impression made in a job interview by an applicant who pronounces words wrong or speaks too loudly or too fast or with too many hesitations. Such a person might find it hard to get employment in some prestigious business firms or to penetrate the upper strata of society in some circles. Although a person's social or business acceptance will probably never depend *only* on vocal cues, there are times when it helps to have correct pronunciation and articulation as part of our credentials.

Research has shown that our vocal cues may accurately reveal the following emotions: contempt, indifference, grief, anger, anxiety, sadness, and happiness. How accurately these emotions are identified depends on the listener. Obviously, what a listener perceives can affect how he or she views our personality. Because we gain insights into our own personality through the feedback of others, listeners' views affect us directly.

It has been observed that if we use great variety in pitch (high or low), we are likely to be perceived as dynamic and extroverted. Males who vary their speaking rate are viewed as extroverted and animated. Interestingly, females demonstrating the same variety in rate are perceived as extroverted, but also high-strung, inartistic, and uncooperative. If our voice is flat, we may be thought of as sluggish, cold,

Consider This

Prospects Slim for Fat Workers, by Joyce Lain Kennedy

Dear Joyce: My son, 28, is having difficulty changing jobs although he has excellent experience. Is it possible his trouble stems from the fact he's overweight? — T.M., Costa Mesa, Calif.

Recent studies strongly suggest fat people are in bad shape in the job market.

Their troubles are indeed largely due to stereotyping, a pattern of traits we lay on other people, often wrongly based on visible characteristics such as race, sex or uniform — the jiving black, the dependent woman, the drunken sailor.

In examining the work-related overweight stereotype, researchers Judith Candib Larkin and Harvey A. Pines ran two hiring simulation studies using middle-class college students. The results, atop earlier studies by others, support the widely-held hunch that the applicant's weight significantly influences the decision to hire.

Drs. Larkin and Pines, both of whom are psychology professors at Canisius College in Buffalo, N.Y., found role-playing hiring overweight models performed identically on work tests as did average-weight "applicants." Specifically, the obese were seen as less competent, less productive, not industrious, inactive, disorganized, indecisive and generally less successful.

Citing earlier studies, Drs. Larkin and Pines note increasing evidence that hiring decisions are not made objectively, but heavily influenced by whether the applicant is in some sense the "kind of person" desired for the job, or fits some preconceived notion — such as that raised by political commentators who speculate on whether the public will be swayed by the fact that a candidate "looks like" a judge or governor. In brief, employers hiring for managerial, professional or technical posts tend to choose applicants who look like themselves.

External pressures come into play too. Consciously or unconsciously, supervisors may fret over whether a fat worker could give outsiders or top management the impression that their departments are loose, sloppy or slovenly.

Baby boom demographics and social trends almost guarantee a glut of middle-managers in the '80s, which means that competition for the best jobs is likely to be the most explosive of any decade thus far this century.

So fair or unfair — unless government intervention makes the obese a protected class along with others in equal opportunity programs — their average-weight competitors are likely to outdistance fat workers in the race for jobs and promotions.

When employers say they want a "heavy weight" for a job, they speak only figuratively.

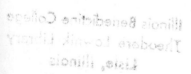

and withdrawn. A person with a nasal voice is often perceived as unattractive, lethargic, and foolish.[51] Whether these perceptions are accurate or not, it's useful for us to know how we are likely to be perceived if we speak a certain way.

Certain vocal characteristics are perceived as revealing interpersonal trust, confidence, and sincerity: when trust or confidence is in jeopardy, excessive pauses and hesitations tend to increase. Also, the number of nonfluencies we use — stuttering, repetitions, slips of the tongue, incoherences — increases in situations where we are nervous or ill at ease.

It should be clear that vocal cues do not just refer to *how* something is said. Frequently they *are* what is being said. Vocal cues, then, can reflect:

1. Attitudes. They can reveal, for example, how much people like each other, or their relationship: superiority or inferiority.
2. Emotions. They can reveal joy as well as sorrow, and many of the range of emotions between these extremes.
3. Control. They can be used to regulate and manage conversations. How something is said can indicate whether the person wants to continue talking or whether he or she will yield to another person. They can be used to coordinate the give-and-take, or ebb-and-flow, of conversations.
4. Personality traits, background, or physical features. Breathiness in males reflects a younger, more artistic person whereas tenseness in a male voice reflects an older, more unyielding, cantankerous person. Breathiness in a female is more feminine, pretty, petite, and effervescent. Tenseness in a female reveals a younger, more emotional, high-strung, less-intelligent person. Increased rate of speaking in both males and females, however, reveals a more animated and extroverted person.[52]

There are also vocal stereotypes that relate vocal characteristics with one's occupation, sociability, race, degree of introversion, and body type, among others.

Although different times, situations, and causes may result in different ways of expressing emotion, it is true that people use vocal cues to judge emotions and feelings. Our total reaction to others may be colored by our reaction to their vocal cues.

READING NONVERBAL MESSAGES

One purpose of learning about nonverbal communication is to increase our understanding of our own actions and reduce the chances of someone misinterpreting us. It's easy to accidentally convey an attitude that may be misleading, inappropriate, or damaging to an interpersonal encounter.

According to Albert Mehrabian there are "only three primary feeling dimensions that are involved in nonverbal behavior": *immediacy or liking, dominance or power,* and *change or responsiveness.*[53] This means of classifying nonverbal communication can be useful both in understanding our own and others' nonverbal behavior. In the following

Try This

Read the following sentence aloud seven times, each time emphasizing a different word in the sentence.

I hit him in the eye yesterday.

Notice how the meaning changes as you change your emphasis. You can get seven more variations by reading the sentence as a question instead of a statement.

Next time you get a telephone call, use this opportunity to make some judgments about the vocal communication that you hear. Which of the following vocal cues did you perceive?

_____	breathiness	_____	throatiness
_____	thinness	_____	orotundity
_____	flatness	_____	increased rate
_____	nasality	_____	increased pitch variety*
_____	tenseness		

Now, having rated the caller on vocal quality, determine which of the following feelings were being conveyed:

_____	affection	_____	impatience
_____	anger	_____	joy
_____	boredom	_____	sadness
_____	cheerfulness	_____	satisfaction**

Was there any relationship between vocal quality and feeling being expressed? Could you find reasons or justifications for what you heard? That is, did your perceptions correspond with your expectations in this situation?

*For descriptions of these cues, see P. Heinberg, *Voice Training for Speaking and Reading Aloud* (New York: Ronald Press, 1964), pp. 152–81.

**For a list of the vocal expressions (loudness, pitch, timbre, rate, inflection, rhythm, and enunciation) connected with these feelings, see Mark L. Knapp, *Essentials of Nonverbal Communication* (New York: Holt, Rinehart and Winston, 1980), p. 217.

discussion, nonverbal behavior is categorized by emotional intent. That is, to understand nonverbal communication, we must consider the emotions from which certain behaviors spring.

Immediacy or liking.   Mehrabian suggested that one of the main determinants in what our nonverbal behavior will be is our tendency to get involved with things we like and to avoid things we don't like. Touching, eye contact, and physical closeness characterize a feeling of immediacy with someone or something; distance, lack of eye contact, and absence of physical contact characterize dislike.

Dominance or power.   According to Mehrabian, another factor that determines our nonverbal communications is our feeling of power or subordination in relation to a particular person or situation. If we feel dominant, we are likely to make large, expansive gestures, stand tall, and move in a relaxed way; we demonstrate submissiveness by avoiding eye contact, maintaining a rigid, erect posture, and making small, tense movements.

Change or responsiveness. A third factor Mehrabian identified as crucial to our nonverbal expressions is our responsiveness to our environment. We respond either positively or negatively to all the stimuli we encounter—the weather, the food we eat, the people we run into, circumstances, events, etc. In every waking moment we are reacting to our environment in some way, and our nonverbal behavior will reflect these reactions.

There Are Limits

In reading the nonverbal cues that others send, we are automatically limited: our eyes can handle about five million bits of information per second but our brain can process only about 500 bits per second.[54] We must be selective. We are also limited by what we decide to look at, and what we can understand. If we can attach no meaning to cues we observe, we are obviously limited in those areas.

Our success in reading nonverbal messages depends on several factors. First, how interested are we in doing it? The more value we ascribe to developing and using our nonverbal skills, the more likely we are to study and improve. Second, what is our attitude toward communication situations as learning environments? If our attitude is, "I want to learn; this looks like fun," it is likely we will find the learning process productive and worthwhile. Third, are we willing to enlarge the scope of our nonverbal knowledge? To develop a skill requires basic understandings; to perfect that skill we must use and expand it by careful observation and conscientious study. Finally, are we actively seeking out opportunities to practice? There is no substitute for experience. The greater the variety, the better chance for improvement, growth, and change.[55]

MISS PEACH

IMPROVING SKILLS IN NONVERBAL COMMUNICATION

As we try to improve our nonverbal communication skills there are three important ideas to keep in mind:

1. Nonverbal communication always occurs in a context. The meanings conveyed are intimately and directly tied to that context. If a man at a party stands with his hips thrust forward slightly, his legs apart, his thumbs locked in his belt, and his fingers pointing down toward his genitals, it may be considered a sexually provocative pose in that context.[56] If he stands the same way as he waits in line for a hamburger with his family, his pose may not carry the same message.

2. No nonverbal cue should be viewed in isolation. Cues must be observed as they interact with each other. In the instance just cited, it was not the man's posture alone that was suggestive, but that cue in combination with the position of his legs, thumbs, and fingers. Cues must be viewed in combination.

3. Although we can learn a great deal from observing nonverbal communication, our conclusions should always be tentative rather than final. Every individual is unique. There is always the possibility of actions occurring that are exceptions to any rule. We should view each behavior as existing at this time only, not assuming it exists permanently or always.

Some people have mannerisms that are habitual and are not meant to convey any special meaning. We must be careful not to read too much into the behavior of people we don't know well and can only guess about. A person's eye may twitch when he or she is nervous; the twitch could be interpreted by a stranger as an enticing wink. We don't have to refrain from making *any* observations, but it is good to be cautious. Remember, whatever meaning we assign to what we see is a meaning that exists *for us*. Meaning is not in the nonverbal cues we observe; meaning is *in us* and because it is in us, it will differ from the meaning other people assign.

Work on your self-awareness. The more we are able to express our selves clearly and accurately and the more in touch we are with our own feelings, the more likely we are to understand the nonverbal communication of others.[57] Our knowledge of our selves can be increased through self-disclosure and feedback. To open up, share, and request feedback from people we trust increases personal sensitivity. Opening channels for healthy, honest, open feedback can be of mutual benefit for us and for our friends. Our effectiveness in receiving nonverbal cues will be increased through self-awareness.

Monitor your own behavior.   It's helpful to review our own communication experiences, whether positive or negative, to become aware of what we are doing. If we discover something we think might be important, we could solicit the help of friends to verify or deny our observations. We should think more about what we do. It is not easy to see our selves as others see us, but difficult or not, it is useful and worthwhile. It would be ideal if we could watch a videotape of our interactions with others over a period of twenty-four hours or so. Since this is not likely to come about, what we *can* do is enlist the cooperation of close friends to help us look for nonverbal cues that cause a disruptive function as we communicate.

Experiment with your behaviors.   There are two reasons for trying out different behavior: to improve communication and to break some of our routine, habitual ways of interacting. When we discover we have certain ineffective or distracting mannerisms, we should try to alter them in a meaningful way to increase our interpersonal effectiveness. If we force our selves to try new approaches, we'll increase the number of alternatives we have for behaving. We can "try on" new behaviors to see how they fit. This is part of the process of growing, changing, and becoming. If we find it very hard to break away from our usual routine, we can at least try to observe how other people handle themselves in similar circumstances. Such observations can give us a framework for monitoring our own behavior in the future.

Respond empathically.   Our nonverbal sensitivity will increase as we train our selves to be empathic. Try to understand how the other person feels. Try to get "the big picture." We should always imagine how we would feel if we experienced the same thing. If we are the twentieth applicant for a job to be interviewed on a certain day and we see a tired, expressionless face on the interviewer, we should try to understand how we would feel if we had just been through a day of interviews. Again, this means trying to see where the other person is coming from. It can explain a lot when we're trying to understand what a certain twitch or posture might signify. Our success in reading nonverbal messages will increase if we try to be *empathic*.

Look for patterns.   The behavior we observe in others is usually reflected in their whole body and not just in their face or hands. We can usually recognize trembling hands as a sign of nervousness, but nervousness may be shown in other ways as well. Nervous people may bite their lips, speak too quickly, squirm in their chairs, always be ready to leave, avoid direct eye contact, or play with paper clips while talking.

Too often we draw conclusions from too little evidence. The face and the hands are obvious and easy to observe, but we must also notice posture, bodily movement, dress, and talk, and try to see patterns of behavior as they relate to different social settings.

Check your perceptions. If we feel that someone's nonverbal behavior is influencing our reaction to that person, it may be wise to find out whether we have correctly understood the behavior. Just because people close their eyes does not mean they are not paying attention. Some people close their eyes to concentrate better on the message by blocking out distractions. If we are talking to Jennifer and she keeps looking beyond, we could ask, "Do you care about this?" or "Are you listening to me?" Something may be occurring behind us that we should also see!

Express your feelings. The cultural norm that says people should not openly express their feelings is powerfully restricting. How can we accurately read other people's nonverbal cues if they are always feeling one thing and trying to show something else? All we can do is try to watch for congruency or noncongruency in the total communication. Some people smile constantly—a pleasant expression has become such a habit with them that they cannot clear their faces of pleasantness even when they are feeling frustration or despair. To understand a person's total message we need to put together the whole communication puzzle—including all verbal and nonverbal elements—and notice which pieces fit together and which don't.

Likewise, we must strive for congruency in our own communication. If we concentrate on not hiding what we feel, it will be much easier to make our nonverbal messages congruent with our verbal messages. In fact, if we are being perfectly honest, we shouldn't have to worry about sending consistent signals—they will take care of themselves. We must discover the potential of our body; what messages does it want to send? Many of us tend to be too restrictive, too closed, and too inhibited in bodily expression. It's healthy to open the channels for sending honest messages.

People are often influenced more by our nonverbal messages than by our words. We tend to believe what we see and the tone of what we hear far more than the words we hear, and rightly so. People generally have more control over their verbal messages than over their nonverbal ones. True feelings, as revealed through nonverbal cues, are difficult to disguise. Becoming aware of our nonverbal communication habits will help us become more expressive. It will also increase our sensitivity to others.

In the next chapter we will have an opportunity to increase our sensitivity in still another area. Tuning in to others means being aware of their verbal and nonverbal communication, but also aware of the attitudes from which their words and actions flow.

OTHER READING

Flora Davis, *Inside Intuition* (New York: New American Library, 1973). Davis provides a comprehensive examination of nonverbal communication. This is a good starting point for learning about this important kind of communication.

Barbara Fast, *Getting Close: Daring to Be Really Intimate With Friends and Lovers* (New York: Berkley Publishing Company, 1978). This book is about relationships and how to reveal our feelings, thoughts, and emotions in those relationships. Although it does not focus on nonverbal communication per se, the dependence of relationships on nonverbal factors—including touch—cannot be escaped. Enjoyable reading.

Julius Fast, *Body Language* (New York: Pocket Books, 1970). This is the book that first created widespread popular interest in nonverbal communication. Fast briefly discusses the major areas of the field and gives a rather superficial glimpse of what it is all about. Easy-to-read and full of examples.

Julius Fast and Barbara Fast, *Talking Between the Lines: How We Mean More Than We Say* (New York: The Viking Press, 1979). Paralanguage is the essential focus of this book. The Fasts discuss the variables of breath, pitch, stress, rhythm, tone, inflection, word choice, and emotional overlay. Their discussion and advocacy of the meta-level of communication will help readers to become better communicators.

Erving Goffman, *Interaction Ritual: Essays on Face-to-Face Behavior* (Garden City, N.Y.: Anchor Books, 1967). Goffman presents six papers dealing with the social organization of spoken contacts. The focus is on social ritual. He discusses the kind of image people need to maintain to give and receive civilities, discourtesies, and other interpersonal gestures. An interesting sociological perspective.

Edward T. Hall, *The Hidden Dimension* (New York: Anchor Books, 1969). In this book Hall focuses on people's use of space—that invisible bubble that constitutes personal territory. He demonstrates how the use of space can affect personal and business relations. This is a well-written, entertaining book full of examples and illustrations.

Edward T. Hall, *The Silent Language* (New York: Premier Books, 1959). Behind the mystery, confusion, and disorganization of life, there is order. Hall urges a reexamination of much that passes as ordinary, acceptable behavior.

Mark L. Knapp, *Essentials of Nonverbal Communication* (New York: Holt, Rinehart and Winston, 1980). This brief textbook is comprehensive and well-written, despite its brevity. The research base is thorough. For an extended version, see Knapp's *Nonverbal Communication in Human Interaction*, 2nd ed. (New York: Holt, Rinehart and Winston, 1978).

John T. Molloy, *Dress for Success* (New York: Peter H. Wyden, 1975). This book is meant for men in business. It is a guide for matching clothes, picking designs, colors, and fabrics, and dressing for leisure. In addition, Molloy provides advice on dressing up office space, and dressing successfully for job interviews. Written in a light, easy-to-read style. Also see his *The Woman's Dress for Success Book* (Chicago: Follett Publishing Co., 1977).

Gerard I. Nierenberg and Henry H. Calero, *How to Read a Person Like a Book* (New York: Pocket Books, 1973). An illustrated handbook of types of nonverbal communication. Although it gives insights into the significance of gestures, one must remember that meaning lies in the speaker and in the listener—not in the gestures. This is a good starting point.

Shirley Weitz, *Nonverbal Communication: Readings With Commentary*, 2nd ed. (New York: Oxford University Press, 1979). Biological rhythms in paralanguage and psychopathology, environmental psychology, touch, smell, and sentics are some of the topics touched on in this volume. Designed for a more serious examination of the topic.

Robert L. Whiteside, *Face Language* (New York: Pocket Books, 1975), and Timothy T. Mar, *Face Reading: The Chinese Art of Physiognomy* (New York: New American Library, 1974). Both of these popularized approaches to this area of nonverbal communication suggest that reading faces insures expertise in getting at the true character of other people. Both books are working manuals that provide specific, simple techniques. Students of interpersonal communication can use these techniques to sharpen their perceptual skills.

NOTES

[1]Flora Davis, *Inside Intuition: What We Know About Nonverbal Communication* (New York: The New American Library, Inc., 1973), p. 55. The direct, unwavering stare is also a threat to some animals. See George Schallar, *The Year of the Gorilla* (Chicago: University of Chicago Press, 1964).

[2]Ibid., p. 58.

[3]Erving Goffman, *Behavior in Public Places* (New York: Free Press, 1963), pp. 83–88.

[4]Davis, *Inside Intuition*, p. 61.

[5]As cited in Mark L. Knapp, *Essentials of Nonverbal Communication* (New York: Holt, Rinehart and Winston, 1980), p. 15.

[6]P. Ekman and W. V. Friesen, "Nonverbal Leakage and Clues to Deception," *Psychiatry* 32 (1969), 88–106. Also see P. Ekman and W. V. Friesen, "The Repertoire of Nonverbal Behavior: Categories, Origins, Usage and Coding," *Semiotica* 1 (1969), 49–98.

[7]Albert Mehrabian, *Silent Messages* (Belmont, Calif.: Wadsworth Publishing Co., Inc., 1971), p. 56. See especially Chapter 3, "The Double-Edged Message," pp. 40–56.

[8]Jurgen Ruesch and Weldon Kees, *Nonverbal Communication: Notes on the Visual Perception of Human Relations* (Los Angeles: University of California Press, 1956), p. 1.

9Jurgen Ruesch, "Nonverbal Language and Therapy," in *Communication and Culture*, Alfred G. Smith, ed. (New York: Holt, Rinehart and Winston, 1966), pp. 209–13.

10Edward T. Hall, *The Silent Language* (Greenwich, Conn.: Fawcett Publications, Inc., 1959), pp. 163–64. He expands upon these in his second book, *The Hidden Dimension* (Garden City, N.Y.: Doubleday & Company, Inc., 1966), pp. 114–29.

11J. K. Burgoon and S. B. Jones, "Toward a Theory of Personal Space Expectations and Their Violations," *Human Communication Research* 2 (1976), 131–46.

12F. N. Willis, "Initial Speaking Distance as a Function of the Speaker's Relationship," *Psychonomic Science* 5 (1966), 221–22.

13F. Erickson, "One Function of Proxemic Shifts in Face-to-Face Interaction," in A. Kendon, R. M. Harris, and M. R. Key (eds.), *Organization of Behavior in Face-to-Face Interactions* (Chicago: Aldine, 1975), pp. 175–87.

14W. E. Leipold, "Psychological Distance in a Dyadic Interview," (Ph.D. diss., University of North Dakota, 1963); and K. B. Little, "Cultural Variations in Social Schemata," *Journal of Personality and Social Psychology* 10 (1968), 1–7.

15R. Schulz and J. Barefoot, "Non-verbal Responses and Affiliative Conflict Theory," *British Journal of Social and Clinical Psychology* 13 (1974), 237–43.

16M. Patterson, "Spatial Factors in Social Interaction," *Human Relations* 21 (1968), 351–61.

17Willis, "Initial Speaking Distance . . . ," 221–22.

18For an excellent discussion of the factors that affect spatial distance, see Knapp, *Essentials*, pp. 81–87.

19Albert Mehrabian, "Orientation Behaviors and Nonverbal Attitude Communication," *Journal of Communication* 17 (1967), 324–32.

20Michael Reece and Robert N. Whitman, "Expressive Movements, Warmth, and Verbal Reinforcement," *Journal of Abnormal and Social Psychology* 64 (1962), 250.

21P. Ekman, W. V. Friesen, and P. Ellsworth, *Emotion in the Human Face; Guidelines for Research and an Integration of the Findings* (New York: Pergamon Press, 1972), pp. 57–65. These authors suggest eight categories. Dale G. Leathers adds the last two in *Nonverbal Communication Systems* (Boston: Allyn and Bacon, Inc., 1976), p. 24.

22C. E. Izard, *The Face of Emotion* (New York: Appleton-Century-Crofts, 1971), p. 216.

23P. Ekman and W. V. Friesen, "The Repertoire of Nonverbal Behavior: Categories, Origins, Usage and Coding," *Semiotica* 1 (1969), 75.

24Dale G. Leathers, *Nonverbal Communication Systems* (Boston: Allyn and Bacon, Inc., 1976), p. 34.

25Knapp, *Essentials*, p. 167.

26P. Ekman, W. V. Friesen, and P. Ellsworth, *Emotion in the Human Face: Guidelines for Research and an Integration of Findings* (Elmsford, N.Y.: Pergamon Press, 1972), p. 107.

27Knapp, *Essentials*, pp. 168–77.

28Mark L. Knapp, *Nonverbal Communication*, 2nd ed. (New York: Holt, Rinehart and Winston, 1978), p. 305.

[29] Erving Goffman, *Behavior in Public Places*, p. 84.

[30] See A. Kendon, "Some Functions of Gaze Direction in Social Interaction," *Acta Psychologica* 26 (1967), 46.

[31] G. Hearn, "Leadership and the Spatial Factor in Small Groups," *Journal of Abnormal and Social Psychology* 54 (1957), 269–72. As cited in Knapp, *Essentials*, pp. 188–89.

[32] R. Exline and L. Winters, "Affective Relations and Mutual Glances in Dyads," in S. Tompkins, and C. Izard (eds.), *Affect, Cognition and Personality* (New York: Springer, 1965).

[33] R. Exline and C. Eldridge, "Effects of Two Patterns of a Speaker's Visual Behavior upon the Perception of the Authenticity of His Verbal Message," paper presented to the Eastern Psychological Association, Boston, 1967, as cited in Knapp, *Essentials*, p. 189.

[34] J. M. Wiemann, "An Experimental Study of Visual Attention in Dyads: The Effects of Four Gaze Conditions on Evaluations by Applicants in Employment Interviews," paper presented to the Speech Communication Association, Chicago, 1974.

[35] Z. Rubin, "The Measurement of Romantic Love," *Journal of Personality and Social Psychology* 16 (1970), 265–73.

[36] M. Argyle and J. Dean, "Eye Contact, Distance, and Affiliation," *Sociometry* 28 (1965), 269–304.

[37] Knapp, *Essentials*, p. 190.

[38] Knapp, *Essentials*, pp. 190–91.

[39] A. Mehrabian, *Nonverbal Communication* (Chicago: Aldine, 1972). This source includes a summary of his work. As cited in Knapp, *Essentials*, p. 135.

[40] A. E. Scheflen, "Quasi-Courtship Behavior in Psychotherapy," *Psychiatry* 28 (1965), 245–57. As cited in Knapp, *Essentials*, pp. 136–37.

[41] Knapp, *Essentials*, p. 138.

[42] Knapp, *Essentials*, p. 138.

[43] Knapp, *Essentials*, p. 140.

[44] Knapp, *Essentials*, p. 141.

[45] Knapp, *Essentials*, pp. 125–33.

[46] Mary Kefgen and Phyllis Touchie-Specht, *Individuality in Clothing Selection and Personal Appearance: A Guide for the Consumer* (New York: Macmillan, 1971), pp. 12–14.

[47] F. Zweig, "Clothing Standards and Habits," in *Dress, Adornment and the Social Order*, M. E. Roach and J. B. Eicher, eds. (New York: Wiley, 1965), p. 164.

[48] J. Schwartz, "Men's Clothing and the Negro," *Phylon* 24 (1963), 164.

[49] Knapp, *Essentials*, p. 106. From W. Wells and B. Siegel, "Stereotyped Somatypes," *Psychological Reports* 8 (1961), 77–78; and K. T. Strongman and C. J. Hart, "Stereotyped Reactions to Body Build," *Psychological Reports* 23 (1968), 1175–78.

[50] See George L. Trager, "Paralanguage: A First Approximation," *Studies in Linguistics* 13 (1958), 1–12.

[51] D. W. Addington, "The Relationship of Certain Vocal Characteristics with Perceived Speaker Characteristics" (Ph.D. diss., University of Iowa, 1963), pp. 157–58. Also see D. W. Addington, "The Relationship of Selected Vocal Characteristics to Personality Perception," *Speech Monographs* 35 (1968), 492–503.

[52]See Addington, "The Relationship . . . ," *Speech Monographs*, 492–503.
As reported in Knapp, *Essentials*, p. 208.

[53]Based on pp. 113–18 from *Silent Messages* by Albert Mehrabian.
Copyright © 1971 by Wadsworth Publishing Company, Inc., Belmont,
California 94002. Reprinted by permission of the publisher.

[54]W. V. Haney, *Communication and Organization Behavior* (Homewood,
Ill.: Richard D. Irwin, Inc., 1967), p. 53.

[55]Knapp, *Essentials*, p. 232.

[56]Julius Fast, *Body Language* (New York: Pocket Books, 1971), p. 85.

[57]J. R. Davitz, *The Communication of Emotional Meaning* (New York:
McGraw-Hill, 1964).

7

Tuning In: Attitudes

"I don't like your attitude!" "How long have you had that attitude?" "You'll never get anywhere with *that* attitude." Sound familiar? Our attitudes are an important part of who we are and how we interact with other people. Yet we are often less aware of our own attitudes than the attitudes of people around us. That's because attitudes themselves are not observable, but the behavior stemming from attitudes *is*. And we are generally not very good observers of our own behavior.

What exactly is an "attitude"? The word is usually taken to mean a tendency to evaluate a person, thing, or idea either favorably or unfavorably.[1] It amounts to sorting our perceptions into two categories: relatively good and relatively bad. In Chapter 2 we saw how perception is the process of attaching meaning to information our senses take in. The attitude we form toward that information is an essential part of the meaning we assign to it.

Our behavior and communication habits are based, to a large extent, on our attitudes. In this chapter I'm going to discuss where these attitudes come from and what they are made of. We'll compare attitudes with beliefs and values, and talk about attitude change and how we can improve our interpersonal persuasive skills.

ATTITUDES, BELIEFS, AND VALUES

A "belief" is a proposition that can be derived from what we say or do.[2] If we say we think something is true, we are saying we "believe" it. It may or may not be true in fact, but our thinking that it *is* true constitutes a belief. Beliefs are not always logical. We may believe our father loves us and act both loved and loving because of it, even in the face of evidence to the contrary. Such beliefs are based on our own unique experiences: they may be confirmed or changed by the beliefs of people we care about and respect.

An "opinion" is usually narrower in focus than a belief. Opinions come and go. They tend to be situational. Our opinion of a certain kind of food may apply to that one particular food and to no other, and this opinion may change. Opinions can be thought of as tentative beliefs. They are our best judgment of a particular situation and they may, in time, come to be beliefs. That is, if we find we have a consistently low opinion of all the pickles we come in contact with, these opinions may evolve into a belief that pickles don't taste good and we will avoid eating them.

An "attitude" may be thought of as a system of beliefs organized around a common subject. We may believe that clothes are too expensive; that clothes we buy in stores are not well made; and that clothes are just not made to fit us properly. As a result of these beliefs, we may develop a negative attitude toward store-bought clothes in general. We may decide not to buy any new clothes for a while—we will either make them or do with what we already have. Our attitude toward store-bought clothes is that they are relatively bad. An attitude is more general and, at the same time, more complex than a belief because it covers more areas. Attitudes usually develop over a long period of time and are not easy to change.

"Values" are still more general (and stable) than attitudes. A value is the common denominator in an attitude system. If we have an unfavorable attitude toward store-bought clothes and prepared convenience foods and manufactured furniture, it may be that we value self-reliance and personal creativity. We probably prefer to make our own clothes and furniture and to prepare our own food because we value our own industry. Values are usually very enduring because they relate to the way we conduct our lives and to the goals we set for ourselves. Because our values are so central to who we are, they influence our communications and our behavior in many ways.

Given the relationship between beliefs, attitudes, and values shown in Figure 1, we can see how it is possible to infer that a person holds certain beliefs and attitudes because of the values we know he or she has. For example, if we know that Margaret values self-reliance and creativity, we might guess that she believes a gift of a ceramic pot made by a friend is preferable to a similar pot bought in a store. We may guess that she would rather plan a trip by herself than go on an organized tour. Guesses such as these can cause us to begin or end a relationship with Margaret. They may also determine how we communicate with her.

Try This

Just to get you started thinking about your own beliefs, opinions, attitudes, and values, list five of each right now. What are five of each of the following that you hold about things (any things) right this minute?

—beliefs

—opinions

—attitudes

—values

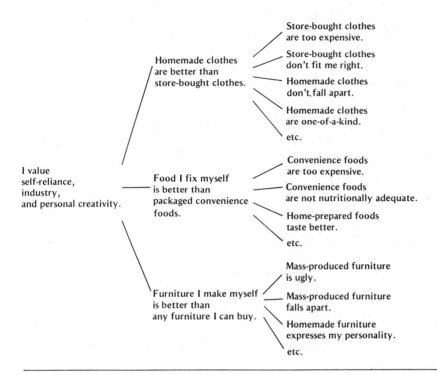

Figure 1.
The relationship of values to attitudes and beliefs.

CHARACTERISTICS OF ATTITUDES

Attitudes exist internally. We derive them from different sources and hold them with different degrees of strength. Attitudes relate to things, people, and concepts. In general, we acquire them as a result of our experiences: we may have a favorable attitude toward animals because our parents allowed us to have pets as children, or toward reading because our parents read to us often. Our peers, teachers, parents, and even television all shape our attitudes. The more we are exposed to, the more varied attitudes we are likely to hold. Each attitude has three dimensions: direction, strength, and salience.

Direction

The *direction* of an attitude is simply whether we like something or not. Direction can be neutral: sometimes we do not care. A positive or negative evaluation reveals the direction of our attitude. Whether we like, do not like, or are indifferent toward someone, we have an attitude toward that person. We have attitudes on just about everything. When other people talk to us, we judge their talk according to our background

Consider This _____

If you are normally a right-handed person, try a little experiment for a half hour or so: Do with your left hand everything that you usually do with your right.

The most simple and obvious acts will become complicated and cumbersome. You will hardly be able to write or cut or eat your food; and you will quickly become baffled, frustrated and exasperated.

Now imagine this lopsided process intensified a thousand-fold, and you may have some idea of how painful and difficult it is to think "with the left hand"—that is, to reverse our customary process of thought.

Why has science made such enormous strides in knowledge and development, while human affairs still remain largely as they were in the days of the Assyrian Empire? Largely because every advance in science is gained by reversing the spool of thought—by thinking in a way that is opposite of the traditional and customary ways.

Of all the habits of mankind the habits of thought are the most persistent, the most tenacious, the most enslaving. We put on an idea in the morning as we put on a shoe, left or right first, unconsciously and without ever varying the procedure by a fraction.

And our resistance against changing our habits of thought is immense and unrelenting. If we try, briefly, we find it as vexing and unrewarding as

---

Try This

For each of the following topics, consider the attitude you hold. What is its direction (positive, negative, or neutral)? Its strength? Its salience?

money
gossip
competition
organized religion
conformity
school spirit
success
patriotism
cats
television
the library
football
hallucinogenic drugs
science fiction
natural foods

of existing attitudes. If we are not familiar with what they are talking about, we will probably form an opinion as a result of the conversation.

Strength

Direction refers to whether our attitude is favorable, unfavorable, or neutral; *strength* refers to how intense it is. We can like a person or we can love that person. We may not like one of our professors, but that dislike may be nothing compared with how we felt toward a high-school teacher whom we still "hate with a passion." In both cases, the direction of the attitude is the same but the strength is different.

Salience

When an attitude is important, it is likely to be prominent and conspicuous—*salient*. Since we have attitudes toward just about everything and many of them reflect the same direction, there must be some further way to distinguish among them. Strength is one way, salience is the other. Some things mean more to us than they do to other people. Some issues involve us more directly. Do not confuse strength and salience: we might really hate it when someone tells vulgar jokes writing a letter with the left hand. What we are used to is comfortable; what is comfortable is good; and what is good is right—this is the unspoken belief of almost all people everywhere.

When a scientist, however, tackles a problem that has hitherto seemed insoluble, he abandons all his preconceptions, and all the preconceptions of the past. Only when he begins to question the basic assumptions he has always held can he make an utterly fresh start, unencumbered by the intellectual baggage of the past.

I am not suggesting that a knowledge of the past is not useful, or that history and tradition have little to offer us—but they must be used as tools, not as points of departure. Our thinking about them must involve a painful revaluation of our most cherished ideas and ideals.

Not one person in a thousand is willing—although many are able—to think left-handed for more than a few minutes at a time. Yet every important discovery has been made in this way, from Harvey on circulation of the blood to Freud on the role of the unconscious. And we know what derision and abuse such men were subjected to for daring to violate the right-handedness of their times.

—Sydney J. Harris, *The Best of Sydney J. Harris*

around us—we have a very *strong* attitude toward vulgarity—but it is not terribly salient to us since the people we know do not tell vulgar jokes. A woman's attitude toward abortion would be much more salient than a man's because he could never experience pregnancy in the same way, though their attitudes may have identical strength and direction.

FUNCTIONS OF ATTITUDES

We acquire attitudes for a number of reasons.[3] According to Daniel Katz, who provides one of the more popular, useful, and accurate approaches to attitudes, they serve four functions:

1. An *adjustment-utility* function, as when we like things that satisfy our needs;
2. An *ego-defense* function, as when we hold attitudes to cover up our insecurities or protect against external threats;
3. A *value-expression* function, as when we use attitudes to express our beliefs and values; and
4. A *knowledge* function, as when we use attitudes to help understand our environment by organizing and structuring it.

Adjustment-Utility

We tend to like things we consider good for us and dislike those we consider harmful. We hold certain attitudes because we think they will help us gain our goals or maintain any present conditions that are similar to past favorable circumstances. If we know that employers look at the college grades of job applicants, we may change our attitude toward the grading system when we realize that good grades increase our chances of being hired. We adjust our attitude to help achieve our goal of getting a job. If we want our tastes to conform with those of our friends, we may adjust our attitudes to the point of liking the music they listen to, the books they read, the movies they see. We will tend to dislike or be apathetic toward things that do not help us gain our goals or bring us pleasure.[4] We are more likely to change an attitude to fit a goal than change a goal to fit a current attitude. When Katz suggests that attitudes serve a utilitarian function, he means that we develop and hold certain ones because they are useful.

A positive attitude toward cooking enables this man to enjoy the reward of creating a good meal.

Consider This _____

Everyone knows that the older you get, the faster time seems to pass. It is a psychological truism that when we are young, each day leading to Christmas can drag like a year; then, as we round middle age, a whole summer seems compressed into a fleeting few days.

This summer seemed to go even faster than ever—just a bright blur between Memorial and Labor days. Everyone I spoke with had the same impression; but, then, all of us were a year older than we had been.

I think that this "telescopic" quality of time can be explained as a matter of proportion, if we look at it arithmetically and not sentimentally. Time actually does "move" faster for us as we increase in age.

When we are young—say, 8 years old—a year represents a full one-eighth of our total experience, and even more than that, for few of us can remember back to our infancies. It is an enormous amount of time in proportion to the little we have known.

By the time we hit 40, a year is only one-fortieth of our total experience. Objectively, it is the same 12-month segment, but subjectively, it is only a small fraction of our remembrance of things past. It is like adding one thin sheet to a fat folio of 39 other sheets.

A child has only a few sheets in his collection, so that adding one more represents a

substantial addition to the memory bank. Time in this respect is much like money.

If you have $30 or $40 saved up, and you add another $10, it seems and is a considerable chunk. But if you have a few thousand saved up and add another $10, it seems insignificant, even though it is the same amount. And the more we have, the less each increment counts.

Thus, when we are quite old, and have 70 or more years behind us, one more year flies by like a week, in comparison with the memories and impressions we have "banked" over the decades. And each year, of course, the amount of experience we add is decreasingly smaller in proportion to the grand total.

So it is not entirely an illusion, or the faulty mechanism of a failing mind, that year by year time seems to increase its pace. It is an arithmetical ratio, like the $10 that dwindles to nothing as we amass more and more capital.

"Time passes," we say. But actually <u>we</u> pass, while time stays on. The hour, the day, the year, maintain their steady pace; it is we who rush faster and faster through eternity. The young at first cannot wait for Wednesday to turn into Saturday; now old, they wonder on Saturday where Wednesday got to.

—Sydney Harris, "Strictly Personal"

Attitudes can cause us to adjust our behavior. If we have a positive attitude toward academic work and like to study, we may seek out jobs that involve some research and writing. We may adjust our behavior by joining groups that have an academic purpose, associating with other people who like to study, and accepting work that has an academic orientation. Our attitudes, in such instances, are useful because they help us attain our objectives.

How clear, consistent, or near to us the rewards for our activities are will be partly responsible for whether we hold an attitude or not. We may think a good grade is useful because it will satisfy our parents. They have always smiled with pleasure when we got good grades—clearly a reward. When we were in high school, perhaps they let us use the car and removed curfews when our grades were good; this is consistent behavior. Also, vacation time is almost here and we may want the peace of mind that comes from having done well; the possible rewards are near. The consequences of our having a particular attitude toward grades are clear, consistent, and near.

Likewise, our attitude toward other people often depends on how we feel they can satisfy our specific needs. We might develop a favorable attitude toward a student who attends class every day and can lend us notes when we miss the class. We may even overlook some of his negative attributes because he can get us those class notes when we need them. True, this is manipulative. We do sometimes use our attitudes in manipulative ways. Katz suggests that the closer people are to satisfying our personal needs, the more likely we are to hold positive attitudes toward them.[5]

Ego Defense

According to Katz, attitudes also function to protect our self-image. It is no secret that we tend to hold attitudes that reinforce our own ideas about our selves. There is nothing wrong with this unless we do it at the expense of truth. Are you honest about your self? Look back at Chapter 3 where you made the "I am" statements. Did your answers accurately reflect who you really are or were you projecting an ideal self?

Sometimes, when we cannot admit that we have a negative trait, we project that trait onto a group or another person. It makes us feel levelheaded to think of other people as being too emotional. The attitude "everyone is a gossip" lets us feel better about talking about other people. We feel superior when we attach the label "inferior" to another person. Our perception of Susan as manipulative may have less to do with how manipulative she actually is than with our own need to

CATHY   **by Cathy Guisewite**

see her that way. These attitudes begin within us. The objects and people to which our attitudes are attached serve as convenient outlets for their expression. The object or person has nothing to do with actually creating the attitude besides being available or convenient; the attitude stems from our own internal conflicts. If no outlet for expression is available, we may even create one.

We hardly ever realize that we are using our attitudes to defend our egos. All people use them this way, to a certain degree. Some people are more defensive than others. And some people are more aware than others of their own reasons for holding certain attitudes. In some cases, we may know that we are doing it but not know why. In other cases, we may not even realize that we are deluding our selves.

Value Expression

The third function of attitudes identified by Katz is value expression. Even if some attitudes we hold keep us from revealing our true selves, others help us express positive things about our central values and about how we see our selves. In fact, an attitude can be said to be nothing more than an outlet for revealing our values—a means of self-expression. If we value honesty, our attitude toward cheating will reflect that value. We may be very specific about crediting others whose information we use; we may sit far away from others during an exam; we may be very careful about lending our lecture notes to people.

What rewards do we gain by sharing our attitudes and values with others? First, simply expressing such things clarifies our self-concept. Second, it may help us mold that self-concept so that it comes closer to what we want it to be. As an example, the way we dress reveals certain things. It shows how we want to be seen. If we dress and talk the way our friends do, we are clarifying our self-concept by establishing our identity with our peer group and rejecting, in part, the identity imposed by other groups. Such clarity in our self-concept is important to growth and development and to a state of mental healthiness. It provides one more answer to the question, "Who am I?" As growth and development occur, it is also important to know that we are the kind of person we want to be.

We may join certain groups so that we can reveal very personal, cherished attitudes without fear. Religious, political, and social action groups provide ideal environments for the expression of values. Such expression is satisfying and psychologically necessary.

Sometimes we join a group and then internalize the group's values. Our own attitudes may be strongly affected. This internalization is

When we join a group and internalize its values, our attitudes and behavior may be strongly affected.

more likely to occur if 1) the group's values are already somewhat consistent with our own; 2) we are indoctrinated to do so; 3) we feel we are given an ample opportunity to participate; and 4) we are given an opportunity to share in the rewards of the group.

When we join a political organization, we seek one that is somewhat consistent with our values. If the values are not entirely or exactly consistent with ours, political speeches, rallies, and discussions serve as an indoctrination program. As a member of the group, we are given a chance to participate in business meetings and perhaps to join a committee. Finally, we share in the rewards of the group: the chance to interact with people who think as we do, the right to use the group's name, and the right to go to its sponsored activities. Group affiliations can be extremely influential in determining the attitudes we come to hold.

Knowledge

The knowledge function of attitudes identified by Katz is one of the most important. Through this function we try to give meaning to an otherwise unorganized and chaotic world. Our attitudes help to provide a frame of reference for comprehending the environment. An attitude we hold becomes a standard against which we apply new information.

We need a certain amount of definition, distinction, consistency, and stability as a background for understanding. We use the attitudes we acquire for further organizing and structuring. A certain religion may help stabilize our world by giving us explanations and a rationale for the way things are. Science may do the same. Einstein's theory of relativity, for example, provided a structure and helped physicists to systematize many other conclusions related to his principle. We

The stereotypical image of the successful business executive is exemplified by these conservatively clad, briefcase-carrying males.

become favorably disposed toward a religion, science, or theory because it helps to give meaning to our world.

Probably the most common example of how attitudes serve the knowledge function is in our use of stereotypes. A stereotype gives us order and structure. We can make sense of a large number of items or random things by labeling and classifying. Notice how this affects our interpersonal communication. We may have a stereotype about aggressive people that says such people tend to be shallow, fake, and in desperate need of attention. This stereotype might keep us from becoming involved with overbearing people. Similar stereotypes may help us categorize and respond to foreigners, old people, young people, fat people, thin people, etc. Although some of our reactions may be limiting or negative, we do need to find ways to make sense of our experience—stereotypical attitudes help us to do this. In this way, our attitudes serve the knowledge function by helping us organize and structure what we experience. They provide order and clarity from an overwhelming set of complexities.[6]

ATTITUDE CHANGE: FOR BETTER OR WORSE

When our attitudes are so deeply ingrained that we are hardly aware of them, they are very difficult to change. And, similarly, it is difficult for us to cause attitude change in others. But there is a process by which attitude change takes place for most of us, especially if we are trying to be less rigid and more open and self-aware. This process can promote growth, as when we rid our selves of an unhealthy bias, or it can be manipulative, as when we try to persuade someone to hold the same attitude as we do. Let's look at how this process takes place.

As a communication source or receiver, we should be aware of what happens when we state an attitude to another person (or vice versa) and when we try to effect successful attitude change. At the outset, it should be clear that we always strive to maintain internal consistency, harmony, or balance among our personal beliefs, feelings, and actions.[7] What this means can be illustrated in one model of attitude change called Heider's Balance Theory.[8] Heider developed a model in which P refers to one person, O represents another person, and X stands for the topic being talked about. This is a useful way to picture the attitude change process.

Think of your self as person one, or P. The relationships between you and O and X will be represented by plus and minus signs. A plus sign indicates a positive attitude; a minus sign, a negative attitude.

Heider proposed that in interpersonal relations, you are in a state of balance if the people you like have the same attitudes you do. You are in a state of balance, too, if people you dislike hold different attitudes than you on the same topics. According to Heider, whenever you have three +'s or two −'s, the relationship will be balanced. (See Figure 2.)

In Figure 2, let X be a certain movie. In A, you like the other person and both of you like the movie (X). In B, you like the other person but neither of you likes the movie. In C, you like the movie and the other person does not, but you really do not care for him or her anyway. In D, you do not care for the other person or for the movie, even though the other person likes the movie. These are all what Heider would call states of balance. We feel comfortable in such situations because everything is stable or in equilibrium.

If, on the other hand, you have three −'s or two +'s, the relationship will be unbalanced. In E of Figure 3, you don't like the other person and neither of you likes the movie. In F, you both like the movie but you don't like the other person. In G, you like the movie and the other person, but the other person dislikes the movie. In H, you dislike the movie but you like the other person and he or she likes the movie. These are all what Heider would call states of imbalance. It's pretty obvious why. You are more comfortable when people you like think the same way you do.

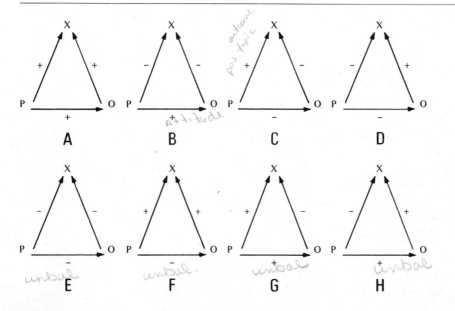

Figure 2.
(P) first person, (O) second person, (X) topic under discussion, (+) positive attitude, (−) negative attitude.

Try This

What are some attitudes that you hold very dear? Are these attitudes likely to change by tomorrow? Next week? How about by next year? List some of these attitudes. Do they have anything to do with

— parents?

— school?

— earning money?

— homework?

— teachers?

— politics?

— selfishness?

— drugs?

— grades?

— how you use your money?

— vacation time?

— cheating?

— the opposite sex?

— music?

— dating?

— free time?

— sex?

— independence?

— religion?

— drinking?

— art?

Straining for Balance

When we are talking with a person we like very much and we realize that the two of us have different attitudes, we may try to bring our attitudes together.[9] How hard we try depends on how strong and how salient our own attitude is. It also depends on how much we like the other person and how important the relationship is to us.

Any strain for attitude balance will affect our interpersonal relationship with this other person. The more we want to make our attitudes like those of someone else, the more likely we are to increase our communication with that person. And greater quantity of interaction—the sheer number of transactions—increases the probability that attitude change will occur.

Consider This

i used to wrap my white doll up in
an old towel
and place her upon my chest
i used to sing those funny old school songs
god bless america
my country 'tis of thee
when i was young
and very colored
— Mae Jackson, "i used to wrap my white doll up in"

Resolving Imbalances

Because we prefer a state of balance, we perceive things so that our balance is not disturbed. Suppose the X in E and F of Figure 2 is the movie *Duck Soup*. We see the movie with Arthur, whom we don't like. In E, we both hate the movie. In F, we both love it. In both cases we are uncomfortable because we don't like Arthur and we would prefer that our tastes were different from his. In G and H of Figure 2, we see *Duck Soup* with Barb, a good friend, but in both of these cases one of us likes the movie and the other doesn't. Again we are uncomfortable because we would like to agree with Barb. How do we resolve these states of imbalance?[10]

1. We could criticize the source of the disturbing message. We could think that Arthur and Barb don't mean what they say or simply don't know their own tastes.
2. We could say it doesn't matter. We may decide that disagreeing with Arthur or agreeing with Barb about this movie really isn't important.
3. We might go out and find additional information or other people to support us. This doesn't resolve the imbalance but it may make us more secure about our position. We could probably find movie reviews that reinforce our feelings whether they are positive or negative.
4. We might misperceive the other person's position. In the case of Arthur, this would mean thinking something like, "He said he didn't like it but really he just doesn't like black-and-white movies" or "He said he liked it but he laughed at all the stupid parts. He missed the really subtle humor." In the case of Barb our misperceptions might be more on the order of "She said she didn't like it but really she was just too tired to enjoy it. She wasn't in the mood" or "She said she liked it but she probably just thought I wanted her to say that."
5. We might tell our selves that our attitudes are not relevant to each other. For both Arthur and Barb, this might mean *we* were looking at the movie from the point of view of a film connoisseur, while *they* were casual moviegoers. Our perspectives are just too different to be relevant to each other.
6. We could try to convince Arthur or Barb that our attitude is the right one. This, of course, means convincing the others that they are wrong. We might try to do this by citing movie reviews or what we perceive as "popular opinion." Or we might simply describe in detail what we thought was good (or bad) about the film.

Try This

For each of the following diagrams, think of an interpersonal situation you recall where the relationships were as shown here:

Which, if any, of these models are balanced? Do you agree that you feel more comfortable when your situation is in a state of balance?

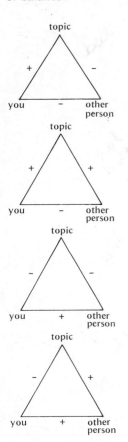

7. We could change our own attitude. We could say we'd reconsidered and really did think *Duck Soup* was great (or terrible).
8. We could consider the imbalance a virtue. We might convince our selves that it is healthy to admit we might agree with Arthur or disagree with Barb some of the time.

These methods of resolving imbalances show what we are up against when we set out to change someone's attitudes. We use some of these methods to protect our selves when we hear disturbing communications just as much as others do. But even if a change in attitude does occur, there is no guarantee that behavior will change correspondingly. Behavior changes will occur only if the direction, strength, and salience of the attitude are significant and if the context is appropriate. If Barb didn't like *Duck Soup* and we want to not only change her attitude but also to get her to go to more Marx Brothers movies, we'll have to convince her of the direction, strength, and salience of our own attitude.

The relationship between attitudes and behavior can be very loose. There is no reason to assume that because an attitude changes, a behavioral change will follow. People can be enthusiastic about something one minute and bored with it the next.

There are problems with looking at attitude change from Heider's perspective alone. The *P-O-X* model makes all attitudes look either positive or negative; of course we know that they vary not only in direction but also in strength and salience. We should realize that all options for resolving imbalance are equally possible; it is difficult to choose the most appropriate one. Finally, there are more alternatives available to us than simply changing one plus or one minus to bring a relationship into balance. We can alter as many elements as necessary to restore balance; the possibilities are infinite.

Temporary and Lasting Change

The point of discussing attitudes is to provide a base for understanding attitude change in our selves and thereby understanding what happens, in a unique way, for every individual. What causes us to change our attitudes? Do we wake up one morning and say, "My attitude toward my family is poor. I think I'll replace it"? Not likely. We need time to realize the need for change and to make that change permanent.

We change our attitudes for a variety of reasons. Another person may give us a reward for changing our behavior or punish us for not changing it. This kind of change is called *compliance*. We may comply for the moment but really not change our attitudes. This kind of change is frequently only temporary. For example, we know we will be punished if we get caught disobeying the speed limit. We may comply with the law, even if we object to it, when the threat of punishment is near—we see a police car—but the compliance is temporary if we speed up when the threat disappears.

We may change our attitudes because of *identification*. If someone we admire holds a particular opinion, we may try to be like that person by adopting similar attitudes. But when we are away from that person, our attitudes may change back to their original position. If we wanted to change another person's attitude through persuasion, one way to do it might be by using identification. We would try to present an honest, trustworthy, and credible image that the other person could identify with.

Internalization occurs when we adopt an attitude because we are truly convinced by it. If someone convinced us to quit smoking because it was harmful to our health, we might change our attitude toward smoking because we were truly convinced we would suffer if we did not. We might be inclined to change our attitude toward a pass-fail grading system if someone convinced us that prospective employers prefer job candidates who took courses for a letter grade. Changes such as these are likely to be long lasting since they are based on intellectual and emotional agreement and do not depend on the presence of arbitrary reward or punishment or on another person.[11]

Up to this point, I've been talking about the ways we deal with challenges to our existing attitudes and how we adjust our thinking to maintain and protect those attitudes. However, we actually do change

_____ **Try This**

When was the last time you changed one of your attitudes? Can you remember the reason why you changed it? Was the change caused by

— compliance?

— identification?

— internalization?

— coercion?

— manipulation?

Were you aware when the change occurred? Did you put up any resistance? What might have been the consequences had you not decided to change? Do you secretly wish that you had not changed?

next

Try This

All advertising is meant to be persuasive. Advertisers assume they have to change our attitude toward their product to get us to buy it. On a *P-O-X* model, we are *P*, the advertisers are *O*, and the product being advertised is *X*. We can assume *O* will always be favorable to *X*. Look at diagrams A, D, F, and H in Figure 2, where the *O-X* relationship is positive. Can you think of some television commercials which each of these diagrams describes? For example, diagram A describes a situation where we like both the product and the commercial itself. In D, we dislike both the product and the commercial. These are states of balance. Obviously, advertisers hope the A situation exists much of the time, but we know that it doesn't. How do you resolve the attitudinal imbalance with advertisers represented by diagrams F and H? Think of the methods discussed in the text.

attitudes at times. There are reasons. For example, we might be coerced to change. If we do something illegal, law enforcement authorities may force us to change. Our attitude toward freedom may result in continual excessive speeding. The authorities may coerce us by 1) giving us a warning, 2) taking away our driver's license, or 3) putting us in jail. We might change our attitudes, too, because of more subtle coercion, or propaganda. An organization may get us to accept its doctrines through "mass hypnosis, constant repetition, loaded language, the subtle use of social pressures, or the appeal to irrelevant loves, hates, and fears."[12]

We might also change our attitudes because of manipulation. A manipulator may exploit us, use us, or control us.[13] This may be blatant control, as when a friend says, "If you have that attitude, you will no longer be my friend." Or it may be more subtle, as when advertisers try to change our attitude toward their product by suggesting it will make us happier and more popular.

The point is, there are many reasons for changing attitudes—some positive and some negative. We need to be aware of the forces at work on us. We also must try to avoid using coercion, propaganda, and manipulation in our interpersonal relations with other people. We should never use our knowledge of others for socially or self-destructive behavior.

It may sound as if attitude change occurs rapidly or as the result of a single conversation. With compliance, this may well be the case. But it takes considerable time and usually a number of interpersonal transactions for important changes to occur. Ongoing interpersonal communication is vitally important in changing another person's attitude.

Creating the Climate for Attitude Change

The problem in dealing with attitudes in any capacity is that we have so many different predispositions to act and so many influences operating. We can never know exactly what factors will work to change someone's attitude.

All we can say with certainty, with respect to changing an attitude, is that some need must be excited to cause attitudes to change. Some relevant cue in the environment must be touched. To do this successfully, we must know what is relevant as far as needs in general are concerned. If old attitudes do not keep up with current interests and needs, a person will be more likely to be open to someone who can suggest a new attitude. For example, if we are no longer happy with our choice of a major, we are susceptible to new attitudes because we are aspiring toward something else, even though we may not know what that something else is. But what should a new major offer us? What would make one major more attractive than another? How could someone convince us to actually make a change? The following lists show some of the needs and environmental cues that might cause us to change our major:

Needs	Environmental Cues
our aptitude is more appropriate	better professors
better personality match	classes are nearby
interest will be greater	better social environment
more likelihood of getting a job	more variety in classes
more likelihood of success and	offered
security	better facilities

Some environmental cues might also be needs. It may be a function of the environment that another major offers more classes, but we may also want a major that offers more classes; thus, an environmental cue becomes a need fulfilled.

IMPROVING SKILLS IN PERSUASION

There are many situations in which we would like to make people think or act differently, where we would like to have an effect, where we would like to persuade another person. "Persuasion," in this discussion, will mean the interpersonal advice, urging, or inducements we use to get another person to think or act in a specific way. "Persuasion" is the label most commonly attributed to the tool used for bringing about changes in other people's attitudes.

The effect we will have on another person through persuasion depends on many variables. We must consider, for example, what the people we are trying to persuade think of us, whether they know we are trying to change them, how much exposure they are getting to our ideas, how committed they are to their present stance, whether they have expressed their position to others, and, obviously, how far apart our views are to begin with. These obstacles alone make our task difficult, but if we're really interested in changing an attitude, being aware of these elements can help us improve the odds. We should also consider how much time we will have to share our ideas and how many different contacts with the people we are likely to have—the sheer number of times we meet increases the likelihood of change. Affecting another person significantly is often a slow process, but if we want to be successful in changing attitudes, we must commit our selves to a long-term effort.

Show them that what you propose is approved by someone important to them. This is the concept I earlier labeled as "identification."[14] If others realize that people *they* consider important accept your ideas, your success will be more likely. Talking about friends, experts, or associates who already believe in the way you are suggesting helps others put their present beliefs or actions in perspective.

Show them that what you propose is consistent with their needs. What are the personal needs of the people you hope to persuade? Abraham Maslow categorized seven types of human needs: needs of physiology, safety, love, esteem, self-actualization, knowledge and understanding, and aesthetics. Think of these as a hierarchy: each level, beginning with physiological needs, must be taken care of before going on to the next one. (See Figure 3.)

Actually, the hierarchy is not as rigid as it sounds. Most people have these basic needs in about the order Maslow suggests, but there are exceptions. For example, there are people who seek self-esteem above all else and highly creative people whose need to create is more important than any other need. Some people, too, have experienced long deprivation which may cause them to be content for the rest of their lives with just having their most elemental needs satisfied. There are also some people who were so deprived of love in the earliest months of their lives that their need to give and receive love as adults is distorted.

Physiological needs. These are the most basic needs having to do with our survival. We need food, water, and sleep to survive. These needs are the strongest because without satisfying them, we cannot pay attention to anything else.

Safety needs. Once our physiological needs are satisfied, our next concern is safety. Our concern for safety in our environment is reflected in our need for shelter, clothing, and protection from heat and cold. We want to prevent any kind of threat; we resist changes that jeopardize our safety.

Love needs. Family and friends help us satisfy our need to love and to be loved. Our membership in groups fulfills a need to belong, to be accepted, and to have friends. Marriage and professional associations also satisfy this social need.

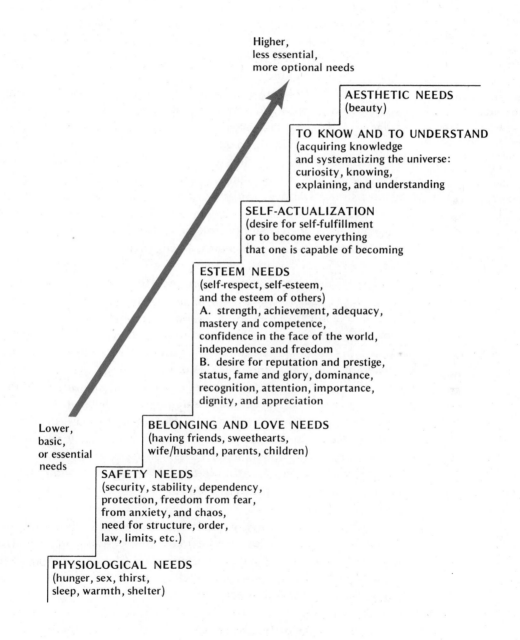

Figure 3.
Maslow's hierarchy of needs.[15]

Higher,
less essential,
more optional needs

AESTHETIC NEEDS
(beauty)

TO KNOW AND TO UNDERSTAND
(acquiring knowledge
and systematizing the universe:
curiosity, knowing,
explaining, and understanding

SELF-ACTUALIZATION
(desire for self-fulfillment
or to become everything
that one is capable of becoming

ESTEEM NEEDS
(self-respect, self-esteem,
and the esteem of others)
A. strength, achievement, adequacy,
mastery and competence,
confidence in the face of the world,
independence and freedom
B. desire for reputation and prestige,
status, fame and glory, dominance,
recognition, attention, importance,
dignity, and appreciation

Lower,
basic,
or essential
needs

BELONGING AND LOVE NEEDS
(having friends, sweethearts,
wife/husband, parents, children)

SAFETY NEEDS
(security, stability, dependency,
protection, freedom from fear,
from anxiety, and chaos,
need for structure, order,
law, limits, etc.)

PHYSIOLOGICAL NEEDS
(hunger, sex, thirst,
sleep, warmth, shelter)

Try This

Try to persuade someone
of something you are not
convinced of. Spend some
time — even several days if
necessary — continuing
your effort.

Notice the effects you
have on your listener.
Were you successful? Why
or why not? What kind of
listener-needs did you appeal to in trying to per-
suade? Did you find some
needs easier to work with
than others?

Esteem needs.   We need to be respected by others. This need has
to do with our desire for status and a good reputation. If we seek
recognition, aspire to leadership positions, desire awards, compliments,
or acknowledgment for our work, our esteem need is operating. Our
need for self-esteem is an important part of this need.

Self-actualization needs.   When our more basic needs are satisfied, we can move toward self-actualization. This is our need to be
everything we can be, to develop our selves to our highest abilities.

The need to know and to understand.   We need to know and to
understand in order to get along in society. For many people, knowledge and understanding are an important part of self-actualization. We
need to inquire, to learn, to philosophize, to experiment, and to explain.

Aesthetic needs.   Have you ever felt uncomfortable in a room
where a picture was hanging crooked on the wall? For many people,
such a situation is aesthetically displeasing and they need to remedy it.
We have a wide range of aesthetic needs, but we all need to have things
around us that we consider beautiful and orderly.

Exactly where our listeners are in their development along this
hierarchy, and what they perceive to be the most pressing needs, will
make a difference in how we approach them. Most college students,
with their needs for physiological safety and security resolved for the
time being because they are in school, can pay attention to their needs
for love, esteem, and self-actualization. Achievement and success are
values prominent in the minds of many college students, but students
generally have the same needs as other people.

If we want to persuade someone of something, we would do well
to tie this to those needs most salient to our listener. If a person is
hungry and desperately trying to feed a family, it is absurd to try to persuade that person to get a job on the grounds that it would be self-
actualizing — the immediate need is for food. If we really want to
change this individual's attitude toward working, we had better relate
working to the most pressing needs.

Show that your proposal is consistent with alternative needs as·well.   If
appealing to one need does not work, perhaps another one will. Do not
assume that satisfying one need is necessarily enough. New times mean
new needs; people are always changing. We may have misperceived the
other person's needs to begin with.

Know the power of fear in attitude change.   Our subconscious fears
are constantly played upon by people who want us to change our attitudes. Advertisers, for example, try to convince us that social or pro-

fessional success hinges on our buying their product. A teacher may say that our grade depends on the successful completion of a project; we complete the project because we fear failure. We may be persuaded to carry a credit card out of fear of what would happen if we lost a large amount of cash.

Fear influences our attitudes and our behavior. There is nothing new or wrong with that—a certain amount of fear is necessary and healthy in many situations. But if we arouse fear to get another person to accept our ideas, we should provide a means for removing the cause of the fear. Parents who persuade their children to wear boots in cold weather by saying they will get sick if they don't should make sure their children understand what they mean. That is, they need not suggest that pestilence and death will necessarily follow a few minutes with wet feet. And parents could say that the main point is not the boots themselves, but that the children are likely to stay healthier if they keep warm and dry.

There is an element of manipulativeness in using the fear approach. Be aware when someone is trying to use it with you. It is a fairly low-level appeal and generally suggests a low evaluation of the other person's intellectual powers. Still, a parent will use fear if necessary to

The political candidate appeals to citizens' needs to win votes.

Consider This _____

Women are expected to behave differently from men in trying to get their way, and so they do, most of the time. Although feminine strategies often work, their use can seriously damage a woman's self-esteem and diminish the respect she gets from others. But if she adopts the more effective techniques used mostly by men, she may be called pushy or aggressive. . . . We asked over 250 college students, divided equally by sex, to write a paragraph on "how I get my way." The essays ranged from the use of blunt and simple argument to Machiavellian plots. . . .

Despite their diversity, the stories fall into certain patterns. First, we discovered that less than a third of the men (27 percent) but almost half of the women (45 percent) say they deliberately show emotion to get their way. They say things like, "I put on a happy face," or "I get mad." Women were responsible for over 75 percent of the negative emotions—sulking, pouting, crying. Fifty percent of the men who reported the use of negative emotion relied on anger; the others adopted a variant of the sad, sulking martyr role. Only 20 percent of the women who used negative emotion mentioned anger. Forty percent persuaded with sadness and sulkiness, and the rest with tears. . . .

To get their way, some people rely on reasoned argument, or at least say they do. Others, slightly fewer in number and with considerable overlap, approach a power play with bargains, hints, deceit, rewards, and coercion. Those in the second group are more likely to be concerned with manipulating the emotional tone of the situation. And they are apt to be women.

—From "How Women Get Their Way" by Paula Johnson and Jacqueline Goodchilds. Reprinted from *Psychology Today Magazine*, October 1976. Copyright © 1976 Ziff-Davis Publishing Company. Reprinted by permission.

keep a child from crossing a busy highway. You must decide for your self if you think arousing fear as a means of persuasion has any place in mature communication.

Offer a reward or incentive.   How much of an incentive we need to offer to get a person to change an attitude depends upon the attitude, the listener, our selves, and the situation. There is no way this can be determined without knowing the variables that operate in a given case. Sometimes another person will go along with an idea if our reward is as simple as saying, "If you do it, I'll go with you." Sometimes it is not so simple. But generally our society operates on a system of rewards and incentives; people want something in return for something. That "something" may be as small as a word of praise at the right time or it may be as elaborate as a large and expensive gift. The reward that works best depends wholly on the circumstances.

Think small. Perhaps the most important suggestion for changing attitudes is to first try to change others in some small way that is consistent with their long-range goals.[16] Small changes are often more acceptable and create less conflict and defensiveness than big changes and may show results more quickly, making bigger changes easier to come by later on.

Our attitudes are influenced by our experiences, including all the attachments we form with other people—people in our family, living area, schools, and social groups. Because of the ties we all have to reference groups and to other people, attitude change is a complicated process. We are likely to encounter opposition, conflict, and defensiveness as we deal with attitudes. Some disagreement is always likely. How to overcome the opposition, conflict, and defensiveness that stand in the way of successful interpersonal communication is the subject of the next chapter.

OTHER READING

Jard DeVille, *Nice Guys Finish First: How to Get People to Do What You Want . . . and Thank You for It* (New York: William Morrow and Company, Inc., 1979). DeVille puts attitude change in perspective by suggesting that you can get whatever you want in life by acting on an understanding and acceptance of other people's personalities. A powerful, interesting book about interpersonal politics.

Andrew J. Dubrin, *Winning at Office Politics* (New York: Ballantine Books, 1978). Dubrin suggests that one cannot get ahead without using sensible office politics at every job level. Much of this involves careful cultivation of one's own image and thoughtful awareness of the attitudes of others.

Philip Lesly, *How We Discommunicate* (New York: AMACOM [American Management Associations], 1979). Engaging in successful attitude change involves the use of specific skills. Lesly provides a program readers can use to improve their personal communication skills and overcome problems of discommunication at the same time.

Jesse S. Nirenberg, *Getting Through to People* (Englewood Cliffs, N.J.: Prentice-Hall, Inc., 1963). This is a realistic, practical book on persuasion that includes discussion of cooperativeness, drawing out people's thoughts, dealing with their emotions, activating their thinking, and dealing with resistance. It is useful and interesting.

John Powell, *The Secret of Staying in Love* (Niles, Ill.: Argus Communications, 1974). Powell discusses the human condition, human needs and the experience of love, love and communication, and the emotions. The author's warm, personal approach is interesting and enjoyable. The exercises provided include an emotional inventory that is effective for developing self-awareness.

Milton Rokeach, *Beliefs, Attitudes, and Values* (San Francisco, Calif.: Jossey-Bass, Inc., 1972). This textbook provides a philosophical and scientific approach to attitude and value formation. It is highly recommended to the student interested in an in-depth exploration of the development of attitudes, beliefs, and values.

Theodore Isaac Rubin, *The Angry Book* (New York: Collier Books, 1969). In this book Rubin encourages readers to understand and work through their feelings about anger. This can lead to greater health, a fuller life, success, and happiness, Rubin contends. A down-to-earth presentation. The author's suggestions appear sound.

Frank Snell, *How to Win the Meeting* (New York: Hawthorn Books, Inc., 1979). Snell dwells on preparation, listening, presentation, persuasion, self-image, timing, and motivation. Other topics are included, too, in this practical guide to effective communication.

David Viscott, *Risking* (New York: Pocket Books, 1977). Engaging in attitude change often involves taking chances. This is a useful examination of what is involved in risking. Viscott shows you how to take necessary risks without fear.

David Viscott, *The Language of Feelings* (New York: Arbor House, 1976). In straightforward, interesting language, Viscott demonstrates how feelings like hurt, anger, guilt, anxiety, and depression can be overcome by freeing the self of emotional debt.

John Wood, *How Do You Feel? A Guide to Your Emotions* (Englewood Cliffs, N.J.: Prentice-Hall, Inc., 1974). This is a book about people sharing their own feelings. It offers new possibilities, new ways to grow, new directions. Wood deals specifically with more than thirty emotions.

NOTES

[1]Irving Sarnoff, "Psychoanalytic Theory and Social Attitudes," *Public Opinion Quarterly* 24 (Summer 1960), 261.

[2]Milton Rokeach, *Beliefs, Attitudes and Values* (San Francisco: Jossey-Bass, 1968), p. 111.

[3]From "The Functional Approach to the Study of Attitudes" by Daniel Katz, *The Public Opinion Quarterly* 24 (1960), pp. 163–204. Reprinted by permission of Elsevier North-Holland Inc.

[4]Attitudes acquired in the service of the adjustment function are either the means for reaching the desired goal or for avoiding the undesirable one. See Daniel Katz and Ezra Stotland, "A Preliminary Statement to a Theory of Attitude Structure and Change," in *Psychology: A Study of a Science*, Vol. 3, ed. by Sigmund Koch (New York: McGraw-Hill, 1959), pp. 434–43.

[5]Katz, "The Functional Approach . . ."

[6]Walter Lippman, *Public Opinion* (New York: Macmillan, 1922), p. 95. Lippman's contribution to the study of attitudes was his description of stereotypes.

[7]William J. McGuire, "The Current Status of Cognitive Consistency Theories," in *Cognitive Consistency: Motivation Antecedents and Behavioral Consequences*, ed. by Shel Feldman (New York: Academic Press, 1966), p. 1.

[8]From "Attitudes and Cognitive Organization" by Fritz Heider, *The Journal of Psychology*, 1946, 21, 107–12. Reprinted by permission. The theory is developed more extensively in his *Psychology of Interpersonal Relations* (New York: John Wiley, 1958).

[9]This is called "symmetry theory," and is developed in Theodore M. Newcomb, "An Approach to the Study of Communicative Acts," *Psychological Review* 60 (1953), 393–404. Robert B. Zajonc, in "The Concepts of Balance, Congruity, and Dissonance," Kenneth K. Sereno and C. David Mortensen, *Foundations of Communication Theory* (New York: Harper and Row, 1970) p. 185, suggests that Newcomb's notion of "strain toward symmetry" will lead to a similarity of attitudes between P and O and X if P is attracted to O.

[10]Herbert W. Simons, "Persuasion and Attitude Change," in *Speech Communication Behavior: Perspectives and Principles*, ed. by Larry L. Barker and Robert J. Kibler (Englewood Cliffs, N.J.: Prentice-Hall, 1971), p. 239.

[11]Herbert C. Kelman, "Processes of Opinion Change," *Public Opinion Quarterly* 25 (1961), 57–78.

[12]Franklyn S. Haiman, "Democratic Ethics and the Hidden Persuaders," in Haig A. Bosmajian, *Readings in Speech* (New York: Harper & Row, 1965), p. 196.

[13]Everett L. Shostrom, *Man, the Manipulator* (New York: Abingdon Press, 1967), p. 15.

[14]Herbert C. Kelman, "Compliance, Identification, and Internalization: Three Processes of Attitude Change," *Journal of Conflict Resolution* 2 (1958), 51–60.

[15]Data (for diagram) based on Hierarchy of Needs in "A Theory of Human Motivation" in *Motivation and Personality*, 2nd Edition by Abraham H. Maslow. Copyright © 1970 by Abraham H. Maslow. By permission of Harper & Row, Publishers, Inc.

[16]A summary of the findings which support this generalization can be found in C. A. Kiesler, *The Psychology of Commitment* (New York: Academic Press, 1971), pp. 14–17.

8   Overcoming Barriers:
Coping with Conflict

So far I have talked a lot about openness, cooperation, and empathy in interpersonal communication. Those positive qualities are at the center of our success in communicating with others. In the last chapter I discussed attitudes and the nature of attitude change. As we attempt to change the attitudes of others, we often run into problems. We all face a certain amount of unpleasantness, hostility, conflict, and defensiveness in our relationships. What do we do about this? We can ignore it. Our society values cooperation and has not taught us how to deal with conflict or even to admit it exists in most cases. But ignoring conflict is not the solution. We can start to deal with conflict by accepting the idea that it is part of life. Next we can learn ways to manage it or cope with it. Finally we can practice those methods or skills.

We'll begin this chapter by considering how our society views conflict and how each of us reacts to it personally. Then I'll discuss ways of coping with conflict with suggestions for some skills to practice. Understanding the nature of conflict will help us to facilitate cooperative behavior, resolve problems, and enhance our interpersonal relationships and contacts. We can't eliminate conflict, but we can start to look at it as something we can handle.

HOW SOCIETY VIEWS CONFLICT

Conflict is considered bad in our society. You may have come to believe that conflicts are the cause for marriages to be dissolved, for employees to be fired, and for demotions, demerits, demoralization, and divisiveness. Certainly arguments, disagreements, and fights do force people

Try This

Can you think of specific people who fit the following phrases?

1. She really is kind.

2. Aren't they friendly?

3. They would do anything in the world for you.

4. He'd give you the shirt off his back.

5. She always has a smile on her face.

6. Isn't he sweet?

7. It wouldn't be a party without him.

8. She really is all heart.

Can you think of other phrases that emphasize the nonaggressiveness we prize in our society?

apart and damage relationships. But more than likely it is not the conflict itself that causes the break in these relationships, but the poor handling of the conflict.

Anger, often one of the underlying causes of conflict, is also considered taboo in our society. This is supposed to be the age of reason and togetherness. Anger is not "gentlemanly," "ladylike," "nice," or "mature." The mere mention of fighting is enough to make some people uncomfortable. They may talk of their "differences" or of their "silly arguments" but not of "fights" because they feel "fight" implies a lack of maturity and self-control. Fighting here means verbal and nonverbal quarreling, not physical battle. Actually, not to admit to conflict or fighting implies a lack of maturity. People who are mature *do* fight. When we are on intimate terms with another person, our closeness may be characterized by quarreling and making up. We may try to live in harmony and agreement with another person but this desire alone creates a need for conflict—just to establish and maintain *our* notion of harmony and agreement.[1]

Our society has conditioned us to dislike and dread personal, aggressive openness. Well-liked people are described with such phrases as, "She is very kind; she'll do anything for anyone" or "He doesn't have a nasty bone in his body" or "She wouldn't raise her voice to anyone." Think of people you know who are admired and the phrases people use to describe them. Nonaggressiveness is praised and admired.[2] We are often taught that nobody will like us unless we are cheerful and that nice people do not fight.

Our society's attitude toward nonaggressiveness may be responsible for the vicarious pleasure many people get from watching the violent acts of other people. Sports such as hockey, football, and boxing include elements of violence; violence is also prominent in the news, in movies, and on television. Anger and aggressiveness are officially taboo, but as a society we are obsessed and fascinated with them and admire them. Our heroes and heroines are powerful, robust, forceful characters. There seems to be a difference between what we give lip service to and what we actually like. There is no doubt that conflict *can be* destructive. Whether it is harmful or helpful depends on how it is used.

HOW YOU VIEW CONFLICT

Healthy interpersonal communication is *not* conflict-free. Conflict is a part of all the relationships we have with other people. It can be constructive or destructive, depending on how we manage it.[3] Conflict is

Consider This

What comes out of the whole range of questions about disagreements, however, is the strong sense that how husbands and wives express their disagreement is much more important than what they disagree about. We asked readers what they are most likely to do when they are displeased with their husbands and what their husbands are most likely to do—say nothing, brood about it, hint that they're unhappy, express their feelings or start an argument. We also asked how often they and their husbands behave in these different ways when they do argue—leave the room, sulk, sit in silence, swear, shout, hit out, cry or break things.

The most happily married wives are those who say that both they and their husbands tell each other when they are displeased and thus try to work out their displeasure together by com-municating in a calm and rational way. They also say that they and their husbands rarely or never fight in any of the different ways we listed; that is, they seldom resort either to the active-aggressive fighting (swearing, shouting, hitting out, crying or breaking things) or to passive-aggressive fighting (leaving the room, sulking or staying silent).

The wives who are most unhappily married are in relationships where one or both partners can't talk calmly about what's bothering them or when one or both do a lot of fighting in the traditional ways. If one partner tends to avoid a fight and the other is a fighter, they're just as likely to be unhappy as if both were fighters.

—*Redbook*, June 1976

often the constructive means we use to challenge established norms and practices and at times it is the means through which we are our most creative and innovative. Conflict often motivates us to summon up our untapped abilities. Some of our most eloquent moments result from impromptu situations that occur when we have been stopped from doing something or need to get our way. We should concentrate on managing interpersonal conflict to gain the maximum benefit, discovering our own best style of handling it in the process.

Any time we get together with another person for more than a short while, conflicts may arise that are serious enough to destroy the relationship if we do not know how to handle them. There are no magic formulas for overcoming barriers and resolving breakdowns. But we can look at those breakdowns in a fresh way. The fact that we are unique and that we experience the world in a unique way is enough to generate conflict because conflict occurs when human differences or uniquenesses meet. In addition to being unique, each of us is also able to make choices. We can decide how to handle the disagreements we encounter.

It may seem discouraging to think that even in the very best of relationships there is going to be conflict and that, on top of that, there is no guarantee that the conflict can be resolved. But we can change the way we deal with it. First we need to confront our own feelings. There are different styles of handling conflict. To know what happens when we disagree is a useful starting point.

Conflict is most frustrating when both sides are inflexible.

WHAT HAPPENS WHEN YOU DISAGREE

Conflict is simply a situation in which we, our desires, or our intentions are in opposition to those of another person. Opposition means incompatibility: if our desires predominate, the other person's will not.[4] If we want to go to one movie and our friend wants to go to another, a state of conflict results. If we feel we deserve an A and our instructor thinks a B is all we deserve, we are in conflict. If we believe that one interpretation of a poem is correct and our classmates think another one is more appropriate, we have another conflict situation. There are, of course, honest differences of opinion that lead to conflict. But there are also barriers and breakdowns in communication that create conflict and can be avoided.

Communication Barriers and Breakdowns

An atmosphere of acceptance is essential to preventing breakdowns in communication. Without acceptance, messages may not be received at all or may be distorted if they are received. Not receiving a message or distorting it causes conflicts. An atmosphere of acceptance can be clouded or destroyed by contrary attitudes, newly acquired contrary opinions, jumping to conclusions, low credibility, and hostility.[5]

Contrary attitudes.   Our prejudices, biases, and predispositions affect the way we interact with and perceive others. When other people's views are contrary to ours, our reactions are aroused through a sense of irritation. This will become a barrier to communication unless we make a concerted attempt to be tolerant, understanding, and personally poised.

Newly acquired contrary opinions.   Converts to a religious belief are generally thought to be stronger believers than those who have been brought up with the belief. The closer we are to the time we acquired a new opinion, attitude, or belief, the more rigid we will be in defending it. And the more rigid we are, the less vulnerable we are to change. Conflict is most frustrating when neither person is willing to be flexible. As time passes, we may begin to be more receptive to contrary ideas, even though we may still firmly hold our original belief. If we are conscious of the effects of the passage of time on creating an atmosphere of acceptance, we will be more careful about our timing when we need to present a new and potentially controversial idea to someone.

Jumping to conclusions.   The problem with jumping to conclusions is that the climate of acceptance is destroyed when we rush to make a decision before we have enough facts on which to base the judgment. When we do not really listen, review the facts, or try to examine all the messages we are receiving, we create an atmosphere of misinformation and distrust which works against effective communication.

Credibility.   Acceptance is affected if one of us perceives the other to be a person of low credibility. If we suspect someone of being unfair, biased, unreliable, hostile, or contradictory, we are not likely to hear what he or she says. This basic lack of acceptance creates a serious handicap to communication. To focus on the content of the message and not on the person will help, but a climate of low credibility is difficult to overcome.

Hostility.   In the presence of outright hostility, it is very hard to achieve an atmosphere of acceptance. Hostility begets hostility. When we become aware of hostility directed toward us, we are likely to respond with a potentially hostile posture — prepared, alert, and equipped for a self-defensive action. Hostility then intensifies and communication is blocked.

Try This _____

See if you can recall a recent conflict that you had. The point here is not to dredge up bad memories but, rather, to focus on some of the reasons why that conflict occurred. Which of the following categories of unproductiveness seemed to be present in your last conflict? To identify these may help you to be more aware of them next time you are in conflict.

1. Were the number of communication channels limited?

2. Did both parties try to make the channels of communication ineffective?

3. Did either party try to close off communication entirely?

4. Did either party try to empathize with the other?

5. Was the position of one person ever restated by the other person, to the other person's satisfaction?

6. Was a third (neutral) party's potential involvement ever rejected when both of you were in a deadlock?

7. Did both of you induce feelings of hostility in the other?

8. Was any kind of cooperation discouraged?

9. Was the concept of decision by joint effort rejected? — even considered?

10. Did both parties try to impose their solutions on the other?

11. Were instruments of power ever resorted to?

12. Was strategy involved? — each party trying to outwit the other?

13. Was there deception (dishonesty) involved?

14. Was that which was finally agreed to, implemented?*

Obviously, these are all negative categories — or negative modes of behavior. To become efficient conflict handlers, we need to become sensitive to these areas.

*Adapted from The Profile of Conflict Characteristics, as reprinted in *New Ways of Managing Conflict*, copyright © 1971 and 1974 by Rensis Likert and Jane Gibson Likert.

Styles of Handling Conflict

Conflict can evolve from situations that are critically important as well as from seemingly irrelevant ones. By "important" I mean situations where basic moral or ethical values are challenged. Such a situation might occur in a family where some members hold politically conservative views and other members have strong liberal tendencies — conflicts may spring up about military service, tax laws, and countless other subjects. Seemingly irrelevant situations occur daily as we must decide what to wear, whether or not to go to class, or where to eat lunch.

It is not for us to judge the importance of conflict to anyone else. What is a conflict situation to one person may not be for another person. Just as people view conflict differently, they deal with it differently. Some people tend to be more conflict-prone than others; they may be less adaptable and their points of view tend to oppose other people's. Some people, too, get certain satisfactions from setting up competitive, win-lose situations. I won't explore all the psychological reasons, but this is a type of person most of us have known. When someone else takes a stand, you can almost predict that the conflict-prone person will stand squarely against that position and an argument will ensue.

Whether we are conflict-prone or not, there are several ways we can deal with such confrontations: we can ignore conflict by actively denying that it exists or by running away from it. We can attack the other person directly by challenging his or her credibility. Direct attacks can take many forms; all are destructive to effective communication. There are, fortunately, some alternatives:

1. We can give in or agree to meet the other person halfway.
2. We can postpone the confrontation, hoping that the passage of time will eliminate the conflict, shed new light on the situation, make one side in the conflict predominate, or cause the other person to forget about it.
3. We can work through the problem until differences are resolved or both of us agree to disagree.

Using the wrong approach can do irreparable damage to a relationship. On the other hand, interpersonal communication can be enhanced if the conflict is handled effectively. People essentially take one of two positions: they may "erupt" or they may "withhold."[6]

"Erupters" tend to enter a conflict situation with vigor. They might lash out at the opposition, bystanders, and whoever else is available, venting their emotions. When these people believe they are right, they may be unwilling to compromise. They may find it hard to apologize or to forgive. They use this means of reacting because they know of no other alternatives, or they know them but do not practice them.

"Withholders" tend to be afraid of conflict. Because of exposure to highly emotional people, because of upbringing, or because of certain personality characteristics, these people may avoid expressing any conflict-oriented feelings. They withhold their frustrations, anger, hate, resentment, irritations, and annoyances. Sometimes these feelings build up and are let out all in one emotional avalanche, but more often they build up inside, causing mental and physical harm. Self-hate is just one of the possible side effects resulting from the containment of strong feelings.

Neither of these ways leads to satisfactory solutions. Only the third way—working through the problem until differences are resolved—makes any sense for strengthening interpersonal relationships, yet this alternative is not often used. I will label people who take this approach "confronters" or "copers."

Try This

Every day we encounter many conflict situations. Of the following, which do you consider critically important? Which seem irrelevant to you?

1. Conflict with another person for control of your life

2. Conflict over what you should eat

3. Conflict about how you spend your money

4. Conflict about how you relate to other people

5. Conflict over how clean you keep your living area

6. Conflict about how you spend your time

7. Conflict over your lifetime goals

8. Conflict over whether or not you should get a job

9. Conflict about your driving habits

10. Conflict over what you want to believe in

11. Conflict over your use of tobacco, marijuana, alcohol, or drugs

12. Conflict about how you think of your self (your self-respect, self-esteem, or ego)

The woman in this conflict situation is an "erupter." She is venting her emotions with vigor—an approach that is seldom constructive.

COPING WITH CONFLICT: A SUCCESSFUL APPROACH

An approach has been designed for managing all stressful conflict situations that puts a high priority on creative coping and on maintaining self-esteem. How successfully we use these coping behaviors depends on our recognition of a conflict situation and on our ability to keep our wits about us as we put this approach into action. The four main elements of this approach to coping are gaining information, organizing our selves, striving for independence, and anticipating conflict situations.[7]

Information: Get Enough of the Right Kind

In any communication setting, whether conflict-laden or not, we act best when we are well informed. In a conflict situation, we need to find out all we can about the problem to assure our selves that we have more than one way to deal with it. The information we pick up may involve the nature of the communication itself or it may involve the other person. Problems with information may develop in three major ways: through overload, manipulation, and ambiguity.

Communication overload. If one person provides another person with more information than he or she can handle, a problem will arise.[8] We call this "overload." The information I am referring to here has to do with the content of a communicator's message to a listener, not with information of a general nature about a conflict situation, as discussed above.

A human being can handle only so much information at one time. This has to do with the capability of the human brain to decipher material but also with the various ways the emotions get bound to certain experiences. Often the root causes for conflict are closely tied to our emotional response pattern. In such cases, as sure as conflicts are bound to come up, so are the emotions that go along with them. If we are having an emotionally involving experience, it is difficult to take on

_____ Consider This

The ways in which one human being can insult another are many and varied. When it comes to being nasty, no other animal can match us. The range and diversity of our derogatory signals are enormous—and that is even before we have begun to open our mouths.

Insult Signals vary in intensity from mild rebuffs to attempts at savage intimidation. They also vary from locality to locality. There are some that we can easily understand almost anywhere in the world, but there are many others that we cannot even begin to interpret without special local knowledge.

How, for instance, would you interpret a gesture in which the tips of the fingers and thumb of the left hand are brought together, and the straightened forefinger of the right hand is moved across to touch the ring of bunched tips? The precise meaning would escape you unless you happened to hail from Saudi Arabia. If you did, you would know that the exact message is: "You are the son of a whore." The clue to the symbolism is given by the literal phrase, "You have five fathers," the five digits of the left hand being the five males in question.

In certain South American countries, a hand cupped just below the chin signals stupidity. It does so because it is meant to indicate an imaginary goiter, which is itself a symbol of stupidity. In parts of Spain, the head is tilted, to rest on a supported hand, as a signal of implied immaturity. The suggestion is that the insulted person is still a baby leaning on its mother.

—Desmond Morris, *Washington Post*, December 4, 1977

Consider This

We swallow it, shelve it, bury it, store it, and ignore it. It comes back. We rationalize it, analyze it, explain it away, and feel guilty. Sometimes, it makes us sick.

Most of us still cannot face our own anger.

"It took me six years to realize that my bad back was a way of taking care of my anger. When the anger got too scary to face, I could give up—become completely helpless—with a backache," Anna, who is 40 years old, said. . . .

Anger, if it's swallowed, contributes to headaches, backaches, ulcers, colitis, hypertension, and a host of other physical ailments, most physicians say.

Still, it scares us.

"Of course, it scares me. Society in general forbids women to get angry—that is a male emotion. We're allowed to cry; men are allowed to yell. We're allowed to sulk; men are allowed to slam doors and kick the waste basket," a successful attorney said.

"In the workplace, we are in a double bind. If we get angry, we're one of 'those libbers.' If we cry, we're unprofessional." . . .

We are afraid of our own anger. We don't know it has limits if we've never tested it. We aren't sure our families could survive it, because we've never given them that chance.

—Niki Scott, "Working Woman"

and fully comprehend a new "load" of information at the same time. Our senses are preoccupied. If someone else tries to share some vital news with us while our feelings are thus tied up, interpersonal conflicts may result. We may experience this when we try to listen to a classroom lecture just after we've heard some upsetting news. The intensity of the emotional experience overshadows any material the teacher could offer. We simply don't have room for any more information; trying to fit it in would be overloading.

Manipulative communication.   Communication breakdowns are likely to occur when a listener feels information is being offered with manipulative intent. You may have experienced manipulation at one time or another when you felt someone was using you or trying to control you. People manipulate other people for various reasons. In some cases, a person looks to others *for support*. Not trusting them to give it, he or she manipulates them to steer them in the right direction. Manipulation may also result *from love*. The problem is described by Everett Shostrom:

> We seem to assume that the more perfect we appear—the more flawless—the more we will be loved. Actually, the reverse is more apt to be true. The more willing we are to admit our weaknesses as

human beings, the more lovable we are. Nevertheless, love is an achievement not easy to attain, and thus the alternative that the manipulator has is a desperate one—that of complete power over the other person, the power that makes him do what we want, feel what we want, think what we want, and which transforms him into a thing, our thing.[9]

Erich Fromm has said that the ultimate relationship between human beings is that of love—knowing a human being as he or she is and loving that person's ultimate essence.[10] Loving someone's "ultimate essence" is just the opposite of manipulation.

A third reason that manipulation occurs is *out of frustration with life*. People who feel overwhelmed may decide that since they cannot control everything, they will control nothing. They become passive manipulators. They may use various devices and tricks to accentuate their helplessness. They will try to get other people to make decisions for them and carry part of their burden, manipulating through their own feeling of powerlessness.

There are two other reasons that people manipulate that appear to be near opposites. People may deal with others ritualistically in an effort *to avoid intimacy or involvement*. An example of ritualistic communication is the teacher who cannot deal with students in other than strictly teacher-student terms. The same type of ritualistic behavior might be seen in employer-employee and doctor-patient relationships.

Another reason people manipulate is *to gain the approval of others*. There are people who think they need to be approved of by everyone.

Consider This _____

> **forces fused together**
> > **from years of fear,**
> **from feasible and unfeasible**
> > **foolishness,**
> **from societal foolery and**
> **from fathoms and fathoms of**
> > **fouled up flash**
> **comes down and clamps down**
> > **so tough**
>
> **'til you**
> > **forget/remember that you are a**
> **force too.**

—Dr. Earl M. Washington, in *Monologue to Dialogue: An Exploration of Interpersonal Communication* by Charles T. Brown and Paul W. Keller

They may be untruthful, trying to please everyone in their quest for acceptance. An example of this behavior is the friend who tells us everything we do is "great" just to keep us as a friend.

Ambiguous communication.   Ambiguous information may contribute to a conflict situation because ambiguity almost always leads to misunderstanding.[11] Ambiguity can result when not enough information is provided or when it is too general. If one of your friends told you that everyone was going to the show tonight and that you should meet them downtown, you might easily misunderstand. Who is "everyone"? Where exactly should you meet them? What time? Also, the more abstract our language is, the more likely it is to be ambiguous and conflict-promoting.

Whenever we find our selves in a conflict situation, we should pay special attention to the kind of information we are exchanging: Is there enough? Is there too much? Is it manipulative? Is it ambiguous? It will be helpful to remember that every receiver of messages creates his or

Consider This

Next time you are angry with your husband, why not try some childlike mannerisms: Stomp your foot, lift your chin high and square your shoulders. Then, if the situation merits it, turn and walk briskly to the door, pause and look back over your shoulder. Or you can put both hands on your hips and open your eyes wide. Or, beat your fists on your husband's chest. Men love this! Or, there is the timid, frustrated manner of pouting, looking woeful or looking with downcast eyes while mumbling under your breath, or putting both hands to your face, saying "Oh, dear!" These are only a few of the childlike mannerisms you can adopt.

Some of these actions may seem unnatural to you, at first. If they do, you will have to be an actress to succeed in childlike anger, even if only a ham actress. But, remember, you will be launching an acting career which will save you pain, tension, frustration, a damaged relationship and perhaps even save a marriage. Is any acting career of greater importance? So, turn on the drama. It is guaranteed to ease tension and bring humor into your life instead of pain.

. . . Acquire a list of expressions or words which compliment masculinity, such as "you big, tough brute," or "you stubborn, obstinate man," or "you hairy beast." Other appropriate adjectives are—unyielding, determined, difficult, hard-hearted, inflexible, unruly, stiff-necked, indomitable and invincible. Be certain that your words compliment masculinity and will not belittle his ego, such as the words little, imp, pip-squeak, insignificant, weak, simpleminded, etc.

—Helen B. Andelin, *Fascinating Womanhood*

"Listen to that rain!" said the woman to her husband. "Will it never stop?"

"What harm is a sup of rain?" he said.

"That's you all over again," she said. "What harm is anything, as long as it doesn't affect yourself?"

"How do you mean, when it doesn't affect me? Look at my feet. They're sopping. And look at my hat. It's soused." He took the hat off, and shook the rain from it onto the spitting bars of the grate.

"Quit that," said the woman. "Can't you see you're raising ashes?"

"What harm is ashes?"

"I'll show you what harm," she said, taking down a plate of cabbage and potato from the shelf over the fire. "There's your dinner destroyed with them." The yellow cabbage was lightly sprayed with ash.

"Ashes is healthy, I often heard said. Put it here!" He sat down at the table, taking up his knife and fork, and indicating where the plate was to be put by tapping the table with the handle of the knife. "Is there no bit of meat?" he asked, prodding the potato critically.

"There's plenty in the town, I suppose."

"In the town? And why didn't somebody go to the town, might I ask?"

"Who was there to go? You know as well as I do there's no one here to be traipsing in and out every time there's something wanted from the town."

"I suppose one of our fine daughters would think it the end of the world if she was asked to go for a bit of a message? Let me tell you they'd get husbands for themselves quicker if they were seen doing a bit of work once in a while."

"Who said anything about getting husbands for them?" said the woman. "They're time enough getting married."

"Is that so? Mind you now, anyone would think that you were anxious to get them off your hands with the way every penny that comes into the house goes out again on bits of silks and ribbons for them."

"I'm not going to let them be without their bit of fun just because you have other uses for your money than spending it on your own children!"

"What other uses have I? Do I smoke? Do I drink? Do I play cards?"

"You know what I mean."

"I suppose I do."

—Mary Lavin, "Brigid"

her own meaning for that communication based upon what he or she perceives. We can never know exactly which stimulus aroused meaning in someone else's head. The kinds of phenomena that can provoke meaning are limitless—there is no way anyone can control with certainty all the variables that will eliminate potential conflict situations.

Finally, remember that the message a receiver gets is the only one that counts in a conflict situation. The message that he or she acts upon may be quite different from the information that was sent. To discover precisely what message was received is useful in coping with conflict. We may need to ask the other person, "Now, what did you hear?" or "What is it that you understand?" or "What are you going to do?" As far as possible, we need to know where the other person is coming from if we are to deal successfully with conflict.[12]

Try This

It is human nature to blame others for conflict in which we find ourselves. More often than not, however, a combination of factors, and our own personality, thoughts, or feelings, are part of the problem. Conduct a self inventory by answering the following questions:

1. Do you consider your thoughts to be more important than those of others?
2. Are your feelings more positive than those of others?
3. Do you speak with authority?
4. Do you like to give orders to people?
5. Do you believe that your principles are superior to those of our society?
6. Do you believe in saying what you feel in dealing with other people?
7. Is your chief concern for your own individuality?
8. Do you admire forceful people more than cooperative ones?
9. Are you able to listen to others when you are annoyed by them?
10. Are you highly tolerant of other people's negative feelings?
11. Do you care for the people with whom you talk?*

If you answered these questions honestly, and if your answers to the first eight questions were predominantly "yes," then it may be that your concern for your self and for control engenders or aggravates much of the conflict in your life.

*Paraphrased from a survey reprinted in Charles T. Brown and Paul W. Keller, *Monologue to Dialogue: An Exploration of Interpersonal Communication* (Englewood Cliffs, N.J.: Prentice-Hall, Inc., 1979), pp. 260–63.

Organization: Sort Things Out

Think of a situation to which you had a powerful emotional response: fear, anger, grief, or passion. If you needed to cope with conflict at that time, you may have found your judgment was affected. To reestablish stability and a sense of right and wrong we need to organize our selves within our selves—we need to get our selves together.[13]

This is not to say we should avoid emotional experiences. Feelings of fear, anger, grief, and passion are healthy and normal and should not be repressed. But when in the throes of extreme emotional experiences, we must remember that our senses are affected, that we cannot depend on our perceptions. This is why, for example, people are wise to make funeral arrangements *before* a person dies. In the emotional aftermath of the death of a loved one, decision making is difficult and judgments are not as rational as they are at other times.

When our perceptions are distorted, conflict is likely to escalate because of the misunderstandings exchanged. One such misunderstanding has been labeled by David W. Johnson as "mirror image." In conflict, "mirror image" occurs when both people think they are right, both think they were the one maligned, both think the other person is wrong, and both think they are the only one who wants a just solution.

Another kind of misunderstanding occurs when one person sees identical acts committed by both sides but considers those of the other person illegitimate, unfair, unjust, and unreasonable while viewing his or her own as legitimate, fair, just, and reasonable considering the circumstances. This is known as the "double standard."

In conflict situations, too, thinking becomes polarized. Both individuals might come to have an oversimplified view of the conflict. In this uncomplicated view, anything the other person does is bad and everything we do is good. Obviously, when such misunderstandings are at work, it is difficult to organize our thinking.

When we are aware that we are not coping rationally, we would do well to seek help from others. It's a good idea to go to trusted friends for help in making decisions and carrying out plans. To recognize that we cannot make competent decisions until we have reorganized our thinking is not a weakness; it is realistic and mature.

To be organized within our selves is an awareness function. People who "have it together" are responsive, alive, and interested. They listen to themselves.[14] The attitudes they express are based on firmly rooted values. An organized person takes time to think, to monitor, and to reevaluate before responding.

Independence: Be Your Own Person

Most conflict situations we deal with on a daily basis are not the extremely taxing kind. The better we know our selves, the better we will be able to cope with daily conflict. The better organized we are, too, the more likely we are to be our own person — autonomous. We need to be free to act and to deal with conflict and we must avoid being pushed into action before we are ready.[15]

The people best prepared to cope with conflict are spontaneous. They have the freedom to be, to express their full range of potentials, to be the masters of their own lives and not to be easily manipulated. Successful copers are open and responsive. They can assert their own independence without trying to stifle another person's. They show their independence by expressing their wants and needs instead of demanding them, by expressing their preferences instead of ordering, by expressing acceptance of each other rather than mere tolerance, and by being willing to surrender genuinely to the other person's wishes rather than simply pretending to submit.[16]

Try This

Can you think of conflict situations where you demonstrated true independence? Think of times when you stuck up for your own feelings, brought your total authentic being to a situation, and contributed to open, honest communication. Consider especially encounters with the following people:

your roommate

a salesclerk

your parents

a close friend

a teacher

a gas-station attendant

your doctor

someone much younger than you

your spouse

a foreigner

a cafeteria employee

someone you did not know

a classmate

a group of people

a brother or sister

your lover

a person of a different race

someone much older than you

CATHY   **by Cathy Guisewite**

Anticipation: Be Prepared for Conflict

Conflicts are more likely to become crises when they catch us totally unaware. Try to anticipate conflict situations. Try to cut your emotional reactions off at the pass. If we are ready for conflict and confident in our ability to deal with it, we'll be much less anxious if and when conflict develops.

By anticipating a conflict situation, we will be more likely to have some control over the context in which it occurs. Instead of focusing, for example, on whose fault the conflict is, we can try to get in touch with where we and the other person are and attempt to work from there.

In addition, with some anticipation, we can take responsibility for our feelings and actions. We can plan, in advance, to say such things as "I am angry" instead of "You make me angry," or "I feel rejected" instead of "You are excluding me again," or "I am confused" instead of "You don't make sense." In this way, we own our feelings—we take full responsibility for them. And we convey our feelings to others, creating trust in the process.

Finally, anticipation can cause us to be more aware. Resolving interpersonal conflict is easiest when we listen to the other person and respond to him or her with feedback. Conflict is likely to be reduced when we try to support and understand the other person.

IMPROVING SKILLS IN CONFLICT MANAGEMENT

The following ideas will aid in developing a constructive approach to dealing with conflict situations.[17] Remember that there are no guaranteed solutions or sure-fire approaches. Remember, too, that not all conflicts can be resolved but that we can always choose how to handle them.

Define the conflict.[18]   How we view the cause, size, and type of conflict affects how we manage it. If we know what events led up to the conflict and especially the specific event that triggered it, we may be able to anticipate and avoid future conflicts. We should learn to see the true size of a conflict: the smaller and more specific it is, the easier it will be to resolve. When a large, vague issue or principle is involved, the conflict itself is often escalated and enlarged. We can get very upset over how the system of higher education stifles individual initiative and growth, but that is a large, vague issue. To narrow the cause of the conflict, we might focus directly on a particular professor we are having problems with.

View the conflict as a joint problem.   There are two general ways of looking at a conflict: as a win-or-lose situation or as a joint problem. If we look at a conflict as a joint problem, there is a greater possibility for a creative solution which results in both of us being satisfied. If we are having trouble with our English professor, we could easily turn the situation into a win-lose confrontation. We might say, "She thinks she's so great, I'm going to show her. I'll go to the department head. . . ." If we perceive the conflict as a joint problem, we might say, "Perhaps she

Consider This

When a child exceeds a limit, his anxiety mounts because he expects retaliation and punishment. The parent need not increase the child's anxiety at this time. If the parent talks too much, he conveys weakness—at a time when he must convey strength. It is at times like this that the child needs an adult ally to help him control his impulses without loss of face. The following example illustrates an undesirable approach to limits:

Mother: I see that you won't be satisfied until you hear me yelling. O.K. [Loud and shrilly] stop it—or I'll beat the living daylights out of you! If you throw one more thing, I'll do something drastic!

Instead of using threats and promises, mother could have expressed her very real anger more effectively:

"It makes me mad to see that!"

"It makes me angry!"

"It makes me furious!"

"These things are not for throwing! The ball is for throwing!"

In enforcing a limit, a parent must be careful not to initiate a battle of wills.

—Haim G. Ginott, *Between Parent and Child*

has a point; maybe if I go in to see her, we could talk about this." The way we label a conflict partly determines the way we resolve it.

Defining conflict as a joint problem means trying to discover the differences and samenesses between our selves and the other person. There is always the question of not just how we define the problem but also of how the *other person* defines the problem and how our definitions differ.

State the problem.   We'll have a better chance of resolving a potential conflict quickly if we have a clear idea of what behavior is acceptable or unacceptable to us and if we express our position to the other person. When we say to another person, "When you interrupt me when we are talking to other people, I feel put down and unimportant" or "Every time you publicly criticize how I dress, I get angry with you," we explain specific behaviors that are unacceptable to us. And we can then discuss or change those behaviors.

When we focus on a specific bothersome behavior, we reveal what is going on inside us. We take responsibility for our feelings by using "I" language instead of "you" language. This lessens the likelihood of defensiveness by not placing the blame on the other person as we would if we said, "You insult me" or "You make me angry."

Once the problem has been stated, however, we must be careful of some of the typical response patterns that may lead to difficulty:

1. Giving in or placating. A response such as "Don't worry, it doesn't matter to me," or "Go ahead and do it, I don't care," leads to no real solution. When people give in like this, they may also speak in a soft or whiny voice. Sometimes they will back up, cower, or look down.

2. Blaming or pouncing. This involves a response such as "You don't know what you're doing; you're such an oaf," or "You know you're wrong, why don't you just admit it?" Such condemnatory responses insult the other person's competence and trustworthiness and imply a conviction of your own superiority. You may be dictatorial. You may also fold your arms, turn your back, or give a strong, silent, condemning stare.

3. Reasoning or computing. Responses such as, "Don't get emotional about this; just stick to the facts," or "Let's remain calm and cool like mature adults," condemn your opponents because they allow their feelings, hopes, wishes, or opinions to enter the conversation. But feelings must be part of conflict situations. Computing people will often give themselves away by their tenseness, lack of expression, and stiff inflexibility.

> Much positive behavior can be clarified when the corresponding negative behavior is clearly understood. For just a moment, engage in some self-diagnosis. Do you use any of these negative styles of behavior? Recalling the last conflict you were in, can you cite at least one thing <u>you</u> said or did that illustrates one of these response patterns?
>
> — giving in
>
> — blaming
>
> — reasoning
>
> — diverting
>
> Are there times when these types of behavior can be positive? Was it positive in your situation? What might have you done, assuming that it was not, to make the situation more positive? Would you just refrain from this kind of behavior, or would you engage in a more positive type of behavior?

4. Diverting or distracting. In this response pattern, a person may skirt the issue by interjecting, "Did you know that Lisa has started going out with Mike?" when you were disagreeing over whether or not an action you took was unfair or thoughtless. Or just as you were getting into a heavy discussion of a controversial topic, one person may say, "Did I tell you what Professor X did in class this morning?" The diverting person tries to ignore the serious situation. Such distracting is often accompanied by random or jerky body movements. Sometimes the distractor will giggle or laugh or look away.

The four styles of behavior described above are not mutually exclusive. It is possible that we engage in each of these styles at different times. These are choices we make depending on the other person, the situation, the nature of the message, and how we feel about ourselves at that moment.

The style of response we choose may also be dependent on our socialization. For example, males in our culture generally are socialized to blame or to reason. Females, on the other hand, are socialized to give in or to divert. To keep your socialization process in mind as you monitor your response style will help you to understand it better.

These response patterns are considered typical—but negative. There is a positive pattern, however, that allows us not only to state the problem in an effective manner but to deal with it in such a way that it

Consider This

DEAR ANN LANDERS: My husband and I are in the U.S. Army, stationed in Munich. We have been reading your column in Stars and Stripes for a long time. When you spoke to the conclave of teenagers in the Bavarian Alps five years ago, we were there, and so were our children.

In exchange for the sound advice you have given us through the years, I would like to share something with you. It is a list of suggestions by army chaplain John Bakle. He calls it "Creative Fighting." Here are the ground rules he has suggested to help strengthen marriages. I hope you will consider them good enough to print.
—LONGTIME ANN FAN

DEAR FAN: I do, and I will. Here they are, with my thanks to you and Chaplain Bakle:
• Express opinions, desires, and concerns as calmly as possible. Listen as well as talk.
• Try to appreciate your mate's point of view, even if it doesn't make much sense at the moment.

• Differences should not be discussed during meals or at bedtime.
• Don't zero in on your spouse's vulnerabilities to gain the upper hand.
• Don't rake up old arguments.
• Don't call each other names.
• Don't use the silent treatment. It ends effective communication and the possibility of compromise.
• Avoid wild accusations, verbal abuse, threats, and shouting the other down.
• Don't play psychiatrist by analyzing the other party.
• Don't drag in children and relatives as allies or go-betweens.
• Physical violence can never be condoned.
        And now, Chaplain Bakle, just to make it an even dozen, may I add one more?
• Never go to bed mad.

—syndicated in *The Blade: Toledo, Ohio*, October 25, 1979

is likely to bring positive results to all concerned. The pattern is called *leveling*. People who level with others engage in the following kinds of positive behavior. They:

—express their feelings, attitudes, ideas, wishes, goals, and expectations
—listen to the feelings, attitudes, ideas, wishes, goals, and expectations of others
—focus on the topic being discussed
—are sensitive and responsive to the location, mood, time available, climate, and other situation variables

Check your perceptions.   Under any circumstances, it is easy to be misunderstood, misquoted, or misinterpreted. Especially in a conflict situation, we should always check to make certain our message has been received accurately. We should also make sure we understand the other person's responses by paraphrasing them before we answer. Because our emotions quicken in times of conflict, further hurt or resentment can occur quickly through distortions caused by expectations or predispositions. Empathic listening is essential. We can determine where we are in our conversation with another person through paraphrases and summaries.

Generate possible solutions.   It is important, once we have shared what is bothering us, to consider how change can occur. We need not come up with all the solutions ourselves. A joint, cooperative solution is more likely to work. Flexibility is important in this process. Julius Fast views flexibility as extremely valuable, calling it "an awareness of alternative solutions as well as the ability to discard one solution if it doesn't work and select another."[19] What is needed? What can the other person do? What can we do? What can be done together? These are realistic questions that should be raised. As we get possible answers to these questions, we should paraphrase and summarize them so that we are certain that both of us know what has been suggested and what alternatives exist.

Reach a mutually acceptable solution.   When we have considered all the possible alternatives we and the other person could generate, we should decide which of them would be mutually acceptable. It is important that we find an answer somewhat agreeable to everyone involved.

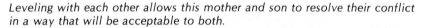

Leveling with each other allows this mother and son to resolve their conflict in a way that will be acceptable to both.

Try This

How would you cope with each of the following situations? Would your reaction help to maintain a positive interpersonal relationship? Your goal should be to effectively cope with the situation without generating new or unnecessary conflict.

1. You have just been accused of cheating and you are not guilty.

2. You have been told that a trusted friend is sharing your intimate secrets with a person you despise.

3. Your roommate is telling you that you cannot use your room at certain times.

4. You have just bought a new car and one of your friends wants to borrow it for the weekend.

5. Some people you like want you to go drinking with them tonight and you have a tough exam in the morning.

6. Your parents have just told you they do not like the people you hang around with.

7. Your closest friend wants to break off your relationship.

8. You have been given what you consider an unfairly low grade by a teacher you have no respect for.

But we cannot stop there. We all should understand the possible outcomes of implementing the solution. What is likely to happen? We should also understand what needs exist for cooperative interaction. In what ways, for example, will a particular solution require us to work together? When we have come to a final agreement on how to settle our conflict, we should make certain everyone fully understands what we agreed on by paraphrasing and summarizing the results.

If we cannot reach an agreement we should stop. Plan another meeting. Try again later. Getting away from the problem for a while may result in new insights being generated.

Implement and evaluate the solution.   Before we put the proposed solution into effect, we should try to agree on how we will check it later to see if it solved the problem. Plan a check-up meeting to evaluate progress. After we implement the solution, we'll want to find out if the results are mutually satisfying. If they aren't, we might have to go back to the beginning, possibly to our original definition of the conflict. We should have some way of knowing how to tell if the implemented solution worked well or did not work at all. If we have moved through the conflict successfully or are at least making progress, some gesture of appreciation might be appropriate.

It should be clear that these suggestions for coping with conflict are designed to provide a framework. No two conflict situations are identical; thus, no two ways of dealing with conflict will be exactly the same. Many of the decisions we face must be made instantaneously; how we cope is often a function of how quickly and accurately we are able to respond. However, successful coping may also result from slow, deliberate action. The discussion of ways to improve our skills in conflict management was designed, not to make the situation more complex than necessary, nor to prolong solutions unnecessarily. The point has been to set the tone or the appropriate frame of reference for decisions, whether quick or slow.

Conflict in interpersonal communication is an inevitable human experience. We are unique, the next person is unique; when these uniquenesses meet, conflict can occur. Conflict does not need to fracture friendships, split marriages, or break up other interpersonal relationships. There is nothing inherently destructive, threatening, or mysterious about conflict. How well we handle it while maintaining our values and our self-esteem and, at the same time, protecting the values and self-esteem of other people will help determine our effectiveness in interpersonal relationships. We are often called to stand up for our rights, values, and beliefs—to be assertive. Assertiveness is the subject of the next chapter.

Consider This

Findings of a University of Akron study of the psychodynamics of anger indicate the importance of getting rid of your anger by sharing it with understanding members of the family, relating the events of the day that have gotten you down and made you mad enough to commit various kinds of mayhem. It is pointed out that "every anger verbalization of this kind, especially when it is done in the presence of loved ones who are not critical but forgiving, makes possible a reduction of the failure feeling that can develop during the day in competitive living. Abreaction (the releasing of repressed emotions by reliving, in words, feelings or actions, the original traumatic situation) is good for the soul, the heart and the mind and should be practiced whenever possible."

It is pointed out in the same study that at times when there are no trusted and sympathetic persons you can talk to, you can abreact "by speaking into a tape recorder and then playing the tape back." And it is noted that while this method of getting anger out of the system is not quite as effective as abreacting before another person, it does get rid of the anger by extraverting it—providing it with means of expression—and thus keeping it from doing damage to the self.

In a University of California study of the psychosocial effects of anger, which evaluates the findings of other leading researches, it is concluded that "One of the most recognizable functions of anger arousal is that it energizes our behavior and increases the vigor with which we act. In addition to strong responses, such as slamming doors or raising the volume of one's voice, this energizing effect can also enable a person to assertively confront provocation or injustice." And it is noted that nearly all social movements have anger as a driving force for efforts at social change. It is also observed that anger serves an important expressive or communicative function in the marriage relationship. It is pointed out that "A healthy relationship depends on the ability of partners to express anger (when they feel it) and give one another negative feedback at times. Some problems never even reach the discussion stage—where they can be aired—until one member of the relationship becomes angry."

—John E. Gibson, *Family Weekly*, April 29, 1979

Consider This

OTHER READING

George R. Bach and Peter Wyden, *The Intimate Enemy: How to Fight Fair in Love and Marriage* (New York: Avon Books, 1968). Fighting is good for you, the authors contend. They provide constructive ways to use fights. This is an excellent book on how to use conflict and defensiveness positively. Many examples and illustrations demonstrate the significance and importance of their suggestions.

Ernst G. Beier and Evans G. Valens, *People-Reading: How We Control Others, How They Control Us* (New York: Warner Books, 1975). This book focuses on what the authors label "unaware communication"— cues delivered without awareness. The authors attempt to answer the questions, "Why do we behave as we do?" and "What kind of information do we have to look for and work with to change behavior?" Beier and Valens encourage the reader to examine and try to improve the whole fabric of unsettling relationships.

Eric Berne, *Games People Play: The Psychology of Human Relationships* (New York: Grove Press, Inc., 1964). Berne's catalog of games that people play in their family and business relationships is designed to heighten awareness. Berne contends that in playing games people are striving for an emotional payoff.

Julius Fast, *Creative Coping: Your Guide to Positive Living* (New York: Perennial Library, 1976). This is a survival manual on how to get along with our fellow human beings. We all use such coping elements as aggression, flexibility, empathy, reason, masking, and control. The methods and examples in this book provide further alternatives and approaches.

Robert J. Ringer, *Winning Through Intimidation* (Greenwich, Conn.: A Fawcett Crest Book, 1974). The purpose of this book, like many of the others, is to promote awareness. To know what intimidation is, how people become intimidated, and how to avoid falling victim to intimidation can be helpful in avoiding conflict situations.

Everett L. Shostrom, *Man, the Manipulator: The Inner Journey from Manipulation to Actualization* (New York: Bantam Books, 1967). All people are manipulators. Many of us do not recognize the manipulation we use and are exposed to. Shostrom explains both the manipulations and the alternatives. There is an excellent chapter on "Teachers and Students."

NOTES

[1]George R. Bach and Peter Wyden, *The Intimate Enemy: How to Fight Fair in Love and Marriage* (New York: Avon Books, 1968), pp. 25–26.

[2]George R. Bach and Herb Goldberg, *Creative Aggression: The Art of Assertive Living* (New York: Avon Books, 1974), p. 82.

[3]Robert J. Doolittle, "Conflicting Views of Conflict: An Analysis of Basic Communication Textbooks," *Communication Education* 26 (March 1977) 121.

[4]Kenneth E. Boulding, *Conflict and Defense* (New York: Harper and Row, 1962), p. 5.

[5]Based on pgs. 172–76 from *Elements of Interpersonal Communication* by John W. Keltner. Copyright © 1973 by Wadsworth Publishing Company, Inc., Belmont, California 94002. Reprinted by permission of the publisher.

[6]Ron Adler and Neil Towne, *Looking Out/Looking In: Interpersonal Communication* (San Francisco: Rinehart Press, 1975), p. 303.

[7]Julius Fast, *Creative Coping: A Guide to Positive Living* (New York: William Morrow and Co., Inc., 1976), pp. 187–88.

[8]W. Charles Redding, *Communication Within the Organization* (New York: Industrial Communication Council, 1972), p. 87.

[9]From *Man, the Manipulator* by Everett Shostrom. Copyright © 1967 by Abingdon Press. Used by permission.

[10]Erich Fromm, "Man Is Not a Thing," *Saturday Review* (March 16, 1957), pp. 9–11.

[11]Richard C. Huseman, James M. Lahiff, and John D. Hatfield, *Interpersonal Communication in Organizations: A Perceptual Approach* (Boston: Holbrook Press, Inc., 1976), p. 99.

[12]Redding, *Communication Within the Organization*, pp. 28, 30, and 37.

[13]Fast, *Creative Coping*, p. 187.

[14]Ibid., pp. 187–88.

[15]Shostrom, *Man, the Manipulator*, p. 50.

[16]Ibid., p. 53.

[17]David W. Johnson, *Reaching Out* (Englewood Cliffs, N.J.: Prentice-Hall, Inc., 1972), pp. 217–19.

[18]This approach is a variation of Dewey's problem-solving method. See John Dewey, *How We Think* (Chicago: D. C. Heath, 1910).

[19]Fast, *Creative Coping*, p. 53.

9

Getting There from Here:
Assertiveness

You are sitting alone in your room one evening. You've done all your assignments and readings for the next day. Everything is quiet. "Now, finally," you think, "I have some time just for my self—to do what *I* want to do." Just then there is a knock at the door. A close friend asks you if you would, as a special favor, go to a meeting with her. You get a sinking feeling in your stomach. You really wanted this time to be alone and yet, after all, this is one of your closest friends! What do you do? How do you feel about your self and your friend as a result of your choice?

We've all had the experience of needing to assert our selves with loved ones, teachers, doctors, salesclerks, and public employees. With friends and with strangers. With children and with people much older than we are. How do we handle it? In this chapter I'm going to consider different ways of coping with situations that too often end up awkward and leave us with bad feelings about our selves and other people. I'm going to look at how our attitudes, ideas, and values affect our choices. I hope to give you information that will help you pinpoint your real feelings and improve your skills in direct, honest, and appropriate communication.

WHAT IS ASSERTIVENESS?

What do we mean by "assertiveness"? Self-assertion usually begins with saying, "I am." It's a hard thing for many of us to say. Equally hard is "I want." Assertiveness means thinking, saying, and acting on the fact that each of us *is* and *wants* certain things. We can be assertive without infringing on the rights of others and feel comfortable about our behavior.[1]

What is being encouraged here is a degree of selfishness, but not the extreme kind of selfishness that is self-seeking, self-satisfying, and egotistical to the exclusion of all else. Most people are taught from childhood that selfishness is wrong, but there is a level of selfishness that is healthy and productive. Caring for one's self is not only good; it is necessary. Like anything else, selfishness can be carried too far, as when we care *only* about our selves or try to satisfy *only* our own desires and the rest of the world be damned. But keep in mind throughout this discussion of assertiveness that selfishness in the sense of self-affirmation is healthy. We must maintain and defend our basic

Try This

Although most of us are capable of communicating in a variety of ways, we often choose to fall back on habitual, familiar, routine approaches to interpersonal situations. We may tend to repeat these styles in certain situations.

Blaming, or Aggressive Style
Do you act in a demanding way? Are you a fault-finder? Do you act in a superior way? Is domination your major goal?

Placating, or Nonassertive Style
Do you try to please everyone? Do you often apologize? Do you seldom disagree? Are you unable to express what you want in a direct and forthright manner? Do you avoid conflict at all costs?

Computing, or Intellectual Style
Do you give the impression of a calm, cool, collected personality? Do you hold your feelings in? Do you emphasize logic and rationality?

Distracting, or Manipulative Style
Do you avoid threatening situations? Do you manipulate yourself out of unpleasant communication encounters? Do you use distracting maneuvers?

Leveling, or Assertive Style
Are you able to stand up for your rights? Are you able to express your feelings, thoughts, and needs directly and honestly? Do you respect yourself?*

Because a range of styles is available, there are different ways to respond. Each style is effective in certain specific situations. But problems occur when we use one style, indiscriminately, for all communication situations. That is why self-diagnosis becomes important.

*Reprinted by permission of the author and publisher. Virginia Satir, *Peoplemaking*, Science and Behavior Books Inc., Palo Alto, California, 1972.

CATHY   **by Cathy Guisewite**

human rights. We have to put our selves forward boldly, at times, to show concern for our selves, to protect our selves, and to *be* our selves.

We have the right to be and to express our selves and to feel good about doing so as long as we do not hurt others in the process.[2] No matter how confident or successful we feel, there are still areas in our lives where we may hesitate to claim our rights, where we are anxious about our feelings, where we are unable to respond to anger, or where we feel powerless in our relations with people. But each of us has the right to be treated with respect. Each of us has the right to have and to express feelings, opinions, and wants; to be listened to and taken seriously by others; to set our own priorities; to be able to say no without feeling guilty; and to get what we pay for. These are some of our fundamental rights.[3]

You might wonder what's wrong with *not* being assertive. I can think of several things wrong with it. By not asserting our selves:

1. We may end up with shoddy merchandise and service;
2. We bottle up our real feelings;
3. We don't do anything to improve a bad situation that already exists and needs improvement;
4. We are cheating another person out of a chance to air the real issues;
5. We get involved in situations we would rather not be in;
6. We end up being a "yes" person—having to do all the work while others sit by and watch;
7. We run into communication barriers because nobody is willing to say what he or she *really* wants.

Consider This _____

If you are reticent about asking for a raise or telling neighbors that their stereo music is shaking the pictures on your walls, bite your tongue no longer. . . .

There is someone who will ask for that raise for you, will tell your best friend that it would be an asset to him if he started using deodorant, and will even tell your loved one that you're in love with someone else.

This someone, with all the gusto and assertiveness that many of us lack, is a 30-year-old Western Springs housewife and mother of two who, for a $5 fee and the cost of making a long-distance phone call, will deliver your message.

Marti Hough began operating her "Speak Up Service" from her home in November after taking an eight-week assertiveness training course.

"Many people in the course would say 'I can't do it, why don't you do it for me' and out of this I saw there was a need for someone to speak for others," she said.

"I've been averaging about six calls per day and have received calls from all over the Chicago area and even calls from as far away as Connecticut and Virginia."

She says that 75 per cent of her callers are men.

Hough will receive calls between 9 a.m. and 5 p.m. Monday through Friday but will deliver messages whenever it's best to reach the designated person.

"The only information I take is the caller's name and number, the name and number of the person to be contacted, when this person can be reached, and the message," she said. . . .

Most just say thanks when they receive the calls, but Hough says a few get furious.

"One man's boss had refused to give him severance pay, and when I called the employer he went crazy and started yelling," said Hough. "Another woman, who lived in an apartment building, was annoying her neighbors because she would get up at 8 o'clock every Sunday morning and make a lot of noise with her heavy soled shoes. She got furious when I phoned and said the neighbors have asked her to wear soft-soled slippers."

—From "For $5, she'll call your boss a jerk" by Carole Carmichael, *Chicago Tribune*, January 23, 1977. Copyright © 1977 by Chicago Tribune Company. All Rights Reserved.

Consider This

ASSERTIVENESS AND COMMUNICATION RELATIONSHIPS

Our society tends to evaluate human beings on scales which make some people "better" than others. In some situations, the "right" person to be is a 40-year-old WASP male. In another situation, the "right" people are black, teen-aged girls. In another, a middle-aged mother is the "right" person to be. Outsiders (anyone else!) can very easily be made to feel out of place by the "better" people in any given situation. Social structures perpetuate this treatment of people in these roles; in them, some people are treated as if they are actually of greater value than others.[4] While society is not likely to change overnight, we can change our perspective about communication relationships. If we see that all human beings are equal and if we recognize that we have the same fundamental rights as the other person in interpersonal relationships, despite roles and titles, we will find it easier to assert our selves and feel comfortable doing it.

What, in any given situation, might make us hold back from asserting our selves? A few possibilities:

1. laziness
2. apathy
3. feelings of inadequacy
4. fear of being considered unworthy, unloved, or unacceptable
5. fear of hurting the other person or making him or her angry
6. fear of getting no reinforcement
7. fear of not knowing how to accomplish our desired goal
8. feeling that if we don't do it, someone else will

No One Is More Equal than Anyone Else

There is a difference between the legitimate exercise of authority and the infringement of another person's rights. Consider an employer-employee relationship. Certain defined, often well-understood relationships exist between an employee and a boss. In a job situation, an employer can literally tell the employee what to do—type this, read that, add this, move that over here. That is not to say a boss might not try to infringe on the rights of an employee and overstep his or her legitimate authority. A boss's authority usually does not extend to telling an employee how carefully to drive or where to go for dinner or interfering in other personal affairs. It does not extend to telling the employee to use personal time on the boss's behalf or to fudge the record books. The illegitimate use of authority, in these situations, becomes an infringement of rights.

Acting in our own best interests is a matter of personal choice. Who knows better than we do what is best for us? The key to assertiveness *is* choice. There are rarely any single ways that we *must* act in particular situations. True, some situations have prescribed or "proper" ways of acting, but even within such guidelines, there is often great latitude for individuality and variety. For example, we know that we would act with a certain amount of deference if we were introduced to the President of the United States—that is a generally prescribed guideline—but within the realm of deference, we can still be our selves. The main point is that we need not be manipulated by circumstances or by people. We must choose for our selves how to act.

Try This

For each of the following situations, think of how you would respond. Be honest. Are you as assertive as you would like to be?

1. You were passed over for a raise.

2. Your grade on your paper was much lower than you expected.

3. A friend wants to use the research you did for a history paper.

4. You have been nominated for a job you do not have time to do.

5. You have been selected to serve on a prestigious faculty-student committee that you have little interest in.

6. You have a friend with a constant problem of body odor.

7. Your friends want you to borrow something from your roommate without telling him or her.

8. You find your seat taken at a ball game but there is one that is not as good several rows higher.

9. A police officer says you were going ten miles an hour over the speed limit when you know you were not.

10. Your parents make some derogatory remarks about your friends.

11. You just got a box of popcorn that is only three-quarters full but there is a line of people waiting for service.

Learning to be assertive involves learning to defend our own best interests.

ASSERTIVENESS, NONASSERTIVENESS, AND AGGRESSION

12. You have just been introduced to a person who did not hear your name correctly and has just called you by the incorrect name.

13. You are in line waiting to get a drink of water and someone has inadvertently stepped directly in front of you.

Did you find you would be assertive in each case? If not, why not? Is there a pattern to your assertive/nonassertive behavior?

You have come to meet with an instructor to discuss a research paper you wrote and that she recently returned. She is a strict teacher who scares you a little in her manner and approach. You put a great deal of time and effort into your paper and you feel the grade is not justified. A girl you know wrote the paper the night before and got an A on hers; you spent the better part of a week on yours and received a low C. She has just begun the conversation with, "Well, I'm glad we are going to have a chance to discuss your paper. . . ."

You have many different options as far as your response to this instructor is concerned. You might reply: (1) "I'm sorry the paper didn't live up to your expectations. I really tried, but . . . you know . . . I guess I just didn't give the paper enough time. . . ." or (2) "You have no right to give me a C on my paper! I worked harder than the girl down the hall and she got an A. Teachers are really unfair; they never give you credit for the work you do. If you don't change my grade, I'm going to see the dean" or (3) "I think you should know how hard I worked on this paper. I spent most of last week researching and writing. I really thought the paper deserved more than a C. Will you tell me your reasons for the grade? Then at least I would know how to approach your next assignment."

These three alternatives are oversimplified for the purposes of explanation. You would, of course, have other options as well. You could discuss the grade and the reasons for it without becoming apologetic or defensive at the outset. Discussion unencumbered by apology or defensiveness is likely to create a positive climate and yield satisfying results as well. Discussion should be conducted in an atmosphere of strength and conviction. That is, you should not sacrifice your values or compromise your standards; you should be able to defend your work and support your overall effort. Discussion is a mutual process of give-and-take that involves *mutual* compromise—not self-sacrifice, apology, or defensiveness. Effective discussion can and should take place in a climate of assertiveness.

Clearly, the (1) and (2) responses above are inadequate. In (1) you apologized and used the "excuse" technique. This nonassertive behavior is both dishonest and unfair. You did not really express your feelings and you denied your teacher honest feedback to her evaluation of the paper. In (2) you showed little sensitivity to the instructor's feelings and used aggressive language that would probably put her off. Only in (3) could you save your self and the instructor embarrassment, hurt, or awkwardness by a straightforward, assertive response.[5] Your initial response sets the tone for all the communication to follow.

A person who is too politely restrained, tactful, diplomatic, modest, and self-denying—whose behavior falls at the extreme *non-assertive* end of the continuum—may be unable to make the choice to act. To act is to be assertive. A nonassertive person says, in effect, he or she will let someone else decide what will happen to him or her. Not to decide is to decide. Freedom of choice and self-control are possible when we develop assertive responses. Being assertive lets others know where we stand. It gives us choices because we are not allowing others to act for us; we act in our own behalf. We reveal a nonassertive style, on the other hand, when we do the following things:

1. Stay in the back of groups;
2. Always stick to the middle-of-the-road position or refrain from taking a stand;
3. Allow others to make decisions for us;
4. Pass by potential friendships because they seem like too much effort;

5. Always keep our voice low or avoid eye contact to keep from calling attention to our selves;
6. Verbally agree with others despite our real feelings;
7. Bring harm or inconvenience to our selves to avoid harming or inconveniencing others;
8. Procrastinate to avoid problems and to keep from making decisions;
9. Always consider our selves weaker and less capable than others;
10. Always escape responsibility with excuses and "good" reasons.

Nonassertiveness can cause the beginning of a negative cycle. For example, we may get a paper back from a teacher with a lower grade on it than we feel the paper deserves. If we go along with the teacher's evaluation without question or discussion, we may acquire a whole new set of doubts—"What is wrong with me? I am not cut out for this. I cannot compete. I'll never succeed." These doubts can lead to further and sometimes intensified inadequate behaviors. (See Figure 1.) We may come to think of our selves as wholly inadequate when, in fact, we may simply have misunderstood the assignment.

Consider This

For its victims, the people perpetually standing on street corners glancing at their watches, lateness touches an amazingly sensitive nerve.

"It's because lateness is regarded as a personal assault, as a hostile, aggressive act," Dr. Brockman [a Chicago psychiatrist] explains. "In order for the late person to make himself feel good, or special, he has to make someone else feel bad. It's as if he's saying, 'You're nothing. You don't deserve to be treated properly.' And that's demeaning."

One of the things particularly galling to victims is the way late people wrap every act of tardiness in a thick blanket of excuses. Sometimes, it's hard to know which is worse, the lateness or the blow-by-blow account of the awful traffic on the Long Island Expressway.

"But the speech is necessary," Dr. Brockman says. "It's the late person's way of trying to explain his behavior to himself. He wants others to believe his explanation, to share his defense, so to speak, so he can protect himself from being discovered. This helps him keep from blowing his cover."

It's the old game of Schlemiel that Eric Berne talks about in his book "Games People Play." A makes a mistake. A apologizes profusely. B forgives him, and A is happy. So a first step toward breaking the cycle is: Stop listening to the apologies, because they're just part of the game.

—Constance Rosenblum, *The Blade: Toledo, Ohio*, October 13, 1977

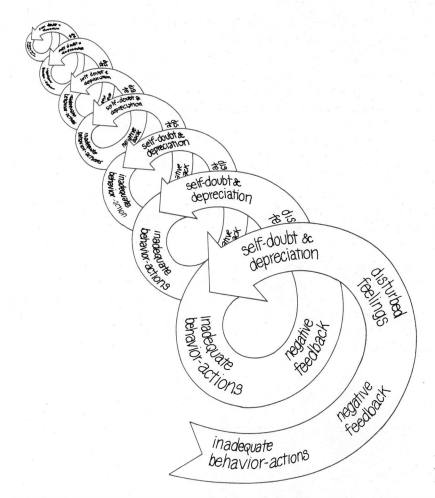

Figure 1.
Self-doubt may lead to further inadequate behaviors.

If we are nonassertive we deny our selves and fail to express our actual feelings. We leave it to someone else to decide what's to happen to us and we may *never* reach our desired goals. This places an unnatural and uncomfortable burden on our interpersonal communications. How do we know how others feel unless they are willing to tell us? Interpersonal communication should not be a game where each person must cleverly try to find out what the other person *really* thinks. Assertive behavior reduces game-playing and makes interpersonal communication more effective.

The *aggressive* style of response is practically the complete opposite of the nonassertive style. If we are aggressive, we might:

1. Interrupt others when they are speaking;
2. Try to impose our position on others;

3. Always make decisions for others;
4. Use and abuse friendships;
5. Always speak loudly and otherwise call attention to our selves;
6. Accuse, blame, and find fault with others despite their feelings;
7. Bring harm or cause inconvenience to others rather than bring harm or cause inconvenience to our selves;
8. Speak beside the issue, distort the facts, or misconstrue the truth to get our solutions accepted quickly;
9. Always consider our selves stronger and more capable than others;
10. Accept responsibility and positions of authority for the purposes of manipulation or to give us a means of vehemently expressing our selves.

If we use aggressive behavior we try to accomplish our life goals at the expense of others. Although we may find this behavior expresses our feelings, we may also hurt others in the process by making choices for them and by implying they are worth less than we are as people.

Although this man's aggressive style expresses how he feels, it does so at the expense of effective interpersonal communication.

Consider This

Since childhood women have been trained to hold back and control their negative feelings. The admonitions come early on: "Forgive and forget" . . . "Not to care" . . . "Someone has to keep peace in the family" . . . "Talk about it when you've cooled off" . . . "Nice girls don't get into fights." This kind of conditioning results in two types of women:

> **Type A:** For whatever reasons, she has never learned to express her anger. Instead she rationalizes, "Men are supposed to be aggressive—it's all right for men to express violent emotions." No matter what the provocation, she clenches her teeth and holds in her resentments. In some cases, she isn't even aware she is angry.

> **Type B:** She too has not learned to appropriately express anger. Instead of ever showing displeasure over the minor, irritating day-by-day episodes that take place in everyone's life, she says nothing at the time. Then, an office mate, salesperson, or friend makes a chance remark that triggers a red flash of rage, and, on an unpremeditated basis, she lashes out in violent anger. This fury has unfortunate consequences: She feels terrible and she alienates people.

Both are extremes. Assertive anger means knowing your rights, appropriately expressing your feelings when someone tries to interfere with your rights, places an obstacle in your path, or violates your dignity. You must also realize that uncontrolled lashing out is not an assertive expression of anger. The hallmark of assertiveness is integrated behavior where, taking everything into consideration, you decide how best to express your anger.

—Jean Baer, *How to Be an Assertive (Not Aggressive) Woman in Life, in Love, and on the Job*

The *assertive* style, in contrast, is self-enhancing because it shows a positive firmness. The assertive style is revealed when we:

1. Allow others to complete their thoughts before we speak;
2. Stand up for the position that matches our feelings or the evidence;
3. Make our own decisions based on what we think is right;
4. Look to friendships as opportunities to learn more about our selves and others and to share ideas;
5. Can spontaneously and naturally enter into conversations using a moderate tone and volume of voice;
6. Try to understand the feelings of others before describing our own;
7. Try to avoid harm and inconvenience by talking out problems before they occur or finding rational means for coping with unavoidable harm or inconvenience;

266 Getting There from Here

8. Face problems and decisions squarely;
9. Consider our selves strong and capable, but generally equal to most other people;
10. Face responsibility with respect to our situation, needs, and rights.

As truly assertive people, we feel free to reveal our selves. We communicate in an open, direct, honest, and appropriate manner. We go after what we want and make things happen. Finally, we act in a way that we, our selves, can respect. We know that we cannot always win. We accept our limitations but no matter what the situation, we always make a good try so that we will maintain our self-respect.[6]

At different times we may be nonassertive or aggressive or assertive. The problems occur when we are nonassertive or aggressive too often—when it is a *habit* for us to be one way or the other. The idea is to be assertive when we want to be—not controlled by the habits of others or by situations. When we can no longer choose for our selves how we will act, the trouble begins.

COPING WITH MANIPULATION: GETTING OUT FROM UNDER

There is some manipulator in all of us, but it might be easier to recognize manipulative behavior if we look at some of the many ways we are manipulated. How can we identify what is being done to us by subtle and overt manipulators so that we can take sensible steps to correct it? There are, of course, times when authority may be legitimately exercised over us. Just because we sometimes have to do things we do not like to do does not necessarily mean we are being manipulated. When we talk about being manipulated we mean those times when we are exploited, used, or controlled or when we are treated as a thing rather than as a person. Some signs of manipulation are.[7]

1. When people in positions of authority pull rank on us—rely wholly on their position to get us to do something. "Do this for me because I'm your boss" or "It's right because I say it's right and I'm your _____" may indicate when this is occurring.
2. When people give in to us too readily, feign extreme sensitivity, or withdraw from the slightest confrontation. "Sorry, I forgot" or "I couldn't hear you" or "I just could not understand" may be examples of this passivity. Sometimes people manipulate by backing off.

Make up an aggressive, an assertive, and a nonassertive response to each of the following questions and statements. This will help you become familiar with the differences between these response styles.

1. Can I nominate you for our organization's president?
2. Would you carry in the things from the car?
3. Prepare a speech for us on why we should abolish grades.
4. Help me with my homework.
5. Could you take me downtown?
6. Would you babysit Saturday night while we go to a movie?
7. Go to the lecture and take notes for all of us.
8. Would you tell him for me?
9. We're all going. Aren't you going to join us?
10. Tell him he expects too much.

With which of the response styles do you feel most comfortable? Most uncomfortable? What other conditions would it be helpful to know in the above examples that would indicate which of the three response styles is most appropriate?

Consider This

DEAR ANN LANDERS: Recently you told a reader, "Show me a person who is repeatedly taken advantage of, and I will show you someone who allows people to kick him around."

Well, dear Ann, I was one of those people who was dumped on a lot and taken advantage of by everybody—until I went in for assertiveness training. I learned a great deal in that course and I would like to share some of it with your readers.

CHARACTERISTICS OF THE NONASSERTIVE PERSON

He confuses the goal of being liked with being respected.

He is conditioned to fears of being disliked or rejected, also fears of anxiety, expressions of anger, or feelings of tenderness.

He is unable to recognize the difference between being selfish in the bad sense and in the good sense.

He allows others to maneuver him into situations he doesn't want.

He is easily hurt by what others say and do.

He feels inferior because he is inferior. He limits his experiences and doesn't use his potential.

CHARACTERISTICS OF THE ASSERTIVE PERSON

He feels free to reveal himself—"This is me. This is what I feel, think, and want."

He can communicate with people on all levels—with strangers, friends, family. This communication always is open, direct, honest and appropriate.

He has an active orientation to life. He goes after what he wants. In contrast to the passive person who waits for things to happen, he attempts to make things happen.

He acts in a way that shows he respects himself, is aware that he cannot always win, and accepts his limitations. He always strives, in spite of the odds, to make the good try, so win, lose, or draw, he maintains his self-respect.

It took me a long time to get all this through my head, but now that I've absorbed these principles and live by them I am a new person.—J.R.M.

—syndicated in *The Blade: Toledo, Ohio,* December 15, 1977

Consider This

3. When people have all the answers, are too quick with their response to any objection, or seem to be outwitting and controlling us at every turn. We see this happening when people only pretend to listen to us but really have already made up their minds and are not about to change them.

4. When people become too dependent on us, wanting constant guidance and asking to be taken care of. "Would you mind doing this for me" or "I just can't seem to figure this out" may signify this kind of behavior is going on. Some people who seem to be always apologizing for their own inadequacy and asking for favors are really trying to manipulate us.

5. When people are overtly aggressive, unkind, or threatening to us. "If you don't do this, I'm going to . . ." or "You'll be sorry. . . ." are their ways of controlling us.

6. When people are excessively, unreasonably affectionate. Some people kill us with kindness. It is difficult to spot this kind of manipulation because these people make things so easy for us and are often very pleasant to be with. They win arguments and achieve their goals through sheer affection and kindness which we can never wholly reciprocate.

7. When people are extremely critical. These people manipulate by bulldozing everyone into accepting their critical standards. They blame others, distrust everyone, and are often resentful. "You can't trust Mark, remember when he . . ." or "Of course, that's all right if you like third-rate schools . . ." are the kinds of statements they might make.

8. When people are overly supportive. They manipulate us with their undying protection. We can always count on them to step in to our defense whether we ask them to or not. "I'll talk to her for you . . ." or "Let me take care of it for you . . ." are the statements they use to reveal their commitment to us.

Try This

Are you a person who is often manipulated? How often do you find yourself in situations where you are being manipulated? Answer the following questions honestly:

1. Does anyone ever pull rank on you?

2. Does anyone ever give in to you very quickly?

3. Does anyone you deal with seem to have all the answers?

4. Is there anyone who is too dependent on you?

5. Is anyone overtly aggressive, unkind, or threatening to you?

6. Is there someone who is excessively, unreasonably affectionate to you?

7. Is there someone who is extremely critical of you?

8. Is there someone who is overly protective of you and your efforts?

It may be that there is no one person who fits any of these categories. But it may be that certain situations cause people to act in these ways toward you. These categories, too, are not mutually exclusive. That is, a person who is trying to manipulate you may use several of these kinds of behaviors—not one alone.

Consider This

The ability to say No can be pyramided into a position of unique influence and authority. This power is usually financial, and manifests itself as a kind of "Scrooge power" in most organizations, in which every request for money, whether it is an investment, an expenditure or a raise, is automatically turned down at least twice, however reasonable, even profitable, the request may be.

Power and money await anyone who can manage to say No all the time, nor are such people easy to find. Almost everybody likes to be thanked and loved, no matter how powerful they are, and saying Yes is therefore a constant temptation for most people. The true "no-sayers" . . . are incorruptible and invaluable, nor do they mind looking ridiculous. Their mode of operation is simple: they say No to everything until overruled, secure in the knowledge that they are likely to be right at least sixty percent of the time and forgiven for the other forty percent. . . .

The most important thing for those who want to play the "no-game" is to be consistent—the moment you start saying Yes to some things, making value judgments, acceding to certain requests because they're reasonable, you've become simply another decision-maker.

—Michael Korda, *POWER! How to Get It, How to Use It*

In situations of manipulation, the kinds of cues listed above are often combined and exaggerated or are revealed consistently only over a period of time. Sometimes they are subtle, sometimes obvious. We, the manipulated, must be cautious in how we respond to them. Too often we see only one side of a person or only what we want to see, but just because we don't like a person it doesn't mean he or she is manipulating us. The crucial thing to watch for is whether our basic rights are being jeopardized or abused.

To get out from under a manipulator requires some understanding of the communication concepts we've been looking at throughout this book. In Chapter 3 we saw how important it is to trust our selves and others. To be assertive requires some basic faith in our selves and in our ability to cope with life. Trust is essential in coping with manipulation. Our perceptual skills are also important in learning how to assert our selves in manipulative situations. We need to be alive, interested, and responsive to our selves and to others. Becoming more aware helps us to make certain we are not just seeing what we want to see and hearing what we want to hear. It is easy for a manipulator to project faults and weaknesses on others without realizing that he or she is guilty of those very faults.

How effectively we listen to others directly affects how well we deal with manipulation. We should listen to discover whether the per-

Try This

Think of people who you feel have manipulated you. Can you picture specific instances where manipulation occurred? Was it with a:

—boss

—worrier

—seducer

—parasite

—hater

—pleaser

—blamer

—martyr

—dictator

—quitter

—con artist

—crier

—shamer

—helper

Can you now think of ways to cope with this manipulation? Are there things that you would do now to cope with this manipulation that you did not do at the time that it occurred?

son has made an error, is misinformed, or is trying to manipulate us. If we suspect manipulation, we must try to discover where the other person is coming from.

It isn't always easy to cope with manipulation and we can't always do it successfully. Trying to be direct and straightforward with others helps. Refraining from hostility also eases the situation. If we approach others confidently yet in a friendly way, we will serve as a model for the manipulator. We can try not to be judgmental and yet feel free to express our own convictions strongly. This is assertive behavior that will help us get out from under those who attempt to manipulate us.

IMPROVING SKILLS IN ASSERTIVENESS

Where do we begin? If we are serious about learning to assert our selves we must understand our rights—the ground on which we can stand and which we can defend just by being a human being. Our assertive rights are the framework upon which we build positive interpersonal relationships. If our rights are often violated, we will begin to find it difficult to express our individual selves to others. Trust may give way to suspicion, compassion may evolve into cynicism, warmth and closeness may disappear, and love (if it exists at all) may acquire an acid bite. The assertive rights that follow are statements about our humanness, about our true responsibilities for our selves and our own well-being, and about what other people should be able to expect of us.[8]

Take responsibility for your self.   This is our primary assertive right from which all the others are derived. If we take the responsibility for our own existence, then we are in control of our thinking, feeling and behavior. When someone, for whatever reason, reduces our ability to be the judge of what we do, we are being manipulated and our most basic right is in jeopardy.

When we can put this primary assertive right into practice, we will learn how to work out ways to judge our own behavior. Just through trial and error we will discover standards of behavior that fit our own personality and life-style. These standards need not be logical, consistent, or permanent; in fact, they may make no sense to anyone else. But our own judgment is *our* guide and it is important to us. This means we take full responsibility for our own happiness and well-being.

We derive our other rights from this one. In a sense, they are everyday applications of this prime right. They provide the foundation for assertive behavior.

"I don't want a raise, Mr. Harlingen. I just want bouquets and accolades and tokens of esteem and bravos and huzzahs and a piece of the action."

Don't overapologize. When we return merchandise, we are accustomed to explaining what is wrong with it. When we cannot go somewhere with a friend, we usually explain why we cannot go. But we often tend to overexplain. We offer lengthy apologies when a brief one would do. While some word of explanation is both polite and helpful, people are hardly ever interested in long, involved excuses. When others demand our explanation to convince us that we are wrong, they are manipulating our behavior and feelings. No friendship should be based upon the requirement that we explain our behavior at every turn. In asserting this right, we should, of course, observe common courtesy. Not to give a reason when one would be helpful may be seen as a negative reaction, especially if we are accustomed to giving reasons and if others expect them from us. But it's best to be brief.

Don't try to rearrange someone else's life. A friend may come to us wanting us to help him or her become healthy and happy. We may be compassionate and we may give advice and counsel, but the person with the problems has the responsibility of solving them. Our best guide in such situations is to assert who *we* are and the limits of what we're

Practice assertive responses for each of the following situations:

1. Someone pushed in front of you in line.

2. You must tell someone you no longer wish to date them.

3. You are trying to study and someone is making too much noise.

4. You are angry with your parents.

5. You must insist that your roommate does his or her fair share of the cleaning.

6. You must ask a friend to do a favor for you.

7. You have been served unsatisfactory food in a restaurant.

8. You want to express your love and affection to a special person.

9. A professor has made a statement that you consider untrue.

10. Someone you respect has expressed an opinion with which you strongly disagree.

11. A friend of yours is wearing a new outfit which you like.

12. A friend has made an unreasonable request of you.

13. A person is being blatantly unfair.

14. A friend has betrayed your confidence.

15. You want to ask a good friend to lend you a few dollars.

16. Someone keeps kicking the back of your chair in a movie.

17. Someone interrupts you in the middle of an important conversation.

18. A friend has criticized you unjustifiably.

able to do. We should help the other person to do the same. As much as we might wish good things for our friends, we really do not have the ability to create mental stability, well-being, or happiness for anyone else. We might temporarily be of some help, but real change requires hard work from the person who wants to change. The reality of the human condition is that everyone must learn to cope on his or her own.

Feel free to change your mind. There is a myth in our society that holds that if we change our minds we are irresponsible, two-faced, scatterbrained, and unreliable. The belief says if we do change our minds, we must justify our new choice or say that we were in error before. We don't want to appear to be wishy-washy because this can affect our credibility: "Don't trust him, he'll just turn around and change his mind!"

Human beings do, however, change their minds. We might make a decision about how to do something, and no sooner do we get started with it than we find a better way. Our goals and interests are constantly changing. Our choices may work for us in one situation, but there is no reason to believe they will work for us in another. To keep in touch with reality, to promote our own well-being and happiness, we must believe that changing our minds is both healthy and normal.

Feel free to make mistakes.   Nobody is perfect; everyone makes mistakes. If we think errors are wrong or should not be made, we leave our selves open to manipulation every time we make one. Often when we make costly errors we feel compelled to retreat and not call attention to our selves for awhile. In that submissive posture, we leave our selves open to people who want to make us pay for our error or who want to put us down for it.

If you make an error of judgment at work, for example, admit the mistake as soon as you realize it. Apologize to anybody who may have been hurt, then forget it. "It seemed like a good idea at the time" is often the most honest, simplest explanation. You may well be genuinely sorry if others were hurt by your mistake; the important thing is not to feel subhuman for having made it. When you realize you've erred, simply show that you are responsible. In this way, you admit that you made the mistake, that it made trouble for the other person, and that, like everyone else, you make mistakes.

Learn to recognize unanswerable questions.   Some questions are unanswerable. Some you may have heard are: "Didn't you know that would happen?" "Why didn't you remember to . . . ?" "What would this world be like if everyone . . . ?" What can we say? "I don't know! I don't know!" We do not need to have immediate answers for questions people ask us.

It is a fact news reporters depend on—most people are very uncomfortable leaving questions dangling, unanswered. Almost everyone will give *some* kind of answer, no matter how preposterous the question. But we should learn to see that questions in themselves do not demand answers. We need not be intimidated by inquiries.

We can recognize other people's attempts to manipulate us by phrases that begin with "What kind of a friend (or son or daughter) would do . . . ?" To deal with questions like this, we simply need to say, "I don't know. What kind of a friend (or son or daughter) would do . . . ?" No one can know all the possible consequences of his or her own behavior. If someone else wants to know, let him or her speculate! This is not a defense of irresponsibility, but there *are* limits to how much we can know.

Feel free to say "I don't know."   There are legitimate, answerable questions that we just do not have the answer to. Either we don't have the facts or we have not had time to think about them or we do not have enough evidence to make a judgment. Whatever, the best response to questions like these is, "I don't know." Sometimes others will try to commit us to a premature response or to quickly answer a question that is complex or confusing. It is better to say "I don't know" than to make the commitment. We should feel free to say we want more time to think about it.

Don't depend on the goodwill of others.   Everyone likes to be liked. Everyone needs to be liked. But although we all need other people, they don't all need to be our brothers and sisters. No matter what we do, someone is not going to like it or is going to get his or her feelings hurt. If we feel that we must have other people's goodwill before dealing with them, we become open to manipulation. All the other people need to do is to cut off goodwill and we are stopped.

Why do you suppose we have the stereotype of the smiling, friendly used-car dealer? Because the assumption is that we will feel liked and will want to keep the dealer's goodwill by buying a car. There are many examples of the "I like you" smile used for manipulative purposes. Parents control children by withholding smiles, politicians win friends with a broad grin, and advertisers generate sales by showing happy, smiling faces.

We are mistaken if we believe we must have the goodwill of anyone we relate with or we cannot deal with them. The belief continues that we need the cooperation of *all* others to survive and it is vital that everyone likes us. The next time you catch your self thinking like this, think again. Do you really care if this salesclerk (or whoever) likes you and the way you live your life? Would you accept this person's judgment on what you should or shouldn't have for lunch? Of course not! So why let him or her judge *you*? We may have great difficulty saying no if we assume that a relationship is impossible to maintain without 100% mutual agreement. We cannot live in terror of hurting other people's feelings. Sometimes we may offend others. Such is life.

Feel free to be illogical.   Logic is not always the answer in dealing with wants, motivations, and feelings. Our emotions occur in different degrees at different times. Logical reasoning may not help in understanding why we want what we want or in solving problems created by conflicting motivations.

Logic is not without its place, of course. We turn a paper in on time because we know if we don't we will lose a grade. We fill up the gas

Try This

Take a moment right now to practice alone saying "Yes, I agree" and "No, I don't think so." Say these phrases over several times just to hear how they sound.

With someone else, practice really listening to what he or she is saying. Don't just nod or smile indiscriminately at whatever is said. After listening, ask your self, "Do I really agree with what is being said?" Use the phrases, "Yes, I agree" and "No, I don't think so" or other emphatic statements. Say them like you really mean them. Let your reaction grow out of your genuine feelings and don't hesitate to speak up.

tank when it's nearly empty because we know that if we don't, we could get stranded. But being logical works best when we are dealing with things we completely understand, and often solutions to problems lie outside these limits. In some cases we just have to guess, no matter how crude that is or how inelegant the results. It is our right to be illogical.

Feel free to say "I don't understand."   It is impossible to understand much of what goes on around us but we survive nevertheless. We understand as a result of experience. But experience teaches us that we do not always understand what another person means or wants. We simply do not understand. People may try to manipulate us by implying we are expected to know something or to do something for them. We may not understand a teacher's explanation of a concept, or a gas station attendant's directions, or any everyday confusing situation. Rather than blame our selves automatically for not "getting" something, we should ask for clarification or restatement. Who says the other person is being as clear as possible?

We can hardly be expected to always understand what other people's needs are. Sometimes when we don't guess correctly, people think we are irresponsible or ignorant. Often, this manipulation occurs after a conflict. People who believe they have been wronged may expect us to understand that they are displeased with our behavior, that we should know what behavior displeases them, and that we should change so that they will no longer be hurt or angry. If we allow this manipulation, we end up blocked from what we want to do and often do something else to make up for wanting to do it in the first place. We have difficulty enough trying to read our own minds, without trying to perform this service for others.

Feel free to say "I don't care."   If we set our selves up to be perfectly informed and concerned in all matters, we will be disappointed and frustrated. It can't be done. Some things will matter more to us, others less. We have the assertive right to say that we do not care about certain things. We do not need perfect knowledge in what someone else has determined to be *the* important category. Some people may try to manipulate us into thinking we need to improve until we are perfect in all things.

The teacher who says, "How can you call your self a history major when you know nothing about medieval England?" and the athletic coach who says, "How do you expect to run the 440 when you eat sugar instead of honey?" are trying to impose their standards on us. If we submit, we fall into the trap of being affected by someone else's arbitrary choice of what constitutes perfection. We end up apologizing for failing in our obligation to become perfect in all things. The only certain way to stop this manipulation is by asking our selves, "Am I satisfied with my own performance and with my self?" We should be free to make our own judgment (remember the first assertive right) about whether or not we wish to make a change.

Being assertive will help us communicate directly, honestly, and appropriately with people we meet in dyadic communication situations. Assertiveness encourages goodwill and self-confidence and aids in pinpointing our real feelings. It is a means of self-expression and has the added advantage of making us feel good about our selves. Asserting our selves is how we get from here to there, from being an object or a pawn to being a human being with rights that should be recognized.

This freedom of positive expression will result in greater openness in the communication of genuine, positive feelings toward other people. Those who are most likely to benefit from our new behavior are those who are closest to us most of the time: our family, our friends, and our work associates. Developing more effective interpersonal communication with these people is the subject of the next two chapters.

OTHER READING

Robert E. Alberti and Michael L. Emmons, *Stand Up, Speak Out, Talk Back!* (New York: Pocket Books, 1975). This is the same material as in *Your Perfect Right*, rewritten in some parts for general readership. This book has more examples and illustrations to which students will be able to relate.

Robert E. Alberti and Michael L. Emmons, *Your Perfect Right: A Guide to Assertive Behavior* (San Luis Obispo, Calif.: Impact, 1974). This is the book that started it all. An excellent, easy-to-follow explanation of how to become an assertive person.

George R. Bach and Herb Goldberg, *Creative Aggression* (New York: Avon Books, 1974). "Creative aggression" is simply a method for expressing natural anger constructively. In this lengthy discussion, the authors present sound, provocative, workable ways to stop the tyranny of unreal "nice" behavior. They offer constructive suggestions on how to live with aggression.

Lynn Z. Bloom, Karen Coburn, and Joan Pearlman, *The New Assertive Woman* (New York: Dell Publishing Co., Inc., 1975), and Bryna Taubman, *How To Become an Assertive Woman* (New York: Pocket Books, 1976). Highly readable, practical books. The former tends to be more scholarly, thorough, and in-depth; the latter is simpler, more superficial, and is based on popular sources.

Henry M. Boettinger, *Moving Mountains: The Art and Craft of Letting Others See Things Your Way* (New York: Collier Books, 1969). Based upon his corporation, university, and armed-forces experience, Boettinger provides an exploration of human nature and how people react to ideas. This is a book full of skills, techniques, and "things to watch." It is about the packaging of ideas.

Jard DeVille, *Nice Guys Finish First* (New York: William Morrow and Company, Inc., 1979). DeVille's chapter headings reveal his focus: "Communicating to Lead," "Creating Interpersonal Awareness," "Listening and Persuasion," and "Offering Winning Options," to name a few. His purpose is to teach you how to predict the attitudes and actions of those you must influence every day.

Andrew J. Dubrin, *Winning At Office Politics* (New York: Ballantine Books, 1978). This is a book about sensible office politics. Dubrin's primary focus is on the strategies needed for gaining both favor and power. It places aggressive, nonassertive, and assertive behavior in a realistic setting.

Wayne W. Dyer, *Pulling Your Own Strings* (New York: Avon Books, 1977). At the heart of assertive behavior is self-strength. Dyer shows the reader how to operate from a position of strength. His chapter on "Being Creatively Alive in Every Situation," is both wise and entertaining. A practical book that puts the power to choose assertive behavior in the hands of the reader.

Herbert Fensterheim and Jean Baer, *Don't Say Yes When You Want to Say No* (New York: Dell Publishing Co., Inc., 1975). Numerous specific suggestions for improving behavior and relationships supported by abbreviated case studies. Interesting and specific. A broad range of applications are provided: eating habits, sexual variants, and assertion on the job are some.

Michel Girodo, *Shy?* (New York: Pocket Books, 1978). Girodo's is a practical book that will help the reader gain self-confidence, become socially and professionally relaxed at both formal and informal occasions, converse with people in a more natural comfortable manner, and become aware of his or her potential. If you are shy, Girodo presents realistic ideas that will help you do something about it.

Jerry Greenwald, *Be the Person You Were Meant to Be (Antidotes to Toxic Living)* (New York: Dell Publishing Co., Inc., 1973). When Greenwald talks of emotionally nourishing behavior, he is talking about assertive behavior. Toxic behavior is nonassertive or aggressive. The point of this book is not to offer answers to specific dilemmas but to help everyone utilize his or her own potentials for standing up and discovering what is needed to live a fulfilling life.

Carole Hyatt, *The Woman's Selling Game: How to Sell Yourself . . . and Anything Else* (New York: A Warner Communications Company, 1979). Although the focus of this book is on the woman in business, Hyatt's ideas about getting and using total career power, meeting the people you want to see, making dates, and selling when the product is you, bear directly on assertive behavior in the professional world, and they relate to the businessman as well as woman.

Stanlee Phelps and Nancy Austin, *The Assertive Woman* (San Luis Obispo, Calif.: Impact, 1975). Same fundamental content as Alberti and Emmons. Many opportunities provided here for analyzing our own behavior. This was the first assertiveness book written by women for women. Well constructed and easy to follow.

Carl Rogers, *On Personal Power: Inner Strength and Its Revolutionary Impact.* (New York: Delacorte Press, 1977). Rogers urges "unconditional positive regard" for the self and for other people as a means of releasing the "constructive power of the organism." An important author writing on an important subject.

Everett L. Shostrom, *Man, the Manipulator: The Inner Journey from Manipulation to Actualization* (New York: Bantam Books, 1967). Manipulation, Shostrom suggests, is the real evil in the world today. In this book, Shostrom provides specific suggestions and ideas that will increase your range of freedom and actualization. It is both interesting and challenging.

Sidney B. Simon, *Negative Criticism: Its Swath of Destruction and What to do About It* (Niles, Illinois: Argus Communications, 1978). Simon focuses on interpreting the motive behind the criticism, sorting out the valid points, dealing with the "attacker," and preserving your self-image. He provides excellent advice, too, on how to handle an attack of criticism positively.

Manuel J. Smith, *When I Say No, I Feel Guilty: How to Cope—Using the Skills of Systematic Assertive Therapy* (New York: Bantam Books, 1975). This is a "how to" book on dealing effectively with the conflicts people have in living with each other. Smith is especially strong in his presentation and explanation of assertive human rights. A well-constructed, thorough, and easy-to-read book.

David Viscott, *Risking* (New York: Pocket Books, 1977). The kind of behavior advocated in this chapter on Assertiveness involves risks for some. Why take chances? How can you best deal with risks? When you seek to control a person or situation, what is the risk involved? Viscott answers these questions and offers practical suggestions on "The Do's and Don't's of Risking."

Philip G. Zimbardo, *Shyness* (New York: Jove Publications, Inc. (Harcourt Brace Jovanovich, 1977). Zimbardo explains what shyness is and what to do about it. He presents realistic, specific suggestions for building your self-esteem and developing your social skills. A thorough, practical book on nonassertive behavior.

NOTES

[1]Lynn Z. Bloom, Karen Coburn, and Joan Pearlman, *The New Assertive Woman* (New York: Dell Publishing Co., Inc., 1975), p. 15.

[2]Robert E. Alberti and Michael L. Emmons, *Your Perfect Right: A Guide to Assertive Behavior* (San Luis Obispo, Calif.: Impact, 1974), p. 6.

[3]Bloom, Coburn, and Pearlman, *The New Assertive Woman*, pp. 11–12.

[4]Robert E. Alberti and Michael L. Emmons, *Stand Up, Speak Out, Talk Back!* (New York: Pocket Books, 1975), p. 14.

[5]Ibid., pp. 36–37.

[6]Herbert Fensterheim and Jean Baer, *Don't Say Yes When You Want to Say No* (New York: Dell Publishing Co., 1975), p. 20.

[7]From *Man, the Manipulator* by Everett L. Shostrom. Copyright © 1967 by Abington Press. Used by permission.

[8]Excerpted from the book *When I Say No, I Feel Guilty* by Manuel J. Smith. Copyright © 1975 by Manuel J. Smith. Reprinted by permission of *The Dial Press*.

10

Experiencing Growth and Change:
Communicating with Family and Friends

We exist only through our relationship to the world around us. Our relationships with family, friends, work associates, and others provide context and meaning for our lives. Growth without these relationships is not likely; it is through them that we learn, share insights, and develop our full potential. It is through them that life takes on meaning.

This chapter is structured differently than those preceding. In other chapters, I developed a concept and then presented specific skills for dealing with it. Obviously the concepts like perception, self-disclosure, listening, and verbal and nonverbal communication are meaningful only in the context of interaction with others. In this chapter we put it all together and discuss the special needs and demands of communicating interpersonally in two vital areas of our lives: family and friends. We all have certain conceptions and expectations for our family and friends. What are they based on? What are our values in these areas?

There are some additional skills we need to gain the most from these important relationships. These additional skills are really emphases rather than ideas I haven't mentioned before. This chapter will focus on these emphases, not specifically on concepts and skills.

FAMILY

"The greatest happiness and the deepest satisfaction in life, the most intense enthusiasm and the most profound inner peace," says Sven Wahlroos in *Family Communication*, "all come from being a member of a loving family."[1] The reverse side of the coin is also true: some of the greatest pain can come from family relationships. But while we choose our friends, we do not choose our family. We can move in and out of relationships with most people, but it is often more difficult with family members. Our choices and our freedom are more limited within family relationships. Family relationships present unique problems and unique satisfactions in interpersonal communication.

The Familiar Question: Who Am I?

Communication within the family is the subject of complete books and is a very complex area of study. Within a few pages here I want to encourage you to consider your place in your own family and some of the

Try This

Which adjectives best describe how you were perceived by other family members as you grew up?*

active	disorderly	kind	self-centered
affectionate	dumb	lazy	self-confident
agreeable	emotional	mischievous	selfish
aggressive	friendly	naughty	shy
alert	generous	noisy	slow
antisocial	gentle	odd	smart
apathetic	gloomy	outgoing	sociable
awkward	happy	peculiar	stable
cautious	high-strung	persistent	stingy
cheerful	hostile	pleasant	strong
complaining	impatient	quarrelsome	stubborn
confident	impulsive	quiet	talkative
cooperative	independent	rebellious	timid
cruel	irresponsible	reliable	tolerant
demanding	irritable	responsible	unattractive

How have these perceptions affected you? Have you seen their influence on your relationships with others? Are there other adjectives that better describe how you were perceived by other family members as you grew up?

*This list of adjectives was borrowed, in part, from David W. Johnson, *Reaching Out: Interpersonal Effectiveness and Self-Actualization* (Englewood Cliffs, New Jersey: Prentice-Hall, Inc., 1972), pp. 29–30.

barriers to communication you may experience and contribute to with your parents or brothers and sisters.

A useful way to begin to think about communicating with our families is to think about the various family roles we all may have assumed or been assigned. "Sister" or "daughter" are some obvious roles, but for must of us things are more complicated than that. There are other influences that decide our roles for us. Whether we are male or female may have determined whether we mowed the lawn or did the dishes, carried out the garbage or cleaned the house, were given freedom in dating or were more controlled — just to cite some obvious examples. Our sex may have affected how we were perceived: forthright, aggressive, athletic, awkward, friendly, or mischievous. Birth order strongly influences family roles. First-born children are often more restricted than those born afterward. Older children, too, are often treated as more mature and responsible; younger children may be spoiled or treated as irresponsible, delicate, or dependent.

Physical and mental attributes also affect the role we may have assumed or been assigned. The physically biggest child in a family may be perceived as the clumsiest or may be given the most responsibility. The smartest may have had "success" in school drilled into him or her since kindergarten. Family members may peg a highly emotional child as the family troublemaker, the one who starts arguments. These qualities (and there are many more) do determine our roles to a great extent. Because they tend to be constantly reinforced, they come to be the roles with which we feel most comfortable. Being perceived as a clown or a peacemaker, moody or jolly, gentle or cruel in family relationships will strongly affect how we relate to people outside the family. It is important to understand where we fit and what our role may be. It is important, too, not to be locked into these roles.

Communication Barriers in the Family

Although the emphasis here is on the family in which you grew up, because of its importance in establishing many of your patterns for communication, some of these things will operate in a family you may form for your self later on. You will be establishing another pattern of roles in that family. These roles will be based, in part, on what your growing-up experience was.

Family roles provide a subtle but continuing influence on our lives. One of the first communication barriers that may develop out of family roles is the tendency for family members to see a person *only* in one role. This does not allow for growth or change. Despite the fact that we may have become an outgoing person or more independent, family members may still treat us as if we are shy or dependent. We may become a corporation president but family members may still perceive us as a helpless kid sister. This not only may limit our own possibilities for change but may cause breakdowns in communication resulting from misperceptions and false assumptions. Our needs, attitudes, beliefs, values, and goals change.

The consciously felt love and good intentions of family members is reinforced when affection is openly expressed.

The second problem results from our assumption that everyone already knows everything about us. We have grown up in the family, a situation where everyone knows us. Communication breakdowns occur when we assume people outside the family know us as thoroughly. We may respond to others with very brief answers to questions, expecting them to fill in the gaps.

There is a related communication problem which is the assumption that no matter *what* we actually say, the other members of our family will understand us.[2] Though family members often communicate with each other very efficiently by means of a kind of communication shorthand, sometimes we come to depend too much on this system of signals and implied meanings. An example of the barrier involved is the fellow who agreed with his father that whenever he wanted to use the family car, he would make arrangements with him in advance. The son used

Consider This _____

At a recent speaking engagement in Florida, I asked 150 women managers how their personal and professional lives fit together. They don't, most of them said.

"You asked how they fit together, and that's a tough question. If you had asked about them individually, I would have said both are in fine shape. But they don't fit together at all—I make each one work in spite of the other," a public-relations expert said.

"I compensate all the time—don't we all?" an office manager asked. "I steal from my family, sometimes, for the sake of my job—then steal from the job for my family. It is a balancing act, and a difficult one at best."

Another woman wrote a page of observations, then summed up neatly when she said, "My husband really hasn't the faintest idea of what I do for a living. He's never shown any interest. And my boss certainly doesn't want to hear about my family problems. So they don't fit together, really, they just coexist—with me in the middle."

Most of these managers said they were satisfied with both their professional lives and their personal lives, however.

Those who are married say (for the most part) their marriages are healthy. Those who are divorced say the marriage would have ended anyway; their jobs are not to blame.

"My career didn't cause the trouble in my marriage, it just gave me a way out of a rotten situation," one wrote. "Without my job, I might have been economically trapped, and the abuse was awful."

Another said: "My marriage hasn't suffered at all because of my career. In fact, it has improved steadily as I've gone along. My husband likes the fact that I can cope in the business world. He respects me much more than he did when I stayed home, and I respect me more, too."

Predictably, most of these highly paid women have older children and most worked while those children were still young. The overwhelming majority said their children benefited, rather than suffered, because they had working mothers.

"I don't feel guilty about my working years. In fact, if I feel guilty at all it's because I waited 10 years to go to work," the mother of a 23-year-old said. "I was miserable at home; my daughter would have been better off with a contented mother those first 10 years of her life."

A mother with four daughters added: "I think watching me have a career was good for all of my girls. They grew up assuming they would work. They're not waiting for Prince Charming to come along and take care of them; they all have good jobs of their own now."

What did trouble these women was the feeling that their careers weren't taken as seriously as a man's would be, given the same success.

—Niki Scott, "Working Woman"

the car and the father accused him of violating the agreement. The son insisted he had told him: "You saw me washing and waxing the car, and you know I never do that unless I'm planning to use it." Our meaning is not always as clear as we might think, even within our family.

In the family relationship, much mutual "picture taking" goes on. That is, members are often involved in forming mental pictures of how others are feeling, reacting, or thinking. As Virginia Satir, a leader in the field of family therapy, states in *Peoplemaking*, "The people involved may not share their pictures, the meanings they give the pictures, nor the feelings the pictures arouse." Those involved guess at meaning and then assume those guesses are facts. This guessing procedure results in a great many unnecessary family communication barriers.

We simply cannot assume the other person always knows what we mean, even if we have grown up with that person. The reason this assumption causes special problems in the family is that people who share such a close relationship feel they *should* be able to read each other's minds. Everyone is supposed to know how everyone else feels—no one needs to say or show what he or she feels. Serious misunderstandings can result when this doesn't work. Think of a time when you felt *very strongly* that the family should take a specific vacation, make a certain purchase, or eat at a certain restaurant. Did you reveal this strong feeling to other family members? Just because you felt it does not mean you showed it to others. We are not as transparent to others as we are to our selves.

This extends to our policy of criticizing and complimenting other family members, too. Whether we're very aware of it or not, we look to our families for reinforcement and rewards. We may not voice praise or gratitude because we expect people to know our feelings without our spelling them out. But our message doesn't always get through, and it should. Not surprisingly, family members are often less inclined to hold back criticisms of each other. When the free and heavy flow of criticism gets to be too much, family relationships may turn into nothing more than opportunities for negative exchanges, with estrangement and resentment resulting. A pat on the back is not only liked but needed from time to time. Wahlroos even goes so far as to say that "the main reason for . . . discord [in families] is simply that the consciously felt love and the good intentions harbored by the family members are not *communicated* in such a way that they are recognized."[3]

Communication Patterns That Fail

Because we see so much of other members of our family, and because we are likely to feel freer and less inhibited with them, stressful situations are more likely to occur in these relationships than in others. Satir discovered certain "universal patterns in the way people communicate" when faced with stressful situations: placating, blaming, computing, and distracting.[4] Leveling, a fifth possible response pattern, is discussed as a remedy or solution.

Although these communication patterns were discussed in Chapter 8, "Overcoming Barriers: Coping with Conflict," they were treated briefly and presented there as responses that are restrictive. Here, they are related to the family and, more specifically, to the roles that are played in the family. It should be clear from the following discussion that these behaviors reflect deeper concerns than a mere categorizing of different responses. They can become deeply ingrained, habitual behavior patterns that negatively affect family relationships.

Placating. If there is a member of your family who never takes a stand, always goes along with what other people say, continually tries to make others happy, and never gets mad, you know how frustrating it can be. This person is a placater. Some people have the notion that the way to keep people happy is never to disagree. They may also feel that in this way everyone will like them; they placate as a means to gain approval.

The person who plays this role to any great extent may find it hard to communicate openly. He or she often reveals an impression of no self-worth or self-esteem. The placater accepts any criticism as if it is deserved; it is as if he or she feels fortunate to have someone communicating with him or her at all. The placater, Satir states, is a "syrupy, martyrish, bootlicking person."

The placater doesn't realize that the most fulfilling relationships are those where ideas, emotions, and opinions are allowed to clash occasionally. Resolving mutual problems and sharing a variety of viewpoints reflects healthy communication. Unfortunately, the placater cannot hold up his or her end of such a relationship. No matter what the placater really feels, his or her response is always an accepting one that offers no opposition or opportunity for growth and change.

Blaming. The blamer is the family member who wants always to look strong in the eyes of others. To show that they are boss, blamers find fault and command others to do their bidding. They always try to reveal superiority, strength, and even perfection. Blamers usually feel that if it were not for everyone else, the world would be perfect. In the eyes and mind of the blamer, nothing is right. It is most important for the blamer to "be somebody," to "act important," to "cut someone down to size," and, thus, to "count for something."[5]

Try This

We have all known people who fit the roles Satir identified. Try to think of one person you have known who best fits each of these communication patterns. What kind of behavior characterizes each of the people?

—placater

—blamer

— computer

—distracter

— leveler

It is difficult to deal with blamers because we can do nothing right. They accuse us of doing things that we did not do. Essentially, the blamer operates from a stance of no self-worth, attempting to lower others, not to raise himself or herself. There are few ways to remedy such a situation; but recognizing that a person is a blamer will help us to understand the communication relationships that involve him or her and the reasons that communication may be blocked.

Computing. There may be a member of your family out of whom you would like to shake some emotion, some feeling, some strength of conviction. The computer, according to Satir, always deals with experience in a logical and reasoned manner. "Calm, cool, and collected," he or she attempts to "sound intelligent." Computers try to impress upon people that they are deep and thoughtful and correct. The display of feelings or emotions would destroy the effect.

Many people assume this posture is ideal. They feel human beings are rational and must deal with information in a cold and calculated manner. They feel it would significantly improve the human condition if interactions could take place in a context devoid of feelings. But humans do have feelings, and when those feelings are suppressed, the communication that results is incomplete. The sharing of feelings brings people closer together—it allows for a more complete communication experience—but most of all it allows people to be people.

The computer attempts to deal with all messages, whether harmful or harmless, in the same manner. He or she may try to reveal self-worth by using large words—even meaningless words—to establish credibility and rationality. It is difficult to deal with such people because they seem to be unfeeling; they react in much the same way to things that affect them deeply and things that they consider trivial.

Distracting. The distracter in the family will ignore threats. Involved in an argument, distracters will change the subject to avoid a confrontation. Rather than respond to the controversial point, they will say something totally irrelevant. Such a role provides relief from responsibility. Although distracters can escape obligations by heading off in an irrelevant new direction each time they are faced with the slightest challenge, their purposelessness can result in loneliness and frustration. They accomplish little, seldom achieve satisfaction, and can maintain only superficial relationships.

Basically, distracters lack a sense of seriousness. Have you ever tried to carry out a serious conversation with a person who assumes a "who cares?" posture? To such a person, all the world's problems are equally meaningless and nonexistent.

Leveling: A Possible Remedy

Fortunately, there is a fifth pattern of communication that is positive and that provides an ideal which family members can work toward. Open, genuine communication between family members is its primary characteristic. Leveling is a means of resolving discord, breaking deadlocks, and restoring communication between people. "In any relationship," states David Viscott in *How to Live with Another Person*, "we need people to wish us well just the way we are and in pursuit of the goals we have chosen for our selves."[6] When we level, we offer another person love and acceptance based on the way he or she is, not on how he or she fits our mold or notion of the world.

Leveling requires honesty. If we make an error, we must be willing to apologize for it. If something happens that we do not intend, we must own up to the situation and admit our predicament. The focus of the apology is on the error or act, not on us as a person. A leveler never apologizes for his or her existence. Leveling responses are content-bound rather than person-bound.

The leveling response allows us freedom to act and to respond as human beings. It provides for the true and open expression of feelings. It provides for change without the need for jumping from one topic to another. It is a genuine response in which nonverbal elements reinforce

_____ Consider This

Dale Didion, 22, has spent plenty of nights waiting for the phone to ring . . .
[He] is part of Rescue Crisis Services' 24-hour crisis counseling program . . .
Listening to other people's problems in the middle of the night can become depressing if you try to assume the caller's worries, Mr. Didion said. But Rescue training teaches volunteers that they can't take on other people's problems—they are there to listen. And that can be satisfying.
Mr. Didion vividly remembers one caller who, tormented by his past in Vietnam, said he felt like taking his motorcycle out on the expressway and running it off the road.
"He said, 'I'm in a telephone booth calling you. I've got no money, no job, and wife problems'," Mr. Didion said. "It sounded really bad. At first I didn't know what to say, but I started talking, and 40 minutes later, he said the worst was over; he wasn't going to hurt himself."
Mr. Didion . . . decided to volunteer to "see what's going on in other people's lives," and to learn about programs available in the area.
Rescue volunteers complete 40 hours of counselor training, learning general counseling skills, listening skills, and how to clarify questions to focus on the caller. "You only intercede for a little time, because they wanted you to," Mr. Didion said.
—Sue Stankey, *The Blade: Toledo, Ohio*, April 24, 1980

verbal statements accurately so that the messages conveyed are direct and true. In the ideal leveler, the body, mind, and emotions are balanced and harmonious. Satir says that in addition to this integration, there is "a flowing, an aliveness, an openness and what I call a *juiciness* about a person who is leveling."[7] We feel safe in the presence of a leveler, able to express our true feelings and reactions.

Levelers are assertive. They are not afraid to make a mistake, to accept criticism from others, to impose on others when necessary, to look inferior or imperfect, or to allow others to leave a relationship. As levelers we respond to people *as they are*, not as we think they should be; we disagree with them because *we* want to; we are responsive, alert, aware—assertive.

If you are a leveler, according to Satir, you are "in touch with your head, your heart, your feelings, and your body." The results, as she presents them, are certainly worth any effort you can exert in this direction. Becoming a leveler "enables you to have integrity, commitment, honesty, intimacy, competence, creativity, and the ability to work with real problems in a real way."[8] In short, a leveler embodies all the values we have emphasized throughout this book for the effective interpersonal communicator.

The point of discussing these various roles is explained by Watzlawick, Beavin, and Jackson in *Pragmatics of Human Communication* when they state that "the behavior of every individual within the family is related to and dependent upon the behavior of all the others."[9] Our attempts at leveling will have a direct influence on other family members. The better we are at leveling, the more likely harmonious and cooperative family interaction will occur.

Other Behaviors That Fail

It may be that the following behaviors cause some of the communication patterns discussed previously. On the other hand, communication patterns such as those discussed may result in some of these behaviors. Or, there may be no cause-effect relationship. It is clear, however, that behaviors like restricting the freedoms of others, allowing emotional build-up, possessiveness, and double standards can cause problems in family relationships.

Restricted freedom simply means less opportunity to behave at any moment just as you please. Living with others may affect the time you may study, eat, sleep, dress, bathe, or even go to the bathroom. When freedoms are restricted, interpersonal stress results. For example, one family member has just come home from a harried day of decision-making. It may be later than usual. As he or she comes in the door, a

Try This

How often have you experienced restricted freedom? How did you respond when any of the following things happened to you?

1. Someone was in the bathroom when you needed to get ready to go someplace.

2. Your parents told you what time to be home from a party or date.

3. It was clearly stated what time dinner was to be on the table.

4. You were told that you could not do something until you had cleaned your room, made your bed, washed the car, mowed the lawn, or done the dishes.

5. You were told that you <u>had</u> to go to church, to visit relatives, to attend a funeral, or to see friends.

6. Your priorities were established for you: "Studying comes first you know," or "Be sure to write _____ a thank-you".

7. You were told whom you could or could not see.

8. You were told how you could or could not talk to someone else.

Are restricted freedoms a necessary part of family life? What is the best way to deal with such restrictions?

new set of decisions may have to be faced: homework that is not finished, television-related requests, civic or community events, invitations from friends, requests for use of the car, and on and on. Such demands and responsibilities are part of family membership, but they can also cause stress. Often they carry with them unstated assumptions and understandings, such as, to be a "good father" you should help Tim with his homework, or to be "good neighbors," we should go over to the Jones' open house tonight, or to be "good parents" or "citizens" we should go to the school board meeting tonight. As well as assumptions and understandings, sometimes such decisions also carry emotional loadings. This can occur when one spouse makes an informal commitment to something, and the other spouse makes a decision that does not correspond with or counters the other. One spouse, for example, may decide to go golfing or bowling when the other believes that that time should be spent with the children.

It may take awhile for a newly-married or live-in person to become "we" oriented. It takes awhile for the feeling to change from unrestricted freedom to restricted freedom—to begin sharing one's space, time, and physical objects with another. To be able to say, in response to a request for your company, "I can't tell you whether or not we can come; I'll have to check with _____," or, "I'll have to check our calendar." As one changes and as one begins to give up some of the

Try This

On what issues do members of your family have strong emotional linkages?
Are they attached to such issues as:

—religion?
—politics?
—sex?
—studying?
—your use of time?
—how seriously you take school?
—what you wear?

—your friends?
—how late you stay up?
—how much you watch television?
—what you read?
—where you go?
—what you eat?
—your appearance?

How do you face these issues—when you know strong emotional linkages are
present? Can you avoid emotional explosions on them? Is avoidance one of
the techniques you use? Is it easier to talk to some family members about
them than others? Do you think complete avoidance contributes to a healthy
interpersonal relationship? Is it likely that emotional linkages will change on
some of the issues above? If so, what may contribute to the change?

freedoms—even the dozens of very small freedoms—one finds that
tension and stress must be accommodated.

Emotional build-ups result when we store up our thoughts and feelings. To the words, phrases, and situations that we are involved in, we
add emotional associations, as previously mentioned. Sometimes the
emotional link is already so strong that all another person has to do is
refer to it, like "I saw Fred today," to activate the emotional avalanche,
"I thought we agreed that you were never going to see him again!" The
more intimate the relationship, the more likely emotional build-ups will
occur. This can be quickly demonstrated. Questions such as "Have you
studied?", "Have you practiced?", "Can I use the car?", or "Can I borrow your tools?" are likely to have powerful linkages because of many
shared past experiences. Think of all the shared recollections that are
likely in such situations: times when studying or practicing was not
given a first or even a high priority, or times when the car was left dirty
or out of gas, or still other times when tools were lost or misplaced.
When these shared experiences have occurred, the question that looks
like a simple request for information is no longer perceived that way.
Emotional linkages will affect the way the question is asked, the way it
is perceived, and the behavior that is likely to follow.

Possessiveness in family relationships occurs when members feel
they have a right to control or influence the behaviors of each other. It
is a normal feeling that grows out of the interpretation of family situations by members belonging to the family. You hear it said, "That's my
girl . . ." or "As long as you live in this house, you aren't going to do

Consider This

At the Center for Family Learning in New Rochelle, N.Y., Dr. Philip Guerin and his staff present courses on family life so that couples, as well as their children, can monitor themselves and their relationships. In the process, couples learn the ins and outs of what amounts to an early warning system for their marital trouble.

As part of an early warning system, Dr. Guerin advises couples to watch these five areas in particular:

Communications. This involves a close look at how well a couple communicate their thoughts and feelings to each other.

Dr. Guerin suggests an experiment to test how much a couple share what goes on inside them: "Go out to dinner alone with no one else along. Notice what you talk about. Is it what color to paint the dining room? Which model car to buy? Ways to cut the phone bill, electric bill, grocery bill? It shouldn't be only one thing after another and none of it concerned with feelings or attitudes towards life and love, attention to what is happening inside each partner—the very stuff of which personal relationships are made."

Toxic Issues. By identifying troublesome issues which are being shunned, a couple can pinpoint issues that can poison their relationship.

"For instance," Dr. Guerin notes, "a lot of people claim they have no trouble talking about sex. But do they talk about their own personal programming in sex as kids, the way their parents dealt with sex, their feelings about themselves as sexual beings, their sexual preferences with their spouses, the times they're satisfied and not satisfied, the times they feel sexual, the times they don't?"

When couples try talking about issues, they soon discover which ones are being avoided and need to be dealt with. They will also find that they are repeating their parents' "toxic issues." Dr. Guerin reassures couples that the reason they have trouble with certain issues is "only in part—and not necessarily very much—tied in with their all encompassing relationship with each other."

Life Cycle. Couples are traveling together on a road covered with "nodal events." These events in the life cycle—births, deaths, sickness,

accidents, changes in jobs, an endless list of stresses—take their toll. Dr. Guerin finds that couples need to be reminded about the ups and downs of the life cycle, particularly when stress strikes.

Emotional Network. Both husband and wife need an emotional and social framework so that a mate is not providing all the feeling of "connectedness." This involves being open and available to their children, parents, brothers and sisters, other family members and friends. Dr. Guerin emphasizes two aspects of this network: "First, there should not be just a social network but also extended family. Second, neither should move into that network in order to complain about a spouse, but to have a relationship in and of itself."

Myth of Freedom: In a marital relationship, a couple pile up what Dr. Guerin labels "relationship debris"—anger, hurt, resentment, etc., in the course of living together. An extramarital affair glitters with the promise of freedom from such "debris." While people make such comparisons all the time, he emphasizes that they are not comparable.

Dr. Guerin adds that marriages can be destroyed unnecessarily because partners don't want to risk being vulnerable again to being hurt. Yet, ironically, no new marriage is going to be risk-free, either.

"It is impossible to have a marriage without conflict," Dr. Guerin explains. "If there is a marriage that seems to have no conflict, you are not taking a good look."

"In order for two individuals to remain really individuals—and that is the only way people can have real intimacy and closeness—they have to expect differences and conflict because they are two different people. Each must take responsibility for the way he or she is—both the nice self and the toxic self. Each has a responsibility to develop a way of dealing constructively with the spouse's toxic self instead of expecting him or her to change for the other's sake and become all nice. If a partner wants change, then the place to begin is with himself or herself. Then changes will take place in the family."

—Edward Wakim, *Family Weekly*, December 3, 1978

that." Or people may make statements like "He's my husband," or "He's my son." There are expectations that accompany these statements and feelings — expectations that imply control.

Parents are known to say such things as, "If you really cared about us, you would . . . ," or "If you loved us, you wouldn't act that way." Parents thus attempt to control their offspring by implying what they expect of them. And people who love others try to please them. It is when others' expectations include changes in behavior that control and possessiveness are demonstrated.

Control and possessiveness tend to make other people defensive. Defensiveness then leads to distortions in communication. Freedom between interactants is less likely to cause defensiveness. Thus, you must expect defensiveness if you show by the following behaviors that you cannot allow freedom:[10]

1. Judgmental behavior: "You should not talk like that," or "Talk like that is bad."
2. Controlling behavior: "When you are in this house, you do it our way."
3. Strategic behavior: "A thoughtful person would have done it without being asked."
4. Neutral behavior: "Let's not get emotional, just give me the facts. Be objective, and you can solve this problem. . . ."
5. Superior behavior: "As your father, I can tell you what *I* would do in such a situation. . . ."
6. Certain behavior: "There is only one way to look at it; only one point of view that is acceptable. . . ."

In his article on defensive communication, Jack Gibb provided parallel, correlated supportive climates for each of the six defense–producing climates mentioned above.[11] To practice each of the following behaviors will help reduce the possibility of defensiveness:

1. Descriptive behavior: "How do *you* feel about the situation?"
2. Problem-oriented behavior: "Let's look at this idea together with no predetermined attitudes or solutions."
3. Spontaneous behavior: "It is important to be straightforward and honest. The best way to deal with situations is by being direct."
4. Empathic behavior: "I think I know how you feel. Perhaps we could talk about the problem a bit more. Sharing feelings like this seems to help."

5. Equal behavior (showing mutual trust and respect): "Isn't it neat that we can discuss problems from the same viewpoint? We can push aside our differences, and really have a meeting of the minds."
6. Provisional behavior: "There are no sure ways to approach this situation; let's just try something and if it doesn't work, we'll try something else."

The purpose of these supportive behaviors, although, perhaps, slightly exaggerated above, is to increase trust between family members. They allow identification to occur: when one family member is able to experience some indication of the emotional tone being experienced by the other family member. In this way, accuracy of communication is likely to increase.

Double standards can also cause problems among family members. Double standards emerge when parents expect their children to follow rules or perform rituals from which they, as parents, are exempt. Parents often follow a "do-as-I-say, not-as-I-do" philosophy. The rules may have to do with lying, stealing, or, on a smaller scale, interrupting others, talking with one's mouth full, speaking correctly, addressing adults, or even standing up straight. Rituals may prescribe proper diets, bed times, teeth brushing, going to church, or other daily or weekly occurrences. The point is, often there is a distinct gap between what the parents do and what they expect of their children.

A double standard may also be operative between other segments of the family. That is, older siblings can impose or expect differences in rules and rituals between themselves and younger sisters and brothers.

Try This

You have undoubtedly found yourself engaged in defense-producing behavior. Can you remember the last time? Which one was it?

—judgment   — neutrality
— control   — superiority
— strategy   — certainty

Can you remember what you said or did that reflected this climate? Which of the following behaviors would have helped reduce the defensiveness?

— description   — empathy
— problem orientation   — equality
— spontaneity   — provisionalism

Is it possible to identify specific behaviors—things you might say or do—that would result in these supportive climates?

Bed times, television rights, or dating or travelling freedoms are just a few areas where these double standards may become obvious. The differences in the language one uses or the books and magazines one reads may be others. Differences between the privileges enjoyed by male and female children may be still another area where what is considered right for one family member may not be considered appropriate for another. A teenage boy, for example, may be allowed to travel alone some distance from home whereas a teenage girl may be somewhat more restricted. The point here is not whether double standards operate, or whether they are good or bad, but simply that they can become points of conflict within a family.

Maintaining Family Relationships

Most of us would like to maintain or improve our family relationships. The familiarity that is an automatic and inseparable part of family life creates tensions and strains. To deal with these tensions and strains requires specific kinds of behaviors. Supportive climates help, naturally, but we can go beyond these. It is imperative to deal directly with roles and behaviors, to face power relationships, to use unrestricted language, and to open communication channels.

Dealing with roles and behaviors.   We must get expectations out into the open. Family conflicts and problems may often occur simply because no one talked about what they expected of others.

Sometimes a problem cannot be discussed immediately because of a high degree of defensiveness or emotional intensity. Then, a brief cooling-off period (about twenty to thirty minutes) is recommended before airing expectations: "It is *your* job to make sure that our checks

MISS PEACH

Consider This

— Janet Cooke, *The Blade: Toledo, Ohio*, July 8, 1979

Although statistics indicate that the divorce rate is climbing steadily, the more than 13,000 hand-holding, kissing, smiling people who gathered in Kent, O., for the national convention of Worldwide Marriage Encounter, Inc., believe that marriage is not only alive and well, but also is on the upswing. . . .

During a Worldwide Marriage Encounter weekend, a series of presentations is made by three Catholic couples and a Catholic priest. At the end of these presentations, couples are asked several thought-provoking questions about marriage; each partner then writes his or her answers and the responses are exchanged. After reading each other's thoughts, the couples privately discuss what they have written. As they leave the encounter weekend, couples are encouraged to continue this exchange of ideas, which the marriage-encounter groups call dialogue, every day.

No limitations are put on the topics to be discussed, and couples are encouraged to explore every area of married life in conversation with each other. . . .

Mr. [Tom] McGuiness and his wife, Jayne, who are from Long Beach, Calif., are the United States executive team of Worldwide Marriage Encounter, Inc. They estimate that more than 300 marriage-encounter weekends take place throughout the country each month, and offer this as evidence that marriage is, as Jayne McGuiness put it, "better than ever."

"A good marriage," Mrs. McGuiness said, "is more than not fighting or not breaking up."

"In a good marriage, you find two people who can communicate openly with one another and who realize that they have something unique and powerful not only to be offered to each other, but also to be shared with the world."

Mrs. McGuiness' belief that so many marriages fail because the partners do not know how to communicate is shared by many in the encounter movement. Most attending the national convention expressed the belief that when marriages and families break down, or when feelings of loneliness, despair, and alienation appear in large segments of the general population, it is because people have not learned how to talk with, or listen to, one another.

don't bounce!" or "Why didn't you make the reservation?" Usually, however, it is best to air expectations as soon as possible after a problem has arisen. To bottle them up, or not to discuss them at all, simply means they will be suppressed and are likely to become highly volatile. If not discussed, they will probably recur with increased intensity, ultimately to explode in proof of extreme volatility!

Facing power relationships.   Families are structured and the power relationships within them are often clearly defined and well understood. Parents have more freedom and more responsibilities than children. Older children usually have more freedom and more responsibilities than younger children. Also, second, third, and fourth children usually have more freedom and responsibility than the first child had at the same age or even than the child immediately older. Differences in power, however, can become blurred, and struggles go on within families to gain or maintain power. One result of such power is a comment like, "My mother?—don't worry about her; I have her wrapped around my little finger!"

The problem with control is that it produces defensive behavior and mistrustful feelings. More often than not, it provokes similar reactions—moves for control—in others. Thus, the best possible atmosphere is one of trust and acceptance. This kind of environment, too, is most likely to create trust and acceptance in others when it is genuine and not just a short-term ploy.

Using unrestricted language. To use language that is unrestricted provides others with an opportunity to understand *why* something is expected or important. Restricted language gives others no reasons for acting. For example, when a parent yells at a child, "Come home now," he or she is using restricted language. It becomes unrestricted when the parent calls, "Come home now; it's time for dinner." Note the differences between restricted and unrestricted language in the following instances:

"Stop eating like that."	—"When you eat like that it sounds very unpleasant."
"Put that down."	—"That was an expensive gift to me, and I treasure it. Please put it down so it doesn't get broken."
"Turn the music down."	—"We're trying to read (or talk on the phone), and we cannot concentrate when your music is so loud."

Children learn to comply because they understand the situation, not because of the tone or the brevity of the command. Unrestricted language cuts through the attitude which requires blind obedience to authority. Parents who are successful in modeling this kind of behavior will sometimes find the children using it when dealing with each other. They begin acting based upon reasonable explanations and upon understandings of possible consequences. Behavior based solely on fear of punishment or hope for reward is reduced and self-discipline is enhanced.

Opening communication channels. The purpose of fostering behaviors that open communication channels is to allow trust to develop. Trust results when family members are:

—open
—honest
—accepting of each other

—displaying empathy toward each other
—listening effectively
—using feedback

One reason why these attitudes are so important is because relationships change. Nothing is static. And yet, in family relationships, we often tend to see others as unchanging, as having a fixed role and assigned place in the family. The failure to recognize constant change in these relationships can cause great trouble. In particular, failing to see and to accept change in our selves and in other family members makes it difficult to grow in a relationship. It becomes cast in bronze and about as alive.

Consider This

PET ["Parent Effectiveness Training," a concept developed by Dr. Thomas Gordon,] encourages parents to engage in what is called active listening with their children. When, for example, a child makes a statement such as "I hate my math teacher," the parent is told to allow the child to continue to express his feelings about math class until a specific problem can be uncovered or the child realizes that, while there may be a problem, there isn't a readily available solution to it.

"You need to keep the door open for continuous communication," Dr. Gordon says, "instead of closing it in the child's face with a remark such as 'You musn't talk about your teachers that way. Now go do your homework'."

Dr. Gordon said that the process of active listening, in which the parent patiently allows the child to express his or her feelings without intervening, moralizing, or offering an immediate solution to a problem, is a difficult task at best.

"It's certainly contrary to what we've been taught about the way a parent ought to behave," he said, "but if you'll really take a look at those old ways, you'll realize that they haven't done very much for us, either. Most of the efforts we've made in this country toward the development of moral, responsible children have failed."

Children try various ways of communicating with their parents, Dr. Gordon said, and often these ways may include making outrageous and attention-getting statements. In order to uncover the child's true intent, the parent must not be put off by things which may at first seem shocking.

Parents also must realize that if a child is to become a responsible adult, he or she must be allowed to begin problem-solving at an early age. Sometimes, just the opportunity to express his feelings to an interested and unemotional listener will lead the child to a reasonable solution to what is troubling him, Dr. Gordon said.

—Janet Cooke, *The Blade: Toledo, Ohio*, November 12, 1978

Consider This _____

Looking at human behavior with all that we know—and can infer—about the life of our human species from earliest times, we have to realize that the family, as an association between a man and a woman and the children she bears, has been universal. As far as we know, both primitive "group" marriage and primitive matriarchy are daydreams—or nightmares, depending on one's point of view—without basis in historical reality. On the contrary, the evidence indicates that the couple, together with their children, biological or adopted, are everywhere at the core of human societies, even though this "little family" (as the Chinese called the nuclear family) may be embedded in joint families, extended families of great size, clans, manorial systems, courts, harems or other institutions that elaborate on kin and marital relations.

Almost up to the present, women on the whole have kept close to home and domestic tasks because of the demands of pregnancy and the nursing of infants, the rearing of children and the care of the disabled and the elderly. They have been concerned primarily with the conservation of intimate values and human relations from one generation to another over immense reaches of time. In contrast, men have performed tasks that require freer movement over greater distances, more intense physical effort and exposure to greater immediate danger; and everywhere men have developed the formal institutions of public life and the values on which these are based. However differently organized, the tasks of women and men have been complementary, mutually supportive. And where either the family or the wider social institutions have broken down, the society as a whole has been endangered.

In fact, almost everywhere in the world today societies are endangered. The difficulties that beset families in the United States are by no means unique. Families are in trouble everywhere in a world in which change—kinds of change that in many cases we ourselves proudly initiated—has been massive and rapid, and innovations have proliferated with only the most superficial concern for their effect on human lives and the earth itself. One difference between the United States and many other countries is that, caring so much about progress, Americans have moved faster. But we may also have arrived sooner at a turning point at which it becomes crucial to redefine what we most value and where we are headed.

—Margaret Mead, "Can the American Family Survive?"

There are times we must change a relationship or break one off. Relationships can become troublesome. People grow apart; they no longer have anything in common. One person may try to suffocate another—to take total, controlling interest. One person may no longer care to work at sustaining a relationship. These may be reasons for terminating relationships.

If the people involved have tried and failed to remedy their problems and are sure that their perceptions are accurate, the best way to break the relationship is through honesty and openness. Without willingness to share true feelings, both people's motives may become open to conjecture and misinterpretation. Self-disclosure is a mature and responsible approach to solving the problem. Honest self-disclosure may expose what turn out to be misperceptions—what we had construed as apathy may turn out to be fear of failure. Such honesty at this point leaves the door open for change and growth.

Just because we perceive the need to change a relationship or break it off does not mean that others perceive it in the same way. It is good to get other points of view.

When we speak of changing relationships, we include many sorts of circumstances. There are important changes that occur in a relationship when two people choose to marry or divorce or to have a child. There are changes that occur when a parent becomes too old to take care of herself or himself and needs looking after. Other sorts of changes take place as a child, once dependent, becomes an independent adult. There is no way to discuss in this space all the psychological and emotional effects of such change, but there are some guidelines for communicating through what can be an exciting but difficult time:

1. Keep flexible. Realize that tastes, perspectives, ideas, and feelings *do* change.
2. Be open and communicative. Do not cut off contact with others.
3. Listen. The best information on your own growth and development will come from others.
4. Accept change. Do not hold on to rigid perceptions of your self or others.
5. Take command. Begin to make decisions and solve problems for your self. Take charge of your life.
6. Stand by your decisions. Support what you do, believe, and feel. Do not be quick to back down at the slightest contradiction or challenge.
7. Seek help from others. You may be surprised how willing others are to provide advice and counsel. Since you are part of a network of interactions, use the network to your advantage.
8. Develop a purpose. Try to accomplish something you can be proud of. Do not spend your time worrying about what others say of you.
9. Be persistent. Life is just as full of setbacks as it is of successes. Persistence produces results.
10. Have a confident, positive attitude. As a free person in a free society, you can excel, find solutions, develop a purpose greater than your self. Act like the person you want to be. Get excited.

FRIENDS

As we saw in the earlier chapters of this book, a great deal of personal growth is possible within our friendships. There are thousands of large and small reasons for forming friendships, for choosing the friends we

Try This

It is important to monitor the relationships we have with our family to help us know when they need attention and/or mending. In monitoring a family relationship, ask:

1. Are you reasonable in your demands on others?

2. Are you clear, specific, open, and honest in making your feelings known?

3. Do you take the feelings of others into account?

4. Do you continually play games with others, using unfair communication techniques?

5. Do you accept the feelings of others and really try to understand them?

6. Are you tactful, considerate, courteous?

7. Are you constantly nagging, yelling, or whining?

8. Are you always joking around? Do you know when to be serious?

9. Are you a good listener?

10. Are you guided by values and principles more important than your self?

These questions get at some of the basic communication barriers that may arise from your side of the relationship. Can you think of other barriers? The decline of a relationship is usually a two-sided problem.

do. Each friendship is unique since each person is unique. We are a slightly different person in each relationship, thus, the interpersonal communication skills we need in one friendship may not be the same skills we need in another one.

Communication Barriers in Friendship

Many of the same barriers that occur in family relationships are likely also to come up in friendships. Some of these stem from freezing-in of roles—from each of us perceiving the other in one role that never changes. Too, we may assume our friend already knows everything about us. We may make guesses about each other and assume those guesses are fact. We may assume our friends know what we mean without our telling them, and hold back from expressing our feelings.

Perhaps the biggest barrier to communication within friendships is the inability of those involved to accommodate change. Too often, friendships are static. They may survive on the circumstances and feelings expressed at the beginning of the friendship. As quickly as these factors become stale, so does the friendship. When friends are unwilling to grow beyond this initial base, communication becomes tired and expressionless. No development occurs.

Another barrier shows up when friends cannot or will not break out of their defense systems, when neither wants to risk anymore. They go as far with each other as they want to and do not open up to further trust. They become prisoners of the relationship and gain little or nothing from it. Communication in such situations is cliché-level and superficial.

Forming and Maintaining Relationships

As we become wiser in the ways of human beings, more sensitive to our selves and more perceptive about others, we become more careful about the kinds of friendships we begin. The more we know about the types of personalities with whom we should or should not become involved, the more likely we are to choose friends with whom a relationship will last a long time.

Often people view the art of acquiring and holding friends as a passive process. They feel fortunate when they find a friend and are happy when that friendship lasts, but they do not realize that friendship involves commitment, giving, and energy. Often people are too lazy to make friendships work. These people never discover what friendships can be and do, and the mutual needs that can be fulfilled. Andrew Greeley, in *The Friendship Game*, calls friendship "the most pleasurable and most difficult of specifically human activities."[12]

Offering our selves to others can be risky, but good friendships are worth it.

In forming and maintaining relationships, all our interpersonal skills come into play. Friendship involves risk, disclosure of self, finding a "rhythm," and practice. It also involves making choices that are not always based on logic. There is a chemistry that occurs between good friends. Sometimes an instant rapport is deceptive and dangerous; we learn to distinguish this from that which is authentic. The skills described here for forming and maintaining relationships assume that you know someone with whom friendship seems likely and you wish to proceed. The purpose of this section is to help you think more clearly about the problems and challenges of friendship.

Taking risks. To develop a friendship we must be willing to run a risk. If we are unwilling to offer our selves to another person, there can be no mutual bond. Offering our selves to another person is the riskiest of all human endeavors because we tend to be ill at ease with people we don't know well. We wonder, for example, if others will like us. The fear that results when we are afraid others will not think well of us may be strong enough to prevent us from taking a risk. Friendship means breaking through this fear of rejection; it means successfully conquering this basic and fundamental barrier.

Try This

To find out whether you have the base for a fruitful and productive friendship, ask your self the following questions. If you can answer yes to most of the questions, it is likely that the friendship will grow and develop; if not, it is likely to become troublesome.

1. Are you willing to risk — to overcome fear of the unknown?

2. Are you attracted to the other person?

3. Do you share values and goals with the other person?

4. Do you have some of the same interests, commitments, and expectations?

5. Are you willing to be open and honest? — to acknowledge your part in the relationship? — to respond to the other person authentically?

6. Can you count on each other to be responsible and reliable?

7. Can you play together — let your self go and have fun without feeling embarrassed or ill at ease?

8. Does the relationship enable you to see your self more clearly?

9. Does the relationship allow you to remain open to other kinds of relationships with other people?

10. Does the relationship feel good?

If your answers here are predominantly no, then you should probably either get out of the relationship or begin at once looking for ways to improve it. Neither solution will be painless, but the longer you wait, the harder it will get.

It is not easy to tear down the walls that separate. For some people it is impossible. But if we view friendship as an invitation, some of the risk may be diminished. As an invitation, we extend to another person a polite request to join us in casting aside fears. We express a desire to comfort, challenge, and support through honest and open conversation. We establish bonds that will hold us and the other person together and that will clearly identify the conditions we both must honor if our friendship is to succeed.

It is easier to do this if we have a strong self-concept. It is easier, too, if we have done it before. Friendship is not something we establish once and then never again worry about — we use our friendship skills over and over. Even in ongoing relationships based on love, in which giving of the self has already occurred, further giving is still challenging and risky and necessary. There would be no challenge or risk if there were no fear, but friendship would be worth neither challenge nor risk if it were not for the satisfactions it holds.

Disclosing the self.   Friendship is not possible unless you offer your self. You must, first, have respect for the self you offer. There is a catch here because you must be strong to be able to offer your self and yet it is through friendship that you become strong. But you cannot rely on the other person for strength. *You* must be strong; to give your self to a relationship does not mean sacrificing your dignity and integrity.

Giving your self to a relationship does not mean throwing your self at another person, either. To do this is to ask for rejection, disapproval, or avoidance. People shy away from sudden, seemingly unexplained change or bombardment. Revealing your self in a relationship must be a slow, steady process which builds on previous revelations. You cannot hurry it, force it, or display it all at once. Through this sometimes painful, sometimes delightful process, you not only expand your self, you also learn about the self that is the other person.

As the other person responds to your self-disclosure with warmth and encouragement, you will discover things about your self that you didn't know before. Self-disclosure is not one-way. If you expect warmth, acceptance, and encouragement, you must be open to the other person's self-revelations as well. But just because you allow some of your self to show does not mean you can expect reciprocal display from the other: one revelation need not evoke an equal or complementary revelation from the other person. Self-disclosure occurs at different times and speeds and requires constant adjustment. Sometimes slow, sometimes fast, the pace is determined by a variety of factors unique to your particular relationship with this other person.

Finding a "rhythm." "Playful rhythm," according to Greeley, is necessary for mutual growth in a relationship. He defines this rhythm as the willingness to lead or be led:

> *At one moment we surrender, and at another moment we conquer. At one moment we seduce; at another moment we let ourselves be seduced. At one moment we support; at another moment we seek support. At one moment we are very fragile and vulnerable; at another moment, very strong and firm. . . . . At one moment we dominate; at another moment we are passive. At one moment we challenge, and at another moment we respond to challenge. The ecstasy of the relationship is perhaps to be found most completely in the very fact of the alternation of roles.*[13]

To allow the alternation to occur, we must be able to see friendship as freedom for play. With this attitude, friends can overcome difficulties and problems together and know they are richer for the effort. Such a situation is growth-promoting. It reveals rhythm.

Practicing the art. If you look at friendship as an art, you will notice that, like any other art, it has some general characteristics. Erich Fromm, in *The Art of Loving* lists four: discipline, concentration, patience, and supreme concern.[14] By practicing these requirements we may be able to move from amateur to artist in our relationships with others.

Consider This

As I've watched those who are deeply loved, I've noticed they all believe that people are a basic source of happiness. Their companions are very important to them, and no matter how busy their schedule, they have developed a life-style and a way of dispensing their time that allows them to have several profound relationships with people.

On the other hand, in talking to lonely persons I often discover that, although they lament their lack of close companions, they actually place little emphasis on the cultivation of friends. . . . They are so occupied earning money, acquiring degrees, or building their stamp collections, that they do not have time to let love grow.

"We take care of our health," observed Emerson, "we lay up money, we make our rooms tight, and our clothing sufficient; but who provides wisely that he shall not be wanting in the best property of all—friends?"

—Alan Loy McGinnis, *The Friendship Factor: How to Get Closer to the People You Care For*

Discipline. We need a lot of self-control to secure and to hold true friends. Often we treat our friends carelessly; friendships cannot survive a great deal of carelessness. While we may be able to sustain a certain level of friendship if we work at it only when we are in the mood, to become a master at the art of friendship we need to rebel against laziness.

Concentration. Have you ever allowed a friendship to be the focus of your attention? We tend to not concentrate on our friendships unless there is something obviously wrong with them. But maintaining a healthy, growing relationship requires attention, too. No friendship can become the center of our attention when we are distracted by trying to do too many things at once. Our friend is only one of many stimuli competing for our attention at any given moment.

Sometimes it seems that surface contacts are what this society is built upon, yet surface contacts are not friendships. Friendships require some intensity. They require an active commitment of both thought and feelings. We need to put distractions aside and make time for friendship.

Patience. Friendship takes time—often so much time that people do not like to wait for it to develop. They are impatient. We live in a society that is always in a hurry. We want to get where we are going quickly. Just as learning to play the piano, paint, dance, or write takes time, so does building friendships. If we want quick results we will neither establish a friendship nor learn an art.

If we rush into intimate disclosures with another person, it is unlikely that the friendship will last. Just as we cannot force a plant to grow by adding more and more water, we cannot force a friendship to flourish by excessive contact or self-disclosure. A plant is likely to live longer if its root system is deep. Friendship needs a well-developed root system as well, and we need to patiently allow time for such growth. Only then can the friendship endure the trials and tribulations that will surely come.

Supreme concern. Supreme concern, according to Fromm, means beginning "by *practicing* discipline, concentration and patience throughout every phase of [your] life." Every dyad really has three parts: you, me, and us. To reveal supreme concern is to focus attention on the "us" of a relationship—the third self. It is not easy because it requires 1) faith, 2) courage, and 3) risk. You need to be faithful to your self and to the other person; you need to demonstrate a spirit of boldness and venturesomeness; and you must realize that in pursuing friendship, you have no guarantee you won't ever be hurt or disappointed.[15]

How do we show supreme concern? We might see evidence of it when a person is unwilling to take a new and better dormitory room because to do so would mean leaving a friend behind. We see supreme concern and sacrifice where one person is willing to give a kidney to save the life of a relative. Extreme sacrifice involves giving up something we want *very* badly so that a friend might be able to have what he or she wants instead. Supreme concern is an expression of deep love for another person.

Changing or Breaking Off Relationships

Friendships are based, in large part, on shared needs or interests. When those needs and interests change, the basis for friendship may disappear. We have all had the experience of having a best friend in grade school and having little in common with him or her by the time we reached high school. The questions arise:

1. When does change or break-up come?
2. What justifies it?
3. How do we do it?
4. How do we feel about it?

When does change or break-up come? Friendship is closely tied to freedom. It is a freedom that involves responsibility, and recognizes the possibility of the end of the friendship. Not to recognize that a friendship can be terminated at any time by either party is unrealistic, naive, and restrictive. In most friendships there will always be certain elements that are imperfect. These need not be causes for break-ups unless they become pervasive or extreme.

Try This

Think of a friendship that has been worthwhile and meaningful for you. How has it required discipline, concentration, and patience? Have you noticed times during the development and maintenance of the friendship where you or the other person showed supreme concern? Think of some specific examples. Would you say that you have shown deep love for each other in this friendship? In what ways?

The pain of breaking out of a relationship comes from leaving something secure and known.

Friendships end for the same reasons that family relationships end. People find they are no longer willing to risk, find nothing attractive about each other, acquire different values and goals, develop interests, commitments, and expectations that are different, or no longer wish to work at the relationship.

What justifies it?   Whether or not the termination of a friendship is justified depends on the particular people and circumstances involved. It is different in every case. If we are aware, for any reason, that a relationship is destroying one or both of us, we must get out of it—even if we have been forced into the situation by the other person. We must carefully take stock of where we are and where we're going in the relationship and make our decision based on whether there is any possibility left for change.

How do you do it?   It is wise to realize that just because we terminate a friendship, the world does not stop revolving. We must go on. Though to end a relationship abruptly is the quickest way to terminate friendship, it is not always the easiest to accomplish. It may mean that we stop seeing each other, terminate all forms of contact, and put geographical distance between us.

The premise here is that we have correctly analyzed the situation and decided that abrupt termination is best. Such abruptness may preclude a variety of other more moderate remedies such as trying to work at some alternatives or compromises:

1. Could you see less of each other?
2. Could you change your behavior or feelings?
3. Could both of you alter your goals or expectations somewhat to bring them into harmony?
4. Are there other ways to change your relationship?

How do you feel about it? Breaking out of a relationship can be either painful or exhilarating or both. The pain comes from leaving something secure and known—from tearing out the roots that are the foundation of the tree. The exhilaration comes from experiencing the novel and unknown—from taking the roots and planting them in a new location. Can we outlive the pain to experience the exhilaration? Is the temporary discomfort worth the risk? Too often people do not accept the risk because of their fear of the unknown.

I have included this chapter on family and friends because it is within such relationships that so much of our interpersonal communication occurs. Our success in these relationships depends largely on how much we care about succeeding. No growth or change can occur if we do not care—if we do not commit ourselves to these relationships.

Our success with family and friends will very likely have a direct influence on another set of relationships that can be very important to us: relationships with work associates. How we use our interpersonal skills as we work with others will be developed and explained in the next chapter.

OTHER READING

George R. Bach and Ronald M. Deutsch, *Pairing* (New York: Avon Books, 1970). This is a book about intimacy: how to establish it and how to keep it going. The authors contend that anyone who can be open and genuine can approach anyone else with a probability of some success. This probability, they add, frees people to explore the potentials of any number of relationships.

Adelaide Bry, *Friendship: How to Have a Friend and Be a Friend* (New York: Grosset & Dunlap Publishers, 1979). Bry's purpose is to show you how to do something to bring more friends into your life. She talks about selecting the right friends, advises about how far one can go in a friendship, and helps one face problems such as jealousies, long-distance friendships, former lovers as friends, and more. This is a warmhearted, sensitive book full of practical suggestions.

Julius Fast, *The Incompatibility of Men and Women and How to Overcome It* (New York: Avon Books, 1971). In a simple writing style supported with numerous examples, Fast explains the nature of compatibility and incompatibility between men and women. His purpose is to formulate ways that men and women can rid themselves of frustration and achieve total personal fulfillment.

Andrew M. Greeley, *The Friendship Game* (Garden City, N.Y.: Image Books, 1971). Greeley examines friendship in relation to love, self-revelation, shame, play, selfhood, freedom, patience, tenderness, and society. Openness and honesty are stressed. Friendship, he contends, is a challenging and demanding game that requires the sharing of common efforts, joys, sorrows, and fears.

Barrie Hopson and Charlotte Hopson, *Intimate Feedback: A Lovers' Guide to Getting in Touch with Each Other* (New York: New American Library, 1973). Intimate feedback, the authors state, is what takes place when we open vital lines of communication. This is a book of games designed to help people tackle commonplace problems. This book touches on basic communication awarenesses and skills.

Jess Lair, *"I Ain't Well—But I Sure Am Better": Mutual Need Therapy* (Garden City, New York: Doubleday & Company, Inc., 1975). Lair's focus is the problem of loneliness, which he considers to be the central problem of human existence. Mutual need therapy, his solution to the problem, is based on establishing relationships with a few intimate friends we can trust, whom we care about and who care about us. In this book, he explains how to form these life-giving relationships.

Alan Loy McGinnis, *The Friendship Factor: How to Get Closer to the People You Care For* (Minneapolis: Augsburg Publishing House, 1979). McGinnis answers questions like "How can I get close and stay close to people I like?" or "What's the key to a successful marriage?" His focus is human relationships and the essential ingredients of warmth and caring. This is a practical book on how to be warmer and more lovable. He also focuses on how to communicate better and how to resolve tension in your relationships with friends, spouse, parents, or children.

Nena O'Neill and George O'Neill, *Open Marriage: A New Life Style for Couples* (New York: Avon Books, 1972). The O'Neills discuss verbal and nonverbal communication as well as self-disclosure, feedback, productive fighting, and fantasy sharing. This bestseller is stimulating and thought provoking.

Nena O'Neill and George O'Neill, *Shifting Gears* (New York: Avon Books, 1974). Continuing in their warm, personal style, the O'Neills offer practical guidelines for achieving full personal potential—centering on identifying real needs, turning crises into opportunities, breaking out of the traps of self-belittlement, and developing a creative life strategy. Their section on creative maturity is especially strong.

Stanton Peele, *Love and Addiction* (New York: New American Library, 1975). Interpersonal relationships are the focus of this book. Peele presents guidelines for analyzing existing relationships. The goal is mutual growth—to be able to share all that people find best in themselves and each other. A well-written, comprehensive book.

Virginia Satir, *Peoplemaking* (Palo Alto, Calif.: Science and Behavior Books, Inc., 1972). Provides basic ideas for helping families discover the causes of some of their problems and offers creative ways of working through them. This is a clear and comprehensive treatment of family living—a workbook designed to enhance self-awareness, to stimulate partner conversation, and to induce new levels of family communication.

Gail Sheehy, *Passages: Predictable Crises of Adult Life* (New York: E. P. Dutton & Co., Inc., 1976). In her thorough and well-documented book, Sheehy describes the personality changes common to each stage of life as people pull up roots, pass through the twenties and thirties, and approach midlife. She compares the development of men and women, talks of couples, and examines the strains that occur in relationships.

Sven Wahlroos, *Family Communication: A Guide to Emotional Health* (New York: New American Library, 1974). This book stresses the importance of communication in both creating and solving problems between human beings. Wahlroos presents twenty communication rules to improve relationships and ten characteristics of emotional health and how to make them your own. This is a useful guide.

NOTES

[1]Sven Wahlroos, *Family Communication: A Guide to Emotional Health* (New York: New American Library, 1974), p. xi.

[2]Virginia Satir, *Peoplemaking* (Palo Alto, Calif.: Science and Behavior Books, Inc., 1972), pp. 51–56.

[3]Wahlroos, *Family Communication*, p. xii.

[4]Satir, *Peoplemaking*, pp. 59–79.

[5]Ibid., p. 67.

[6]David Viscott, *How to Live With Another Person* (New York: Arbor House, 1974), p. 143. See especially Chapter 12, "Living with Your Family."

[7]Satir, *Peoplemaking*, p. 74.

[8]Ibid., p. 77.

[9]Paul Watzlawick, Janet Helmick Beavin, and Don D. Jackson, *Pragmatics of Human Communication: A Study of Interactional Patterns, Pathologies, and Paradoxes* (New York: W. W. Norton & Co., Inc., 1968), p. 134.

[10]From "Defensive Communication" by Jack R. Gibb, *Journal of Communication*, vol. 11:3 (1961), p. 147. Reprinted by permission.

[11]Gibb, "Defensive Communication," 147.

[12]From *The Friendship Game* by Andrew M. Greeley. Published by Image Books, a division of Doubleday & Company, Inc., 1971, p. 15. See also pp. 25–32, 46–56, 74–83, and 135.

[13]Ibid., p. 80.

[14]Erich Fromm, *The Art of Loving* (New York: Harper & Row, 1956), pp. 108–10.

[15]Muriel James and Louis M. Savary, *The Heart of Friendship* (New York: Harper & Row, 1976), p. 155.

11

Entering the World of Work:
Communication and Your Job

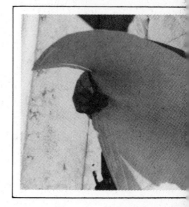

Much of your adult life will be spent on the job. More than any other single factor, the way you speak—verbally *and* nonverbally—will reveal more about you—your intelligence, personality, and character—than anything else you do. Thus, your ability to get a job, to get a better position, or to gain recognition may relate to what you say and how you say it.

Just as landing a job, getting a raise, or attaining a promotion may relate to effective communication, so may your satisfaction with your work. Aubrey Sanford, writing on human relations, says that the conditions which most often lead to job satisfaction include experiencing a sense of achievement; deserving and receiving recognition for the work we do; finding our work interesting, challenging, and varied; taking responsibility for outcomes; and discovering potential for growth and advancement.[1] Harry Shaw, author of a book entitled *Better Jobs Through Better Speech*, claims that "More time, money, opportunities, and even friendships are lost through thoughtless and unacceptable speech than through any other activity of people's lives."[2] Your satisfaction with your work, then, is likely to improve if you can express yourself clearly, accurately, concisely, and openly with both employers and fellow employees.

The encounters that are likely to matter most in the world of work are person-to-person. What others know about you will depend on your ability to communicate. If you have a unique idea, an exciting proposal, or an unusual solution, it will make little difference if it cannot be communicated in an acceptable and effective manner. The impression you make on others will become crucial to the successful implementation of your ideas.

The application of the interpersonal skills discussed so far in this book is similar when we move into the sphere of work, but we must now contend with a culture that is built on interrelated, competitive, and interlocking roles. A work environment is a system for processing information, setting goals, making plans and decisions, implementing action, and evaluating results. It has a problem-solving orientation. Within this context, stress points occur that bear on the interpersonal communication that takes place within the system. Certain kinds of interpersonal behavior become appropriate, other kinds inappropriate.

It is likely that your contribution to the company that employs you will depend on your intelligent use of interpersonal skills. Whether or not you earn recognition within this context may also depend on those same skills. Thus, it is helpful to understand the range of situations in which interpersonal skills are important. You will be dealing with the immediate boss as well as higher-ups and you will be dealing with peers as well as people below you in the hierarchy of the organization. Situations are likely to be simultaneously informative and persuasive. They may include conferences, meetings, and interviews as well as more informal talks at the office drinking fountain or over coffee. The point is, you will probably be on display more than you realize, and your interpersonal skills will have an impact on those with whom you interact.

In this chapter we will first look at the role of communication in the job-hunting process. We will then discuss various types of work-related interviews and outline several of the communication barriers likely to be experienced on the job. The final section of the chapter will wrap it up by examining the many opportunities that arise on the job which challenge people to use and improve communication skills.

LOOKING FOR THE RIGHT JOB

When we look for a job, we invest a good deal of our time, energy, and hope in the search. Effective interpersonal communication is crucial to finding a job—the right job. For most of us, a personal interview is the way we gain entrance to employment. Not only is this occasion vital for the interviewee, it can be just as important for the interviewer. Before talking specifically about the actual interview, we should first understand a little about what precedes it. What precedes helps to determine the quality of the interview—and its outcome. Thus, we need to consider how to obtain the interview and how to prepare for it.

Consider This

Looking for a job is a job, and like any other work, mastery of the system can greatly ease its difficulty. What's more, job-hunting techniques are well worth mastering. Experts say that the average worker under 35 goes through a job switch once every 18 months, and the worker over 35, once every three years!

Taking stock. Even if you already have a general idea of the job you're looking for, it's important to take time before the job hunt to pinpoint exactly what you want. You don't want to accept a new position only to discover that it has some of the same pitfalls you thought you were escaping.

"Start by examining your own job," says Carol Feit Lane, a career development specialist with New York University. "What do you like about it? What do you dislike? Do you like the functions you perform but dislike the environment? Or do you like the people and the environment, but dislike the functions? The more clearly you identify what you're looking for, the better your chances of really enjoying your next job."

After listing your on-the-job likes and dislikes, you need to consider the other skills you have which you'd like to use. What do you enjoy doing and do well? These may be skills you've developed in volunteer work or your hobbies.

These lists are the key to identifying the position you're looking for. If you can't think of a job that suits your skills, consult friends and contacts. Find out what their jobs entail, and ask if they know of any work that suits your skills.

—Kate Kelley, *Family Weekly*, July 29, 1979

The Initial Inquiry

The purpose of the initial inquiry is to obtain an interview. There are three ways to do it: 1) the inquiry by letter, 2) the telephone inquiry, or 3) the in-person inquiry.[3] Because first impressions are so important, the way you conduct yourself in that initial inquiry can make a significant difference.

No matter which of the three methods of inquiry are used, you will need a "home" base from which to operate. That is, there must be some way for prospective employers to contact you. It is a good idea to establish regular hours, to let others know those hours, and to stick to them. If there are times when you cannot keep regular hours, use an answering service, a telephone answering device, or provide the number of a friend who can take messages for you. You need to be businesslike in responding to telephone calls and letters, just as you do in setting hours. Respond promptly. Consider such responses necessary commitments that convey a businesslike attitude.[4]

The *inquiry by letter* is, perhaps, the most common inquiry. It is usually accompanied by a brief résumé. It is best if it can be addressed to a specific person rather than to "Personnel Director," "Department

Try This

Compose a letter of inquiry of your own for an ideal position of your choice. If you do not have an ideal position, check the want-ads section of your local newspaper and select a position you would like to find out more about. Make this letter neat, formal, and brief. Assume that once it is completed and typed, you could actually send it.

Chairperson," or "To Whom It May Concern." If you do not know a person's name, it is worthwhile placing a telephone call to ascertain this information. Make certain you get the proper spelling of the name and the person's title.

The inquiry by letter should:

1. Be brief.
2. Be businesslike (serious and formal).
3. Reveal a positive attitude about the firm.
4. Show what you can offer the company.
5. Indicate confidence (but maintain your distance).
6. Be courteous in its opening and closing greetings.
7. Give some indication of your individuality.
8. Have no typing, spelling, or grammatical errors.
9. Stimulate the reader's interest.
10. Explain why you want to work for this company.

A sample letter of inquiry might read like the following. Remember to express your own unique style in such a letter.

May 1, 1981

Mr. Robert Davis, President
The Patrick Company
5101 State Street
Ann Arbor, Michigan 48105

Dear Mr. Davis:

Sunday's <u>Ann Arbor News</u> carried notice of an opening for the position of Sales Representative with your company. I am very interested in this position.

As indicated on my enclosed résumé, I have majored in Speech Communication with emphases in business, economics, and marketing. The several sales positions I held during summer months gave me practical experience in these areas as well. I am looking for a career position that will build on this base of education and experience. The position you advertised would not only be a challenge to me, but also would offer me an opportunity to capitalize on my talents and abilities. Perhaps I should add that I grew up in Ann Arbor; thus, I am already familiar with that sales area.

I would like to visit the Patrick Company and discuss this position with you, as well as some of my ideas on sales. I look forward to hearing from you.

Sincerely,

Douglas Mainstrom

Douglas Mainstrom
668 Central Street
Dublin, Ohio 43221
(419) 653-1883

The *telephone inquiry* requires forethought. For example, before placing or receiving a call, make certain you have a paper and pencil handy. If numerous inquiries are going to be made, these could be recorded on index cards for easy filing. Essential information that should be recorded would be:

—name of firm
—name of person to be contacted (or contacting). Be sure to get this name down exactly right; ask for the correct spelling and pronunciation.
—address
—phone number
—days and hours person can be contacted
—short job description, if known
—impressions or suggestions about how to proceed next time

Think about what you plan to say. The telephone inquiry is usually brief; every word is important. Prepare a *short* summary of who you are, your background, and what you can do. You should not have to flounder when asked for your credentials. But you should not offer a full résumé either. Because you know the facts well and have probably repeated them before, be careful not to rush. Speak loudly, enunciate clearly, and avoid sounding either bored or as if you have memorized your speech.

If the person you want is out when you call, be certain to get the name of the person who answered the phone. You might also jot down the time you called. It may be useful later when you *do* make contact. For example, it sounds responsible and mature to say in response to a question about when you tried to call, "I called yesterday at 2:15, but Mrs. Smith said you were in a conference." Also, you will then be able to greet Mrs. Smith by name if you come in for an interview. Going out of your way to be courteous and polite is not just good manners, it is appropriate behavior in the business world.

An initial telephone inquiry may sound like the following:

Respondent: Hello, Mr. Stevens. My name is Lisa Martin. I saw your company's advertisement in the <u>Chronicle</u> and would like to know something about the position you are advertising.

Interviewer: The position we've advertised, Ms. Martin, is that of staff writer in our public relations department. It requires a college degree . . .

Respondent: I will graduate from State University in May with a bachelor's degree in business communication.

Interviewer: Good. Of course, the job involves a great deal of writing—press releases and so on. Have you had much writing experience?

Respondent:	I have a minor in journalism and have taken English courses in both technical and creative writing. I also worked on the college newspaper, as a writer and a copy editor.
Interviewer:	Fine. Do you have any other questions I can answer?
Respondent:	It sounds like the kind of position I'm looking for, Mr. Stevens. I'd like to talk with you about it in person.
Interviewer:	Yes, I think we should discuss this at greater length. When are you available for an interview?
Respondent:	I'm free any morning during the week. What time is best for you?
Interviewer:	Does next Monday at 9:30 a.m. sound all right?
Respondent:	Yes, that would be convenient. Where is your office located?
Interviewer:	(Explains best way to get to office.)
Respondent:	That seems clear. I should have no trouble. I look forward to seeing you next Monday at 9:30 a.m. Thanks, Mr. Stevens, for your time.

The *in-person inquiry* has several advantages. It will allow you to learn what positions are available, the various job requirements, and a little about the firm as well. You can also find out who the people are that you will need to see. By observing the organization and the people who work there, you will learn a great deal about the company that will help you in the job interview. If you can talk to anyone on the job, this will also help.

In the in-person inquiry, make certain you

1. Present yourself professionally in both appearance and manner.
2. Get the information you need efficiently and succinctly. Be prepared to write down the necessary facts.
3. Repeat names, places, times, or other data to make certain you recorded them accurately.
4. Plan to collect the same information outlined previously under telephone inquiry.
5. Come prepared for an interview at once, if you can get one. This may save you another trip. Do not let this circumstance take you by surprise.
6. Leave a copy of your résumé, if possible.

The Résumé

There is no single right way to prepare a résumé, but it is an essential part of the job-application process. The nature of a résumé will be determined by your qualifications and by the job. Its purpose is to pro-

---

Create the dialogue for a telephone inquiry. You are attempting to secure an interview for a job. Pretend that this is the job that you really want—your ideal position. Provide both sides of the dialogue—your side as well as the person on the receiving end.

In an actual telephone contact, you should make certain that you are clear and to the point. In telephone situations there is a need for instant understanding as well as immediate recall. Pay particular attention to your

1. Voice. Do not be abrupt or harsh.

2. Manner. Do not be tactless, unkind, or unpleasant.

3. Articulation and enunciation. Because telephone conversations do not include nonverbal elements, you must be sure that the sounds of the language are formed carefully (articulation) and, also, that they are clear and distinct (enunciation).

If you have a tape recorder available, tape your inquiry. When you play it back, check yourself on the factors: voice, articulation and enunciation, and feedback. How did you measure up?

vide other people with a concise summary of your qualifications. Minimal requirements for the résumé include:

—overall neatness
—no misspellings, typographical errors, or grammatical errors
—no erasures
—typed or professionally printed presentation

Since most people send in résumés printed on white-stock paper, a résumé printed on light-colored paper could give the applicant an edge. Remember, above all, that an employer will accept your résumé as an indication of the type of person you are. Present your résumé as you would yourself. Let it be an accurate reflection. Most often, a one-page résumé is sufficient. Employers usually skim the page for the information they are seeking; don't hide the relevant facts about yourself in a jumble of unnecessary details. The following is an abbreviated sample of the kind of information which should be included in a résumé.

Please note that details such as race, religion, and age are no longer appropriate on the résumé, since it is illegal for employers to base hiring decisions upon these factors. That is why such information does not appear in the sample.

Emily G. Russell
1927 Pine Avenue West
Denver, Colorado 80210
(303) 462-3387

Objective: Entry level position that will draw upon my interest and
training in business and my proficiency in Spanish.

Qualifications: Good analytic skills, creative thinker, enthusiastic, bilingual.

Education: 1980. B.S., University of Wisconsin at Madison. Major in
business, minor in Spanish.

1979. Four-week summer seminar in International Business
Law at Stanford University. Received certificate of satisfactory completion.

January 1978 to May 1978. Attended La Universidad de
Guadalajara as student in intensive Spanish language program. Awarded Honors Certificate.

1976 to 1977. Attended Miami University, Oxford, Ohio.

Professional
Memberships: National Linguistic Association
Institute for International Business Management

Work
Experience: September 1979 to May 1980. Part-time bookkeeper for La
Baguette (French bakery and café) in Madison, Wisconsin.
Responsible for preparing payroll, submitting monthly tax
statements. Suggested method for collecting on outstanding
accounts, which was successfully implemented.

1979 summer. Apprentice clerk for import/export firm in
Denver. Learned and assumed responsibility for invoicing,
translated documents.

October 1978 to May 1979. Part-time clerk in grocery store,
Madison. Duties included cashiering, stocking, taking
inventory.

1977, 1976 summers. Swimming and waterfront counselor
at camp for inner-city children. Responsibilities included
supervising water games, teaching canoeing.

References: Mrs. Madeleine LeGrand
La Baguette
123 Pace Street
Madison, Wisconsin 53706

Mr. Joseph Perrino
Armand's Imports
1020 Arapaho Drive
Denver, Colorado 80210

Mr. Mario Lopez
Mario's Finer Foods
14 Capitol Street
Madison, Wisconsin 53706

Ms. Lane Mitchell
Director, High Peak Camp
P. O. Box 192
Boulder, Colorado 80302

Preparing for the Personal Meeting

You have now secured an interview. Preparing for it must begin at once. (You probably do not have a great deal of time!) The purpose of this preparation process is to assemble as much information as you can to be ready for the interview. There are several areas in which preparation can be made: 1) personal areas, 2) the company, 3) the job, and 4) other areas (environment).

Personally, you should begin to consider your own professional needs and goals.[5] What are *you* looking for? Try to narrow down both your goals and your occupational choices. It is almost certain that you will be asked questions in this area. What are your interests and attitudes? Your answers to questions like this one will indicate how interested you are in professional growth. What past experience, education, or training have you received? You will undoubtedly be seeking a career that will build on your expertise. Your qualifications will, then, add to your confidence and self-worth. What considerations need to be made with respect to your physical stamina and general health? Certain

Prepare an accurate, up-to-date résumé for yourself. Make certain that it is complete—including all of your recent education, personal qualifications, and work experience. For references, choose those people who could comment specifically on your ability. Cite no more than three references.

In this résumé, include a short paragraph in which you describe, as specifically as possible, your career goals and ambitions. This statement should reflect some positive quality about you—something that you believe is one of your strongest assets.

This résumé should also include as many of the following optional items as are appropriate:

1. Honors, awards, and trophies (with the award title, the granting agent, and the date received).*

2. Professional publications (with title, publisher, and date).*

3. Professional workshops and conferences.*

4. Professional consulting experience.*

5. Community service (with a description, the agency involved, and the date completed).*

6. Hobbies, interests, and activities (with a description, location, the time involved, and the date—list sparingly and only if meaningful).

*When a time sequence is involved, list individual items in reverse chronological order; the most recent awards or activities should appear first.

jobs may overextend you, inundate you, or box you in. To know this beforehand will help ensure that you do not get into the wrong type of job.

Knowing in advance of the interview your most valuable educational experiences, your most rewarding work experiences, your most successful projects and accomplishments, and your strengths and capabilities will help you to avoid hesitating when asked any of these personal questions. Your forthright answers to such questions will indicate self-confidence and strength.[6]

To find out about *the company* may require some digging. You may have to consult reference publications in the library. Sometimes, the local chamber of commerce can provide information. The *Industrial Index* may be another source, as may the public relations department of the company you are investigating. The kinds of information you might wish to know would include the following:

1. How long has the firm been in business?
2. What is its product line?
3. What have been its sales over the past five years?
4. What is its growth potential?
5. Who are the company's biggest competitors?
6. What reputation does the company have?
7. How many employees are there? What training do they receive?
8. What are the company's future plans?
9. What are the company's expectations? traditions? regulations?
10. What is the company's financial profile? size of payroll? amount of debt?
11. Who are the major shareholders? Who owns the company?[7]

These questions are only a beginning. The more background information and knowledge you have, the better your letters, phone conversations, and interviews are likely to be. If you have completed this kind of investigation, your future employer will surely discover that you have done your homework. This indicates not only your enthusiasm but also your sincerity and determination.

The job is also of importance to you. Some questions that you need to ask would be:

1. What specialized ability or knowledge does this job require?
2. Is the job long- or short-range? permanent or temporary?
3. What are the opportunities for advancement?
4. What are the working conditions? (safety, desirability, comfort)
5. What likelihood is there for changes in working conditions? mobility? travel? relocation?

6. What are the salary and fringe benefits offered (insurance, retirement plans, health care, stock options)?
7. What are the provisions for overtime, sick leave, personal leave, maternity leave, vacation time, lunch facilities, paid holidays?
8. Can you detect any hidden expectations? off-duty standards, modes of conduct, or expectations?
9. Must you provide your own car? equipment? tools? uniforms? materials? Are they insured? Do you receive compensation for using your own?[8]

You may lack the time or the resources to find answers to all these questions. The point is, however, a thorough investigation would provide answers to many of them. And if you think of this job as a permanent, lifetime commitment, you can see how important such answers are. The more you know, the more intelligent and specific will be your questions in the interview. The more likely, too, that you will be able to get just the information you need without a big loss of time. In business, as in many other facets of life, time is money!

Besides personal preparation, information about the company and job, you should also think about *other possible areas* where questioning might occur. Try to anticipate the situation as much as you can. For example, what about the locality and environment? How about churches, schools, and recreational facilities? What about the cost of living? desirable housing? Do you find the climate desirable? tolerable? What are the social and cultural norms of the local society? Would you and your family be accepted there? How about educational opportunities?[9] Could you pursue your hobbies and sports interests there?

THE JOB INTERVIEW

Now that you have written the letters, sent out the résumés, made the telephone calls, and secured basic information, you are ready for the interview. So far you have dealt with basically inanimate objects; now you have to perform. You will be meeting a person face-to-face. Based on this meeting, a decision about you will be made.[10]

It is clear from the preceding discussion that the best interviews result from solid preparation, pre-examination, and thought. Expectations by both interviewee and interviewer are usually well-defined. In this section we will first discuss the nature of the interview situation as a whole, then the role of the interviewer in the job interview, and finally that of the interviewee.

The *nature of the situation*, of course, varies with the job, the loca-

Try This

Select a local company in which you might have some interest. Do a complete profile on this company answering the questions on this page. From where did you get most of your information? How reliable or accurate do you think this information is? Would you want to work for this company based on what you know now? What are its major strengths? weaknesses? Are there things that you would still like to know? Are there questions that you could ask an interviewer? Can you see the advantage of doing a company profile before engaging in a job interview?

tion of the interview, and the company holding the interview. But whatever the variations in these factors, personal appearance is always important in establishing the first impression. You should dress as others do in the occupation you are seeking. In addition, be clean and neat. It is probably advisable to be more conservative in dress than liberal in these situations. Avoid faddish styles, garish colors, and junk jewelry. Simplicity and appropriateness help others know that you are mature, thoughtful, and responsible. "If you care about your attire," others are likely to think, "you will probably care about your job."

The interviewee must also be sensitive to the tone of the interview. An interview can be positive or negative. The tone is often reflected in feedback from the interviewer. The interviewee may detect indicators of tone in face, bodily position, muscular tension, vocal quality, and eye contact. Interviewers have bad days, long days, or troublesome interviews, just as you do. If you detect tension or fatigue you can sometimes change the tone by:

1. Relaxing. Try to enjoy the interview and learn from it.
2. Adding a bit of humor.
3. Asking a question.
4. Striving, despite the circumstances, to give a good impression.[11]

The *interviewer's* job is to hire someone, not to play games. The intent is to hire the person who will best fit into the organization and have something important to contribute. The interviewer is usually prepared to give the interviewee a fair hearing. After all, he or she is taking the time to interview you.

In most cases interviewers will have carefully reviewed applicants' résumés and applications to familiarize themselves with the basic information. During the initial interview, an interviewer will attempt to fill gaps, explore ranges of experience, determine expertise in certain areas, discuss the interviewee's career goals and potential usefulness to the organization, probe the interviewee's attitudes toward the company, its products, or its services, and assess the prospective employee's personality and character.

Employment interviews often follow progressive stages of development. In many cases there will be an initial screening interview. This interview is designed to decrease the total pool of prospective candidates. Depending on the size of the pool, it can be reduced by making the job specifications more specific, thereby eliminating those who do not fit the position rather precisely, or simply eliminating those who do not meet certain criteria, such as level of education or job experience. Either way, once the pool is substantially reduced, second-stage screen-

The job applicant, knowing that a decision about him will be made based on the interview, should prepare carefully for that face-to-face meeting.

ing interviews can take place. The number of stages involved is likely to depend on the size of the reduced pool at each stage and the difficulty in finding just the right person for the job.

Interviewers often look for interpretive information that is not conveyed on a résumé or application. For this reason, they are likely to ask open-ended questions that have few restrictions on the applicant's answers. That is, they will try to get the interviewee to expand and elaborate: "How do you feel about . . . ?" "What would be your reaction to . . . ?" or "What would you do if such-and-such happened?" Closed questions are restrictive and usually ask for a "yes" or "no" response: "Did you take any courses in business?" "Have you any job experience in this area?" or "Based on what I have outlined, then, does this job still interest you?" They do not allow the interviewer much insight into the personality and character of the interviewee. Open questions elicit subjective responses, and they take longer to answer. Thus, interviewers often use open-ended questions or a combination of both open and closed.

After interviewers get an answer to a question, they will often use a follow-up, or secondary, question to probe the interviewee more deeply. "Why did you choose to do that?" "Did you find that ex-

Consider This

Three out of every four job applicants are rejected during the preliminary or screening interview. Sometimes the reasons are obvious: unwillingness to relocate, say, or lack of proper qualifications. More often, however, the interviewer is turned off by inarticulateness, lack of enthusiasm or poor appearance.

"One of the best ways to impress an interviewer is to ask good, thoughtful questions. This shows that you have been attentive during the interview, you have done your homework on the company and you're interested in working there," says Donald H. Sweet, director of employment for the Celanese Corp. and co-author of Job Hunting for the College Graduate (D. C. Heath & Co., $5.95).

But asking the wrong questions can be as harmful as not asking any, Sweet warns. Particularly bad are immediate queries about salary and benefits—it's better to discuss money in a second interview—and putting the interviewer on the spot at the end by asking how you did or what your chances are.

To help you survive that first interview, Sweet suggests you ask questions such as these:

- What would be a typical first assignment for someone like me?
- Which of your locations might need someone with my abilities?
- Is there a formal training program?
- What might I look forward to in terms of promotions?
- How often would my performance be reviewed?
- Would I have opportunities to continue my schooling? Is there a tuition-reimbursement plan?
- Has the company had to lay off people in my specialty in the past few years?

If you're particularly interested in a company, don't hesitate to say so—and why—at the end of the session. "This is a good way to end the interview on a high note," says Sweet.

He also advises writing a thank-you letter, including in it points that you were not able to make during the screening. This helps the interviewer remember you and also shows off your writing skills which is important to most employers.

—*Money,* April 1979

---

perience meaningful?" or "Can you see the benefits of this?" are some examples of secondary questions. These require the interviewee to expand on his or her answers. They are designed to show how the interviewee thinks and feels—to get behind obvious or superficial responses.

Secondary questions also help interviewers "measure" attitude and personality. Certainly no single question provides a direct line into another person's soul, but from questions like "How do you feel about that?" "What difference do you think such-and-such makes?" or "How would you respond in that situation?" help them gauge commitment, responsibility, maturity, and other leadership qualities. Is the interviewee fiercely independent, or able to work with others? Does the interviewee appear eager and enthusiastic, or lazy and complacent? Secondary questions can provide insights into such areas.

Interviewers also work under certain restraints. Title VII of the Civil Rights Act of 1964 forbids discrimination on the basis of race, sex, religion, nation of origin, or age in personnel decisions. The Equal Employment Opportunity Commission (EEOC) enforces Title VII, getting its power to take companies that do not follow Title VII guidelines to court from the Equal Employment Opportunity Act. And, for employers, ignorance of the law is no excuse. Thus, unless certain characteristics regarding a person's ethnic origins, race, sex, religion, age, or marital status are directly related to effective performance on the job, questions on these areas are illegal. This means that an interviewer cannot ask you if you are married, single, or divorced; whether or not you attend church; if you and your spouse plan to have children; if you have been arrested; what your age, height, or weight is; whether or not you own your own home; if you are living with anyone; whether or not you practice birth control; what social clubs or lodges you belong to; how your parents earn their living; how you might feel working with people of other races, or those of the opposite sex; or even how your spouse may feel about your having a career.

Questions like these are an invasion of privacy and, in most cases, irrelevant to job requirements. If an interviewee provides such information, the interviewer should discourage further comment and inform the interviewee that this information cannot be pursued because of EEOC regulations. Also, an interviewer should never add information to the application form. The interviewee can be requested to fill in missing information or it can be left blank. Even doodling on a candidate's form could be interpreted as evidence of an interviewer using a code to transcribe illegal information.

Try This

Conduct a practice interview session with a friend. Tell your friend about the ideal kind of job you would like. Provide as many details as you can. Then ask your friend to ask you <u>any</u> appropriate questions — playing the role of the future employer. In your answers to your friend's questions, make certain that you

1. Avoid any nervous habits.
2. Speak up.
3. Refrain from giggling.
4. Speak to the point.
5. Avoid being too abrupt or curt.
6. Give an adequate answer, but not an overlong one.
7. Make no offensive or off-color comments.
8. Appear confident, alert, and responsive.

If a tape recorder is available, tape the practice interview. Then listen to the tape, analyzing your responses. How did you sound?

The interviewee's job is to make a good impression. If you have thought about the interview and job in advance, you will be prepared to get the information you need. One thing you can plan to find out from the interview is whether or not you really want this job. Interviews are not one-sided. Not only does the interviewee have a choice, but he or she also has a certain personal responsibility to find out information. How often are performance reviews conducted? What are the chances for promotion or advancement? How does the organization promote employee advancement? through educational grants? training programs? Are employees unionized? Do union and company administrators cooperate or work amicably together? Are there contract difficulties? no-strike clauses in the contract? What are company policies regarding layoffs? Are there grievance procedures? Are clear channels set up whereby employees can communicate with superiors? What are the future plans of this organization?

Asking intelligent questions indicates that you have already thought about the interview and position. Also, it lets the interviewer know that you are serious. A serious job-seeker wants to know more than how long the working week is, how much the job pays, and what fringe benefits are available. To limit yourself to such questions—as important as they are—provides interviewers with a fairly clear set of interviewee motives and attitudes—a set that is unlikely to result in a job for the applicant displaying it!

An interviewee can make other decisions during the interview as well. For example, you can decide which questions should be answered briefly and which require elaboration. If questions are ambiguous, you should ask for clarification and avoid responding too hastily. It is a sign of good judgment to make sure that you understand the exact nature of a question before you answer it.

You can also make certain that the questions asked are relevant to professional or personal qualifications only. Finally, you can decide if the job requirements outlined by the interviewer are too restrictive. Sometimes interviewers may entertain unreasonable expectations for a prospective employee. If the interviewer has provided a fairly complete job description, the interviewee has a right to question responsibilities that go along with the job. You can also show how your own special qualifications or abilities make up for not satisfying some of the other qualifications the interviewer has outlined.

Finally, the interviewee should not leave without determining what further information the interviewer may want. What follow-up steps are likely to be taken? How will the outcome of the interview be determined? How will you learn about the outcome? Can you call next week for an answer? Interviewees need to know what is going to come next and who is to be responsible for it.

Some writers specializing in job-hunting techniques suggest that the interviewee should take the follow-up initiative with a "thank-you" letter or phone call. Such a letter or call can also be used to clarify ambiguous points or offer further information about the candidate's qualifications.

OTHER TYPES OF INTERVIEWS

In this section we will examine several situations—other than job-seeking—when interview skills can be used at work. Much communication on the job occurs in interpersonal encounters of various kinds. For example, the situation may be that the boss wants some information, wishes to appraise your performance, needs to reprimand you, or needs to get you to believe or to do something.

If you are the interviewee in any of these situations, you should realize that your rights as a human being—outlined in Chapter 9, "Getting There from Here: Assertiveness"—must be protected and preserved. You may often find yourself in a position where it is up to you to maintain this protection and preservation. You need not, for example, apologize for your background or lack of experience. Everyone must start somewhere. You should feel free to change your mind during an interview or to make a mistake. This is part of being human. You should also feel free, when questioned, to answer "I don't know." No one is expected to know everything. Also, you can say "I don't understand." Remember, this is a new situation. Interviewers have information with which you are not familiar. They may assume that you know things when in fact you do not. The best way to handle such situations is to admit that you do not understand and to ask for more information.

The *information-gathering interview* is, perhaps, the least threatening type of interview. Bosses must get specific information from subordinates. They usually know in advance exactly what they need to find out. Their questions are likely to require clear, specific responses. Interviewees in these situations should plan to be

1. Certain what is being asked, or what is being requested. Listen carefully. Paraphrase a request to make sure the meaning is clear.
2. Brief and clear. Keep your responses tied directly to the request. Do not digress or waste time.

3. Complete. Try to give all information that may be useful.
4. Honest. Do not use ambiguity or evasiveness to mask a situation where you do not have the information or have not done the work. Be straightforward and honest.

The *appraisal interview* is designed to assess the performance of workers. It can be distasteful to everyone involved because it can become an opportunity for the boss to tell you all that you are doing wrong. This is why many appraisal interviews are conducted in a defensive climate. But this interview should be more than an occasion to criticize the worker. It should be an opportunity for interviewees to learn the employer's expectations. Also, it can reveal strengths as well as weaknesses and lead to changing demands and responsibilities. For the employer, the interview can determine whether workers are perceiving the job correctly. Conducted in a supportive climate, appraisal interviews often avert problems before they arise. They keep open important channels of communication.

Another function of the appraisal interview can be goal setting. This type of interview provides an opportunity for the interviewee to set objectives: tasks to be accomplished within a specified time. Further meetings can be planned to assess progress toward goals. This process has been referred to as management by objectives, and it requires that all participants approach these interviews in a positive, open, and supportive manner.

Interviewees should consider the appraisal interview constructively. The interview will achieve its positive potential more fully if you, as interviewee, strive to

1. Find out specific information. General reactions of "goodness" or "badness" will not be useful to you unless they are related to specific behaviors or actions.
2. Express your own expectations clearly. Seek boss or supervisor support of these in order to provide yourself with specific direction and understandable future objectives.
3. Offer a well-defined picture of what you have accomplished, what you are doing now, and what you plan to be doing, as well as why.
4. Understand in detail how your personal activities and behaviors fit into those of your unit, or of the organization as a whole.
5. Do your part, to the extent that you can, to keep the interview focused on performance, not personality.

Reprimand interviews occur when a supervisor finds violations in organizational policies, principles, or procedures. Usually the boss will engage in an information-gathering interview first to find out why the violation occurred. Was the policy known? Was the violation purposeful? Once this information is discovered, the remaining part of the interview follows naturally.

The interviewee, in this situation, must do several things:

1. Provide accurate, complete information.
2. Seek clarification about the nature of the violation and how the organization views it.
3. Gain a full explanation of the penalty, if one is to be imposed, its implementation, effect, and extent. What is its duration? How will it be monitored? (Some of these questions may not be asked directly because of the nature of the situation.)
4. Offer an apology, if appropriate, and a statement that will assure the boss that such a situation will not occur again.

The *persuasive interview*, the final type, occurs when one person wants to change a belief or course of action. When a boss or subordinate wants to convince another person of a new idea, he or she is likely to engage in a persuasive interview. Although all the preceding interviews are persuasive to a degree, this one has the expressed purpose of sales: selling an idea or course of action. The skills necessary in such a situation are identical to those outlined in Chapter 7, "Tuning In: Attitudes," in the section labeled "Improving Skills in Persuasion."

A subordinate may not have a choice when a boss wants a change. But these circumstances are less persuasive and more informative. That is, if a boss decides that employees are taking too long at coffee breaks, all he or she may need to do is inform them of this situation to bring about a change. On the other hand, if the solution is negotiable, if several alternatives are included, or if opinions are solicited, then the subordinate may need more information, and the questions that follow may help.

1. Who approves of the change? Is it authorized?
2. Is the change consistent with my needs or the needs of my job?
3. Is the change likely to help others in the organization or the organization as a whole?
4. What rewards or incentives are being offered to persuade me to change?
5. How big, important, or long-range is the change being requested?
6. What side-effects is the change likely to bring about? Does the change raise more problems than it solves?
7. Am I allowed time to consider my response? Can I think about it before deciding whether to go along with the change?

Consider This

Public employees who complain to their bosses privately enjoy the same free-speech protections as those who go public with their criticism, the U.S. Supreme Court ruled Tuesday.

Voting unanimously, the justices struck down a lower court's ruling that applied such First Amendment rights to public statements only.

"Neither the amendment itself nor our decisions indicate this freedom is lost to the public employee who arranges to communicate privately with his employer rather than to spread his views before the public," Justice William Rehnquist wrote for the court.

An employee fired because of such a talk with his or her boss must be reinstated if the evidence shows that the worker would not have been fired "if the constitutionally protected conduct had not occurred," Justice Rehnquist said.

—(AP) *The Blade: Toledo, Ohio,* January 10, 1979

Try This

Practice the skills required by the following types of interview situations:

1. Information-gathering: you missed a class or lecture and must find out from another student what went on.

2. Appraisal: you are working with another person on a class project and you are pleased with the results and the contribution the other person has made.

3. Reprimand: you are unhappy with your roommate for transgressions on your rights. (Your roommate is leaving the room a mess, entertaining in your room often and asking you to leave, or borrowing things that belong to you without asking permission.)

4. Persuasion: you are trying to convince a teacher that a new policy is unfair. You are trying to convince your roommate to spend more time studying.

Can you think of other realistic settings where the above types of interview skills could be practiced?

If a worker is trying to persuade the boss that a new procedure—like posting all directives that relate to employees on the bulletin board—should be adopted, the boss becomes the interviewee in this situation. Some of these questions may be appropriate in this situation too.

WORK-RELATED COMMUNICATION BARRIERS

Work settings provide numerous opportunities for interpersonal communication. As such opportunities increase, so do the possibilities for breakdowns in communication. Some barriers to effective communication occur because people are people and some occur because of the nature of an organization. It is the latter, those that occur because of the nature of an organization, that concern us here. (We looked at the former in Chapter 8, "Overcoming Barriers: Coping with Conflict.") The four major problems to be addressed here concern (1) poorly defined roles, (2) difficulty in making needs known, (3) negative attitudes, and (4) work as escape.

Poorly Defined Roles

Problems with role definitions occur when people do not know exactly what the limits of their jobs are. When job specifications are not spelled out clearly in a contract, or in other written form, employees may be asked to do far more (or less) than what they expected when hired. This problem can often be traced back to the job interview. Many interviewees are so anxious to get a job that they do not find out enough about the employer's expectations. When the interviewee accepts an open-ended contract, the employer has the upper, controlling hand, and the situation becomes difficult by lack of definition.

The employee should recognize, however, that role definition can be a two-sided coin. That is, it *can* work to his or her advantage as well as disadvantage. Lack of role definition may allow for variety and change. It may allow freedom where freedom might not otherwise exist. Specific role definitions may restrict individual effort, motivation, and initiative. What if it is you who wants to go beyond your role? What if you want to demonstrate your ability at another related or tangential job? What if you want to demonstrate your worthiness for promotion? What if you want to prove that you are invaluable to the company? In these cases, all a specific role definition will offer is a clear indication to your supervisor when you are exceeding specified limits. Whether or not to exceed the limits depends on so many undefined variables peculiar to specific situations that the decision must be a matter for personal discretion.

Making Needs Known

Making your needs known may be difficult in work situations because of the complexity of organizations. Employees often feel like an anonymous cog in a massive machine. What good would it do to make needs known, some employees undoubtedly feel. Who would listen? Who would care? What difference would it make? The problem occurs when you do not express your needs and others begin to take advantage of you, to overlook you, to define your needs for you, or to manipulate you.

The employee must recognize, once again, what was outlined in Chapter 9, "Getting There from Here: Assertiveness." You have certain basic rights as a human being, and no one can take those rights from you. Neither the size of an organization, nor the nature of a firm's hierarchy of positions (and how you fit into that hierarchy), can justify a denial of basic human rights. And it pays to be wise when making your protest heard. Before you reply—when rights have been jeopardized—you should consider the short-range vs long-range benefits, as well as effects, of your action. That is, seeing someone in person and speaking to them may bring immediate results, but these may be short-range only. A letter may have far-reaching ramifications and be more effective in the long run. Weigh responses and desired effects before making your move.

When your needs as an employee require expression, or when your rights are in jeopardy, you should do some or all of the following:

1. Determine proper channels for expressing yourself.
2. Assess your situation carefully. Think about your goals and responsibilities. Do not act impulsively.
3. Find out if others are experiencing the same problem. If so, solicit their help. There is likely to be more power in numbers.
4. Present the problem directly, clearly (but not aggressively) to the appropriate employer or supervisor. Do not talk to those who are not concerned or involved, or to those who can do nothing about it.
5. Be patient. The larger the organization, the slower the wheels of change will turn within it.

Consider This

For many employed mothers—and a growing number of fathers—the most welcome change would be less rigid workdays. "We know job satisfaction has declined," says business Prof. Stanley Nollen of Georgetown University, "and we know one of the reasons is that there are conflicts between work life and home life." To ease them, an estimated 17 per cent of U.S. companies and 237 government agencies are now trying "flextime," which enables workers to pick their own starting and quitting times, as long as they work a required number of hours and are present during a certain "core" period. A mother might come in at 7 a.m., for example, leaving a child in the father's care, and go home when school lets out at 3 p.m. Although impractical for some assembly lines, flextime boosts morale and reduces lateness, according to the American Management Association, and a Georgetown report says that it also increases productivity by 5 to 15 percent. By 1990, Nollen estimates, 30 per cent of all American workers will be flexing their own schedules.

—From "The Superwoman Squeeze" from *Newsweek*, May 19, 1980. Copyright 1980, by Newsweek, Inc. All Rights Reserved. Reprinted by permission.

Negative Attitudes

Poor or negative attitudes toward work may be another barrier to communication. People who love their work are rare. It would be nice if we could all have the luxury and the opportunity of doing creative, fulfilling work in the field of our choice. As we well know, life is not like that.

Consider This

Two basic principles of the Dana Corp. are that employees should "talk back to their bosses" and that "the only dumb question is the one not asked," Ren McPherson, chairman and chief executive officer, said at the Second National Seminar on Individual Rights in the Corporation.

A realistic organizational chart places the chairman at the bottom and the people at the top, he said. "I work for the people and the shareholders, and if our top managers are not encouraging all of our people to speak up, we are not managing correctly."

Mr. McPherson was the keynote speaker at the seminar, being held this week in New York.

Among top priorities at Dana are to simplify goals and procedures, to be flexible to change, and to admit mistakes, he said. "If we promote expression without responding, we lose all the credibility we sought to achieve and are right back to ruling with an iron fist."

The best expert in any job is usually the person performing it, Mr. McPherson said, adding that to ignore that person is to waste knowledge.

Dana's chairman said that the company's incentive plan has increased productivity by getting employees to work "smarter as well as harder." . . .

Mr. McPherson said that one of the most effective ways to fight inflation is to increase productivity.

And he said that the answer to America's problem of declining productivity is to simply ask, every day, "What do you think?"

—*The Blade: Toledo, Ohio*, June 27, 1979

Many people will tell us that the main reason they go to their jobs every day is that they are paid to do so.

Although some people have the idea that work is *inherently* dignified or fulfilling, actually work is simply part of the process of life. It is what we bring to it that is rewarding, exciting, and challenging, or punishing, boring, and demeaning. Our attitude toward work affects what we put into it and what we get out of it. If we simply tolerate our work, enduring it as a necessary evil, we are not likely to see the potential that it holds, the joy that might possibly result from it. We need to stay open to *all* experience, work included. This attitude can open communication channels and broaden our range of experience.

"Dignity of the work," says Jess Lair, "comes from inside the person doing the work."[12] It's a known fact that some people work more productively when they are proud of themselves and the job they're doing. It's when people feel they are performing a meaningless task in a meaningless organization that they experience real job dissatisfaction.

Work as Escape

The final barrier occurs if we use our work to insulate us from our selves and from reality. Our society is work-oriented. Lair facetiously identifies one of its sacred commandments as, "Thou shalt work thyself to death." When we assume our role of "worker" to the exclusion of all others, it lets us escape from discovering information about our selves. It allows us, too, to flee from our friends, family, community, and from many responsibilities. Lair adds that "work is an escape only if it is on top of us and we can bitch and moan and groan and feel miserable and yet occupy ourselves with our grief all day long."[13]

When we find our selves assuming the following things, it may be that the work ethic has become ingrained in us to the detriment of our interpersonal relationships and communications:

1. Everything in our job revolves around us; without us nothing would get done.
2. To say no to additional jobs or responsibilities is a sign of weakness.
3. Work comes first; whatever time is left is given to family and friends.
4. Getting the good things in life is solely dependent on work.

When work is everything, we experience the frustration of being a "workaholic" and we share this pain with our work associates. They are likely to respond by rejecting us—workaholics do not make the best companions. Communication is ended.

We must turn escape around. If we are so immersed in our work that we have no time for anything else, we limit our own future. Since we find out about our selves through other people, if our work takes us away from them, we remove the mirror of information. But if we hate our work, too, we tend to be preoccupied with our intense emotions of dislike and to use up emotional energies that we might have applied in a more productive direction. Then communication breakdowns occur.

We *can* do something about the barriers we create for our selves. We can do less about those others create. Perhaps we work in an atmosphere that does not encourage self-expression. We can try to find a job that allows self-expression. As much as we are able, we must try to find situations where we are free to develop our own potential.

USING YOUR INTERPERSONAL SKILLS ON THE JOB

Let's look briefly at the roles self-concept, perception, listening and feedback, language, conflict, and assertiveness play in a work situation.

Try This

Consider each of the following occupations. Which of them do you feel you could work well at? Which do you think you would not be suited for? (There may be some jobs listed here with which you don't have enough experience to guess about your suitability.)

chiropractor	business executive	plumber
airplane pilot	accountant	musician
secretary	interior decorator	coal miner
cabinetmaker	lawyer	researcher
teacher	golf pro	architect
beautician	contractor	writer
engineer	electrician	social worker
psychologist	dentist	doctor
nurse	bank teller	truck driver
store manager	salesperson	public relations director
artist	optometrist	real estate agent
pharmacist	mortician	minister/priest/rabbi
auto mechanic	telephone operator	insurance agent
disc jockey	radio/TV announcer	law enforcement officer
cook	barber	school principal
farmer	mail carrier	designer

You will notice that you feel comfortable with some occupations and not with others. Why is this? Are there occupations not listed here which you are interested in? Being in touch with your self gives you a better base for making these judgments.

Self-concept and Work

It is obviously preferable to find a job that will help us grow rather than stifle our growth. It should be challenging and enriching. Not only does our self-concept help dictate the kind of job that would be appropriate, but the kind of job we choose has a direct bearing on our self-concept. Have you ever had a job where you had a job title you weren't proud of? It's not uncommon for people to think more of themselves or less of themselves depending on their current job status. A job where we have a great deal of latitude, responsibility, and room for creative development will make us feel good about our selves and our potential. We will want to progress because we will feel strong about what we do and who we are.

Letting a negative self-concept get the upper hand is self-defeating. A low opinion of our selves can lead to a low opinion of our boss, our co-workers, and our whole job situation. We *do* have some control over our situation insofar as we can change a negative self-concept to positive. This isn't easy, as we saw in Chapter 3, but it can be done. The advantage of a positive self-concept extends beyond just the obvious. Sometimes we look at our job as a separate part of life, and yet we tend to spend more time on the job than we do in most other pursuits. A positive self-concept will help us get as much out of the work situation as we can. It will improve communication channels as well so that the feedback and reinforcement we get is continuous and open. To review, what can we do to develop a positive self-concept?

1. Assess our strengths and weaknesses.
2. Act on our needs for self-improvement.
3. Handle our feelings constructively.
4. Initiate change as well as accept change.
5. Assess situations and design approaches to them.
6. Revise our values and establish new goals.
7. Cope with problems inventively and realistically.
8. Stockpile successes as guides to future self-direction.
9. Set and accept reasonable, realistic situational limits.
10. Keep growing steadily in the direction we want to go.
11. Reach out and up for peak experiences in the process of being and becoming.[14]

Perception and Work

Remember as we briefly discuss perception here that the way we perceive is directly related to our self-concept because our self-concept helps determine what we process. Remember, too, that perception is simply the process of gathering information and giving it meaning. It is through perception that we gain a meaningful picture of our job and our work associates.

We function best in any situation when we have sufficient information. Too often we operate with blinders on. We perceive our selves as a tiny cog in a very large machine, as if we don't make a difference. With such a perception, we close our selves off to the big picture—we see our personal cog but not the whole machine. In so doing we protect our selves but we limit the amount of information we attain and become rigid and inflexible. *We become machinelike and not like an active, responding, involved human being.*

Our job restricts our perceptions because it affects what we expect, need, and believe. If we get a job with great potential for upward mobility, we might start thinking about our future more concretely than we ever have before. Jobs can affect perceptions even more directly

Good listening habits on the job are important; we can't afford to let our minds wander.

than that. If we teach, we might start perceiving people according to the kind of student we guess they are or were. If we sell insurance, we might start thinking of people we meet as possible clients. If we sell, we might start seeing the world as consisting of two kinds of people: buyers and nonbuyers. If we work as a waiter or waitress, we might start thinking of people as potentially big tippers or potentially small tippers. The list could go on and on.

There's nothing wrong with letting a job affect how we perceive the world. It can give us insights into people and behavior we could not have gotten any other way. The problem comes when perceptions acquired in this way come to dominate our thinking. People we meet may *well* be possible clients, big tippers, etc., but they have many other aspects we don't know about. We shouldn't presume to know them based on our limited view.

Listening/Feedback at Work

Many instructions get misinterpreted and many directives are never carried out because people fail to listen on the job. Work-listening usually requires more concentration than social listening because work situations tend to be oriented toward action and productivity where social

Consider This

"Poor listening is one of the most significant problems facing business today," [chairman J. Paul Lyet of Sperry Corp.] says. "Business relies on its communications system, and when it breaks down, mistakes can be very costly. Corporations pay for their mistakes in lower profits, while consumers pay in higher prices."

If you're a poor listener, you're much more apt to make mistakes on important business matters. Letters must be retyped, appointments rescheduled, and shipments reshipped—all because the proper information wasn't heard, or understood, when first given.

If you're in the majority, though, you don't overrate your own listening abilities. For instance, 85 per cent of those asked rate themselves as "average" listeners or less, while fewer than 5 per cent rate themselves as "superior" or "excellent."

But your listening ability can be improved. In the few schools which have adopted listening programs, listening comprehension among students has as much as doubled in a few months.

How can you improve your job performance and money management skills through better listening? Sperry, with the aid of Dr. Lyman K. Steil, an authority on listening from the University of Minnesota, suggests these guidelines:

• Don't tune out "dry" subjects. Be an opportunist and ask "What's in it for me?" What you don't ask can hurt you in the long run.

• Don't judge the speaker's delivery. Instead, pay attention to the content. You may not like how your boss talks, but you can learn a lot from what he says.

• Don't be argumentative. Stay quiet until you have completely understood what the speaker is really saying. This will give you time to think of constructive comments and to make a positive impression when you do enter the discussion.

• Do listen for ideas, not only to facts. If you restrict your attention to facts alone, you may completely miss the point. Not only that, common sense will tell you that at times, facts can be exceedingly deceiving.

• Do keep your mind open. Try not to overreact to emotional words or the emotional impact of certain words. Instead, concentrate on why your speaker is using them.

• Do capitalize on the fact that thought is four times faster than speech. You can use this time to challenge, anticipate, mentally summarize, and listen between the lines to the speaker's tone of voice, as well as to what the speaker is saying on the lines.

• Do, finally, work at listening. As a good listener, you'll be a step ahead both in your business and in your personal affairs. As a poor listener, you almost surely have been causing havoc in your personal business affairs and having a negative impact on your own work.

Try this little test on a member of your family or a group of friends this evening. Read this column at your ordinary reading speed, wait 10 minutes, then ask how much of the content has been truly understood, properly evaluated, and retained. I'll wager you'll be appalled at the results.

—Sylvia Porter, "Your Money's Worth"

situations are not. Our supervisor may say something to us only once— if we don't get it the first time, we don't get it at all. We can't afford to let our mind wander. Especially if our work involves dealing with the public, we must listen well to understand requests and instructions quickly in order to perform efficiently.

The important thing about listening is that we must consider it an active process. We have to make an emotional and intellectual commitment as well as arrange the best opportunity for the physical process to occur. Many on-the-job communication breakdowns result from half-hearted and lackadaisical responsiveness. People who get ahead in business are alert and responsive; they listen effectively.

Alertness requires getting instructions and directives correct. As an employee, we may feel subservient to our employer. Because of this difference in status, we might adjust our communication patterns to fit the situation. We may accept rather than question and challenge things our employer tells us. But we shouldn't abandon what we know to be good listening habits that work well for us in non-job circumstances. To check our listening, we can still question and paraphrase. Feedback is the way to make certain mutual understanding has occurred in any situation. It results in more accurate message transmission. It lets us know we are understanding our instructions as we are meant to understand them.

In providing feedback to a boss or co-worker, work to make your message complete. Do not assume they know what you mean. Monitor the responses you get to determine if you are being understood. Do not assume others know all the facts you do.

Language and Work

We may find that our job has a vocabulary all its own. One of our first tasks, on taking a new job, is to learn the special meanings that certain words have in that workplace. We want words to mean the same things to us as they mean to the people we work with.

The most important part of language as it relates to a work situation is that we need to get others involved in our frame of reference. This means asking them questions—how do they feel about what we say? Doing this opens channels for the give-and-take necessary for effective communication. It is the best way to catch misunderstanding before it results in loss of time, energy, or money.

Conflict at Work

There are many work situations that produce conflict. How we deal with that conflict can determine how happy we are at work, with our work associates, and with people outside the work environment. We need to deal successfully with conflict because our peace of mind, not to mention our efficiency, depends on it. In some cases our security on the job may even be at stake.

The best way of establishing a base for coping with conflict situations is to make sure we have enough information. We need all the options and alternatives we can get. We need to find out all we can about potential problems and solutions.

Try This

What is your first reaction to the following potential conflict situations?

1. The boss has accused you of coming to work late and leaving early.

2. A co-worker has become angry because you are working too hard and thus raising the boss's expectations.

3. The boss has suggested your unit is taking too long at coffee breaks.

4. Somebody has suggested that you and he are doing the same work but that you are getting paid much more for it than he.

5. Your boss is suggesting you take on some new duties that you feel are beneath you.

6. A coworker accuses you of "brown-nosing" and becoming too good friends with the boss.

The second thing to realize about conflict situations is that there is no way we can keep them from occurring. There are simply too many variables over which we have no control. There is no reason to become discouraged just because you see a conflict shaping up in the future. Conflicts will happen. We have to be ready for them so we can cope in a mature way.

In any situation, but especially in on-the-job conflicts, we need to determine the nature of the situation from the other person's vantage point. How is that person coming at the message or situation? What did he or she hear, perceive, and understand? What are his or her plans? Conflict can be reduced when all the people involved see the situation in a similar way, as much as this is possible.

It's important to stay calm in conflict situations. Relax. The emotion generated by the current conflict is already enough to distort perceptions, meanings, and understandings. Further emotion will just add fuel to the fire.

Finally, try to anticipate conflict situations. We put our selves in a difficult situation when we have to act hastily or respond on the spur of the moment. We may make an impulsive decision we later regret. To avoid impulsive behavior entirely is impossible, but to eliminate many such situations is possible if we think ahead. Anticipation is the difference between a mature, well-thought-out response, and an immature, careless one.

Assertiveness and Work

The work situation, often by definition, encourages superior-inferior relationships. We are often reluctant to assert our selves in such circumstances. It is especially important in the work environment to not be manipulated by circumstances or by people. We must choose for our selves how to act, knowing that there is probably no one right way.

The best guidelines for assertive behavior at work are:

1. Feel free to reveal your self to your co-workers and boss.
2. Communicate with them in an open, honest, and appropriate manner.
3. Act in a way *you* can respect.
4. Be aware of your own limitations—what you can and cannot do.
5. Maintain an active and aware orientation to life. Be interested.

Remember the basic assertive rights outlined in Chapter 9. They will remind us we are human beings with rights that must be protected.

There is often a close relationship between how we feel about our work and how we feel about our associates at work. If we like the people we work with, it can make even unpleasant work tolerable. If we find our work confusing or if we are frightened by the demands, deadlines, and dilemmas that we must face daily, it may be that we don't see our need for the people around us. We *do* need them. They are an important part of our ultimate job satisfaction. Ideally, the person who finds his or her work thoroughly enjoyable and fulfilling will be unable to distinguish it from play, and will find work pleasurable and happy.[15] Understandably, this attitude results in more effective relationships with the people we work with.

OTHER READING

William H. Banaka, *Training in Depth Interviewing* (New York: Harper & Row, Publishers, 1971). The author focuses on all facets of the information-gathering interview. This is a succinct training manual that covers the planning, setting up, conducting, transcribing, and analyzing of the in-depth interview. A useful chapter, too, shows how to evaluate your interviewing skills.

Edwin C. Bliss, *Getting Things Done: The ABC's of Time Management* (New York: Bantam Books, 1976). This little book includes time-saving advice on cutting paperwork, overcoming mental blocks, making lists, meeting deadlines, and overcoming procrastination. Bliss provides straightforward information on managing your time.

Henry M. Boettinger, *Moving Mountains or The Art and Craft of Letting Others See Things Your Way* (New York: Collier Books (A Division of Macmillan Publishing Co., Inc., 1969). Boettinger covers both how one thinks and how one presents thinking. How do you find new ideas? How do you structure your presentation? How do you get your message across? His book surveys the concepts of attention, style, visual aids, and jargon, as well as psychology and cross examination.

Carl R. Boll, *Executive Jobs Unlimited: Updated Edition* (New York: Macmillan Publishing Co., Inc., 1979). Boll's is a practical book that covers preparing résumés, getting interviews, conducting interviews, and many other topics. One of his basic ideas is that "in order for other people to find out about you, you must have the ability to communicate your ideas."

Richard N. Bolles, *What Color Is Your Parachute? A Practical Manual for Job-Hunters & Career Changers.* 5th ed. (Berkeley, Calif.: Ten Speed Press, 1979). This collection of current data, sources, and thinking on job-hunting is updated every year. It is written in a simple, candid, and entertaining style. Job-seekers, this should be on your "must buy" list.

Melvin W. Donaho and John L. Meyer, *How to Get the Job You Want: A Guide to Résumés, Interviews, and Job-Hunting Strategy* (Englewood Cliffs, N.J.: Prentice-Hall, Inc. (A Spectrum Book), 1976). This highly

Consider This

Debbie Arbinger, 26, is responsible for auditing coal contracts, and the costs associated with the rising cost of coal, in her job as an accountant and statistical analyst with Toledo Edison.

She feels a two-fold responsibility as a woman in management—she must prove herself as an accountant and as a female executive in a man's field, she said.

"In the beginning, you have to really prove yourself, because they're listening to see if you are knowledgeable," she said. "You have to gain their respect and prove that you have expertise, that you're not just a token woman."

She also hopes to move up to a higher-level executive position, and the way to do this is by performance, and by "letting them know you're interested in moving up, that you're not just here for a job, but a career. You have to speak up and be aggressive and ambitious, and make sure people know it."

—Sue Stankey, *The Blade: Toledo, Ohio,* December 10, 1979

practical, readable book answers many employment-seeking questions. It provides valuable directions for approaching jobs in a professional manner. It gives readers greater confidence and increases their chances for success.

Andrew J. Dubrin, *Winning at Office Politics* (New York: Ballantine Books, 1978). To ignore office politics, Dubrin suggests, "is to ignore those underlying forces that account for the differences in success between equally talented people." (p. vii) He offers an understandable explanation of office politics and then outlines strategies for gaining favor and power. In the final section, Dubrin treats misfortune, mistakes, and misdeeds. Readable, practical, useful.

Robert L. Genua, *The Employer's Guide to Interviewing: Strategy and Tactics for Picking a Winner* (Englewood Cliffs, N.J.: Prentice-Hall, Inc., 1979). This practical guide is designed for those in the position of hiring employees. It covers the basic strategies, techniques, and tools for interviewing—the face-to-face skills needed to become an effective interviewer.

Margaret Hennig and Anne Jardim, The Managerial Woman (New York: Pocket Books, 1977). In case study after case study, the authors have identified specific traits that successful managerial women possess. What have they done? What can you do to compete in the male-dominated corporate structure? A persuasive book designed to help women "move forward to attack those issues which threaten all of our rights to a just, decent and rewarding work life." (p. 239)

Carole Hyatt, *The Woman's Selling Game: How to Sell Yourself . . . and Anything Else* (New York: Warner Books, Inc., 1979). This is a guidebook that shows women how they can use their unique life-skills to sell themselves, their ideas, their products, their services, and their talent. It is a simple, clearly written book full of enthusiasm and interest.

H. Anthony Medley, *Sweaty Palms: The Neglected Art of Being Interviewed* (Belmont, Calif.: Lifetime Learning Publications (A Division of Wadsworth Publishing Company, Inc., 1978). This is a book designed for the interviewee. It covers preparation, types of interviews, enthusiasm, questions and answers, assumptions, honesty, confidence, dress, sex, salary, discrimination, and more. An enjoyable, practical book full of good ideas.

Letty Cottin Pogrebin, *Getting Yours: How to Make the System Work for the Working Woman* (New York: Avon Books, 1975). This is a guidebook on the pitfalls and possibilities of the working world. Although designed for the career-minded woman looking for a job opportunity, it is useful for anyone who wants to get ahead in a career. The book is filled with facts, advice, and solid information.

Adele M. Scheele, *Skills for Success: A Guide to the Top* (New York: William Morrow and Company, Inc., 1979). Every now and then we need a shot of adrenalin, an ego boost, or a warm statement of support or encouragement. This book, with its enthusiastic style of writing, can provide just that. Scheele tells readers how to present themselves, take new risks, show off their talents, and achieve recognition. She also includes interviews with four successful people. Enjoyable.

Frank Snell, *How to Win the Meeting* (New York: Hawthorn Books, Inc. Publishers, 1979). Snell presents the meeting as a decision-making body. This is a book about force and persuasion—a practical approach to being more direct, thinking more quickly, and learning how to use this communication situation more effectively. This book will help you learn how to control the decision-making process of organizations.

Lawrence L. Steinmetz, *Interviewing Skills for Supervisory Personnel* (Reading, Massachusetts: Addison-Wesley Publishing Company, 1971). Steinmetz discusses in detail how to conduct a successful interview. It is designed to help the manager or supervisor improve his or her interviewing skills and, thus, select employees more effectively. It is thorough and complete.

Charles J. Stewart and William B. Cash, Jr., *Interviewing: Principles and Practices*, 2nd ed. (Dubuque, Iowa: Wm. C. Brown Company Publishers, 1978). One of the most popular textbooks on interviewing, this is thorough and comprehensive. Easy to read, it includes many practical suggestions and ideas.

Jean Tepperman, *Not Servants, Not Machines: Office Workers Speak Out* (Boston: Beacon Press, 1976). Tepperman brings together the experience of women office workers, and she provides practical information on how to improve the situation of a whole group of women through collective action. Most of the book consists of interviews with office workers. It offers a close examination of what work is like for this set of women.

NOTES

[1]Aubrey C. Sanford, *Human Relations: Theory and Practice* (Columbus, Ohio: Charles E. Merrill, 1973), pp. 175–76.

[2]Harry Shaw, *Better Jobs Through Better Speech* (Totowa, N.J.: Littlefield, Adams & Co., 1979), pp. 1–2.

[3]Marion Sitzmann and Reloy Garcia, *Successful Interviewing: A Practical Guide for the Applicant and Interviewer* (Skokie, Illinois: National Textbook Company, 1976), p. 1.

[4]Sitzmann and Garcia, p. 1.

[5]These ideas have been adapted from Melvin W. Donaho and John L. Meyer, *How to Get the Job You Want: A Guide to Résumés, Interviews, and Job-Hunting Strategy,* © 1976, p. 77. Reprinted by permission of Prentice-Hall, Inc., Englewood Cliffs, New Jersey.

[6]Donaho and Meyer, p. 80.

[7]Donaho and Meyer, pp. 81–82.

[8]Donaho and Meyer, p. 81.

[9]Donaho and Meyer, p. 82.

[10]H. Anthony Medley, *Sweaty Palms: The Neglected Art of Being Interviewed* (Belmont, Calif.: Lifetime Learning Publications (A Division of Wadsworth Publishing Company, Inc., 1978), p. xi.

[11]Sitzmann and Garcia, p. 8.

[12]Jess Lair, *I Ain't Well—But I Sure Am Better* (Garden City, N.Y.: Doubleday & Company, Inc., 1975), pp. 171–72. See Chapter 10, "Loving our Work."

[13]Ibid., p. 175.

[14]Raymond F. Gale, *Who Are You? The Psychology of Being Yourself* (Englewood Cliffs, N.J.: Prentice-Hall, Inc., 1974), p. 68.

[15]Abraham H. Maslow, *Motivation and Personality*, 2nd ed. (New York: Harper & Row, 1970), p. 179.

Index